AN INTRODUCTION
TO
MULTINATIONAL
ACCOUNTING

AN INTRODUCTION TO MULTINATIONAL ACCOUNTING

FREDERICK D.S. CHOI
University of Hawaii

GERHARD G. MUELLER
University of Washington

Prentice-Hall, Inc., Englewood Cliffs, New Jersey 07632

Library of Congress Cataloging in Publication Data

CHOI, FREDERICK D.S.
 An introduction to multinational accounting.

 Includes bibliographies and index.
 1. International business enterprises—Accounting.
I. Mueller, Gerhard G., joint author. II. Title.
HF5657.C543   657'.95   77-12799
ISBN 0-13-489302-6

©1978 by Prentice-Hall, Inc., Englewood Cliffs, N.J. 07632

Printed in the United States of America

10 9 8 7 6 5 4

Prentice-Hall International, Inc., *London*
Prentice-Hall of Australia Pty. Limited, *Sydney*
Prentice-Hall of Canada, Ltd., *Toronto*
Prentice-Hall of India Private Limited, *New Delhi*
Prentice-Hall of Japan, Inc., *Tokyo*
Prentice-Hall of Southeast Asia Pte. Ltd., *Singapore*
Whitehall Books Limited, *Wellington, New Zealand*

To Lois and Coralie ... with fond aloha.

CONTENTS

PREFACE

Only twenty years ago terms such as *international accounting* or *multinational accounting* were regarded with much academic and professional suspicion. "Fad or fact?" was then the standard query. Multinational (or international) accounting is still thought of by some as a trivial specialization of the general theory and practice of accounting. But contrary evidence is mounting. Academe now requires an international component in higher education for business, as a condition for school and curriculum accreditation. Professionals fill their journals with numerous articles on various multinational dimensions of accounting, and they expend vast resources on all manner of international committees, conferences, study groups, and pronouncements. We assert that multinational accounting has come of age.

Agreeing to the validity of multinational accounting specialization and teaching the subject are two quite different things. An absence of appropriate text readings and/or case books makes an organized and sustained teaching effort difficult. To surmount this difficulty, this book was written. We believe that it is the first comprehensive textbook in the field.

Textbooks assimilate many different sources and wide ranges of ideas, as well as practices. In this respect our effort is no exception. Among the antecedents of our book, we gratefully acknowledge Professor Mueller's *International Accounting* (1967), relevant research studies by the American Institute of Certified Public Accountants and the Canadian Institute of Chartered Accountants, papers and proceedings of many international conferences and seminars, and, last but not least, the great volume of proprietary publications on various multinational accounting topics made available by the large international public accounting firms. The financial press has also provided many leads and facts. Their growing attention to the topic has been a blessing to our writing effort.

The co-authors personally know many of the accounting faculty who teach multinational accounting courses, both in the United States and abroad. Many of these individuals have encouraged us, quite a number have made syllabi and other course materials available for guidance, and still others have responded to a number of idea "trial balloons." To all of these individuals we express our collective thanks. We have also benefited from several classroom tests of our material with students at the Universities of Hawaii and Washington. Comments received from these student groups were carefully considered and appreciatively acknowledged. Moreover, manuscript portions of this book were used in executive development seminars between 1975 and 1977; some of these seminars were conducted abroad. We certainly appreciated the input received not only from seminar participants but also from organizing directors.

Several individuals warrant special credit. Professors Irving Fantl, of Florida International University and Dhia D. AlHashin, of California State University at Northridge reviewed the entire manuscript for this book and provided many useful hints and suggestions. Mr. Warren Wee, a graduate student first at the University of Hawaii and now at the University of Washington, gave considerable assistance with finding, classifying, and annotating most of the case materials referenced throughout the book. We have a better product as a consequence of the contributions received from these individuals, and we wish to acknowledge their assistance with a personal note of thanks.

No book can be produced without capable and efficient manuscript production. In this respect we were most fortunate to have the able assistance of Ms. Sylvia Christensen at the University of Washington and Ms. Shirley Kamins at the University of Hawaii. To both of them, our sincere "Mahalo!"

Finally, the publisher's personnel have great influence over almost every aspect of a new book—including its physical appearance and the time of publication. We were more fortunate to be able to work with a publisher's production team who is second to none. Their continuous and cheerful help and advice yielded many improvements throughout the publishing period.

However hard one tries to avoid them, a number of errors are certain to occur in a project of this type. As authors we accept full responsibilities for any failures in judgment, communication, or physical production of the manuscript. We would much like to have the opportunity of receiving comments from all those who have occasion to use this book.

Frederick D. S. Choi
Honolulu, Hawaii

Gerhard G. Mueller
Seattle, Washington

AN INTRODUCTION
TO
MULTINATIONAL
ACCOUNTING

Chapter 1

MULTINATIONAL DIMENSIONS OF ACCOUNTING

Multinational (international, transnational, or global) accounting has established itself as a legitimate subarea in the accounting field. Enormous amounts of resources are devoted each year to further development and refinement of multinational accounting. Worldwide, various national and local organizations and institutes are producing volumes of discussion papers, professional and technical recommendations, and numerous monographs and articles, all devoted to this subject matter.

International CPA firms have permanently organized international departments, and large corporations are increasingly creating separate top executive positions for their multinational controllers and treasurers. Many business schools now teach courses in this subject area. In the United States two examples of this trend can be seen. The American Institute of Certified Public Accountants (AICPA) has established an International Practice Division as a formal part of its line organization. Further, the American Accounting Association (AAA) officially established an International Accounting Section in 1976.

In the past, some critics have charged that separate recognition of multinational accounting would mean acquiescence to a fad, would lead to proliferation of the procedural aspects of accounting, or would waste resources on what intellectually was asserted to be a "nonarea." Today there is no need to defend a small textbook devoted to multinational accounting. The business and social environment of the last quarter of the 20th century has made multinational accounting a reality—for reasons and purposes amply demonstrated throughout this book.

1

In synopsis, the raison d'être of multinational accounting divides itself into four major contributing factors:

1. Historical antecedents.
2. Rise of the multinational enterprise.
3. International nature of some special accounting problems.
4. Academic curiosity.

Each of these factors is sketched briefly in the paragraphs that follow.

Historical Antecedents

The history of accounting is an international history. Double entry book-keeping, generally thought of as the genesis of accounting as we know it today, emanated from the Italian city states of the 14th and 15th centuries. "Bookkeeping after the Italian fashion" then migrated to Germany to assist the merchants of the Fugger era and the Hanseatic League. At almost the same time some Dutch business philosophers sharpened ways of calculating periodic income, and some Frenchmen applied the whole system to governmental planning and accountability.

In due course, double entry accounting ideas reached the British Isles, where the ideas received further attention and development. Britain's world economic position during the 17th and 18th centuries made her an ideal missionary on behalf of accounting. Thus, British influence spread the banner of accounting not only to North America but well throughout the British Commonwealth as it then existed.

Parallel developments are, of course, observable for other spheres of socio-economic and/or political influence. Thus the Dutch carried the brand of accounting that they had developed at home to Indonesia, among other places. The French made sure that Polynesia and French-administered territories in Africa would use French accounting systems, and the Germans extended their accounting influence to nations like Japan, Sweden, and czarist Russia.

As the United States' economic power grew during the first half of the 20th century, she quite naturally developed a corresponding sophistication in matters of accounting. Business schools assisted in this development by fostering the conceptual dimension of accounting and eventually having it recognized as an academic discipline in its own right on college and university campuses. Hence it seems quite natural that, after World War II, United States accounting influence made itself felt almost throughout the Western world, particularly in Germany and Japan. To a lesser extent the same factors are directly observable in countries like Brazil, Israel, Mexico, the Philippines, Sweden and Taiwan. Moreover, a degree of similar influences has surfaced in regional accounting developments, such as those underlying the accounting directives of the European Common Market or the companies law development for the five Nordic (Scandinavian) countries.

The paradox of the international heritage of accounting is that in most individual countries accounting has become an intensely nationalistic affair—with national standards and practices deeply anchored into national laws and professional regulations. There is little understanding of or patience for parallel requirements in other countries. In this respect, accounting is much like law—both have developed their own national systems and both are subject to very nationally oriented rules and interpretations. Yet, both serve people and organizations whose activities are increasingly transnational in scope.

Multinational Enterprises

A multinational enterprise is loved and hated, praised and condemned—all at the same time. But it is proliferating, and all the experts see sustained further growth. In 1977, there are about 1,000 corporations that could be classified as multinational and whose total annual sales volume each exceeds $250 million. Among themselves, these multinationals produce approximately one-fifth of the world's total economic output. The economic power of multinational enterprises, as a group, is substantial and unquestioned.

How have the multinationals survived in the face of all the criticism and attacks leveled at them? "Because they have adapted to the world as it is," opines Karl Mayer, Business Planning Director of ITT (*Dun's Review,* July, 1976, p. 56). Mayer goes on to say, "If the legislators don't like the results, they may change the ground rules. Well-managed multinationals will simply adapt to the new ground rules and continue to do a good job of reallocating resources in a new optimum manner." ITT was incorporated in 1920, and 80 percent of its total business was overseas as late as 1959. Then it increased its United States investments to 50 percent in a single decade. But when United States antitrust efforts severely restricted ITT's United States business merger activities in 1969, the corporation again switched its major investments and attention to Europe.

The very adaptability of the multinationals and their willingness to shift resources on a worldwide scale are reasons for the existence of multinational accounting. As previously stated, accounting developments around the globe have been predominantly nationalistic in nature. The resulting differences are reinforced by environmental differences. For instance, a sociological view of accounting would hold that different socio-economic environments require different types of decision-making and therefore different accounting systems and procedures. The accounting needs of a centrally controlled economy like that of the Soviet Union are quite different from those found in an administered market economy.

Similarly, accounting in a developing country has functions that are different from those in highly developed countries. Multinational enterprises must somehow bridge these accounting differences, if real benefits are to be gained from worldwide optimal resource allocation patterns. Thus the accounting problem for the multinational enterprise is the usefulness of differing local accounting standards and practices that are often in conflict with one another.

The paradox with regard to multinational business operations is that any type of worldwide resource allocation system requires a reasonably centralized management decision-making system (suggesting, among other things, *worldwide* accounting standards). Multinational enterprises are very eager, however, to lose their strict national identities in favor of multinational acceptance in many host countries. For instance, Philips of the Netherlands feels best if Germans see it as a German enterprise, Autralians as an Australian company and United States citizens as a United States corporation (suggesting acceptance of *national* accounting standards and practices). A multiple approach might eventually be the answer here. Chapter 4 provides additional discussion on this topic.

Specific Accounting Problems

International commerce started as foreign trade of the export/import variety. Trading goods outside one's own national borders requires the use of foreign currencies—either to receive payment from a foreign source for one's exports or to be able to utilize one's national currency to pay for desired imports. Either way, transactions of this type require measurements in two national currencies and hence create foreign exchange translation problems—a unique element of multinational accounting.

Consolidations of foreign subsidiaries are another special accounting problem unique to the multinational setting. For instance, German companies law since 1965 *requires* consolidation of controlled domestic subsidiaries *only*—controlled foreign subsidiaries have the option of consolidation. Related to the consolidation problem are general purchasing power adjustments of financial statements. Suppose one has a wholly owned subsidiary company operating in another country and the parent company is required to prepare financial statements on the basis of general price level adjustments. Should the home country price index or the subsidiary's country price index be used for the restatement of the subsidiary company's financial statements?

Aside from the foregoing, does one first translate foreign currency effects and then restate for price level effects; or does one, in reverse, "restate and then translate"? Financial statement effects are not the same under these two alternative procedures. This concept is further discussed in Chapter 3.

Recasting financial statements from one set of applied accounting standards and procedures to another set (as Dutch-based multinational enterprises do when they recast their own partially replacement cost-based financial statements to largely historical cost-based statements required and understood in the United States) or grappling with the format of the reports of independent auditors (attached to financial statements), which differ significantly from country to country, are but two examples of accounting problems unique to the multinational domain. In the absence of international trade and business activities, these special accounting problems would not exist.

Academic Curiosity

When tens of thousands of people make their living by working in the multinational accounting field; when institutes and organizations feel compelled to make major resource commitments to multinational accounting agencies; and when speeches, committee reports, and articles suggest time and again that a number of issues and problems prevail within the reaches of multinational accounting, a certain amount of intellectual curiosity is triggered. As a result, a degree of academic attention is produced. Academics take many of the problems they work on from practice. Multinational accounting is no exception.

As practical problems in this area surfaced more and more—generally through papers presented at international conferences and articles appearing in the professional literature—a number of accounting Ph.D. dissertations addressed multinational accounting phenomena. In turn, this effort generated some academic expertise on multinational accounting problems and, as one would expect, still more contributions to the literature on the topic. Not every academic trial balloon will float. The multinational accounting one did though! Hence we have, in 1977, a level of academic attention to multinational accounting that is vastly larger than its counterpart was a few years ago. There is every expectation that this trend not only will continue but will further accelerate. Curiosity has developed into attention, and attention into real progress. This chain of events is explored further in the final chapter of our book.

THE IDEA OF MULTINATIONAL ACCOUNTING

Human ideas probably occur and undergo refinements in cycles. Nations seem to rise and fall; clothing styles seem to come and go at fairly regular intervals; so why should not human ideas also have their ups and downs?

From the philosophy of science viewpoint, Kuhn (*The Structure of Scientific Revolutions*) sketches the cycle of human ideas very succinctly. He points out that given bodies of ideas can become widely (or "generally") accepted at one time only to be found deficient later. As inconsistencies and unpredictability begin to be observed in any established pattern, new ideas and proposals are advanced to remedy the deficiencies. At this point, the corresponding field of inquiry becomes confused and often contradictory. Then a crisis occurs! Attempts to patch up such a crisis with various adaptations of the old patterns and negotiated "compromises" between the old and the new ideas might well cause an entire field to sink into oblivion. On the other hand, if the logic and usefulness of the new ideas are strong enough, they will ultimately prevail and push the respective field of inquiry to new heights. Then a new equilibrium pattern of ideas and related standards and procedures emerges. The pattern of cyclical behavior of bodies of human ideas seems quite plausible.

A related and much more generally espoused and accepted philosophy of scientific viewpoint is that fields of inquiry come and go according to a fairly simple pattern. This pattern appears to be one wherein successively higher levels of abstraction are reached as knowledge in a field progresses. Broadly, the following six steps are often recognized:

1. Descriptions of phenomena observed.
2. Systematic classification of observations according to a generally useful taxonomy.
3. Comparisons and analyses of the observed phenomena according to classes and subclasses.
4. Abstraction of general characteristics and principles from the analyses undertaken.
5. Determination of a relatively few basic concepts underlying the evolving field of inquiry.
6. Theory (model) building and testing, congruent with the foregoing developmental steps and aimed at predictive processes.

After realistic models of properly classified and analyzed phenomena have been built, predictions of future cause and effect relationships become possible, at least within broad ranges. At this point, Kuhn's equilibrium plateau is reached. Either a new field of inquiry has been born (e.g., cybernetics, computer sciences) or an existing field has received a new orientation (e.g., Einsteinian physics superseding Newtonian physics, or social psychology expanding psychology).

Where Are We?

Utilizing the notions mentioned above from the philosophy of science tool kit, we observe that the development of multinational accountng as a separately identifiable area of inquiry is generally at the step of comparing and analyzing observable phenomena. Multinational accounting has not yet reached a level of abstraction that would permit separate conceptualization or model-building! These authors are not aware of any "basic concepts" of multinational accounting—let alone any multinational accounting theories. No attempt is made in this book to push the field further up on the abstraction ladder by postulating a group of basic concepts or formulating what might be called a theory. The book addresses multinational accounting at the level of its current state—with a relatively small amount of crystal-ball gazing in a few selected passages only.

A second line of thought that springs from the earlier discussion is that multinational accounting is best seen as a subarea of accounting; in much the same interrelationship that exists between economics and international economics, anthropology and social anthropology, law and international law of the seas, etc.

Multinational accounting is therefore placed most advantageously within the context of the accounting discipline as a whole. It does not seek to supersede or replace existing accounting thought and practices; rather, it strives to "stretch" the existing field as a whole by giving it more conceptual precision as well as more practical usefulness. These authors perceive the interface between accounting in total and multinational accounting quite similar to that which exists between accounting and behavioral accounting or accounting information systems. Not every accountant needs to be a multinational accounting expert. But a well-informed accountant should know what the core problems of multinational accounting are and in which direction appropriate solutions are being developed.

A third introductory assessment is definitional in nature. In 1971, Weirich, Avery, and Anderson (*International Journal of Accounting*) distinguished among three approaches: (a) a universal system, (b) a descriptive and informative approach covering all the methods and standards of all countries, and (c) accounting practices of foreign subsidiaries and parent companies. They named and defined these definitional approaches, respectively, as follows:

> *World Accounting.* In the framework of this concept, international accounting is considered to be a universal system that could be adopted in all countries. A worldwide set of generally accepted accounting principles (GAAP), such as the set maintained in the United States, would be established. Practices and principles would be developed which were applicable to all countries. This concept would be the ultimate goal of an international accounting system.

International Accounting. A second major concept of the term international accounting involves a descriptive and informative approach. Under this concept, international accounting includes *all* varieties of principles, methods and standards of accounting of *all* countries. This concept includes a set of generally accepted accounting principles established for each country, thereby requiring the accountant to be multiple principle conscious when studying international accounting.... No universal or perfect set of principles would be expected to be established. A collection of all principles, methods and standards of all countries would be considered as the international accounting system. These variations result because of differing geographic, social, economic, political and legal influences.

Accounting for Foreign Subsidiaries. The third major concept that may be applied to 'international accounting' refers to the accounting practices of a parent company and a foreign subsidiary. A reference to a particular country or domicile is needed under the concept for effective international financial reporting. The accountant is concerned mainly with the translation and adjustment of the subsidiary's financial statement. Different accounting problems arise and different accounting principles are to be followed depending upon which country is used as a reference for translation and adjustment purposes.

The definitions advanced by Weirich, Avery, and Anderson have withstood the test of time. Your authors have built upon them—only to make five rather than three basic distinctions in the subject matter of multinational accounting. Table 1 – 1 portrays the classifications used to organize the topics of this book.

As with all classification schemes, borderlines between classification groups are not so precise as to avoid overlap. Nonetheless, it is useful to point out how the subject matter to be covered relates to different developmental levels within multinational accounting as a field and how the different areas relate to classifications commonly recognized for the accounting discipline as a whole.

As a final step in our introduction to multinational accounting, we elaborate somewhat the column entitled *General Orientation* in Table 1 – 1. Our purpose is to provide sufficient tie-in between the familiar ground of accounting generally and multinational accounting so that the latter will be seen as more than a succession of interesting but unrelated topics.

ACCOUNTING AND MULTINATIONAL ACCOUNTING

Most definitions of accounting agree that it is a discipline concerned with measurement and information. Accounting information is used over a wide range of public and private sector financial and economic decision-

TABLE 1—1. Subject Matter of Multinational Accounting

CHAPTER NO.	CHAPTER TITLE	GENERAL ORIENTATION	LEVEL OF ABSTRACTION	DESCRIPTION
2	International Accounting Patterns	Academic	Classification	Discernible Clusters or Groups of Existing Patterns of Accounting
3	Accounting for Foreign Currency Translation and Inflation	CPA Professional	Description and Analysis;	Different Methodologies for Foreign Currency Translation Accounting and Recognition of Inflation Effects, Including Foreign Subsidiary Consolidation Problems
4	Transnational Financial Reporting and Disclosure	CPA Professional	Description and Analysis: Also Comparisons	Present Forms of Transnational Reporting, Including Auditors' Reports; Proposals for Changes
5	International Accounting Standards and Organizations	Institutional	Description; also Policy Oriented	Existing Diversity of Nationally Accepted Accounting Standards and Efforts at Worldwide Harmonization
6	EEC Accounting	Institutional	Description; also Policy Oriented	Highlights of Accounting in EEC Countries and Efforts to Harmonize Regionally
7	Financial Planning for Multinational Operations	Managerial	Analysis	Project Evaluation, Financial Sourcing, and General Financial Risk Management from an Accounting Point of View
8	Management Information Systems and Control	Managerial	Analysis	Information/Information Systems/Functional Organization/Control/Management Audit in Multinational Business Operations
9	Multinational Taxation and Transfer Pricing	Managerial	Description	Issues, Practices, and Tradeoffs in Multinational Taxation and Transfer Pricing
10	Current Issues and Developments	Public Interest	Description	Multinational Aspects of Special Purpose Accounting: Behavioral, Developing Countries, Public Sector, Social Responsibility, and International Balance of Payments

making. Substantial use of accounting information occurs in (a) financial markets of various types, (b) planning and operating private business enterprise activities, (c) planning and operating public sector organizations and programs, and (d) initiating and administering financial and economic policies at state, national, and international levels. In addition, accounting information is used in such varied activities as collective bargaining, nomination and election of or confirmation of persons for public office, applications for personal credit, employment growth opportunities with individual firms or other organizations, and many other endeavors that have financial or economic dimensions. Thus *usefulness* of accounting information is the critical variable that justifies its existence as a field of study and application.

Multinational accounting, as specified earlier, is largely concerned with accounting applications. Its utility derives principally from its service to multinational financial markets, to worldwide enterprise operations, and to international governmental activities and policy-making. Another way of looking at this is to see multinational accounting as a microcosm of each commonly recognized subarea of accounting in general, except for the more academic accounting theory construction and verification.

Academic Pursuits

Chapters 2 and 7 are academic in their basic orientation but both chapters are also quite different. Chapter 7 relies on existing finance theory to develop key points and procedures suitable for financial planning in multinational operations. Chapter 2, on the other hand, recognizes that no usable multinational accounting theory is presently available. It therefore restricts itself to almost pure classification as (a) a way to understand the totality of accounting worldwide, (b) a tool of analysis in individual country or regional accounting applications, and (c) a cautious initial step toward eventual conceptualization of multinational accounting.

Chapter 2 draws a distinction between centrally controlled and administered market economies. It also points toward patterns of accounting derived from simple groupings of existing practices to those leaning on economic or legal frames of reference. It further distinguishes accounting patterns according to types of companies or types of industries in which a given enterprise is operating. Thus, several alternatives are provided for categorizing the world accounting scene.

Academic accounting has recently shifted from a search for pure theory to an analysis of the socially relevant contributions of the discipline. The Trueblood Commission searched for "objectives" for financial statements. The so-called empirical branch of academic accounting seeks to establish links between published accounting data and market price behavior of securities. Accounting policy-makers recognize that good theory alone does not necessarily offer socially useful accounting applications.

Chapter 2 fits the evolving emphasis on inductive academic research in accounting. It holds a certain amount of interest for the accounting theorist at large. More important, it yields a recognition framework for multinational accounting and possibly provides a stepping stone toward its eventual conceptualization. Chapter 2 subject matter is a particularly suitable area of study for graduate students.

Professional Concerns

Certified public accountants (CPA's) render services as both professional accountants and independent auditors. As expert accountants, they (a) supervise the procedural discharge of the accounting function at all levels and sectors of the economy; (b) establish, through special boards and institutes, socially useful accounting policies in the form of standards and principles; and (c) utilize their expert judgement in applying agreed upon (generally accepted) accounting standards and principles to complex new or otherwise difficult business events and transactions.

As independent auditors, CPA's perform an attest function aimed primarily at establishing and maintaining the integrity of financial information. They are accounting review specialists whose efforts improve the reliability and fairness of financial statements made available to third parties. The objective of their ordinary audits (examinations) of financial statements is an expression of a professional opinion on the fairness with which the financial statements present financial position and operating results of an enterprise. The auditors' reports are the medium through which auditors either express or disclaim their opinions.

Chapters 3 and 4 describe and analyze the role of CPA's in multinational accounting. Since no binding international accounting standards exist at this time, financial accounting policy-making in this realm is categorized separately in the following section under "Institutional Developments." The institutional framework is significant in its own right.

Accounting for foreign currency translations is probably the most pervasive technical multinational financial accounting problem and therefore lies at the core of the professionally oriented issues in Chapter 3. The principal use of foreign currency translation occurs during the *consolidation* of the financial statements of foreign subsidiaries; another major subject covered in Chapter 3. The very essence of financial planning, budgeting, and reporting of multinational business activities goes to the aforementioned two subjects. Thus they have significant importance, not only for the professional CPA but also for the financial executive of the multinational enterprise.

In some ways the adjustment of historical cost-based financial statements for the effects of general price level changes is related to foreign exchange accounting. Both procedures restate financial transactions from one unit of account to another. Of course, foreign exchange translations employ a real market price (a foreign exchange rate) as the translation coefficient, whereas general price level adjustments utilize a statistically derived index. The objectives of the two procedures also differ. These ramifications are explored toward the end of Chapter 3.

Chapter 4 delves into the main ideas of transnational financial reporting. When corporate securities are held totally within the country in which the issuing firm is incorporated, dissemination of financial information to investors and others concerned with accounting data is generally covered by accounting standards and principles generally accepted in that country. Both the preparers and the consumers of the information have the responsibility of being familiar with applicable rules. While this state of affairs does not guarantee effective communication in all cases, a mutual understanding of the ground rules that apply at least minimizes distortion.

International ownership of corporate securities presents a new problem. Past, present, and future securities owners in various countries outside the corporate domicile differ from one another not only in their cultural and social attitudes, their life-styles, and general behavior patterns, but also in the understanding they have of the accounting principles underlying the financial statements that they encounter.

Aside from meeting the needs of different national financial reporting "audiences of interest," multinational enterprises are often forced into multiple reporting practices when a subsidiary company operating in Country A must (a) report for local purposes under locally accepted accounting principles and laws to local authorities, often referred to as *statutory reporting,* and (b) report to the parent company in Country B for investment control and consolidated financial reporting purposes, often referred to as *business reporting.* One key issue in all this is whether financial statements, like companies, have a domicile that cannot be changed at will.

Since auditing standards are also not uniform worldwide, the meanings of auditors' reports involved in transnational financial reporting processes are not always clear. In fact, on reading financial statements of multinational enterprises located the world over, one is sometimes not even sure whose accounting standards and practices were used in a given set of statements! Yet the multinationals must annually publish financial statements. Little wonder that there is much diversity worldwide when it comes to financial reporting across national borders!

Institutional Developments

Should accounting standards and rules be established in the private sector or by political fiat? Can one force all enterprises in different industries and of varied sizes, plans, and goals into a single uniform financial accounting methodology? What makes good accounting standards and practices— good theory, social fairness, and equity or desired allocation patterns for economic resources? Is it that which is easily understood and widely applicable? These are difficult questions and, of course, they are difficult to answer.

In the United States, where the private sector houses the professionally oriented mechanism for determining financial accounting policies, the unsuccessful search for *basic accounting concepts* was a major element in the 1957 demise of the AICPA's Committee on Accounting Procedures. The successor body, the Accounting Principles Board, also ran into difficulties. Among other things, it was unable to find or establish *basic accounting postulates.* In 1973, the Financial Accounting Standards Board became the most authoritative financial accounting rule-making body in the United States. Despite much effort, it was not until late 1976 that the FASB formulated its initial attempt at a *Conceptual Framework for Financial Accounting and Reporting.* If there is this much difficulty with basic accounting development within a single country, what hope is there for worldwide harmonization of accounting?

Chapters 5 and 6 address the background, the institutional settings, and the prospects for the eventual evolution of international accounting standards—possibly on a regional rather than a global basis. As in any single country, there is a whole range of relevant difficulties. Even if we had international or regional standards, who would enforce them and how? Should business managers and CPA's, who are the basic users of accounting standards and principles, be a party to the determination of such standards and principles in the first place? Should international agencies like the United Nations get into the act? And who should pay for international accounting organizations and for the international "manufacture" of standards and principles?

In Chapter 5, the existing diversity of nationally accepted accounting standards and principles (first mentioned in Chapter 2) is sketched. We then catalog the long list of conferences and organizations devoted to the worldwide harmonization of accounting and financial reporting. The chapter ends with a description of the work of the International Accounting Standards Committee and the even more recently established International Federation of Accountants. If judged on the basis of time and money spent, international accounting standards should soon be a reality!

Between diversity from country to country and worldwide harmony lies the possibility of regional harmonization. If economic policies, national security, social programs of various kinds, and international assistance can be regionalized, why not pursue the same course of action for accounting? The European Economic Community (EEC) has moved some distance toward political and economic as well as social and international integration. It is, of course, also busy with efforts to harmonize accounting within the jurisdictions of its nine member countries. The antecedents of these efforts, their present status, and their future prospects are the subjects of Chapter 6.

Managerial Applications

In many ways managerial accounting is better integrated and less nationalistic than financial accounting. Professional accountants and enterprise managers have complete discretion over managerial accounting matters. Conversely, political bodies, administrative agencies, courts of law, and many other third parties heavily influence what happens in financial accounting. While there exists a fairly major conflict within many multinational enterprises between decision-making centralization at headquarters (i.e., close coordination worldwide) and locally autonomous decision-making (i.e., more participatory management), it seems a fair assessment that managerial accounting techniques are far more uniform than financial accounting standards and principles.

The most critical managerial aspect of multinational accounting is that a fairly high degree of complexity marks its nature. Domestic managerial accounting problems become cumbersome and involved when extended to the multinational dimension. Take, for instance, foreign exchange rate forecasting problems. The number of cause and effect relationships that come to bear on these particular exercises are so numerous that not even a comprehensive listing of them exists as yet!

As stated earlier, Chapter 7 tackles financial planning topics for the operation of multinational enterprises. By borrowing some concepts from managerial economics as well as from finance theory, this chapter analyzes how a multinational project or investment can be evaluated, financed if affirmatively decided upon, and managed as to attendant risks. Some unique dimensions appear in each of these phases of multinational operations. How do you quantify political stability before building a plant abroad or entering a merger with a company in another country? If you are performing a large international construction project that is financed by funds available in several different currencies, which currency do you use first to avoid unnecessary exchange risks and conversion fees? At a time of a big expansion abroad, do you borrow from local banks, finance through the parent company, or tap the international financial markets? Chapter 7 catalogs and analyzes these very problems.

The emphasis shifts to information and information systems (i.e., control) in Chapter 8. Here we establish that managers of multinational operations need a greater expanded information base vis-à-vis their domestic counterparts. But does this necessarily mean a specially designed information system? One wonders, for instance, what a financial executive would do with a special multinational operations information system if he is not fluent in the foreign languages or with the characteristics of the host countries. Should one, in fact, have a separate financial executive organization for international operations? Chapter 8 develops these and related topics to the point of analysis. It also covers internal management audits in multinational business operations.

When it comes to multinational taxation and transfer pricing, Chapter 9 is designed to shed some light on the issues involved. We recognize that cash and working capital management are inextricably intertwined with taxation and transfer price policies. We also are aware that multinational enterprises typically transfer greater proportions of their total output between related companies than do domestic enterprises.

Now suppose a transfer price favors the parent company in the domicile country. This implies many things: a taxation advantage to the domicile country, foreign exchange exposure away from the domicile country, indirect profit remission to the parent company, and more opportunities for centralized cash and working capital management. These types of analysis chains permeate Chapter 9.

Multinational taxation and transfer pricing are of particular interest to Third World countries and to a number of commissions established at the international level. If one were to speculate, it seems likely that greater disclosure of transfer pricing policies as well as ways and means of tax payments by the multinationals is a likely occurrence in the near future. Chapter 10 expands upon the latter point.

The Public Interest

The title of Chapter 10 is fairly descriptive of its contents. As in domestic accounting, public interest considerations are strongly felt in multinational accounting matters.

The aggregate economic power of the multinational enterprise has become massive and, therefore, its political and social influence potentially pervasive. Smaller nation-states tend to see the multinationals as a direct challenge to their national sovereignties. Labor unions assert that the multinational enterprise is able to "import" or "export" jobs. Publics at large have become concerned because they are told that even general standards of living in a given country may well be affected by the collective influence of multinational business activities. The foreign exchange value of their country's currency may be significantly affected by direct foreign investment strategies decided in a very small number of boardrooms abound the world. Public welfare may be influenced by arbitrary allocations of corporate tax payments between countries, by substantial under-the-table payments to officials in other countries, and by a long string of still other asserted multinational corporate manipulations. Many of these concerns translate directly into accounting measurement and financial reporting consequences.

In Chapter 10, from a public interest point of view, measurement and reporting of corporate social responsibilities are briefly described as they relate to the multinational enterprise. A similar brief is afforded to international balance of payments accounting that impacts broadly not only the formulation of national economic policies but individual pocketbooks when export/import availabilities or external exchange rates are affected.

The concerns of developing countries are also given some attention, especially the relationship between economic development and accounting development. The chapter concludes with a few observations about behavioral and public sector accounting, wherein the international dimension has not yet gained much foothold.

SELECTED REFERENCES

1.1   BERG, KENNETH B., GERHARD G. MUELLER, and LAUREN M. WALKER (Ed.), *Readings in International Accounting,* Boston: Houghton-Mifflin, 1969, 305 pp.

1.2   CHOI, FREDERICK D. S., "Multinational Challenges for Managerial Accountants," *Journal of Contemporary Business,* Autumn 1975, pp. 51 – 67.

1.3   DASCHER, PAUL E., CHARLES H. SMITH, and ROBERT H. STRASSER, "Accounting Curriculum Implications of the Multinational Corporation," *International Journal of Accounting,* Fall 1973, pp. 81   97.

1.4   EITEMAN, DAVID K., and ARTHUR I. STONEHILL, *Multinational Business Finance,* Reading, Mass.: Addison-Wesley, 1973, 399 pp. (See especially Chapter 13, "Accounting and Reporting," and Chapter 14, "Controls.")

1.5   KUBIN, KONRAD W., and GERHARD G. MUELLER, *A Bibliography of International Accounting* (3rd ed.), Seattle: University of Washington, International Accounting Studies Institute, 1973, 144 pp.

1.6   KUHN, THOMAS S., *The Structure of Scientific Revolutions*, 2nd Ed., Chicago: University of Chicago Press, 1970, 210 pp.

1.7   MAHON, JAMES J., "Some Observations on World Accounting," *Journal of Accountancy*, January 1965, pp. 33–37.

1.8   MOORE, RUSSELL M., and GEORGE M. SCOTT, (Ed.), *An Introduction to Financial Control and Reporting in Multinational Enterprises.* Studies in International Business No. 1. Austin, Texas: The University of Texas, 1973, 89 pp. (Adapted from "Report of the Committee on International Accounting," *Accounting Review*, 1973 Supplement, pp. 120–167.)

1.9 MUELLER, GERHARD G., *International Accounting*, New York: Macmillan Company, 1967, 225 pp.

1.10 MUELLER, GERHARD G., "An International View of Accounting and Disclosure," *International Journal of Accounting*, Fall 1972, pp. 117–134.

1.11 MUELLER, GERHARD G., "A New Breed of Accounting Innovators: Multinationals Flex Their Muscles," *Proceedings*, Accounting and Finance in Europe Conference, London: The City University, Graduate Business Centre, 1976, pp. 93–109.

1.12 NATIONAL ASSOCIATION OF ACCOUNTANTS, *Management Accounting for Multinational Corporations*, Vol. I and II, New York: Author, 1974, 383 pp. and 317 pp.

1.13 PARKER, ROBERT H., "Some International Aspects of Accounting," *Journal of Business Finance*, Winter 1971, pp. 29–39.

1.14 PREVITS, GARY JOHN, "On the Subject of Methodology and Models for International Accountancy," *International Journal of Accounting*, Spring 1975, pp. 1–12.

1.15 RUESCHHOFF, NORLIN G., *International Accounting and Financial Reporting*, New York: Praeger Publishers, 1976, 172 pp.

1.16 SCHOENFELD, HANNS-MARTIN, "Some Special Accounting Problems of Multinational Enterprises," *Management International Review*, No. 4/5, 1969, pp. 3–20.

1.17 SEIDLER, LEE J., "International Accounting—The Ultimate Theory Course," *Accounting Review*, October 1967, pp. 775–781.

1.18 WATT, GEORGE C., *Accounting for the Multinational Corporation*, New York: Financial Executives Research Foundation, 1977.

1.19 WEIRICH, THOMAS R., CLARENCE G. AVERY, and HENRY R. ANDERSON, "International Accounting: Varying Definitions," *International Journal of Accounting*, Fall 1971, pp. 79–87.

1.20 ZENOFF, DAVID B., and JACK ZWICK, *International Financial Management*, Englewood Cliffs, N.J.: Prentice-Hall, 1969, 550 pp. (See especially Chapter 12, "Management Control of Foreign Operations," and Chapter 13, "Managerial Accounting for Operations Abroad.")

DISCUSSION QUESTIONS

1.1 With reference to economic development, sociologists have posited the so-called *convergence hypothesis.* This hypothesis suggests that economic and social systems become more and more alike as different countries reach similar stages of economic development. Is there any evidence of convergence in the multinational accounting field?

1.2 Consider international law and multinational accounting. Identify five similarities and five dissimilarities between these two fields.

1.3 What is the *paradox of the international heritage of accounting?*

1.4 North American accounting was imported from Great Britain late in the 19th and early in the 20th centuries. Would you expect British and United States accounting to be quite similar today? Why or why not?

1.5 List five specific financial accounting problems that a multinational enterprise is likely to be faced with and explain the nature of each of these problems in the form of a short paragraph.

1.6 Find a copy of the latest annual report of the International Telephone and Telegraph Corporation (ITT). What percentage of disclosed worldwide consolidated sales represents sales outside the United States? Which formal FASB statement requires the disclosure referred to?

1.7 It seems reasonable to suspect that most multinational enterprises are subject to highly centralized management decision-making at corporate headquarters. Explain why you agree or disagree with the foregoing assertion.

1.8 Describe concisely what you understand to be the theory of multinational accounting.

1.9 Identify the six steps often recognized as successively higher levels of abstraction in the development of knowledge for a given field of study. At which step is today's state of the art in multinational accounting?

1.10 Define, in your own terms, the notions of (a) world accounting, (b) international accounting, and (c) accounting for foreign subsidiaries. Do these definitions imply that subareas are already developing within the multinational accounting field?

1.11 List and briefly explain five different factors that distinguish managerial from financial accounting in the multinational setting. Are these distinctions the same as for the uninational setting?

1.12 On the basis of your study of Chapter 1 materials, prepare an abbreviated working outline of a possible multinational accounting research project.

1.13 How do individuals rendering professional CPA services become involved with multinational accounting problems? If you have not had practical accounting experience that allows you to answer the foregoing question, list 15 multinational accounting problems in which a practicing CPA *might* become involved.

1.14 Distinguish between institutional and managerial aspects of multinational accounting.

1.15 Some observers suggest that multinational enterprises are fairly tightly controlled by a great number of (and often conflicting) national laws. Others contend that there is no effective international law governing the multinationals, which allows them too many freedoms and privileges. What are the implications of these two positions for future developments in multinational accounting? Provide your answer in the form of two concise paragraphs.

ANNOTATED TEACHING MATERIALS

1.1 *CPA Examination Coverage.* Some years ago, the U.S. Uniform CPA Examination occasionally required the foreign currency translation of the trial balance of a foreign branch. This practice has given way to shorter (multiple-choice type) questions in more recent examinations.
   a. Have students prepare a multinational accounting content analysis of the most recent six CPA Examinations.
   b. Assign the preparation of a multinational accounting problem appropriate for the theory part of a future CPA Examination.

1.2 *The Broken Hill Proprietary Company Limited (ICCH Case 9 – 175 – 268).* Broken Hill Proprietary Company Limited (BHP) is a vertically integrated Australian manufacturing company that used current value accounting selectively in the preparation of its 1974 annual report. Criticisms were raised about BHP's departure from conventional practices. The questions of concern are the need for the revaluation of fixed assets, the ethics involved with respect to raising new money capital, the determination of reasonable earnings figures, and related effects on stock market prices. Included with the case is a partial 1974 annual report (*Note:* In 1976, Australia was the first country to adopt a formal professional accounting standards recommendation in favor of current cost accounting. Also see the technical discussion in Chapter 3.)

1.3 *Manners Europe* (Centre for International Business Studies Case; University of Western Ontario, Canada). The Managing Director of the European Operations of a United States corporation is reviewing operations after 2½ years of a 3-year assignment. During this period he has seen the European sales of building supplies and home improvement materials increase from $1.5 to $10 million. Now he is planning for future expansion. Problems have arisen in the past that have plagued previous attempts in this direction; therefore, some of the internal accounting subsystems must be evaluated.

Cultural problems persist. In Germany, Denmark, and Sweden some of the company's policies are still ignored. In Denmark, for example, the chief accountant is very reluctant to shift idle cash balances to the corporate account so that short-term borrowings are obviated. Receiving reports are not sent to headquarters in time. In Germany, credit sales are made to employees who are ineligible for credit under company policies. Consequently, the internal accounting systems have to be revised.

1.4 *Current Research Inventory.* Abstracts of Ph.D. dissertations are one guide to current research in a given field. Assign a project that lists and briefly describes a specified number of recently completed dissertations on multinational accounting topics. (*Note:* This project may be expanded to cover topics pending in the International Accounting Standards Committee. Also see the discussion in Chapter 5.)

1.5 *Chronology of Important Dates.* History is prologue. An effective teaching device is the construction of a historical chronology of important multinational accounting events. The selected literature references at the end of the chapter will provide sufficient inputs for such an exercise. Various classification possibilities exist, e.g., personalities, organizations, issues, literature content, or countries associated with specific developments.

Chapter 2
INTERNATIONAL ACCOUNTING PATTERNS

In society, accounting performs a service function. This function is put in jeopardy unless accounting remains above all technically and socially useful. Thus, it must respond to ever-changing needs of society and must reflect the cultural, economic, legal, social, and political conditions within which it operates. Its technical and social usefulness depends on its ability to mirror these conditions.

The history of accounting and accountants reveals continuing change—a process that accounting seems to undergo fairly consistently. At one time, accounting was little more than a recording system for certain banking services and tax collection schemes. Later it responded with double entry bookkeeping systems to meet the needs of trading ventures. Industrialization and division of labor made possible cost behavior analysis and managerial accounting. The advent of the modern corporation stimulated periodic financial reporting and auditing. More recently, accounting has revealed a capacity for public interest responses in such forms as human asset accounting and measuring, reporting, and auditing the social responsibility of various organizations. At present, accounting operates in the behavioral, public sector and international spheres, among others. It provides decision information for huge public securities markets—both domestic and international. It has even extended into the management consulting area. It is clearly concerned with its environment. Parenthetically, it might be noted that the developmental processes in accounting have many parallels to those operating in the field of law.

From an environmental point of view, various developments in society affect accounting. This is the source, for instance, of the worldwide concern with inflation accounting. It also accounts for the very serious preoccupation of United States accountants with the needs of United States securities analysts. To cite yet another example, the first formal opinion on accounting principles issued by the Swiss Institute of Certified Accountants addressed the problem of accounting for foreign currencies. This seems very natural when one considers that huge Swiss-based multinational enterprises, like Nestle or CIBA-GEIGY, do as much as 98 percent of their business outside the country of incorporation.

But accounting also affects its environment. Many economic resources are allocated to specific business uses on the basis of relevant accounting information. Taxes are collected through the use of accounting procedures, and labor unions often base wage demands on accounting-type information. Rate cases of regulated companies are based primarily on accounting data and so are most cases initiated in areas like antitrust or professional liabilities of CPA's. In some measure, even national and international economic policies are formulated on information emanating from corporate financial statements.

Therefore, accounting both reflects environmental conditions and influences them. If we then accept the proposition that the environments in which accounting operates are not the same in different countries or even in different organizations, it stands to reason that accounting must necessarily differ from case to case if it is to retain the sharp cutting edge of social utility.

The thesis of environmentally stimulated and justified differences in accounting runs directly counter, we might observe, to efforts at worldwide harmonization of accounting (explored in Chapter 5). Despite this apparent contradiction, it is a fact that the present world of accounting is characterized by diversity and that worldwide harmonization (or standardization) is still only a goal for the future. Understanding accounting as it exists requires an appreciation of how accounting operates in different environments and also of the different developmental patterns that have produced today's state of the art in accounting.

In an attempt to explain these two elements, the remainder of this chapter is divided into four sections:

1. An abbreviated listing of environmental circumstances likely to affect accounting development.
2. Groups or clusters of financial accounting principles now in use.
3. Various economic systems as determinants of different types of accounting.
4. Basic developmental patterns of accounting in market-oriented economies.

RELEVANT ENVIRONMENTAL CIRCUMSTANCES

In his pioneering book, *Forging Accounting Principles in Five Countries: A History and an Analysis of Trends,* Professor S. A. Zeff first demonstrates that accounting principles development does not come from specific scientific theory but from interactions among theory, practice, and various social, economic, and political influences. Corollary to this major conclusion is Zeff's proposition (based on a substantial amount of research in the five countries concerned—Canada, England, Mexico, Scotland, and the United States) that the formulation of accounting principles cannot be achieved by an accounting profession alone but necessarily depends on the tacit or expressed support of the real "power centers" in an economy, e.g., governmental agencies, industry associations, and investor groups and their representatives.

What are the environmental circumstances, then, that determine the process of "forging" accounting? Despite the considerable amount of research devoted to this topic, no definitive list of such circumstances exists. Both the process of searching for them and the circumstances themselves are rather subjective and therefore defy statistical specifications. Moreover, the latter are aggregate in nature and therefore subject to a great variety of specific (or micro) cause and effect relationships. Nonetheless, it is useful in multinational accounting analysis to specify at least a number of the environmental circumstances that apparently affect accounting development directly.

1. Type of Economy Involved. National economies vary in nature. Some are purely agricultural, while others depend heavily on the exploitation of natural resources (iron ore in Canada, oil predominantly in the Near East, gold and diamonds in South Africa, copper in Chile, etc.). Some economies rely mainly on trade and institutions (Hong Kong, Lebanon, Switzerland), while still others depend largely on tourism (many Polynesian Islands). The largest and most powerful economies are highly developed and highly diversified and include a great many different economic and financial activities. For example, the absence of publicly held corporate securities and masses of subsidiary companies will give accounting a very different orientation from that in an economy in which those two circumstances are present. Inventory methods, accounting for accretion or discovery of natural resources, audit functions being performed by state agencies, or decrease of refinement in cost accounting techniques—all have some relevance to the type of economy that is involved.

2. Legal System. Codification of accounting standards and procedures appears natural and appropriate in Roman or code law countries. By contrast, the nonlegalistic establishment of accounting policies by professional organizations working in the private sector of an economy is more in keeping with the system prevailing in common law countries. Under martial law or other national emergency situations, all aspects of the accounting function may be regulated by some central governmental court or agency. This was the case, for instance, in Nazi Germany when intensive war preparations and later World War II itself required a highly uniform national accounting system for purposes of total control of all national economic activities.

3. Political System. It seems almost self-evident that an accounting system which is useful to a centrally controlled economy must be different from an accounting system which is optimal for a market-oriented economy. In the former, the state owns all fixed assets and land; there is very little or no private ownership of business equities; "outside" auditors are simply government employees from another government agency; and the concept of periodic profit determination makes no sense. Accounting in centrally planned economies is discussed further on p. 36.

Of course, political systems also export and import accounting standards and practices. For instance, British accounting, as it existed at the turn of the 20th century, was exported in large measure to other Commonwealth countries. As mentioned in Chapter 1, the Dutch did the same with the Philippines and the French with their possessions in Africa and Asia. The Germans used political sympathy to influence accounting in Japan and Sweden, among others. Modern-day political systems have even larger impacts upon accounting. The example of the European Economic Community is so pervasive that Chapter 6 is devoted entirely to it.

4. Nature of Business Ownership. Widespread public ownership of corporate securities suggests financial reporting and disclosure principles different from those applicable to predominantly family- or bank-owned corporate interests. For instance, the huge public interest in corporate securities in the United States has produced many so-called "sunshine" accounting standards of wide open disclosure, whereas the virtual absence of public participation in corporate equities ownership in France has limited effective financial communications there largely to "insider" communication channels. Heavy bank ownership of corporate equities in West Germany produces still different accounting responses. In the United States, a 1977 committee of the AICPA made special recommendations for particular financial accounting standards and practices to be used by smaller, closely held enterprises.

5. Differences in Size and Complexity of Business Firms. Self-insurance may be acceptable for a very large firm but not for a small firm. Similarly, a large firm mounting an extensive advertising campaign directed at a specific market or season may be justified in deferring part of the resultant expenditure, whereas smaller programs in smaller firms may need to be expensed directly. This dichotomy extends over the entire range of parent company/subsidiary company accounting and specific technical problems like research and development expenditures or restructuring of long-term debt.

The complexity argument is equally applicable. Large conglomerate enterprises operating in significantly different lines of business need financial reporting techniques different from those for a small firm producing a single product. Similarly, multinational enterprises need accounting systems different from those for strictly domestic firms. Product testing (and accounting for it) is a different matter for a worldwide pharmaceutical firm than it is for a local firm producing only oil additives in a provincial capital in Mexico.

6. Social Climate. Developments in the United States point toward public reporting and examination by independent auditors of efforts to discharge corporate social responsibility by individual enterprises. There is also public reporting of both foreign and domestic corporate (possibly illegal) payoffs. "Consumerism," as it is called, is beginning to produce accounting changes.

In contrast, the social climate in Switzerland is still much more conservative and therefore demands considerably less financial disclosure by large Swiss companies. Italians still play tax games and hence are suspicious of anything and everything having to do with accounting. In some Eastern and South American countries, accounting is equated with bookkeeping and regarded as socially disagreeable—remaining underdeveloped and largely ineffective.

7. Relative Stability of the Currency of Account. If a currency is quite stable over time, historical cost-based accounting might be indicated. Significant currency instability often produces forms of price index adjustments, which depend largely on the types of indexes available and their reliability. France, Germany, Japan, and several South American countries experimented with general price index adjustments of accounting information after World War II—and some countries still do today. (*Note:* Current cost, replacement cost, or current market value alternatives to historical cost measurements are not predominantly inflation accounting responses, even though relative price stability may be a factor in their respective choice.)

Accounting for foreign currencies is related to accounting applications of price indexes—but is not the same. The topics of inflation and foreign exchange are explored in Chapter 3.

8. Level of Sophistication of Business Management and the Financial Community. Highly refined accounting standards and practices have no place in an environment where they are misunderstood and misused. A complex technical report on cost behavior variances is meaningless unless the reader understands cost accounting well. Statements of changes in financial position are useless unless they can be read competently. Capitalization of leases, consolidation of foreign subsidiaries, separate parent company financial statements, or financial forecasts are all counter-productive accounting techniques in the hands of the unsophisticated.

9. Degree of Legislative Business Interference. Tax legislation may require the application of certain accounting principles. This is the case in Sweden where certain tax allowances must be entered into the accounts before they can be claimed for tax purposes; this is also the situation for LIFO inventory valuations in the United States (which the U.S. Treasury Department attempted to extend to all foreign subsidiaries of domestic parent companies). Varying social security laws also affect accounting standards. Severance pay requirements in several South American countries are one illustration of this effect. Pension accounting in the United States is another.

Of course, in regulated or nationalized industry situations the legislative interference effect may be total. Sometimes the interference is indirect. For instance, new legislation was drafted (but *not* adopted) in Germany in 1976 under which only those corporate securities would be admitted to official trading in Germany that had been listed on a German stock exchange, issued by a company with residence or stock exchange quotations inside the EEC, or offered for official trading in an EEC member state after being scrutinized and admitted by a competent authority. In accounting terms, this would have been a way of enforcing German or EEC approved accounting standards upon all corporate securities officially traded in Germany.

10. Presence of Specific Accounting Legislation. In some instances there are specific legislative provisions for certain accounting rules and techniques. In the United States, the Cost Accounting Standards Board operates under the force of Federal law in prescribing certain cost accounting requirements for larger contracts with Federal Government departments and agencies. The United States Securities and Exchange Commission (SEC) prescribes accounting and disclosure standards for larger companies, but it does so by relying heavily on the authoritative and private sector Financial Accounting Standards Board (see SEC Accounting Series Release No. 150).

In most other countries of the Western world, local companies acts contain accounting provisions that are binding upon the accounting profession and business firms. So-called royal commissions propose changes to companies acts in the United Kingdom. Hence new accounting provisions emanating from successive British companies acts come essentially from the private sector. In Germany, on the other hand, companies legislation is predominantly a political process and therefore any accounting changes promulgated through such legislation are determined largely in the political arena. These different *systems* naturally have different consequences for accounting development.

11. Speed of Business Innovations. Business combinations became popular in Europe only a few years ago. Before that, European countries had little need for accounting standards and practices relating to mergers and acquisitions of going concerns. Very small stock distributions (so-called "stock dividends") occur most generally in the United States. Again, this is a business innovation that has directly affected United States accounting. Examples of this type abound. For instance, equipment leasing is not practiced in a number of countries at all, and consequently there is simply no need for lease accounting standards in those situations.

12. Stage of Economic Development. A one-crop agricultural economy needs accounting principles different from those of a sophisticated, industrialized country. In the former, for example, there is probably relatively little dependence on credit and long-term business contracts. Thus sophisticated accrual accounting is out of place, and basic cash accounting is needed.

13. Growth Pattern of an Economy. Companies and industries seem to grow, stabilize, or decline. The same applies to national economies and other organized forms of human endeavor. If growth and expansion are typical, the capitalization of certain deferred charges is more feasible than in stable or declining conditions. Stable conditions intensify competition for existing markets and thus require more restrictive credit and inventory methods. Declining conditions may dictate write-offs and adjustments not warranted in other situations. Protracted civil war (as in Ireland or Lebanon) may dictate accounting patterns quite different from those prevailing in politically stable environments.

14. Status of Professional Education and Organization. In the absence of organized accounting professionalism and native sources of accounting authority, standards from other areas or countries are likely to be utilized in filling existing voids. Adaptation of accounting factors from Great Britain was a significant environmental influence in accounting the world over until about the end of World War II. Since that time international adaptive processes have relied more on United States sources. Native or adapted, accounting development is unlikely to succeed unless environmental circumstances such as those enumerated in the present list are fully considered.

15. General Levels of Education and Facilitating Processes. Statistical methods in accounting and auditing cannot be used successfully where little or no knowledge of statistics and/or mathematics exists. Likewise, computer principles are not needed in the absence of working EDP installations. A plant accountant in a factory of a foreign subsidiary may have difficulty understanding the accounting and reporting requirements of the parent company unless adequate professional training is provided.

A good illustration of these interrelationships is the French general accounting plan that has enjoyed wide acceptance in France because it is easily understood and readily usable by those with average levels of education and without sophisticated accounting training. Independent audit requirements legislated in Italy during 1975 are still not implemented 2 years later because educational facilities are insufficient to produce the number of needed auditors in short order. This means, in turn, that the big international CPA firms will probably get most of the new Italian professional audit business—which was not at all the intent of the legislation!

CLUSTERS OF FINANCIAL ACCOUNTING PRINCIPLES

It goes almost without saying that significant differences characterize generally accepted accounting principles as applied in various countries. While these differences are material for a number of individual accounting standards and practices, they should not obscure the equally important observation that there are also a great many similarities between the generally accepted accounting principles of different countries. The differences, of course, are the sources of frequent and substantive problems in multinational accounting practice.

Does this mean that each member country of the United Nations has its own and distinct set of generally accepted financial accounting principles?

The answer is an emphatic no. Probably at least half of the total group of politically recognized independent countries does not have what might be called a national set of generally accepted accounting principles and, for the other half, differences exist in degree only. The accounting standards and practices applied in the United States and in Canada are so similar that for all intents and purposes they might be defined as a *cluster* of accounting. Similarly, Commonwealth practices in the United Kingdom, Australia, New Zealand, and South Africa are such close relatives that again they might be defined as a cluster. Ten to twelve distinct and identifiable groups or clusters of financial accounting standards and practices are sufficient to encompass all financial accounting as it is known today. Beyond the fairly substantial differences from cluster to cluster, variations are really a matter of degree only. Multinational accounting is not as fragmented as some of the descriptive literature suggests.

Evidence of Clustering

How does one go about sorting existing accounting principles into clusters and know, in fact, when one has such a cluster on hand? Two methodologies have been employed. One involves subjective classification on the basis of descriptive literature. The other extends statistical analysis to the problem.

An overwhelming amount of descriptive literature has become available in the last 15 years. All the larger international CPA firms publish individual "Doing business in ... " brochures for 75 to 100 different countries—each containing appropriate descriptions of locally accepted financial accounting principles. Government departments of commerce and economic development do likewise. Banks also publish economic information about different countries, including respective accounting requirements. Commercial newsletter services on accounting abound around the globe. Traveling accountants fill the pages of their professional journals with descriptions of what they found abroad in a veritable flood of reporting.

Three reference books are particularly useful in drawing together the entire multinational accounting descriptive literature. These books are (a) *Professional Accounting in 30 Countries,* published by the AICPA, (b) *Financial Accounting Principles—A Survey in 46 Countries,* published by Price Waterhouse & Co. International, and (c) *Accounting in Europe,* published by Michael Lafferty, a Financial Times (London) correspondent.

The AICPA book is, in essence, the "official" professional United States viewpoint. The editor of this book is a retired partner of a Big Eight international CPA firm. He assigned each of the 30 chapters in the book to a United States-based international CPA firm for preparation and review. Hence the professional/institutional frame of reference. The principal difficulty with the book is that it fails to make clear whether professional or other requirements are indeed applied in practice and reflected in periodic financial reports.

The Price Waterhouse & Co., compilation is a survey result produced by that firm's own worldwide offices. It is a very useful reference tool that provides a quick multinational overview of what is and what is not acceptable from country to country. If one constructs an overlay of the countries included in the survey and the individual accounting principles used, one eventually has a world "map" of accepted or acceptable accounting practices.

The Lafferty volume is geographically restricted to the EEC countries (see Chapter 6), but it contributes something fresh since Lafferty's style is journalistic and his perspective that of a world-renowned financial daily. Lafferty "calls it as he sees it"—and thereby makes a unique contribution to the descriptive multinational accounting literature.

Taken as a whole, descriptive multinational accounting materials suggest clustered effects between groups of countries or geographic regions and groups of accounting standards and principles.

The appendix to this chapter contains a simple classification of some informal evidence of clustering. For instance, Australia fits the United Kingdom pattern, Brazil and Columbia apparently "cluster," and Japan and Germany are not very far apart.

Earlier in this chapter we suggested that environmental circumstances are strong determinants of accounting thought and practice. No doubt these circumstances, together with historical and other more indirect factors, have produced the accounting clusters we now observe. But accounting is dynamic and socially responsive. This suggests that the cluster configuration of world accounting is probably undergoing continuous change. As the field of multinational accounting matures, it should attain some capability for forecasting both direction and intensity of these changes.

Cluster Analysis

Formal statistical analysis was employed by Hani Mahmoud Abu-Jbarah in 1972 at the University of Wisconsin (Madison) to group countries by dominant economic characteristics for purposes of recommending line of business (segmented) financial reporting according to the clusters he found. If the environmental influence thesis can be accepted, then Abu-Jbarah's clusters should be a reasonable guide to corresponding groups or sets of financial accounting principles.

The eight economic characteristics that Abu-Jbarah used for purposes of his data base are:

1. Per capita national income.
2. Private consumption expenditure as a percent of GNP.
3. Gross capital formation as a percent of GNP.
4. (Exports minus imports) as a percent of GNP.
5. Share of agriculture of all gross domestic products.
6. Rate of growth of real domestic products (at factor cost).
7. Change in the foreign exchange rate.
8. Change in the consumer price index.

After running 72 iterations on a computer model of interactions between the foregoing variables, eight separate clusters of countries with an observable degree of economic homogeneity were identified. The national "membership" in each of the separate clusters is shown in Table 2-1.

Utilizing a judgmental approach, Mueller reached similar conclusions in 1968. He based his analysis on four elements of differentiation—namely:

1. States of economic development.
2. Stages of business complexity.
3. Impact of political persuasions.
4. Reliance on some particular system of law.

Starting with the preceding four differentiating characteristics, Mueller came to the conclusion that ten distinct sets of business environments exist—each different from all others in at least one important respect. Mueller's list is as follows:

1. United States/Canada/The Netherlands—There is a minimum of commercial or companies legislation in this environment. Industry is highly developed; currencies are relatively stable. A strong orientation to business innovation exists. Many companies with widespread international business interests are headquartered in these countries.

2. British Commonwealth (excluding Canada)—Comparable companies legislation exists in all Commonwealth countries and administrative procedures and social order reflect strong ties to the mother country. There exists an intertwining of currencies through the so-called "sterling block" arrangement. Business is highly developed but often quite traditional.

3. Germany/Japan—Rapid economic growth has occurred since World War II. Influences stemming from various United States military and administrative operations have caused considerable imitation of

TABLE 2-1.   Clusters of Countries According to Observed Economic Characteristics

CLUSTER NUMBER	NUMBER OF COUNTRIES IN THE CLUSTER	COUNTRIES IN THE CLUSTER	CLUSTER NUMBER	NUMBER OF COUNTRIES IN THE CLUSTER	COUNTRIES IN THE CLUSTER
1	20	Burma			Denmark
		China (Taiwan)			Finland
		Costa Rica			France
		Cyprus			Germany
		Egypt			Iceland
		Greece			Italy
		Guyana			Japan
		Ireland			Luxembourg
		Jamaica			Netherlands
		Mauritius			Norway
		Nicaragua			Sweden
		Panama			Switzerland
		Peru			New Zealand
		Portugal			United Kingdom
		South Africa			
		Spain	4	7	Ethiopia
		Syria			Ghana
		Thailand			India
		Trinidad and Tobago			Nigeria
		Tunisia			Pakistan
					Sudan
2	19	Bolivia			Tanzania
		Cameroon			
		Ceylon	5	5	Jordan
		Columbia			Korea
		Dominican Republic			Malawi
		Ecuador			Singapore
		El Salvador			Viet Nam
		Guatemala			
		Honduras	6	4	Argentina
		Iran			Brazil
		Ivory Coast			Chile
		Kenya			Uruguay
		Malaysia			
		Mexico	7	3	Iraq
		Morocco			Venezuela
		Paraguay			Zambia
		Philippines			
		Sierra Leone	8	3	Israel
		Turkey			Puerto Rico
3	19	Australia			Malta
		Austria			
		Belgium			
		Canada			

SOURCE: Hani Mahmoud Abu-Jbarah, "A Subentity Basis for Financial Reporting by Multinational Firms: A Cluster Analysis Approach" (unpublished Ph.D. dissertation, University of Wisconsin, 1972), p. 99.

many facets of the United States practices, often by grafting United States procedures to various local traditions. The appearance of a new class of professional business managers is observable. Relative political, social, and currency stability exists.

4. Continental Europe (excluding Germany, The Netherlands and Scandinavia)—Private business lacks significant government support. Private property and the profit motive are not necessarily in the center of economic and business orientation. Some national economic planning exists. Political swings from far right to far left, and vice versa, have a long history in this environment. Limited reservoirs of economic resources are available.

5. Scandinavia—Here we have developed economies, but characteristically slow rates of economic and business growth. Governments tend toward social legislation. Companies acts regulate business. Relative stability of population numbers is the rule. Currencies are quite stable. Several business innovations (especially in consumer goods) originated in Scandinavia. Personal characteristics and outlooks are quite similar in all five Scandinavian countries.

6. Israel/Mexico—These are the only two countries with substantial success in fairly rapid economic development. Trends of a shift to more reliance on private enterprise are beginning to appear; however, there is still a significant government presence in business. Political and monetary stability seem to be increasing. Some specialization in business and the professions is taking place. The general population apparently has a strong desire for higher standards of living.

7. South America[1] — Many instances are present of significant economic underdevelopment along with social and educational underdevelopment. The business base is narrow. Agricultural and military interests are strong and often dominate governments. There is considerable reliance on export/import trade. Currencies are generally soft. Populations are increasing heavily.

8. The Developing Nations of the Near and Far East[1]—Modern concepts and ethics of business have predominantly Western origins. These concepts and ethics often clash with the basic oriental cultures. Business in the developing nations of the orient largely means trade only. There is severe underdevelopment on most measures, coupled with vast population numbers. Political scenes and currencies are most shaky. Major economic advances are probably impossible without substantial assistance from the industrialized countries. OPEC member countries are developing more rapidly since 1973.

[1] These areas are obviously treated very generally; exceptions exist for a few given countries.

9. Africa (excluding South Africa)¹—Most of the African continent is still in early stages of independent civilization and thus little native business environment presently exists. There are significant natural and human resources. Business is likely to assume a major role and responsibility in the development of African nations.

10. Communist Nations—The complete control by central governments places these countries in a grouping all of its own (see related discussion in the next section of this chapter).

While the foregoing analyses did not specifically address multinational groupings of financial accounting principles, *they suggest very strongly that such groupings in fact exist.* Furthermore, it is likely that each grouping represents a given pattern of accounting development rather similar to existing patterns of economic and social development.

Some unanswered developmental questions are (a) will additional clusters emerge—and if so, when, where, and how? (b) is more harmonization within existing clusters a better developmental strategy than worldwide harmonization of financial accounting principles? and (c) are past rates and directions of development within a cluster useful predictors of future accounting development patterns?

INFLUENCE OF ECONOMIC SYSTEMS

World economic systems, as presently in operation, vary from almost completely unfettered reliance on free market forces (e.g., Switzerland) to almost total central control (e.g., the Soviet Union and the Peoples Republic of China). Along this spectrum are varied degrees of central government interference in economic market forces. If we recognize three basic types of economic systems, (a) the administered market system of most Western countries, (b) the controlled market system of the developing countries, and (c) the tightly controlled systems of the Communist/Maoist countries, we can readily assert that each requires an accounting pattern unlike the other two. If all three were forced into a single uniform pattern, nonsensical results would be produced, and accounting would lose its social usefulness.

Market Systems

In market-oriented systems, even if they are administered or regulated to a certain degree, market prices are powerful factors that guide economic decisions and therefore the allocation of economic resources. Many observers feel that these systems make possible the preservation of private property rights and individual freedoms on the one hand, together with orderly economic organization on the other. While wastes of resources occur in this system and business cycles tend to inflict economic hardships during periods of recession, the general economic well-being, at comparatively high levels, of individuals who are a part of these systems is noteworthy.

Professor J. M. Yang, in a 1959 essay entitled "Accounting in a Free Economy," produced a classical statement of the role of accounting in market-oriented economic systems. Professor Yang specifically analyzed accounting as a basis of (a) business enterprise management, (b) economic productivity, and (c) product and service distribution. He also considered the significance of accounting in terms of its contribution to social cooperation. He concludes that accounting serves an important role in education and social welfare. Systems of taxation could not operate without appropriate forms of accounting. Through accounting, he maintains, "People maintain suitable control over the activities of the government. This is true fundamentally of all forms of civic organizations as well as private institutions, which carry on work for cooperative welfare." (Note the relevancy of the 1975 City of New York's financial debacle to the point made here.)

Similar benefits are seen for accounting in relation to regulated industries like insurance, transportation, and utilities. Moreover, "in many industrial establishments today an attempt has been made to secure the representation of employees on management committees to supply their representatives with accounting reports so that they may understand the financial position of their enterprise ... this is clearly ... a step in the direction of establishing a firm basis for genuine cooperation." (See Chapter 6 on the so-called "two tier" boards of directors in Europe).

The accounting standards and principles needed to assure the discipline's utility in market-oriented economic systems rest on such key concepts as transactions and events measurements; systematic and periodically complete accumulation of data; measurement of periodic business income; and the entire process of periodic financial reporting, full disclosure, and outside review of accounting reports presented by management. Concepts are expounded and refined in a plethora of textbooks, handbooks, and other literature to the point where they are by and large self-evident to students and practitioners. While our scope does not permit further cataloging of the concepts, standards, and principles involved, they are, we would remind our readers, undeniably a function of the economic system within which they operate.

Developing Economies. The specter of *third-world accounting* is raised in Chapter 10 as one of the most significant emerging issues of multinational accounting. Thus only three critical considerations are put forth at this time.

First, emerging countries usually have several special characteristics—burgeoning and often starving populations, severe lack of capital, inadequate educational and other social institutions, high dependence on world markets for export of agricultural products or mineral resources, plus political turmoil. Usually, there is little native accounting expertise to deal with the accounting dimensions of these characteristics.

A second consideration is the inordinate scope of accounting demands made upon third-world countries. Native industries are often labor intensive, organizationally simple, and single-product oriented. This type of enterprise requires basic, cost-efficient accounting. Yet when it comes to the analysis of new capital projects or the financial reporting requirements of international financial institutions such as the International Bank for Reconstruction and Development, the needed accounting systems and techniques are as sophisticated as they come! Due to these contradictions, ineffectiveness and inefficiency often plague accounting in developing countries.

The third factor, which is the one most directly relevant to the present discussion, relates to the uniqueness of the circumstances in most emerging nations. Local governments often play major roles in the developmental processses, whether through heavy regulation of market enterprises or under the aegis of central planning. Systems for national income accounting and other social indicator series must be devised and implemented. Taxation systems must be established and enforced. All kinds of institutions must be developed and brought into the mainstream. And, as far as accounting is concerned, simple importation of accounting paraphernalia from other countries is typically more counter-productive than helpful. Here, again, a particular economic system requires a particular pattern of accounting. This is easier said than done when it comes to Third World countries.

Centralized Control

In economies that are centrally planned and controlled, the role of accounting is relatively larger and more important than its counterpart in market-oriented economies. The entire system of prices and costs in central systems are really established through accounting procedures rather than through market processes. In the Soviet Union, for instance, single enterprises are not financially independent, and few decisions turn on whether calculated earnings are positive or negative. A firm has access to new resources basically through planning and control processes rather than through past economic performance.

Accounting, statistical, and technical records are all typically kept within a single system in Soviet enterprises. Accounting rules and procedures are very formalized and subject to uniform central control. Standard accounting procedures and reports exist for each major industrial classification. Naturally, there is little controversy over different ways in which any one economic transaction might be handled.

R. H. Mills and A. L. Brown wrote in 1966

> The purpose of such rigidly constructed [accounting] reports is to facilitate better centralized control and planning. The reports are used in the evaluations of the administrative organizations and resource allocation process and are an integral tool in developing regional and national economic plans.
>
> One area of considerable interest and importance, for several reasons, is cost accounting. The virtual absence of the influence of the market mechanism on prices ... necessitates the determination and fixing of prices primarily on the basis of cost accounting reports. These reports are valid only to the extent that they have been properly prepared and reflect accurate cost data.

Professor R. W. Campbell, who is an authority on Soviet accounting systems, has summarized the main deficiencies of their cost accounting as resulting primarily from poor estimates of depreciation allowances, improper allocation of current expenditures among individual kinds of output, failure to charge certain outlays to costs of products, and the use of broad aggregative accounts with the result that expense flows through a plant are poorly traced, costs of individual products or of separate processes are often not ascertainable, and so on. While this is not the place to delve into the details of Soviet accounting, we might observe that cost accounting is as critical to the Soviet system as periodic income determination is to the United States system. Furthermore, accounting for land in a Communist system is pointless since all land is owned by the state. In fact, what Western accountants might call balance sheet accounting is really accounting for working capital in a centralized system, since their individual enterprises have virtually no control over long-term assets of any type. It stands to reason that patterns of accounting appropriate for the two sides of the Iron Curtain cannot and should not be similar.

BASIC DEVELOPMENT PATTERNS

In addition to the concept that fundamentally different economic systems should develop and use correspondingly different accounting systems, there are at least four distinct approaches to accounting development that can be observed among Western nations with market-oriented economic systems. These four approaches, or patterns, of accounting development are:

1. The macroeconomic pattern.
2. The microeconomic pattern.
3. The independent discipline approach.
4. The uniform accounting approach.

These four patterns (or approaches or frameworks) were developed in the predecessor to this book (see reference 1.8, p. 16) and are therefore accorded only summary treatment here.

Macroeconomic Pattern

If the mass of research and writing in business and economics were reduced to two central propositions, we would probably find that (a) individual firms establish formal and informal goals and then gear their operations toward optimizing these goals and (b) nations establish formal and informal national policies and then adopt administrative procedures toward optimal implementation of these policies. Firm goals and national policies are not always clearly defined, and they are often perceived differently by different individuals or groups. Yet that does not invalidate the assertion that such goals and policies exist and that they become guides to actions for the organization concerned.

Business firm goals are necessarily narrower than national economic policy. A firm has more specific purposes to accomplish, often operates in more circumscribed space and time dimensions, and is accountable to more identifiable interest groups. As a consequence, firm goals normally follow rather than lead national economic policies. This is not an absolute condition since business firms are a part of the public interest that influences and directs national policies; hence, reciprocal cause and effect relationships exist.

If the foregoing views of a developed economic environment are accepted, the following three propositions might be postulated:

1. The business enterprise is the essential unit in the economic fabric of a nation.
2. The business enterprise accomplishes its goals best through close coordination of its activities with the national economic policies of its environment.
3. Public interest is served best if business enterprise accounting interrelates closely with national economic policies.

What are the accounting implications of such a formulation? Let us postulate, for example, a policy of relatively full employment. This implies, above all, sustained efforts toward economic and business stability. It also means administrative efforts to minimize effects of business cycles or, better yet, avoidance of pronounced swings in business cycles altogether. Accounting could be adapted to such a policy through, for example, requiring some averaging of reported business income for the firm over the length of the typical business cycle.

Another national policy might be the achievement of a predetermined rate of economic growth. Here accounting might adjust its depreciation and amortization procedures with regard to firms or industries that are most likely to be significant contributors to the rate of economic growth in a given period. Moreover, accounting might incorporate the measurements on a firm's contributions to gross national product or on changes in rates of productivity. For example, an accounting system could readily encompass information on percentages of utilization of resources. Expressed differently, accounting could measure the waste of resources.

Many of our newer accounting concerns appear to fit into the macroeconomic pattern of accounting development. Accounting for corporate social responsibilities and reporting and auditing the "social conscience" of a firm clearly fits the picture. So does accounting for human resources. Even the public interest, i.e., "consumerism," concerned with corporate payoffs for illegal purposes, contributions of corporate funds to charitable organizations, and disclosure responsibilities to the public at large rather than to existing and prospective shareholders only are manifestations of macroeconomically oriented developments.

Periodic income smoothing, as found in Europe and South America, is one application of the macroeconomic pattern. German income statements, which report as revenues amounts realized from the sale of goods and services plus amounts of value created by a firm's construction or development of assets intended for its own use plus amounts of value added to inventories of goods and materials, are another.

Macroeconomically oriented financial accounting might formally recognize discovery values of mineral or oil deposits, might compute depreciation charges on productive equipment on a unit of production basis wherever possible, and might permit fast write-off of certain costs when this would be in the interest of regional or national economic development. In the past, such write-offs have aided the Scandinavian shipbuilding industry, construction of employer-owned dwellings for employees in Germany and France, and capital expenditures for defense purposes in the United States during World War II under certificates of necessity. The country in which the macroeconomic development pattern of accounting has found the relatively most comprehensive acceptance is Sweden. In this connection, the accounting procedures surrounding Swedish capital investment reserves are of special interest.

The Microeconomic Approach

Market-oriented economies, including those with some degree of central government administrative interference, entrust much of their economic well-being to the business activities of individuals and of individual business firms. Therefore, in these economies, a fundamental orientation exists to the individual cells of economic activity. This is so deeply ingrained in Western economic organizations that it is simply assumed for many business, judicial, legislative, and social processes.

The intellectual part of economics reflects this orientation as well. The tradition of Western economic thought is overwhelmingly a tradition of microeconomic thought. To be sure, more recent decades have seen a broadening of economics into areas such as social economics, national income models, econometrics, and economic forecasting. These specialty areas are not, however, the foundation of the economics discipline in Western culture. They are an outgrowth of it. The traditional elements of Western economic thinking come from the band of great political economists and economic philosophers among whom we find Hume, Locke, Marshall, Mill, Ricardo, and Smith. Their oratory and writings have shaped much of what remains fundamental in economics to this day.

With private and business activities at the core of the economic affairs in a market-oriented economy and with accounting oriented to a service function for business and business enterprises, it seems natural enough that accounting would seek to orient itself to the same micro considerations that are so strongly represented in its environment. In fact, in many European universities, accounting is typically considered as a tool area of microeconomics.

Several propositions can again be postulated using a microeconomic framework for accounting:

1. Individual firms provide focal points for business activities.
2. The main policy of the business firm is to ensure its continued existence.
3. Optimization in an economic sense is a firm's best policy for survival.
4. Accounting, as a branch of business economics, derives its concepts and applications from economic analysis.

The central accounting concept in a development pattern based on microeconomics is that the accounting process must hold constant in real terms the amount of monetary capital invested in the firm. This is essential on three counts: (a) The continued survival of the firm is impossible if its real capital base is eroded away by tax or dividend payments that fully or in part invade the real investment capital base; (b) the permanently invested capital is the economic root of the firm and, therefore, the capital investment in the firm must receive key considerations as long as the firm itself is the focal point of business activities; and (c) an effective separation of capital and income is prerequisite to evaluating and controlling the firm's business activities.

Most advocates of the microeconomic approach to accounting conclude that an accounting measurement system based on replacement costs fits microeconomic concepts best. A brief illustration of the replacement cost measurement idea is provided in Chapter 3. Under this approach, monetary amounts needed to maintain invested capital in real terms are not considered a part of periodic accounting income. Vice versa, changes in replacement costs are a part of accounting income to the extent that they are not needed for required capital investment adjustments. A full set of operational accounting standards and principles has been developed along this line—for instance, by several multinational enterprises based in Holland.

When microeconomics plays a heavy role in accounting considerations, a general managerial emphasis prevails in *all* accounting reports, including those issued to shareholders annually *and* quarterly. Segmented reporting (by product lines, market areas, or international sectors) for revenues, gross business assets, and other important financial indicators is one logical consequence. Others would be accounting reports detailing compositions of wages and other production costs, giving a fair airing to internal enterprise affairs in categories like pension schemes, listings of firms' securities on different stock exchanges, long-term commitments not yet accountable, and so forth. Accounting, as advocated and practiced in the Netherlands, represents the most comprehensive example of the microeconomic pattern of accounting development.

Independent Discipline

History has not accorded much glamour to business people. Scholars have scorned business studies as void of theoretical complexity and as too commonplace for intellectual pursuits. The moneychangers of the Bible were little more than outcasts of society. While artisans and craftsmen (often through their respective guilds) flourished during the Middle Ages, merchants were seldom able to improve their lowly social status. Even in the early decades of the present century, businessmen found relatively little sympathy for their skills and abilities. Today they are indicted as wasters of social resources, polluters of the environment, and unethical payers of bribes and kickbacks. The chronicles of business are filled with Scrooges and slave traders—people of great greed and little social distinction. The perpetration of spectacular financial swindles only added coals to smouldering fires of public wrath.

Reflecting upon this historical background, there is little wonder that business has become introspective. It has turned primarily to itself for analysis and innovation. Good business practices have become identified with those practices that are profitable and effective in generating more business. A deep-seated respect for pragmatism developed.

Factors of judgment and estimate cannot be eliminated from business processes. Business deals significantly with human want satisfactions whose origins and patterns are forever changing. From the inception of producing a product or a service to its final sale to an actual user, a very complex fabric of human emotions and reactions must be accommodated. Add to this the ever-present condition of uncertainty, and the significance of business judgment becomes all too apparent.

Thus business people have learned to use intuition. They find and use signs of changes that are not evident to the inexperienced. The trial and error method is often the only avenue open to them, and they manage to use it with facility and expediency. The ability to make sound business judgments often is the most important attribute of a successful business person.

Earlier discussions in this chapter suggested a direct interrelationship between accounting and its environment. If business is the main interest served by accounting and if accounting provides primarily an efficient and effective service to business, the inevitable question is, should not accounting and business practices have the same basis and follow the same pattern of development? If the answer to this question is affirmative, a case is made for regarding accounting as an independent discipline. If business can produce its own concepts and methods from experience and practice, the argument follows that accounting can (or should) do the same. If business can develop itself from within, why should accounting not be capable of doing the same?

Viewing accounting as a service function of business provides ample room for concluding that accounting can construct for itself a meaningful framework derived essentially from the business processes it serves. When this is held possible, conceptual support from a discipline like economics is not needed. Accounting, in other words, relies on itself—it becomes an independent discipline.

When so perceived, accounting adopts a rather pragmatic approach for its development. Induction from existing business (accounting) practice is then the most important foundation for establishing accounting standards and principles. Many prominent accountants view accounting exactly in this vein. Note George O. May's most important work, *Financial Accounting* (Macmillan, 1943), pages 2 – 3:

> Many accountants were reluctant to admit that accounting was based on nothing of a higher order of sanctity than conventions. However, it is apparent that this is necessarily true of accounting as it is, for instance, of business law. In these fields there are no principles in the more fundamental sense of the word on which we can build; and the distinctions between laws, rules, standards and conventions lie not in their nature but in the kind of sanctions by which they are enforced. Accounting procedures have in the main been the result of common agreements between accountants. Though they have to some extent, and particularly in recent years, been influenced by laws or regulations.
>
> Conventions, to have authority, must be well conceived. Accounting conventions should be well conceived in relation to at least three things: First, the uses of accounts; second, the social and economic concepts of the time and place; and third, the modes of thought of the people. It follows that as economic and social concepts or modes of thought change, accounting concepts may have to change with them.

Regarding accounting as an independent discipline with roots in the practical affairs of everyday business implies, first of all, that a cohesive and complete conceptual structure of accounting is difficult to erect. In the United States, for example, we have struggled through the 1938 Sanders, Hatfield, and Moore study and the long and arduous efforts of both the AICPA's *Committee on Accounting Procedure* and *Accounting Principles Board* without much success in this respect. At present, the *Financial Accounting Standards Board* is trying its luck with its "Objectives for Financial Statements" project.

A second point is that the piecemeal approach to evolving and establishing accounting standards is the only possible avenue of approach in the absence of a comprehensive conceptual framework for the discipline. Under the independent discipline philosophy, each individual accounting standard or principle has to meet the conditions of practical business usefulness and therefore has to reach back to related and proved business practices. Interrelationships and consistency among various accounting standards and principles are of only secondary importance under this approach because the general business community does not seem greatly concerned about the intellectual niceties of a single conceptual structure.

A strictly conventional definition of business income is yet another hallmark of this particular approach to accounting development. *Income* here is simply a defined quantity that seems useful in practice. Even though "constructed" pragmatically, this income notion enjoys wide acceptance and has found its way into business literature, accounting textbooks and handbooks, and even legal cases and positions. It is a significant illustration of a pragmatic response to the practical needs of the business communities affected.

Full and fair disclosure in published financial reports has developed over the years into one of the more important standards of accounting within an independent discipline development pattern. One might go so far as to say that the full and fair disclosure tenet might be seen as a substitute for a comprehensive conceptual framework under this approach.

The United Kingdom and the United States are comprehensive examples of countries in which accounting has developed as an independent discipline.

Uniform Accounting

Accounting development based on a pattern of uniformity in accounting has long intrigued scholars and others concerned with accounting information. Most important in this regard is probably the long quest to make accounting more scientific. At a time when society broadly seems to rely more and more upon the application of the scientific method for many of its undertakings, it is not difficult to find supporters for the proposition that accounting should conform to this trend and also become more scientific. In the views of many, more uniform accounting means more scientific accounting.

A second reason why the uniformity pattern of accounting development holds much appeal is the *cameralistic* aspect of accounting—as the phrase is used in Europe. *Cameralistic* can be translated roughly to mean that something is an ideal administrative device. Thus, when used in the accounting sense, it can be employed to control a small, one-person business as well as a giant government apparatus. In government, in particular, it can become the central tool of administration. Accounting procedures can allocate funds to functions, measure performance by assuming proportionality between administrative effectiveness and fund changes, classify functions in terms of monetary rewards and vice versa, and perform other similar functions.

Beyond administrative convenience, however, accounting also presents itself as a tool for economic and business control by government. This was suggested earlier in the chapter and is clearly demonstrated in totalitarian regimes like Nazi Germany or several present-day communist countries. As mentioned previously, centrally directed economies plan, administer, control, and reward many facets of their societies on the basis of accounting information. But they can do this only if accounting is as uniform as their systems are absolute.

A third major appeal of accounting uniformity lies in the simplicity it affords. Uniformity is a pattern that is very simple on most counts—recording and classifying financial data, manipulating the data toward financial reports, and finally understanding and interpreting financial reports. For example, the French plan of accounts provides instruction for the recording of the simplest of all transactions as well as a completely detailed pre-numbered chart of accounts. *Alternative* financial accounting principles is something such a system does not know!

Most tax accounting systems are uniform accounting systems. Thus a uniform system for financial accounting often holds advantages for the corresponding tax accounting system.

Three practical approaches to the uniform accounting development pattern can be distinguished. Each is identified in the paragraphs immediately following.

Business Approach. Here accounting uniformity is oriented specifically to particular users of accounting data. The business approach takes full account of the business characteristics and the business environment under which the data are collected, processed, and communicated. It is a pragmatic approach that relies heavily on convention and is employed most frequently in the design of sectional uniform charts of accounts, i.e., for a branch of industry or trade. Railroad or utilities companies' accounting in the United States falls into this category by reason of the governmental regulations to which it is subject. The Swedish "M – Chart" is another example. It is a blueprint for a comprehensive accounting system for Swedish companies in the metal-working industries prepared by the industry association in question.

Economic Approach. The economic approach to accounting uniformity is in essence a macro approach. It links accounting to public policy. Public laws and regulatory agencies are used to enforce the system established within such a pattern of development. Technical accountng considerations are secondary, and national economic policy considerations uppermost. H. W. Singer sketches this approach as it was utilized in Nazi Germany between 1937 and 1945.

> The new aims of the German economy call for increased output and efficiency from business undertakings. The fulfillment of this great task requires a thorough knowledge and close control of all business transactions. Thus a well-developed accounting system is a primary factor in the reorganization of industries. The public interest, and in

particular the aims of the four-year plan, demand that the accounting system of all firms should be arranged on uniform principles. Systematic mutual exchange of experience, especially in the form of comparative analysis of companies, will help toward this end (from the 1937 Nazi regime decree which made uniform accounting mandatory in Germany).

Technical Approach. The technical accounting approach to uniformity development is by and large the work of academics. This approach is *analytical* in that it attempts to derive uniformity schemes from the basic tenets of double entry bookkeeping. It is also a *general* approach because direct attention is paid to specific business characteristics of accounting transactions or accounting processes. Finally, the broad orientation of this approach is *theoretical* in nature. For example, it seeks to establish linkages between accounts of the same type so that they can be treated consistently within the overall framework of a particular scheme (i.e., to group accounts by functions or by substance but not indiscriminately). European professors identified with generalizing accounting processes from comprehensive flow charts of accounts include K. Käfer (Switzerland), L. L. Illetschko (Austria), E. Schmalenbach (Germany), and A. ter Vehn (Sweden). France, without doubt, is the country most identified with the uniformity pattern of accounting development.

As we turn our attention now to practical and institutional problems of multinational accounting, we suggest keeping in mind the more conceptual framework established in the preceding two chapters. This will help not only with definitions and classifications but also with problem identification and analysis inherent in the material that follows.

SELECTED REFERENCES

2.1   ABU-JBARAH, HANI MAHMOUD, "A Subentity Basis for Financial Reporting by Multinational Firms: A Cluster Analysis Approach," Unpublished Ph.D. Dissertation, University of Wisconsin, 1972, 150 pp.

2.2   ALHASHIM, DHIA D., and S. PAUL GARNER, "Postulates for Localized Uniformity in Accounting," *Abacus,* June 1973, pp. 62 – 72.

2.3   AMERICAN ACCOUNTING ASSOCIATION, "Report of the American Accounting Association Committee on International Accounting, 1974 – 75," *Accounting Review,* Supplement 1976, pp. 70 – 196.

2.4   AMERICAN INSTITUTE OF CERTIFIED PUBLIC ACCOUNTANTS, *Professional Accounting in 30 Countries,* New York: Author, 1975, 792 pp.

2.5   BEVIS, HERMAN W., *Corporate Financial Reporting in a Competitive Economy,* New York: Macmillan, 1965, 212 pp.

2.6   CAMPBELL, ROBERT W., *Accounting in Soviet Planning and Management,* Cambridge, Mass.: Harvard University Press, 1963, 315 pp.

2.7   CHASTNEY, JOHN G., "On to International Accounting," *Accountancy*, July 1976, pp. 76, 78–80.

2.8   GORELIK, GEORGE, "Soviet Accounting, Planning and Control," *Abacus,* June 1974, pp. 13 – 25.

2.9   HENDRIKSEN, ELDON S., *Accounting Theory* (rev. ed.), Homewood Ill.: Richard D. Irwin, 1970, 643 pp. (See especially Chapter 1, "The Methodology of Accounting Theory.")

2.10 KÄFER, KARL, *Theory of Accounts in Double Entry Bookkeeping,* Monograph No. 2, Center for International Education and Research in Accounting, University of Illinois, 1966, 76 pp.

2.11 LAFFERTY, MICHAEL, *Accounting in Europe*. Cambridge, England: Woodhead, Faulkner, Ltd., 1975, 425 pp. (Published in association with National Westminster Bank.)

2.12 MILLS, ROBERT H., and ABBOTT L. BROWN, "Soviet Economic Developments and Accounting," *Journal of Accountancy,* June 1966, pp. 40 – 46.

2.13 MUELLER, GERHARD G., "International Experience with Uniform Accounting," *Law and Contemporary Problems,* Autumn 1965, pp. 850 – 873.

2.14 MUELLER, GERHARD G., "Accounting Principles Generally Accepted in the United States Versus Those Generally Accepted Elsewhere." *International Journal of Accounting,* Spring 1968, pp. 91 – 103.

2.15 MUELLER, GERHARD G., "Academic Research in International Accounting," *International Journal of Accounting,* Fall 1970, pp. 67 – 81.

2.16 PERRIDON, LOUIS, "Accounting Principles, An Academic Opinion," *Journal UEC,* October 1974, pp. 213 – 224.

2.17 PRICE WATERHOUSE & CO. (U.S.A.), *Guide for the Reader of Foreign Financial Statements* (rev. ed.), New York: Author, 1975, 71 pp.

2.18 PRICE WATERHOUSE INTERNATIONAL, *A Survey in 46 Countries: Accounting Principles and Reporting Practices* (Text in English, French, German and Spanish). London: Author, 1975, 264 pp. plus Index.

2.19 YANG, J. M., "Accounting in a Free Economy," *Accounting Review,* July 1959, pp. 442 – 451.

2.20 ZEFF, STEVEN A., *Forging Accounting Principles in Five Countries: A History and an Analysis of Trends.* Champaigne, Ill.: Stipes Publishing Company, 1971, 332 pp.

DISCUSSION QUESTIONS

2.1   Identify, in one sentence each, five environmental factors which influence the nature and scope of financial accounting and five accounting factors which influence the environment in which accounting operates. Be sure that at least one-half of these factors are multinational in character.

2.2   Authoritative and sophisticated observers seem to agree that financial accounting policy-making is increasingly becoming a political process.

Relying on the findings in Professor Zeff's book (Ref. 2.20), do you agree with this assertion? Defend your position in a concise two-paragraph response.

2.3   The chapter lists 15 environmental circumstances that are said to have a direct effect on accounting development. From your own personal vantage point, rank order these 15 items from most to least important as far as accounting development is concerned. Then write brief justifications for both the top and bottom items in your ranking.

2.4   Let us arbitrarily divide accounting development stages into a spectrum of five categories: (a) highly developed and complex; (b) well developed and mature; (c) reasonably developed, with a character of its own; (d) beginning development, mostly under outside influences; and (e) little or no measurable development. Now attempt to place five countries in each of the five categories established. Make sure that you can justify each individual selection.

2.5   In your nearest library, find a published book review of the AICPA's 1975 *Professional Accounting in 30 Countries.* From this review, determine and capsulize the three most distinguishing features of this particular reference work.

2.6   What is *cluster analysis* and how does it work? Can you think of five easily quantifiable factors that might be employed in applying this formal statistical methodology to financial accounting and reporting?

2.7   Suppose that financial accounting and reporting the world over can indeed be grouped into 10 to 12 distinct clusters. What conditions or circumstances might cause a particular country to shift from one such cluster to another? Provide your response in the form of a brief essay.

2.8   Late in 1976, the FASB published a set of tentative conclusions concerning objectives of financial statements. Could similar conclusions have been reached in Poland, Uganda, and West Germany? As far as possible, list specific reasons in support of your answers.

2.9   Read three relatively recent articles in the periodical accounting literature dealing with accounting in the Soviet Union. Then outline (don't actually write!) a reasonably comprehensive essay on the nature and system of accounting in the Soviet Union.

2.10 In 1965, Paul Grady published the AICPA's Accounting Research Study No. 7 entitled *Inventory of Generally Accepted Accounting Principles for Business Enterprises.* On pages 23 to 24 of this study, Mr. Grady lists 10 basic concepts to which accepted accounting principles are oriented. Prepare similar lists of basic concepts for accounting appropriate to (a) developing economies and (b) centrally controlled economies.

2.11 The chapter text distinguishes among four basic accounting development patterns. Naturally, these four patterns overlap and hence are not found in completely pure forms.

Thinking of generally accepted accounting principles in the United States, LIFO inventory pricing methods are available for financial purposes only if they are also applied in parallel fashion for tax accounting purposes. This is a good example of the uniform approach to accounting development.

Identify three specific United States financial accounting standards, principles, or practices that illustrate each of the other three basic accounting development patterns cited in the text.

2.12 Identify and briefly describe three key differences between the macroeconomic and the microeconomic patterns of accounting development.

2.13 Assume that The Netherlands is a good representative of the microeconomic pattern of accounting development and that the United States best represents the independent discipline approach. Has one of these two development patterns been more successful than the other? How might one go about measuring the success of these two different patterns? Please develop your answer in essay form.

2.14 During the 1960's the "uniformity versus flexibility" issue was ardently debated in the United States but has since lost momentum and appeal. On the other hand, the French not only like uniform accounting but are actively proposing its acceptance throughout the European Economic Community (EEC). The uniformity issue is alive, well, and gaining in France.

Why this difference between the United States and France? Is one wrong and the other right? What future developments do you foresee with regard to uniformity in France on the one hand and the United States on the other? Write a concise explanation of this apparent paradox.

2.15 Keeping in mind the entirety of the materials discussed in Chapter 2, write an executive memorandum to the members of the FASB outlining to what extent, if any, they should consider "international accounting patterns" as inputs to their work. Be as specific as you can. Use short examples or illustrations to underscore major points. Remember that FASB Discussion Memoranda are issue-oriented. Your memorandum should be likewise.

ANNOTATED TEACHING MATERIALS

2.1   *Introduction to European Accounting* (ICCH Note 4-174-043). The purpose of this note is to describe the major differences between United States and European financial accounting practices. The differences are classified into three groups: (a) business and political factors, (b) specific accounting differences, and (c) trends within Europe. Each of these groups of differences is presented in some detail to highlight contrasts.

2.2   *Philips N. V.* (ICCH Case 9-108-003). This case describes the accounting practices of Philips N.V. of the Netherlands. Philips departs from the historical cost model of accounting and financial reporting by using replacement (current) cost valuations. This involves the policy of capitalizing and expensing fixed assets and inventories on the basis of replacement values (current costs). General information and background material on Philips is provided as well as an explanation of Philips' treatment of major balance sheet items. Some questions are raised concerning Philips' version of applying replacement value (current cost) accounting.

For specific additional readings, refer to:

a. J. Vos, "The 1971 Annual Report: Replacement Value is Continued Though Applied Differently," *Philips Administration Review,* December 1972, pp. 2 – 13.

b. C. Nijs, "The Application of Replacement Value Theory in Balance Sheet and Profit & Loss Account Reconsidered," *Philips Administration Review,* September 1976, pp. 34 – 38.

2.3   *Update of Informal Cluster Analysis.* The appendix to Chapter 2 presents a 24-way, cross-country analysis of selected accounting practices. The descriptive methodology underlying it was considered as informal cluster analysis in the text. The data base used is the initial edition (1971) of the Price Waterhouse & Co. publication *A Guide for the Reader of Foreign Statements.*

This *Guide* was revised and republished in 1975. To provide a possibility for comparative exercises, the initial edition was deliberately used to develop the Chapter 2 appendix.

As a learning exercise, students may secure a copy of the 1975 edition of this *Guide* from their nearest library or Price Waterhouse & Co. office. The 1975 data can be restated to the Chapter 2 appendix format and then compared to determine the changes that have taken place over the 5-year period involved. A less ambitious project would be to select a cluster of countries from the appendix and then analyze the changes occurring between 1971 and 1975.

2.4   *Comparative Influences upon Accounting Development.* Professor Gary John Previts (University of Alabama) wrote an article in the Spring 1975 issue of *The International Journal of Accounting.* This article carries the title "On the Subject of Methodology and Models for International Accountancy." One "block" of research suggested in the article is

An evaluation of the contemporary role of accounting in other nations in the multinational community in order to draw inter-country comparisons and analyze contemporary influences (positive step).

Design and execute a limited test of the methodology suggested by Professor Previts to "analyze contemporary influences" upon multinational accounting. As part of this project, limitations and advantages of this methodology should be explored and the usefulness of its results analyzed.

2.5 *Introduction to Accounting in Japan.* In 1976, Robert J. Ballon (Sophia University, Tokyo) published a book, *Financial Reporting in Japan.* Many other references to accounting standards and practices in Japan are now available in the English language, including those cited in Ref. 1.5 (p. 16).

From relevant materials available to you, construct a teaching note similar to the one cited under 2.1 above. In carrying out this project, do not over-emphasize technical accounting aspects and give adequate attention to environmental and multinational influences.

APPENDIX TO CHAPTER 2. Classified Summary: A Guide for the Reader of Foreign Financial Statements (Price Waterhouse & Co., 1971)

ASSET MEASUREMENT

Exchange losses on liabilities capitalized..
   (inventories and fixed assets)
Fixed assets at appraisal (current) value ....
Price level adjustments ....
Decline in permanent investment values not recognized ....
Some capital purchases are expensed ....
Inventories sometimes above historical cost..
Majority-owned subsidiaries not carried on equity basis ....
Cost rather than cost or market in inventories ....
Interest on fixed assets capitalized after completion ....
Fixed assets revalued on arbitrary bases...

LIABILITY MEASUREMENT

Known liabilities or losses not provided for ....

OWNERS' EQUITY MEASUREMENT

Unusual gains (losses) directly to retained earnings ....
Capital gains directly to capital reserves..
Goodwill written off directly to capital or revenue reserves.....................................
Negative goodwill from consolidation directly to capital reserve ....
Current items sometimes directly to retained earnings ....

PERIODIC INCOME DETERMINATION

Income taxes:
   Not allocated ....
   Allocated on a discounted amount ....
Above cost charges for asset replacement ....
Special ommissions (e.g., bad debts, depreciation) ....
Goodwill (intangibles) not generally amortized ....
Deliberate shifting between periods ....
Income taxes not on accrual basis..
Pensions on cash basis ....
Overconservatism (e.g., inventory, contingencies) ....
Exchange gains not allowed until realized...
Direct costing allowed..
Installment sales on either cash or installment basis ....

GENERAL ABSENCE OF DISCLOSURE

Book and tax accounting differences ....
Monetary effects of accounting changes...
Rental commitments on long-term leases..
Equity in majority-owned subsidiaries ....
Subsequent events ....
Contingent liabilities ....
Retained earnings restrictions ....
Capital commitments..
Uninsured risks ....
Depreciation methods ....
Consolidated statements not required ....
Tax losses ....

Argentina	Australia	Belgium	Brazil	Candad	Chile	Columbia	France	Germany	India	Ireland	Italy	Japan	Mexico	The Netherlands	New Zealand	Peru	Phillipines	South Africa	Spain	Sweden	Switzerland	United Kingdom	Venezuela
×			×		×	×			×				×			×	×						
	×			×					×	×			×		×							×	
		×	×		×																		
			×						×							×							
											×												
				×	×																		
				×				×															
						×										×							
																×							
																×							
			×													×						×	
	×								×	×		×			×	×	×	×		×		×	
	×	×			×				×	×					×			×	×	×		×	
	×									×					×							×	
	×									×					×							×	
		×	×							×	×	×				×			×			×	
×		×	×		×	×		×					×				×			×	×		
														×									
	×									×					×	×			×				×
	×									×									×				×
	×									×					×	×							×
		×	×		×		×				×					×			×	×			
		×									×						×						
						×		×			×					×							
		×				×	×	×			×	×							×	×	×		
							×																
									×														
													×										
×			×	×		×	×		×	×			×								×	×	
×		×	×	×		×	×					×				×			×	×	×		×
×	×	×	×		×	×	×	×	×	×	×	×	×		×	×	×		×	×	×	×	×
×		×	×		×	×	×	×	×		×	×	×			×			×		×		×
		×	×			×	×				×					×			×		×		×
			×			×										×							
			×																				
								×															
									×														
									×														
																	×						
																						×	

Chapter 3

ACCOUNTING FOR FOREIGN CURRENCY TRANSLATION AND INFLATION

Chapter 2 outlined, in general fashion, some of the major accounting patterns that exist internationally. This chapter adopts a narrower orientation. It demonstrates some practical/applied multinational accounting problems.

Two problems in particular have been chosen for elaboration; namely accounting for foreign currency translation and inflation. These two practical problems have proved especially troublesome to multinational companies that, for reasons to be explained shortly, find it desirable to prepare consolidated financial statements incorporating the results of their network of foreign affiliates. The reader will discover that many of the problems associated with foreign currency translation stem from the fact that foreign exchange rates used to accomplish the translation process generally fluctuate from period to period. Operating results can differ markedly from financial results as the latter may also reflect gains or losses caused by exchange rate changes. Furthermore, if any translation gains or losses are deferred to future accounting periods through the use of balance sheet reserves, the financial statements affected may lose a significant degree of usefulness as indicants of a firm's performance.

The other problem examined here is related to the first and concerns accounting for changes in the relative purchasing power of various currencies due to inflation. This modern disease, which affects both developing and industrialized countries alike, has reached epidemic proportions and promises to present accountants with some of the more difficult challenges they are likely to encounter over the balance of this decade. Thus, can one consolidate the results of operations conducted in a number of different inflationary environments and come up with aggregate numbers that are meaningful? Are there practical ways of adjusting for the effects of differential inflation rates and impacts at home and abroad? Does it really matter whether we adjust financial accounts for inflation or not? These and other questions are addressed in the sections to follow.

CONSOLIDATED FINANCIAL STATEMENTS

More and more companies are being drawn into multinational operations. Indeed, international business activities have grown to such an extent that if you were to purchase shares of any major corporation in the United States or abroad, you would more than likely be investing indirectly in a number of foreign operations. Understandably, then, more and more companies are presenting themselves to the financial community on the basis of consolidated financial statements that include the results of both foreign and domestic operations.

Consolidated statements essentially convey the results of operations and the financial position of a group of companies as if they were a single economic unit regardless of any legal distinctions that exist among the separate corporate entities. Principles of consolidating foreign accounts are similar in most respects to those followed in consolidating purely domestic subsidiaries. Hence, accounts ·of the parent company and its foreign subsidiaries are generally combined on a line-by-line basis by adding together like items of assets, liabilities, revenues, and expenses. Intercompany transactions, including intercompany sales, charges, and dividends, are eliminated. The major issue on consolidation of foreign accounts, therefore, is not so much a case of *how* but *whether to or not.*

Consolidation Criteria

In the United States, subsidiaries are commonly excluded from consolidation in circumstances where the ability of the United States parent to control the financial operating policies of the foreign subsidiary is limited. Control is usually presumed to exist if the United States parent owns more than 50 percent of the voting shares of the subsidiary. In other countries, it is often considered appropriate to exclude from consolidation any subsidiary whose business activities are so dissimilar to those of the parent that combined financial statements would not be meaningful (e.g., when banks and insurance companies are subsidiaries of industrial companies). Additional grounds for nonconsolidation of foreign accounts include impracticality of consolidation, insignificance of foreign accounts in terms of amounts involved, the likelihood of disproportionate expense or delay in preparing consolidated statements, or the opinion of the company's directors that the effects of consolidation would be misleading or harmful to its business.[1]

Companies electing not to consolidate the accounts of foreign subsidiaries may account for these investments in one of two ways: the cost method or the equity method. Under the cost method, an investment in the shares of a foreign investee is recorded at cost. The parent company subsequently recognizes income from such an investment only to the extent that dividends are distributed by the investee. In most cases, however, recognition of income on the basis of dividends received is not an adequate measure of the income actually earned. Dividends received may bear little relation to the real performance of the investee; that is, dividend distributions can be varied to meet the income or cash needs of the parent.

This state of affairs is largely eliminated under the equity method of accounting for investments whereby the carrying value of the investee is adjusted to reflect the investor's proportionate share of the investee's profits or losses. Dividends received from an investee are treated, in turn, as reductions in the carrying value of the parent's investment.

Many criteria have been advanced to aid in the decision whether to consolidate foreign accounts with those of the parent. The authors feel that the decision to consolidate depends on two broad factors: (a) the significance of the degree of consolidation to the various users of the financial statements and (b) the meaningfulness of the consolidated statements that report in a single currency what in fact occurred in several.

Uses of Consolidated Financial Statements. Principal users of consolidated statements of multinational companies include creditors of the parent corporation, creditors of the foreign subsidiaries, stockholders of the parent corporation, stockholders of the foreign subsidiaries, and managers of the parent company.[2]

Long-term creditors of the parent corporation have a genuine interest in consolidated statements as they must ultimately look to the profitability of the enterprise as a whole for satisfaction of their claims. Creditors of a foreign subsidiary, while primarily interested in the financial statements of the subsidiary, are also interested in consolidated statements, especially in those instances where the debts of the subsidiary carry parent company guarantees. In the latter case local creditors, in effect, become creditors of the parent company as well.

Shareholders of the parent company are interested in consolidated financial statements since the value of their equity investments is directly

---

[1] Accountants International Study Group, *Consolidated Financial Statements* (New York: Author, 1973), paragraphs 28 – 33.

[2] This classification is based on David K. Eiteman and Arthur I. Stonehill, *Multinational Business Finance* (Reading, Mass.: Addison-Wesley, 1973), pp. 319 – 326.

related to the wealth of the entity as a whole. From an economic standpoint, the fact that two segments of the parent company's activities are domiciled in different legal-political systems is immaterial. In those instances where the parent company's investment abroad is represented by a joint venture arrangement with foreign stockholders, the latter group would also be interested in consolidated financial statements as a source of information about the joint partner's financial strength. In addition, parent company guarantees of foreign subsidiary obligations generate interest among foreign shareholders in consolidated statements. Anything that weakens the position of a foreign subsidiary's creditors directly affects the interest of its foreign shareholders as well.

Finally, while historical consolidated statements may be of little use to management in planning and controlling day-to-day operations, managers still have a very real interest in consolidated statements as their performance is often gauged in terms of the combined results of the group as a whole. In this respect, consolidated statements may be viewed as the external relations side of international management.

Institutional Support for Consolidated
Financial Statements

The practice of consolidating foreign accounts varies from country to country. A reader of published United States financial statements typically finds that only consolidated results are disclosed. Separate statements of either the parent company or its subsidiaries are not included even as supplementary data. While a few countries currently share the United States view, Price Waterhouse International's *A Survey in 46 Countries: Accounting Principles and Reporting Practices* (1975) reveals that in 23 countries both parent company and consolidated financial statements are issued simultaneously.

Especially noteworthy is the fact that no fewer than 18 countries currently publish only parent company financials. Three recent events on the international scene, however, promise to change this picture. The first event was the 1976 issuance of a proposed *directive* by the European Economic Community (EEC) calling for annual publication of consolidated financial statements.[3] This directive is the seventh in a series of pronouncements designed to achieve uniform legal requirements in all member countries.

---

[3] The EEC started as a customs union for both industrial and agricultural goods involving the abolition of all restrictions on trade among member countries and the erection of a common external tariff. It has since adopted the more ambitious objective of incorporating full economic union with free movement of persons, services, and capital, as well as progressive harmonization of social, fiscal, and monetary policies among member countries. Belgium, Denmark, France, Italy, Ireland, Luxembourg, the Netherlands, the United Kingdom, and West Germany are presently EEC members.

Thus, if formally adopted by the EEC, the provisions of the proposed directive will be written into each member nation's laws. Informed observers feel that eventual passage is likely. EEC accounting is discussed more fully in Chapter 6.

The second event was agreement (also reached in 1976) by the 24 member countries of the Organization for Economic Cooperation and Development (OECD) on guidelines for the conduct of multinational corporations.[4] The accounting dimensions of these guidelines call for the annual publication of financial statements for each enterprise as a whole. Supplementary disclosures on a consolidated basis are also entailed. Although strictly voluntary, these guidelines will probably be adhered to by big multinational companies in the member countries (see Chapter 10 for further details).

The third event was the 1976 issuance of a formal standard on the subject of consolidated financial statements by the International Accounting Standards Committee (IASC), a truly international professional body established to promulgate worldwide accounting principles (Chapter 5 contains additional information about IASC):

> A parent company should issue consolidated financial statements, except that it need not do so when it is a wholly owned subsidiary.
>
> A subsidiary should be excluded from consolidation if: (a) control is temporary, or (b) the subsidiary operates under conditions in which severe long-term restrictions on the transfer of funds impair control by the parent company over the subsidiary's assets and operations.
>
> Uniform accounting policies should preferably be followed by companies in the consolidated financial statements . . . .
>
> Investments in associated companies . . . and in subsidiaries which are not consolidated . . . should be included in the consolidated financial statements under the equity method of accounting.

FOREIGN CURRENCY TRANSLATION

Companies with significant operations abroad cannot prepare consolidated financial statements unless their accounts as well as those of their subsidiaries are expressed in terms of a homogeneous currency (or measurement or reporting) unit. Thus, one cannot use in the same accounts Argentine pesos to express current assets, Japanese yen to state long-term assets, Swiss francs for liabilities, South African rands for owner's equities, Iranian riyals for revenues, New Zealand dollars for expenses, and so on. Doing

---

[4] The OECD is an organization of the industrialized countries of the world that provides a framework for harmonizing national policies in many fields vis-à-vis the less developed countries (including development assistance programs).

so would be akin to adding apples and oranges in trying to obtain meaningful results. Accordingly, a single currency framework is required and this,
traditionally, has been the reporting currency of the parent company. The
process of restating various foreign currency balances to single currency
equivalents is called *translation*.

It is important that we clearly distinguish the terms *translation* and
conversion. Until recently, much of the literature dealing with foreign currencies in accounts used the terms *conversion* and *translation* synony-
mously. This usage is no longer acceptable. Conversion now refers to the
physical exchange of one currency unit for another. Thus, a United States
citizen vacationing in London would convert dollars into pounds if he were
interested in purchasing British goods. Similarly, a Canadian importer
would make an actual payment to an Indonesian exporter by ordering a
bank to exchange Canadian dollars for Indonesian rupiahs so that payment
may be effected. Such currency transactions, whether direct or indirect, are
conversion processes.

Translation, on the other hand, is simply a change in the monetary expression of a foreign currency balance. An account expressed in the currency of one country is merely restated to the currency equivalent of
another country. In this case, no physical exchange occurs. There is no
movement of funds and no accountable transaction takes place. Indeed, the
concept of foreign currency translation is no different from translating a
book written in the German language to one written in English.

Reasons for Translating Foreign
Currencies in Accounts

Additional reasons for foreign currency translations are (a) recording foreign currency transactions, (b) reporting international branch and subsidiary activities, and (c) reporting the results of independent operations
abroad. Subsets of each basic translation category are expounded throughout the literature.

The need to translate foreign currency transactions is similar to the
need for consolidation procedures; namely financial statements cannot be
prepared from accounts that are expressed in various currencies. A company whose exports or imports are invoiced in terms of a foreign currency
unit must translate those amounts to their domestic currency equivalents
before entering the transactions in its books of account. Despite separate
record keeping on the basis of local currency units, accounting reports
resulting from such records must often travel internationally and be understood and used in countries other than those in which the reports are
originally prepared. This, in fact, is why the problem of translating foreign

currencies in accounts arises. Someone removed from the local scene must understand and utilize locally-oriented accounting reports.

Branch and subsidiary activities are another case in point. Branch activities are normally quite closely planned, administered, and controlled by the parent organization. Since both branch and parent are integral parts of a closely knit whole, it makes little sense to view the accounts of either by themselves. They must be combined so that a fair and complete total financial picture evolves. Again, foreign currency translation procedures are called for. As the parent's viewpoint prevails in other organizational and business matters, so it should in accounting. The parent must evaluate its investment in the branch, judge the operations of the branch, and generally direct branch activities. Thus it is necessary to have the accounts of the branch available in terms of the home currency of the parent both for independent evaluation and in combination with the parent's own accounts. Outsiders should see these accounts only in combined form.

In contrast to branch activities, subsidiary companies have a separate legal existence apart from their parent companies, even though the parent usually exercises administrative and operational control over majority or wholly-owned subsidiaries. The subsidiary companies enjoy a greater degree of autonomy by virtue of their separate legal existence. Nevertheless, foreign currency translation procedures are called for. Parent company consolidation requirements are often in effect for subsidiary companies. In addition, parent companies must continually evaluate their investments in subsidiaries and thus need accounting information that allows close comparisons between the results of the subsidiaries' operations and those of the parent. Also, planning and administrative functions of parent company management cannot be performed effectively unless accounting information is available about the subsidiaries and unless the information has substantially the same basis as that of the parent.

It is important to note, in this connection, that subsidiaries in other countries are quite likely to rely heavily on local management talent. This means that there is a strong need for accounting information prepared according to local accounting concepts and practices and in terms of local currency units. This is the type of information that local managers are accustomed to and need for their own management purposes. Also, evaluation of local competitive conditions and comparisons with similar local firms are difficult unless locally-oriented accounting information is available. Therefore, accounting information requirements of a parent company should generally not be allowed to overshadow local accounting information requirements. In effect, two distinct sets of information requirements exist and they require translation and reconciliation back and forth.

Finally, the expanded scale of international investment activities increases the need to convey accounting information about an independent company domiciled in one country to readers in another. This occurs, for example, when a company wishes to have its shares listed on a foreign stock exchange, contemplates a foreign acquisition or joint-venture arrangement, or simply desires to communicate the results of its operating performance and financial position to its foreign stockholders. Under these circumstances, a parent company translates its financial statements in their entirety from the domestic currency to the currency of the statement recipient's domicile.

Translations of accounts of independent companies are fundamentally distinct from translations of branch or subsidiary accounts. The former serve information purposes only. They are executed primarily for the convenience of a firm's foreign financial reporting audiences-of-interest and do not involve any restatement of accounting principles or adaptation of the original data base (see further discussion on this point in Chapter 4). In short, financial statements translated solely for information purposes have a single accounting domicile—the country in which the translated accounts are originally prepared. Exhibit 3 – 1 illustrates one such "convenience" translation. It shows the 1976 balance sheet of the Japanese Mitsui & Co., Ltd. translated into English and United States dollar amounts.

Foreign Exchange Rates

The traditional medium for translating foreign currency amounts is the foreign exchange rate. This rate may be thought of as the price of a unit of currency in terms of all other currencies. A financial statement prepared in terms of Dutch florins cannot be translated into United States dollar amounts unless appropriate translation rates (foreign exchange rates) are available. Similarly, before two international trade partners can agree upon settling their obligations through conversion of certain currencies, they must establish conversion rates or a settlement cannot take place. Rates of exchange underlie the entire structure of foreign exchange transactions as well as the translation of foreign currencies in accounts.

If foreign currency exchange rates were relatively constant, the translation process would be quite straightforward and no more difficult than, say, converting inches or feet to their metric equivalents. Exchange rates, however, are seldom stable as their values tend to vary in response to rather complex forces of supply and demand. This, in turn, introduces a host of difficulties in foreign exchange translation and conversion procedures.

There are many causes for changes in foreign exchange rates. Foremost is the state of a country's balance of international payments. Its significance has been described as follows (Chemical Bank, New York, *Foreign Exchange Exposure Management,* 1972, p. 4):

EXHIBIT 3-1. Mitsui & Co., Ltd. (Mitsui Bussan Kabushiki Kaisha)
And consolidated subsidiaries
Consolidated Balance Sheet
March 31, 1976 and 1975

ASSETS	MILLIONS OF YEN		TRANSLATION INTO THOUSANDS OF UNITED STATES DOLLARS (NOTE 1)	
	1976	*1975*	*1976*	*1975*
Current Assets				
Cash...............................	¥ 103,124	¥ 97,812	$ 343,747	$ 326,040
Time deposits.......................	222,100	154,978	740,333	516,593
Marketable securities................	72,978	21,713	243,260	72,377
Trade receivables:				
Notes and loans...................	869,654	814,272	2,898,847	2,714,240
Accounts	936,287	964,087	3,120,957	3,213,623
Unconsolidated subsidiaries and				
associated companies............	211,821	231,877	706,070	772,923
Allowance for				
doubtful receivables..............	(40,902)	(35,457)	(136,340)	(118,190)
Unearned interest				
and commissions	(19,238)	(14,421)	(64,127)	(48,070)
Inventories...........................	294,233	338,563	980,777	1,128,543
Advance payments to suppliers........	186,901	204,599	623,003	681,997
Deferred income taxes	2,591	8,951	8,637	29,837
Prepayments, etc.	88,478	68,841	294,926	229,470
Total current assets............	2,928,027	2,855,815	9,760,090	9,519,383
Investments and Non-current Receivables				
Investments in and advances to unconsolidated subsidiaries and				
associated companies..............	308,865	276,154	1,029,550	920,513
Other investments..................	214,401	185,835	714,670	619,450
Non-current trade receivables,				
less unearned interest	456,154	399,097	1,520,514	1,330,324
Property leased to others – at cost, less accumulated depreciation: 1976, ¥4,640 million – $15,467 thousand; 1975, ¥2,667 million –				
$8,890 thousand....................	12,112	10,918	40,373	36,393
Total investments and				
non-current receivables	991,532	872,004	3,305,107	2,906,680
Property and Equipment —At cost				
Land, land improvements,				
and timberlands....................	53,984	54,868	179,947	182,893
Buildings, including				
leasehold improvements...........	74,959	69,720	249,863	232,400
Equipment and fixtures	74,230	68,999	247,433	229,997
Ships	7,953	2,741	26,510	9,137
Projects in progress	36,615	16,813	122,050	56,043
Total	247,741	213,141	825,803	710,470
Less accumulated depreciation	58,248	50,229	194,160	167,430
Property and equipment – net ..	189,493	162,912	631,643	543,040

EXHIBIT 3 – 1. Continued

Miscellaneous Assets				
(less amortization)	23,233	27,987	77,443	93,290
Total	¥4,132,285	¥3,918,718	$13,774,283	$13,062,393

LIABILITIES AND SHAREHOLDERS' EQUITY	MILLIONS OF YEN		TRANSLATION INTO THOUSANDS OF UNITED STATES DOLLARS	
	1976	*1975*	*1976*	*1975*
Current Liabilities				
Short-term bank loans................	¥ 921,783	¥ 916,647	$ 3,072,610	$ 3,055,490
Current maturities of long-term debt	186,944	150,391	623,147	501,303
Trade notes and acceptances payable...	957,724	923,449	3,192,413	3,078,163
Trade accounts payable...............	508,570	479,721	1,695,233	1,599,070
Notes and accounts payable – unconsolidated subsidiaries and associated companies..............	104,792	116,171	349,307	387,237
Accrued expenses:				
Income taxes......................	5,571	20,226	18,570	67,420
Interest	17,895	18,746	59,650	62,487
Other	22,110	27,317	73,700	91,057
Advances under incomplete transactions.............	124,197	129,201	413,990	430,670
Deposits	18,397	27,922	61,323	93,073
Total current liabilities..........	2,867,983	2,809,791	9,559,943	9,365,970
Liability for Severance Indemnities and Accrued Pension Costs.....	18,815	17,927	62,717	59,757
Long-term Debt, Less Current Maturities	1,048,449	890,659	3,494,830	2,968,863
Minority Interests...................	3,875	3,559	12,917	11,863
Deferred Income Taxes – Non-current	24,873	22,386	82,910	74,620
Deferred Foreign Currency Exchange Gains.................	930	4,837	3,100	16,123
Shareholders' Equity:				
Common stock, ¥50 par – authorized: 1976 – 2,500,000,000 shares, 1975 – 1,700,000,000 shares; issued and outstanding: 1976 – 688,581,554 shares, 1975 – 680,554,093 shares	34,429	34,028	114,763	113,427
Capital surplus.......................	32,533	30,582	108,443	101,940
Special surplus	1,620	1,620	5,400	5,400
Retained earnings:				
Appropriated for legal reserve	5,539	4,922	18,463	16,407
Appropriated for sundry reserves.....	32,741	28,779	109,137	95,930
Unappropriated	60,498	69,628	201,660	232,093
Total shareholders' equity.......	167,360	169,559	557,866	565,197
Commitments and Contingent Liabilities				
Total	¥4,132,285	¥3,918,718	$13,774,283	$13,062,393

The fundamental determinant of the supply/demand relationship among currencies is, of course, long run developments in the balance of payments of individual countries, particularly the major trading nations. A basic balance of payments disequilibrium, whether it takes the form of persistent surpluses or deficits, inevitably leads to pressures resulting in parity changes in the form of revaluations or devaluations. Such a disequilibrium can result from numerous sources. These include, to name only a very few, interest rate differentials, the loss of a key export market, changes in the propensity to import, the existence of differential rates of inflation among key trading nations, a desire to invest heavily abroad, foreign military commitments and aid programs, and tariff and anti-tariff restrictions on trade. Of these causes, the most basic is the development of differential rates of inflation among a group of trading nations. If prolonged, such a development will invariably erode the competitive position of the country or countries with the most rapid rate of inflation. Exchange rate (parity) changes are certain to flow from such a situation.

Janssen cites "extrapolated expectations" as another major factor causing exchange rate fluctuations.[5] This means that whatever speculators and other traders in foreign currency think the market is most likely to do in the future is what it will do.

Until recently, the foregoing complex supply and demand factors were controlled, to some extent, by rather predictable governmental interactions in the foreign exchange market. Under the Bretton Woods system, currencies of countries that adhered to the International Monetary Fund (IMF) agreement were anchored to a common standard of value; namely, gold and certain "reserve currencies" that were readily convertible into gold. Governments of the IMF member countries committed themselves to limiting the fluctuation of their exchange rates within certain prescribed limits. When it appeared that the limits were likely to be exceeded, the monetary authorities of the nations concerned intervened in a number of ways to stabilize respective exchange rates. If the exchange rate movement could not be contained, the country whose currency was under pressure devalued or revalued its currency relative to other currencies. *Devaluation* means that more units of the devalued currency are needed to acquire a given number of units of another currency. *Revaluation* means just the opposite.

The Bretton Woods system came to an unexpected and abrupt end in late 1971 when fixed exchange rates were abandoned. Today the currencies of most industrialized countries are free to find their own values relative to

---

[5] Richard F. Janssen, "Inflation, Interest Rates Seen As Part of the Answer to Currency Fluctuations," *The Wall Street Journal,* June 1976, p. 1.

one another, with governmental intervention much more constrained and unpredictable to moderate these fluctuations. A system of so-called *floating* exchange rates now prevails.

Translation Methodology

Varying exchange rates give rise to a number of conceptually distinct methods for the accounting translation process. In the past, companies have often adopted a combination of these methods to suit their own particular needs and circumstances, thereby creating additional options. Four translation methods can be clearly distinguished: (a) the current-noncurrent method, (b) the monetary-nonmonetary method, (c) the temporal method, and (d) the current rate method.

TABLE 3-1. Exchange Rates Employed in Different Translation Methods For Specific Balance Sheet Items

	CURRENT-NON-CURRENT	MONETARY-NON-MONETARY	TEMPORAL	CURRENT	HYBRID 1	HYBRID 2
Cash	C[a]	C	C	C	C	C
Accounts Receivable	C	C	C	C	C	C
Inventories:						
Cost	C	H	H	C	C	H
Market	C	H	C	C	C	H
Investments:						
Cost	H[b]	H	H	C	H	H
Market	H	H	C	C	H	H
Fixed Assets	H	H	H	C	H	H
Other Assets	H	H	H	C	H	H
Accounts Payable	C	C	C	C	C	C
Long-Term Debt	H	C	C	C	C	H
Common Stock	H	H	H	C	H	H
Retained Earnings	*[c]	*	*	*	*	*

[a] C = current rate.
[b] H = historical rate.
[c] * = residual, balancing figure representing a composite of successive current rates.

Table 3−1 summarizes the treatment of specific balance sheet items under each of the four methods. Hybrids 1 and 2 represent additional treatments often found in practice.

The Current-Noncurrent Method. This method, until quite recently, was the most authoritative method of translating foreign currency accounts in the United States. Although it has been replaced by a more recent construct—the temporal principle of translation to be described shortly—its use is still advocated in the authoritative literature of countries outside the United States.

Under the current-noncurrent method (described in Chapter 12 of *Accounting Research Bulletin No. 43* of the AICPA), a foreign subsidiary's current assets and current liabilities are translated into their domestic currency equivalents at the current exchange rate, i.e., the actual exchange rate in effect at the balance sheet date. Noncurrent assets and liabilities are translated at historical rates of exchange, i.e., rates prevailing when the respective assets were acquired or liabilities incurred.

Income statement items, with the exception of depreciation and amortization charges, are translated at average exchange rates applicable to each month of operation or on the basis of weighted averages covering the whole period to be reported. Depreciation and amortization charges are translated at rates in effect when the related assets were acquired. Realized gains or losses on foreign exchange conversion and/or translation are taken directly to current results of operations. Unrealized losses are also charged against current operations, but unrealized gains are to be carried to a suspense account. To the extent that unrealized gains offset prior provisions for unrealized losses, the former are credited to the account previously charged.

This methodology, unfortunately, suffers from a number of shortcomings. For example, it lacks adequate conceptual justification. Present definitions of current and noncurrent assets and liabilities do not explain why such a classification scheme should determine which rate to use in the translation process. Furthermore, fluctuating exchange rates may produce translations that distort operating results between accounting periods. Inventories are a case in point.

Under conditions of a deteriorating exchange rate, assume that inventories are shipped from a United States parent company to one of its foreign subsidiaries during the last quarter of year 1 when the prevailing rate of exchange was one foreign currency (FC) unit per United States dollar. Assume also that these inventories remain unsold at year end, the date of the financial statements. The inventories have a United States dollar cost of $100,000. Thus, the foreign subsidiary would record this transaction on its books at FC 100,000. The subsidiary operates with a 50 percent markup on cost, which leads to a selling price of FC 150,000 for the inventory.

Now assume that the foreign exchange rate falls to $ 0.90 = FC1 by year end. Under the current-noncurrent translation method, the FC 100,000 of inventories are translated at the current rate and yield a translated figure in United States dollars of $90,000. Therefore, a translation *loss* of $10,000 appears in the accounts and year 1 earnings are reduced by the same amount.

If the inventories in question are then sold for FC 150,000 during the first quarter of year 2, and the average rate of exchange during this quarter is $ 0.95 = FC1, the sale transaction yields approximately $142,500. The gross margin on the sale is then reported at $52,500 in year 2, whereas it should be reported at $42,500—the real difference between cost and selling price in terms of United States dollars. In this example,

1. There really is no foreign exchange "loss" in year 1. The decline in the foreign exchange rate simply reduces the originally anticipated gross profit margin.
2. Reported operating results for both years 1 and 2 are distorted because of an unrealistic foreign exchange translation method.

Partially as a result of these shortcomings, other translation methods were developed. One such method, the monetary-nonmonetary approach, is described next.

The Monetary-Nonmonetary Method. Among the earliest advocates of needed changes in translation methodology was the late Professor Samuel R. Hepworth of the University of Michigan. His 1956 research monograph entitled *Reporting Foreign Operations* called for (a) abandoning the traditional distinction between current and noncurrent items for translation purposes and substituting a more realistic dichotomy of monetary versus nonmonetary items, and (b) changing the method of accounting for exchange gains and losses. Under his approach, *monetary* assets and liabilities—representing rights to receive or obligations to pay a fixed number of foreign currency units in the future (cash, receivables, and payables, including long-term debt)—are translated at the current rate. *Nonmonetary* items—fixed assets, long-term investments, and inventories—are translated at the historical rate. Income statement items are translated under procedures similar to those described for the current-noncurrent framework.

In accounting for foreign exchange gains or losses, Hepworth departed from earlier dogma by recommending that such items be included as part of the overall operating results of international business operations, though separately disclosed.

The Hepworth thesis proved influential. A research report published in 1960 by the National Association of Accountants (*Management Accounting Problems in Foreign Operations,* p. 17) described the current-noncurrent distinction as one that "seems to reflect the use of an established balance sheet classification for a purpose to which it is not relevant." In turn, the practice of translating *all* payables and receivables at current rates of exchange was given official recognition with the issuance of *Accounting Principles Board (APB) Opinion No. 6.* This modification of ARB (Accounting Research Bulletin, AICPA) No. 43, in effect, permitted firms to employ the monetary-nonmonetary method of translation.

Note, however, that the monetary-nonmonetary method, like its predecessor, relies on a classification scheme to determine appropriate translation rates. Since translation is concerned with measurement and not with classification, the characteristics of assets and liabilities that determine their financial statement classification are not necessarily relevant for selecting appropriate translation rates. The monetary-nonmonetary method may also be criticized in that

> ... no comprehensive principle of translation can be derived solely from the monetary-nonmonetary distinction. Nonmonetary assets and liabilities are measured on different bases (for example, past prices or current prices) under different circumstances, and translation at a past rate does not always fit. Translating nonmonetary items at a past rate produces reasonable results if the items are stated at historical cost, but not if they are stated at current market price in foreign currency. For example, if a foreign operation purchases as an investment 100 shares of another company's common stock (a nonmonetary item) for FC 1,000 when the rate is FC 1 = $1, the cost of that investment is equivalent to $1,000. If the investment is carried at cost by the foreign operation, treating the investment as a nonmonetary item and translating it at the historical rate is appropriate. However, if the investment is carried at market price, translating that basis by the historical rate usually produces questionable results. For example, if the current market value of the investment is FC 1,500 and the current rate is FC 1 = $1.25, translating FC 1,500 into $1,500 using the historical rate does not result in the current market value measured in dollars (FC 1,500 × 1.25 = $1,875) or the historical cost in dollars. The monetary-nonmonetary method can produce the $1,875 current market value only if it recognized that, under the method, the current rate is the applicable historical rate for nonmonetary assets carried at current prices. The point has been confusing enough to cause some proponents of the monetary-nonmonetary method to argue that nonmonetary assets, such as investments and inventories, should become monetary assets if they are carried at market price.[6]

The Temporal Method.   To remedy the aforementioned situation, Lorensen introduced what has come to be known as the *temporal principle* of translation.[7] Under this method, assets and liabilities are translated in a manner that retains their original measurement bases.

---

[6] Financial Accounting Standards Board, "Accounting for the Translation of Foreign Currency Transactions and Foreign Currency Financial Statements," *Statement of Financial Accounting Standards No. 8* (Stamford, Conn.: Author, October 1975), pp. 58–59.

[7] Leonard Lorensen, *Reporting Foreign Operations of U.S. Companies in U.S. Dollars,* Accounting Research Study No. 12 (New York: American Institute of Certified Public Accountants, 1972).

To elaborate, Lorensen holds that since translation is a measurement conversion process (restatement of a given value), it cannot be used to change the attribute of an item being measured; it can only change the unit of measure. Translation of foreign inventory balances, for example, restates the currency denomination of these inventories but not their actual valuation. Under United States generally accepted accounting principles, the asset cash is measured in terms of the amount owned at the balance sheet date. Receivables and payables are stated at amounts expected to be received or paid in the future. All other assets and liabilities are measured at money prices that prevailed when the items were acquired or incurred. In short, there is a time dimension associated with these money values.

According to Lorensen, the best way to retain the accounting bases used to measure foreign currency items is to translate their foreign money amounts by exchange rates in effect at the dates to which the foreign money measurements pertain. The temporal principle thus states that

> Money, receivables, and payables measured at the amounts promised should be translated at the foreign exchange rate in effect at the balance sheet date. Assets and liabilities measured at money prices should be translated at the foreign exchange rate in effect at the dates to which the money prices pertain.

Under this principle, then, cash, receivables, and payables are translated at the current rate. Assets carried on the foreign statements at historical cost are translated at the historical rate. Assets carried at current values are translated at the current rate (see Table 3 – 1). Revenue and expense items are translated at rates that prevailed when the underlying transactions took place, although average rates are suggested when revenue or expense transactions are voluminous. Foreign exchange gains or losses are accorded the same treatment as under the Hepworth proposal.

The latitude in selecting translation methods that was allowed United States multinational companies under previous pronouncements was eliminated in 1975. Standard No. 8 issued by the Financial Accounting Standards Board (FASB), the principal rule-making body for the United States accounting profession, requires all United States companies to adhere to the temporal principle of translation. A comprehensive tabulation of the rates at which certain common balance sheet accounts are to be translated under Standard No. 8 is contained in Table 3 – 2.

It is interesting to note that the translation procedures resulting from the temporal principle are virtually identical to those produced by the monetary-nonmonetary method when the historical cost accounting framework applies. The results would differ markedly, however, if other valuation constructs were generally accepted, such as replacement cost, market values, or discounted cash flows.

TABLE 3-2. Rates Used to Translate Assets and Liabilities Under FASB Standard No. 8

	TRANSLATION RATES	
ASSETS	*Current*	*Historical*
Cash on hand and demand and time deposits	X	
Marketable equity securities:		
Carried at cost		X
Carried at current market price	X	
Accounts and notes receivable and related		
unearned discount	X	
Allowance for doubtful accounts and notes receivable	X	
Inventories:		
Carried at cost		X
Carried at current replacement price or		
current selling price	X	
Carried at net realizable value	X	
Carried at contract price (produced under		
fixed price contracts)	X	
Prepaid insurance, advertising, and rent		X
Refundable deposits	X	
Advances to unconsolidated subsidiaries	X	
Property, plant, and equipment		X
Accumulated depreciation of property, plant, and equipment		X
Cash surrender value of life insurance	X	
Patents, trademarks, licenses, and formulas		X
Goodwill		X
Other intangible assets		X
LIABILITIES		
Accounts and notes payable and overdrafts	X	
Accrued expenses payable	X	
Accrued losses on firm purchase commitments	X	
Refundable deposits	X	
Deferred income		X
Bonds payable or other long-term debt	X	
Unamortized premium or discount on bonds or		
notes payable	X	
Convertible bonds payable	X	
Accrued pension obligations	X	
Obligations under warranties	X	

The Current Rate Method. All the methods described thus far have their origins in official United States accounting pronouncements. When we examine the literature outside the United States, we find advocacy of still another translation method—namely the *current* or *closing rate* method. Under this model, *all* of a foreign subsidiary's assets and liabilities are translated uniformly at the current rate of exchange. Foreign currency revenues and expenses are treated likewise.

The method was first supported by the Institute of Chartered Accountants in England and Wales in their 1968 *Statement N25,* "The Accounting

Treatment of Major Changes in the Sterling Parity of Overseas Currencies.'' This document concluded that both the historic rate method (i.e., the
United States current-noncurrent construct) and the closing (current) rate
method are equally acceptable.[8] The Scottish Institute took an even stronger
stand on the question of appropriate translation methods by expressing an
exclusive preference for the current rate method.[9] Canada has not, as yet,
issued a formal standard on the subject. Parkinson, under the auspices of
the Canadian Institute's Accounting and Auditing Research Committee,
published a research monograph in 1972, however, which supports the current rate method under certain circumstances. It also appears that Australia
will soon join the ranks of those formally advocating adoption of the current rate method.

Diversity in the Application of Foreign Currency Translation Methods

So much for concepts and official pronouncements. But what of practice?
Paradoxically, one finds that foreign currency translation is one of the few
areas in accounting in which practice pretty much follows precept! Empirical evidence suggests that multinational companies employ all the methods
described above and others.

   In the United States, the Financial Executives Institute conducted a research study *prior* to the issuance of FASB Standard No. 8 and found some
companies employing the current-noncurrent method, others following the
monetary-nonmonetary method, but the majority adopting a blend of the
two—the hybrid methods 1 and 2 appearing in Table 3 – 1. While United
States practices are now more uniform as a consequence of the required
application of FASB Standard No. 8, general international practice remains
widely diverse. *A Survey in 46 Countries: Accounting Principles and
Reporting Practices,* (the Price Waterhouse International study already referred to on p. 57) reveals the following:

1. A majority of companies in Argentina, Australia, Brazil, Chile, Fiji,
   Mexico, New Zealand, Uruguay, and Venezuela employ the monetary-
   nonmonetary method.
2. A majority of firms in Bermuda, Canada, Columbia, Iran, Pakistan,
   and South Africa employ the current-noncurrent method.
3. A majority of enterprises in Denmark, France, India, Japan, the
   Netherlands, Norway, Switzerland, and the United Kingdom employ
   the current rate method.

[8] Institute of Chartered Accountants in England and Wales, *Member's Handbook,
Statement N25* (London: Author, 1968), paragraph 14.

[9] "The Treatment in Company Accounts of Changes in the Exchange Rates of International Currencies—A Scottish Institute Research Study," *The Accountant's Magazine*
September 1970, pp. 415 – 423.

Similar results have been reported by Evans in the June 1974 issue of *The CPA Journal* ("Foreign Currency Translation Practices Abroad," pp. 47 – 50).

It is interesting to observe how translation methods used tend to cluster geographically. The patterns exhibited in this clustering lend some additional credence to the accounting patterns thesis set forth in Chapter 2.

Financial Statement Effects

Given the variety of translation methods that exist both in theory and practice, let us now examine some of the financial statement implications of this diversity via a hypothetical example. Before proceeding, however, it may prove helpful to clarify the statement effects of using historical versus current rates of exchange as foreign currency translation coefficients.

Historical exchange rates generally preserve the original cost equivalent of a foreign currency item in the domestic currency statements. From the perspective of a United States parent company, assume that a piece of equipment was acquired by a foreign subsidiary for FC 1,000 when the exchange rate was FC 2 = $1. This asset would appear in the United States consolidated statements at $500. Now assume that the exchange rate declines from FC 2 = $1 to FC 4 = $1 by the next statement date and that the equipment is still on hand. Will the United States dollar equivalent of the equipment now change to $250? Clearly not. As long as we translate the original FC 1,000 cost at the rate that prevailed when the asset was acquired, it will appear in the United States financial statements at $500: its historical cost expressed in United States dollars. The point is that historical rates shield financial statements from foreign currency translation gains or losses, i.e., increases or decreases in the dollar equivalents of foreign currency balances due to fluctuations in the translation rate between reporting periods. Use of current rates directly gives rise to translation gains or losses. Thus, in our previous example, translating the FC 1,000 piece of equipment at the current rate would yield a translation loss of $250 (FC 1,000 ÷ 2 − FC 1,000 ÷ 4).

With this distinction in mind, let us now proceed with our hypothetical example. Table 3 – 3 illustrates the translation gains or losses that stem from using differing translation methods, assuming that the foreign currency devalues relative to the dollar. The balance sheet of a hypothetical foreign subsidiary of a United States based multinational corporation appears in the first two columns of the table. The third column depicts the United States dollar equivalents of the foreign currency balances when the exchange rate is FC 1 = $1. Assuming that the foreign currency loses 50 percent of its foreign exchange value in relation to the dollar (now FC 1.5 =

TABLE 3-3. Translation Gains and Losses Under Differing Methodologies Assuming a Foreign Currency Devaluation[a] (Illustration of Table 3-1)

FOREIGN SUBSIDIARY BALANCE SHEET IN FOREIGN CURRENCY — Amount	Assets	U.S. DOLLARS BEFORE DEVALUATION: FC 1 = $1	Current-Noncurrent	Monetary-Nonmonetary	Temporal	Current Rate	Hybrid 1	Hybrid 2
			U.S. DOLLAR EQUIVALENTS AFTER DEVALUATION FC 1.5 = $1.0					
FC 300	Cash	$ 300	200	200	200	200	200	200
300	Accounts Receivable	300	200	200	200	200	200	200
	Inventories: Cost (FC 900)							
600	Market	600	400	600;b	400	400	400	600
1,500	Fixed Assets, Net	1,500	1,500	1,500	1,500	1,000	1,500	1,500
FC 2,700		$2,700	2,300	2,500	2,300	1,800	2,300	2,500
	Liabilities and Owners' Equity							
FC 600	ST Payables	600	400	400	400	400	400	400
1,200	LT Debt	1,200	1,200	800	800	800	800	800
900	Owners' Equity[c]	900	700	1,300	1,100	600	1,100	900
FC 2,700		2,700	2,300	2,500	2,300	1,800	2,300	2,500
—0—	Translation Gain (Loss)	—0—	(200)	400	200	(300)	200	—0—

a Note that if the exchange rate remained constant over time, the translated balance sheet would be the same under all translation methods.

b Under some interpretations, this item would be reclassified as a monetary item and translated at the current rate.

c In the translated statements, Owners' Equity is a residual balancing figure.

73

$1), a number of different accounting outcomes are possible. (Brackets appearing in Table 3 – 3 identify foreign currency balances affected by exchange rate changes giving rise to translation gains or losses.)

Under the current-noncurrent method, rate changes (changes in the current rate) affect only current assets (CA) and current liabilities (CL) in the current period. Therefore, a firm's net working capital position always determines whether the translation process results in a gain or loss. In financial analysis, a firm's net working capital position is usually referred to as a firm's balance sheet *exposure* to foreign exchange risk. Thus, if a foreign subsidiary is in a positive net working capital position (CA > CL), the parent company incurs a loss on translation if the foreign currency devalues. It incurs a gain on translation if the foreign currency gains exchange value. In our example, translation under the current-noncurrent method yields a $200 translation loss since the dollar equivalents of the foreign subsidiary's net working capital position *after* devaluation is $400 ($800 – $400) whereas the dollar equivalent *before* devaluation is $600 ($1,200 – $600).

Under the monetary-nonmonetary method, a firm's exposure is measured by its net monetary asset or liability position. Exposure under the temporal principle depends on whether the subsidiary's inventories are valued at cost or current market value. Under the current rate method, balance sheet exposure is measured by a firm's net asset position as *all* assets and liabilities are translated at the current rate and hence affected by exchange rate changes. The reader is encouraged to work through the example until all translation gains or losses that are produced by each of the remaining constructs can be traced.

To summarize, the different translation methods illustrated offer a wide array of accounting results—ranging from a $300 loss under the current rate method to a $400 gain under the monetary method. This is quite a variation in light of the fact that all the results presumably describe the same factual situation!

Problem Areas

Considerable controversy and unresolved accounting problems characterize the foreign currency translation issue. Three, however, emerge as more basic than others: (a) the choice of appropriate translation procedure, (b) the choice of an appropriate current rate, and (c) accounting for translation gains and losses.

Translation Procedure. The quest for a comprehensive translation methodology has engaged the energies of accountants for many years. Numerous writers have suggested their particular ideal translation modes to end the confusion that has characterized this aspect of international financial reporting. Most have premised their constructs on the traditional assumption that a single translation method can be appropriate for all circumstances in which translations occur and for all purposes which translation serves. We feel that the assumption just cited is categorically wrong. First, circumstances underlying foreign exchange translation differ widely. Translating accounts from a stable to an unstable currency (e.g., from Swiss francs to Argentine pesos) is not the same as translating accounts from an unstable currency to a stable one (e.g., from Chilean escudos to United States dollars). Likewise, there is little similarity between translations involving import- or export-type transactions and those involving a permanently established affiliate or subsidiary company in another country that reinvests its local earnings and does not contemplate repatriating any of its funds to the parent company in the near future.

Second, translations are undertaken for different purposes. Translating the accounts of a foreign subsidiary for purposes of consolidating such accounts with those of the parent company has very little in common with translating the accounts of an independent company primarily for the convenience of various foreign audiences-of-interest.

The problem of translation procedure thus has three dimensions:

1. Is it reasonable to employ more than a single translation method?
2. If so, what should the acceptable methods be and under what conditions should they be applied?
3. Are there situations in which translations should not be undertaken at all?

With respect to the first question there seems little doubt that, given the underlying conditions of multinational business today, a single translation methodology cannot logically serve equally well translations occurring under different conditions and serving different purposes. Thus, more than one translation method seems warranted.

Regarding the second question, three different translation approaches seem called for: (a) the historical method, (b) the current method, and (c) no translation at all.

Financial accounts of some or all foreign entities can be translated either in terms of a parent company perspective or in terms of a local perspective. Under the former, the object of translation is to change the unit of measure for financial statements of foreign subsidiaries from one defined in terms of a foreign currency to one defined in terms of the domestic currency. Another objective is to make the foreign statements conform to accounting principles generally accepted in the country of the parent company. In short, foreign-based operations are viewed as extensions of the parent company, as in the preparation of consolidated financial statements. These objectives, in the opinion of the authors, are best accomplished by the use of translation methods incorporating historical rates of exchange. While several historical rate methods have been identified and described, we prefer the temporal principle as it generally retains the accounting principles used to measure assets and liabilities originally expressed in foreign currency units. Since foreign statements under a parent company perspective are first adjusted to reflect parent country accounting principles (*before* translation), the temporal principle is appropriate as it changes only a measurement in foreign currency into a measurement in domestic currency without changing the basis of measurement. This is the key rationale of FASB Standard No. 8, which the authors support.

Because the historical rate translation method inherently involves a conceptual dimension, it is easily adapted to processes that make accounting adjustments in the course of the translation. When this is the case, adjustments for differences between two or more sets of accounting concepts and practices are made in addition to the translation of currency amounts. For example, inventories or certain liabilities may be restated according to accounting practices different from those originally used. The temporal principle can accommodate any asset valuation framework whether it be historical cost, current replacement price, or net realizable values.

While the primary purpose of historical rate translation is the consolidation of the financial statements of an international branch or subsidiary company with those of a parent company, this method also serves additional accounting purposes. For example, the method is useful for special management information or administrative reports. Furthermore, it is useful in compiling national statistics about international investments and about international balance of payments questions as they concern individual countries.

Using a current rate of translation for all financial statement items is another method of achieving translation of foreign currencies in accounts. This method, it should be noted, has no accounting orientation. It simply changes a medium of expression. It is straightforward translation from one "language" to another. There is no change whatever in the nature of the accounts. Only their particular form of expression is changed.

The current rate method is first of all appropriate when the accounts of foreign subsidiaries are translated in a fashion that retains the local currency as the unit of measure; i.e., all foreign entities are viewed from a local, as opposed to a parent, company perspective. This view recognizes that a foreign-based operation is a separate business unit whose business transactions are effected in a foreign currency. What a difference from the parent company perspective that translates as if the transaction had been in the domestic currency to start with! Translation at the current rate, furthermore, does not change any of the initial relationships (e.g., financial ratios) in the foreign currency statements as all account balances are simply multiplied by a constant. This approach is most useful when the accounts of an independent company are merely translated for the convenience of foreign stockholders or other external user groups.

A second use of the current rate method comes about when price level adjusted accounts are to be translated to another currency. If reliable price level adjustments have been introduced into a given set of accounts and if the domestic price level changes for the currency involved are reflected closely in related foreign exchange rate movements, then the current rate translation of price level adjusted data yields results that are comparable to translating historical cost accounts under the historical rate translation method. This topic is covered on p. 95.

Now to repeat a question raised earlier, "Are there situations in which translations should not be undertaken at all?" We would argue in the affirmative. No translation is appropriate between highly unstable and highly stable currencies. Translation of one into the other will not produce meaningful information under any translation method. For example, historical dollar costs of inventories carried by an Argentine or Chilean subsidiary are a poor guide to pricing decisions in the face of heavy recent inflation in those countries.

No translation would also mean nonconsolidation of financial statements. This seems to be a reasonable conclusion. If a currency turns so soft as to put account translations into question, it should also act as a bar to financial statement consolidation. Should reporting of operations in extremely volatile currency areas be necessary, separate reports might be rendered. There is no reason why several rather soft currency operations could not be combined into a single report as long as this report is separate and clearly distinct from the main report.

No translation is necessary when financial statements of independent companies are issued for purely informational purposes to residents in another country that is in a comparable stage of economic development and has a comparable national currency situation. For example, a Canadian company reporting to United States stockholders should not be required to translate its accounts provided, of course, that it fully discloses the expression of monetary amounts in Canadian dollars.

Finally, translation should not take place for certain special management reports. Effective international managers should be able to evaluate situations and reach decisions in terms of more than a single currency unit. They need to develop "multilingual" capabilities with reference to different national currencies. Hence some internal company reports may well have several different columns of monetary amounts, each in a different currency unit. Certain other reports, for instance those on a possible international acquisition, may leave no choice about translation because historical foreign exchange rate information may simply not be available—even if subsequent consolidation or other accounting procedures would eventually require use of (often reconstructed!) historical rates. Still other types of reports may translate current or monetary items only and leave other items untranslated.

Appropriate Current Rate. Thus far we have referred to rates of exchange used in various translation methods as either *historical* or *current.* Average rates are often employed in income statements for purposes of expediency. In practice, the choice of an appropriate exchange rate is not clear-cut because there are a number of exchange rates in effect for any given currency at any one point in time. There are buying rates and selling rates, spot rates and forward rates, official rates and free-market rates, with numerous gradations of rate differentials in between. While this list is far from exhaustive, it does illustrate the problem that arises in trying to identify an appropriate rate when foreign currencies trade at significantly different rates depending on types of transactions and temporal dimensions involved. It is not difficult to cite examples of currencies whose official rates have varied significantly above or below free-market rates. At one time, a single United States dollar would officially buy 1,000 Brazilian cruzeiros, while the free market would offer more than twice that amount. And remember today's current rate becomes tomorrow's historical rate!

In our present world of floating exchange rates, there are few limits to permissible degrees of fluctuations in currency values. Under these circumstances, Parkinson recommends the use of a standard bookkeeping rate that would approximate actual exchange rates for converting foreign currencies. He doubts whether the precise exchange rate prevailing at any specific date is particularly relevant for translation purposes.

To quote Parkinson directly,

> As a general rule, the accounts of a foreign subsidiary should be translated to Canadian currency at bookkeeping rates of exchange which need only approximate actual rates for converting the foreign currency. Once established, a bookkeeping rate should not be changed until, because of changes in actual exchange rates, it becomes clearly inappropriate; a new translation rate should be selected as soon as practical after a currency revaluation, as distinct from a mere currency fluctuation.[10]

While foreign exchange translation is only a distant cousin of foreign exchange conversion, your authors feel that an appropriate translation rate

[10] MacDonald R. Parkinson, *Translation of Foreign Currencies* (Toronto: Canadian Institute of Chartered Accountants, 1972), p. 26.

should seek to achieve the greatest possible correspondence to economic and business reality. Thus the rate selected should be the free-market rate quoted for spot transactions in the country where the accounts to be translated originate. This is the only rate that appropriately measures current transaction values. For example, if the translation of the financial position of a Philippine subsidiary company were to be accomplished for the purpose of consolidation with the financial position of its United States parent company, the free United States dollar spot rate quoted by a major Philippine bank at or near the date of the financial statements should be used as the appropriate current translation rate.

In attempting to achieve certain national objectives, a country may apply different exchange rates to different transactions. At times, different simultaneous exchange rates occur for payments of imports, receipts for exports, dividend remittances, and so forth. In these situations, a choice from several existing rates must again be made. Several possibilities have been suggested: (a) use of dividend remittance rates, (b) use of free-market rates, and (c) use of any applicable penalty or preference rates, such as those associated with imports or exports.

Your authors are of the opinion that free-market rates are preferable with one exception. In cases where specific exchange controls are in effect (i.e., when certain funds are definitely earmarked for specific transactions to which specific foreign exchange rates apply), the specifically applicable rates should be utilized. For instance, if a Latin American subsidiary of a United States parent has received permission to import certain goods from the United States at a favorable rate and has set aside certain cash funds to do so, the earmarked funds should be translated to dollars at the special preference rate. The current year-end free-market rate should, of course, be applied to the balance of the foreign cash account. This procedure has the effect of translating portions of a foreign currency cash account at two or more different translation rates. Nothing is wrong with this as long as economic reality is properly and fully reflected thereby.

Translation Gains and Losses. Table 3-3 illustrates five respective translation adjustments resulting from the application of various translation methods to foreign currency financial statements. Accounting treatments accorded these adjustments are as diverse as the underlying translation procedures. Hence, reasonable solutions to problems of how to treat these translation "gains or losses" are urgently needed.

At the outset, however, a distinction between conversion and translation must again be acknowledged. In the former case, there is actual conversion of one currency into another. Thus, if a United States parent company borrows FC 1,000 when the exchange rate is FC 2 = $1 and then converts the proceeds to dollars, it will receive $500. If, at the time of repayment, the foreign exchange rate rises to FC 1 = $1, the United States parent will actually have to pay out $1,000 to discharge its foreign currency debt. A $500 conversion loss has taken place. This loss has been realized and accountants generally agree that such losses (or gains) should be reflected immediately in period income.

Translation adjustments, on the other hand, may be thought of as "unrealized" gains or losses (i.e., "paper" items) that result from the application of different translation rates to individual foreign currency account balances. In this instance, the appropriate accounting disposition is less obvious. Should translation gains or losses receive the same accounting treatment as conversion gains or losses? Should the former be deferred in the balance sheet and taken into income in one or more future accounting periods? Or should they never be brought into the income statement at all?

In view of our earlier comments on translation procedures, it is clear that the objectives of translation have a bearing on the nature of any potential translation adjustment. Accordingly, if a local currency perspective is maintained, reflection of a translation adjustment in current income would appear unwarranted. Recall that a local company perspective should call for use of the current rate translation method—the purpose being to preserve relationships existing in the foreign currency statements. Increasing or decreasing current income by any translation gains or losses would, in our opinion, distort original financial relationships and possibly mislead rather than enlighten users of such information. Translation gains or losses should be treated here as adjustments to owners' equity much like those made when a company's fixed assets are restated for changes in the purchasing power of the monetary unit.

If the reporting currency of the parent company is used as the basic unit of measure for the translated financial statements (a parent company perspective), translation adjustments can be accounted for in a number of ways.[11] Unfortunately, the scope of the present chapter does not permit a detailed enumeration of all conceivable possibilities. What follows, instead, is a brief sketch of some of the basic issues involved in accounting for translation adjustments when a parent company perspective applies.

Accountants have always had difficulties with the disposition of translation gains or losses from the viewpoint of a parent company. The traditional approach has been to recognize losses as soon as they occur, but to recognize gains only to the extent realized. The problem with this approach

---

[11]For an excellent discussion of possible accounting treatments, see Financial Accounting Standards Board, *Discussion Memorandum,* "An Analysis of Issues Related to Accounting for Foreign Currency Translation," 1974, pp. 82–100.

has been the absence of any explicit criteria to determine when realization of a translation gain occurs. In addition, those favoring deferral of translation gains are at a loss to determine how much should be deferred. In the past, companies have followed a procedure of netting current gains against prior losses and deferring the difference. But this implies that translation gains or losses are not period items and are expected to wash out over the longer run. If this is indeed the case, should any deferrals occur at all?

An opposing viewpoint argues that both foreign exchange translation gains *and* losses should be reflected immediately in current income. This represents, in essence, a market-value approach to foreign exchange similar to that taken with respect to the valuation of marketable securities by some mutual funds in the United States. But there is no cash equivalency test on which to base a realization criterion in the foreign exchange translation case! If realization is required in some form, the implication is that any revenue transaction must undergo two realization steps—one for the initial recording of the transaction in local currency units and a second one in terms of the currency in which the local accounts happen to be translated. In those instances where foreign affiliates have no intention of repatriating funds to the parent company, the entire concept of realization in connection with translation becomes extremely nebulous.

Your authors agree with the proposals originally advanced by Hepworth and adopted in 1975 by the FASB; that is, all gains or losses from foreign exchange translation should be considered a part of the overall operating results of the enterprise whose foreign accounts are being translated. No deferrals should be effected and no separate realization conditions should be imposed. Translation gains or losses should be reported separately, to be sure, but they should receive full recognition as soon as they can be calculated.

The procedure supported by us (in conformity with FASB Standard No. 8) may very well entail financial statement effects deemed undesirable by certain groups. Multinational companies, in particular, are likely to report larger fluctuations in their periodic earnings as a consequence. No longer will they have the option of smoothing the impact of fluctuations in the exchange values of national currencies. Indeed, available evidence suggests rather startling results for United States companies that have adopted the FASB's prescription (see Table 3–4). Due to the strengthening of the United States dollar relative to many of the world's major currencies in mid-1975, International Harvester's 1975 third-quarter earnings of $0.16 a share were reportedly wiped out by a $4.5 million translation loss. For ITT (International Telephone and Telegraph), that figure was more like $52 million.[12]

[12]"Learning to Live with Currency Fluctuations," *Business Week,* January 20, 1976, pp. 48–52.

TABLE 3-4. Big Impact of Foreign Exchange[a]

Under new accounting rules, adjustment for fluctuations in foreign exchange rates can make a significant difference in a company's earnings. Here are some of the companies that showed the biggest gains and losses in 1975 from currency changes, according to a study by Investors Management Sciences.

| | EARNINGS PER SHARE | | |
	BEFORE CHANGE	AFTER CHANGE	PERCENT LOSS
Itek	$0.11	$0.06	83
Graco	0.56	0.39	44
Cramer Electronics	0.12	0.09	33
Uniroyal	0.92	0.80	15
Rexnord	5.20	4.62	12
Norton	4.67	4.26	10
Tokheim	2.04	1.88	9
Nashua	0.37	0.34	9
American Cyanamid	3.61	3.35	8
American Air Filter	2.16	2.00	8
	EARNINGS PER SHARE		
	BEFORE CHANGE	AFTER CHANGE	PERCENT GAIN
Sonesta Int. Hotels	1.38	1.77	28
Crompton & Knowles	1.20	1.51	26
Overseas Shipholding	3.14	3.71	18
Cummins Engine	0.75	0.91	21
Cincinnati Milacron	2.33	2.70	16
Rogers	0.46	0.53	15
Vitramon	0.29	0.33	14
Reynolds Metals	2.89	3.29	14
Gleason Works	0.48	0.53	10
Kaiser Aluminum	4.32	4.78	11

[a] Adapted from *Dun's Review* (June 1976), p. 68.

Expressing downright chagrin at having to book such losses, some executives maintain that recording unrealized translation gains and losses is not in accord with economic facts. For, unless conversion of foreign currency investments actually takes place, there is no effect on foreign currency cash flow.

Pending further research on the capital market effects of foreign currency translation processes, we feel that much of the adverse reaction to FASB Standard No. 8 is probably exaggerated. Admittedly, immediate recognition of translation effects may be a somewhat arbitrary and expedient choice. We continue to support this treatment, however, if for no other reason than the fact that accruing an item that is simply a financial statement "plug," or deferral of an item without explicit criteria for its subsequent realization, is even more arbitrary and, in all likelihood, mere historical accident. Furthermore, as long as the nature of translation gains and losses is fully disclosed, we seriously doubt whether intelligent investors and other statement readers are "fooled" by the present procedures.

ACCOUNTING FOR INFLATION

Fluctuating currency values, as we have seen, are today an integral feature of the international business scene. Another environmental consideration is the phenomenon of inflation. It is equally complex and perplexing. Accounting for the effects of inflation is especially germane to managers of multinational enterprises who must, among other things, consolidate the accounts of subsidiaries domiciled in a number of inflationary environments.

The subject of changing price levels is not new. What is new is the fact that inflation today has assumed global dimensions. Rising prices not only continue to plague the economies of the less developed countries but "double-digit" inflation now engulfs many nations of the industrialized world as well. National commitments to rapid economic growth and full employment, together with spiraling costs of energy, account for a goodly portion of the world's current inflationary tendencies.

The international consequences of severe global inflation are disturbing in the extreme. As inflation erodes the standards of living of those on fixed incomes and significantly complicates business decision-making, widespread political and social unrest are likely outcomes. Economic resentments undoubtedly account for many political upheavals that have characterized world politics in recent years.

Economists have posited that inflation is a principal cause of gross liquidity and capital formation problems worldwide. Given the presumed relationship between capital formation and economic growth, it is little wonder that economic summit meetings attended by world leaders have declared inflation to be the most important issue facing all societies today.[13]

Unfortunately, while agreement generally exists about the nature of the inflation problem, little has happened by way of solutions. Governments the world over have experimented with a number of potential inflation remedies. Included in this category are restrictive fiscal and monetary policies, mandatory wage and price controls, and other regulatory activities. All of these policies have been less than successful in containing for very long any national inflation malady.

---

[13]A joint-nation policy statement to this effect was issued in connection with the Rambouillet Agreement of 1975.

A direct implication of the foregoing, for business at least, is that inflation is a phenomenon largely beyond management control and one with which managers must learn to cope. Especially important is management's ability to evaluate the effects of inflation on enterprise performance and financial position. Accounting data that reflect the effects of inflation thus seem both necessary and appropriate.

Accepted accounting principles in the United States and many other countries are, however, premised on an assumption of essentially stable price levels. Therefore, significant distortions in accounting measures of enterprise performance and financial position frequently result. Matching revenues realized during an inflationary period against the historical costs of resources acquired in the past when price levels were lower generally results in overstatements of enterprise income. It has been reported, for example, that while after-tax profits of United States nonfinancial corporations amounted to $66 billion in 1974, real earnings (after adjusting for the effects of inflation) were only $21 billion—43% less than real earnings for these corporations a decade earlier.[14] Overstatements of enterprise income, in turn, may lead to:

1. Increases in proportionate taxation.
2. Demands by shareholders for more dividends.
3. Demands for higher wages by labor or their representatives.
4. Reduced confidence in the credibility of enterprise accounting reports.

In pronounced inflationary situations there is always the danger that a firm may not preserve sufficient resources with which to replace specific assets whose prices have risen. Inventories and plant and equipment are important asset categories in this regard. Failure to adjust corporate financial statements for changes in the purchasing power of the monetary unit makes it difficult for statement readers to interpret and compare reported operating performances of companies both within and between countries. Purchasing power gains and losses that arise from holding monetary items are also ignored under conventional accounting procedures. This further distorts business performance comparisons during inflationary periods.

General Versus Specific Price Level Changes

When it comes to accounting for price level changes, we must be careful to distinguish between general and specific price movements. In the past the term *inflation* has been applied indiscriminately to both.

A *general price level change* occurs when the prices of all goods and services in an economy move on the average, i.e., the purchasing power of

---

[14]Robert Mims, "More Realism in Inflation Accounting," *Business Week,* January 19, 1976, p. 26.

the monetary unit changes in terms of its ability to command goods and services in general. A *specific price level change,* on the other hand, refers to a change in the price of a specific commodity. In the context of a business enterprise, it refers to changes in the specific prices of a firm's resources, e.g., inventories, plant and equipment, and supplies.

Statistical series that measure changes in both general and specific prices do not generally move in parallel fashion. For example, while the Wholesale Price Index (measuring average changes in prices of about 2200 commodities sold in primary markets in the United States) rose about 8% between 1974 and 1975, the relative price changes of some of its specific components exhibited the following pattern: agricultural chemicals, up 47.8%; gas fuels, up 33.6%; construction machinery and equipment, up 21.6%; heating equipment, up 11.6%; but lumber, down 7%; hides and skins, down 10.9%; grains, down 13.2%; and inedible fats and oils, down 25%.[15] These data apply only to the United States. The dispersion of specific price changes internationally would probably be even greater.

In addition, each type of price change has a differing effect on measures of a firm's financial position and operating performance and should be accounted for, consequently, with different objectives in mind. Hereafter, accounting for the financial statement effects of general price level changes is referred to as the *general price level model* and accounting for specific price changes is referred to as the *specific price level model.* The term *current(cost) value model* is also employed when appropriate.[16]

In explaining the accounting objective of the general price level model, let us briefly review the concept of enterprise income. Income may be defined as the change in an entity's wealth position over time without regard for new capital investment or withdrawals. Hence income represents the amount of an entity's wealth that can be disposed of during a given period of time while leaving the entity as well off at the end of the period as it was at the beginning. For instance, under conventional accounting doctrine in the United States, a firm's wealth position at any point in time is reflected by the original acquisition costs of its net assets. Now assume conditions of stable price levels. If a firm's net assets equaled $100 at the beginning of the period and $150 at the end due to profitable operations, income would be equal to $50 ($150 − $100)—assuming again that disposing of the $50 (perhaps in the form of dividends to existing stockholders) would leave the firm with as much money capital at the end as it had at the beginning, namely $100.

Once we depart from the assumption of stable prices, the $50 may no longer represent the amount of a firm's disposable wealth. The general price

---

[15] *Survey of Current Business,* May 1976, pp. 9–10.

[16] For an expanded discussion of the concepts treated here, the reader is referred to Robert G. May, Gerhard G. Mueller, and Thomas H. Williams, *A New Introduction to Financial Accounting* (Englewood Cliffs, NJ.: Prentice-Hall, Inc. 1975).

level model takes this into account by measuring income in such fashion that it represents the maximum amount of resources that could be distributed to various income claimants during a given period while preserving the firm's ability to command as many goods and services, *in general,* at the end of the period as it could at the beginning.

Using the previous example, assume now that the general level of prices, as measured by an appropriate price index, increased from 100 at the beginning of the period to 120 at the end. This implies that it takes $120 at the end of the period to purchase, in general, what $100 would have purchased at the beginning. Income, under the general price level model, is thus measured by taking the difference between wealth at the end of the period ($150) and wealth at the beginning adjusted to its end of period purchasing power equivalent ($100 \times 120/100 = \$120$) or $30.

The specific price level model, on the other hand, holds that income is the amount of resources a firm can distribute during a given period while maintaining its productive capacity or earning power. This may be achieved by adjusting a firm's beginning and ending net asset position (usually by appropriate specific price indexes) to reflect changes in *specific* price levels during the period. Continuing our previous example, if during the same period prices of the firm's specific assets had increased from an index level of 100 to 140, income under the specific price level model would be measured as $(150 - 100 \times 140/100)$ or $10. Distributing no more than $10 would therefore assure that the firm at least preserves internally enough resources to enable it to replace specific assets whose prices have risen during the period. Thus, while the general price level model seeks to preserve the general purchasing power of an enterprise's original money capital, the specific price level model seeks to preserve a firm's productive capacity or earning power. The latter concept underlies the United States Securities and Exchange Commission's (SEC's) replacement cost measurement and disclosure requirements as stipulated in Accounting Series Releases No. 190 and 203 and elsewhere.

An International Perspective on Inflation Accounting

Various accounting solutions to the price level problem have been adopted in different countries over the years. For the purpose at hand, three categories of price level accounting are discussed.[17] They include (a) use of balance sheet reserves to provide for the increased cost of replacing assets or

[17]Based on R. W. Scapens, *The Treatment of Inflation in the Published Accounts of Companies in Overseas Countries* (London: Research Committee of the Institute of Chartered Accountants in England and Wales, 1973).

for the additional depreciation that would be required if fixed assets were valued at current values; (b) upward revaluation of specific asset categories with or without the restatement of depreciation; and (c) use of comprehensive price level accounting systems using either general or specific price level adjustments, or some combination of the two.

Balance Sheet Reserves. This approach involves a charge to current income or unappropriated retained earnings to establish a reserve for the higher replacement cost of a firm's assets. The rationale: In times of rising prices, depreciation of assets valued on the basis of lower acquisition costs may not shelter adequately cash flows from operations to finance the replacement of a firm's specific assets. Appropriations of current income or retained earnings are thus undertaken to reduce the dividend declaration base so that the firm will not disburse funds that it needs to preserve its productive capacity.

Appropriation of retained earnings to create inflation reserves is reportedly used in countries where alternative methods of dealing with price level changes are lacking. Extensive use of the procedure has occurred in Australia, Canada, the United Kingdom, and the United States. More recently, Price Waterhouse International's *A Survey in 46 Countries* revealed that the creation of inflation reserves by means of charges to current income is employed by a minority of companies in Argentina, Belgium, Brazil, Chile, Denmark, Ethiopia, Jamaica, the Netherlands, Pakistan, South Africa, Switzerland, Trinidad, Uruguay, and Zaire.

The use of balance sheet reserves suffers from a number of shortcomings. For one thing, the creation of an inflation reserve does nothing to indicate the effects of inflation on a firm's resources and operations. As such, the information content of this procedure is minimal. In most cases, amounts appropriated to inflation reserves are based on arbitrary criteria. Appropriations based on available "profits" are often favored over more accurate estimates of actual price level distortions.

Asset Revaluations. This approach to inflation accounting overcomes some of the limitations mentioned above. It typically involves restating the amounts of certain assets by using appropriate price level indexes or other measures of current exchange values. The general object of a revaluation scheme is to disclose the current economic values of assets employed in generating revenues. It facilitates, to some extent, intercompany comparisons and more accurate evaluations of a firm's wealth position. Moreover, if depreciation is taken on the revalued amounts, operating income also reflects the effects of inflation. If allowed for tax purposes, revaluation depreciation helps to minimize management's often heard complaint of "capital confiscation through taxation."

Asset write-ups were commonly employed during the aftermath of World War II. Germany is a case in point. Hyperinflation, which characterized Germany's war-torn economy in the late 1940's, made the preparation of meaningful historical cost-based financial statements impossible. After the major German currency reform in June 1948, all companies were allowed to revalue their assets at their current replacement costs to provide a common reference point for future financial statements. Depreciation was permitted on the revalued amounts both for tax and financial reporting purposes.

Legislation permitting similar revaluations was also effected in Austria, France, Italy, and Japan. While maximum revaluations were established by statute, companies in these countries were usually granted considerable leeway in deciding which assets to revalue.

In view of the persistent and significant rates of inflation that characterize the countries of South America, asset revaluations now occur on a regular basis in this part of the world. Brazilian companies are required to revalue their assets each year using a government supplied price index. Depreciation is then permitted on the revalued amounts. Interestingly, the revised figures are not treated as supplementary statements but are, instead, an integral part of a company's published accounts.

In both Chile and Argentina, annual restatements of fixed assets for both tax and financial reporting purposes became mandatory in 1963 and 1972, respectively. In 1975, as part of the new military junta's reform program, price level adjustments were extended to all real assets in Chile. As in Brazil, depreciation is permitted on the asset write-ups. While similar practices exist in Uruguay, they are not mandatory there. Revaluation is considered to be a generally accepted accounting practice in Uruguay, however, and auditors have been known to render qualified opinions where the revaluations and related higher depreciation expenses are not recorded in the financial statements. Considered in total, South American approaches to inflation adjustments may be distinguished by the use, in most instances, of government supplied indexes that measure changes in *general* rather than *specific* price levels.

Occasional revaluations of fixed assets are also practiced in Australia, Belgium, Denmark, Norway, Sweden, the United Kingdom, and (to some extent) Canada. In contrast to the South American examples, however, depreciation on restated asset values in these countries is usually not allowed for tax purposes. Another major distinction is that asset restatements in countries outside South America tend to be based on *specific* as opposed to *general* price level changes.

Despite the fairly widespread use of asset write-ups as a means of recording the effects of inflation in company accounts, this procedure is generally regarded as providing only a partial remedy to the inflation problem.

Note that, in the examples cited, price level adjustments are applied only to certain asset categories or only intermittently. Accordingly, more comprehensive systems of inflation accounting are currently being sought.

Comprehensive Price Level Accounting Systems. This approach to inflation accounting entails adjustments of *all* financial statement items— assets, liabilities, revenues, and expenses—for the effects of changing price levels. The two rival, though not mutually exclusive, methods employed are the general price level model and the specific price level model discussed earlier. Recall that the general price level model calls for adjusting financial statements by applying a single general index such as the United States Gross National Product Implicit Price Deflator or the United Kingdom Consumer Expenditure Deflator. The specific price level model, on the other hand, seeks to adjust financial statement items in terms of their current exchange (market) or replacement (current) cost values.

Both adjustment models possess their own unique attributes. At the same time, comprehensive price level accounting systems, as we have defined them, are not yet common practice in most countries. Chile probably stands alone in this respect as the only country to have replaced historical cost accounts with general price level adjusted statements officially. Companies in other countries are, however, experimenting with various adjustment systems. Indeed a few, such as the Philips Lamp Company of the Netherlands, have unique inflation recognition accounting systems well established.

In January of 1973, the Accounting Standards Steering Committee of the Institute of Chartered Accountants in England and Wales issued a provisional accounting standard entitled "Accounting for Changes in the Purchasing Power of Money." This document recommends the provision of supplementary statements in which figures appearing in published accounts of British companies would be restated into pounds sterling of current purchasing power (our general price level model) at the end of the financial year. Although this recommendation has since been rejected in favor of another proposal, to be discussed shortly, a number of British companies have already complied with the earlier recommendation. Exhibit 3–2 contains the 1975/1976 general price level adjusted supplementary accounts of the Royal Dutch/Shell Group of Companies.[18] Note the significant differences between adjusted and unadjusted amounts revealed in the financial ratios appearing at the bottom of p. 90.

---

[18]Royal Dutch is a holding company that, in conjunction with the Shell Transport and Trading Company, Limited (United Kingdom), owns, directly or indirectly, investments in the numerous companies comprising the Royal Dutch Shell Group. Arrangements between Royal Dutch and Shell Transport provide that both companies share in the aggregate net assets and dividends and interest received from Group Companies in the proportion of 60:40.

EXHIBIT 3 – 2. Royal Dutch/Shell Group of Companies' Supplementary Financial Statements—Current Purchasing Power Basis

SUMMARIZED STATEMENT OF INCOME

	HISTORICAL BASIS	CURRENT PURCHASING POWER BASIS	
	1976 £ million	1976 £ million	1975 £ million
Total revenues	20,903	22,342	18,925
Total costs and expenses (other than the following items)	(16,744)	(18,334)	(14,888)
Depreciation, depletion and amortization	(536)	(1,142)	(1,419)
Taxation on income	(2,237)	(2,391)	(2,783)
Income applicable to minority interests	(156)	(126)	(96)
Gain on net monetary liabilities	–	350	503
Net income for the year	1,230	699	242
Add UK Advance Corporation Tax allocated to Shell Transport	70	71	61
Net income divisible under 60: 40 arrangements	1,300	770	303

SUMMARIZED STATEMENT OF ASSETS AND LIABILITIES

	HISTORICAL BASIS	CURRENT PURCHASING POWER BASIS	
	1976 £ million	1976 £ million	1975 £ million
Property, plant and equipment (net)	6,545	11,006	10,295
Investments in associated companies	487	1,425	1,557
Long-term receivables and deferred charges	456	456	480
Excess of current assets over current liabilities	3,521	3,741	3,527
Total assets less current liabilities	11,009	16,628	15,859
Deductions:			
Long-term provisions	(1,164)	(1,164)	(1,072)
Long-term debt	(2,534)	(2,534)	(2,228)
Minority interests	(735)	(1,401)	(1,288)
Net assets	6,576	11,529	11,271

FINANCIAL RATIOS

	HISTORICAL BASIS	CURRENT PURCHASING POWER BASIS	
	1976	1976	1975
Income[a] as % of average net assets	21.1%	6.8%	2.7%
Long-term debt as % of total capital employed	25.7%	16.4%	15.1%

[a]income = net income divisible under 60: 40 arrangements

EXHIBIT 3-2. Continued

1 Basis of Restatement

The supplementary Statement of Income and Statement of Assets and Liabilities show in summarized form a restatement of the historical sterling amounts in pounds of current purchasing power at December 31, 1976.

Since the conventional historical Group financial statements are translated into sterling (on the bases described in the Accounting Policies on page 32) the restatement has been made by applying the United Kingdom retail price index, which indicates a rate of inflation since December 31, 1975, of 15.1%.

Restatement is effected by adjusting non-monetary items for the change in the purchasing power of sterling since acquisition and by measuring the purchasing power losses and gains in holding monetary assets and monetary liabilities. Property, plant and equipment (including that of associated companies) and stocks have been treated as non-monetary items; all other assets and liabilities have been treated as monetary items. The restatement of property, plant and equipment and other non-monetary assets does not purport to represent appraisal, replacement cost or any other measure of the current value of assets or the prices at which transactions would take place currently.

2 Change in net assets

	HISTORICAL BASIS	CURRENT PURCHASING POWER BASIS	
	1976 £ million	1976 £ million	1975 £ million
Net assets at beginning of year	5,774	11,271	11,389
Net income for the year	1,230	699	242
Dividends to parents	(428)	(441)	(360)
Net assets at end of year	6,576	11,529	11,271
Increase (decrease) in net assets	802	258	(118)

3 Change in net income divisible under 60:40 arrangements

The adjustments to convert the Statement of Income to a current purchasing power basis are as follows:

	1976 £ million	1975 £ million
Revenues net of costs and expenses	92	138
(other than items shown below) This increase in income is caused principally by the change in the index between the average date at which the transactions occurred during the year and the end of the year.		
Stock change	(396)	(529)
The additional charge is caused by restating the opening and closing stocks according to the period in which they were acquired.		
Depreciation	(606)	(730)
The higher depreciation charge is caused by the increase, in terms of current purchasing power, of property, plant and equipment on which the depreciation charge is based. It includes a loss in current purchasing power terms on disposal of property, plant and equipment amounting to £111 million (1975: liabilities £299 million).		

91

Exhibit 3-2. Continued

Gain on net long-term monetary assets	427	535
and		
Loss on net current monetary assets	(77)	(98)
Monetary liabilities exceed monetary assets and there is therefore a net gain on these two items in terms of current purchasing power.		
Minority share of income	30	(3)
Updating of 1975 figures to account for the decrease in purchasing power of pounds sterling during 1976	–	40
Decrease in net income divisible under 60:40 arrangements	(530)	(647)

REPORT OF THE AUDITORS ON THE SUPPLEMENTARY CURRENT PURCHASING POWER FINANCIAL STATEMENTS

> *To Royal Dutch Petroleum Company and The "Shell" Transport and Trading Company, Limited*

We have examined the supplementary current purchasing power financial statements for the years 1976 and 1975 which appear on pages 42 and 43 herein.

In our opinion these supplementary statements fairly restate in summarized form the historical financial statements of the Royal Dutch/Shell Group of Companies for such years expressed in terms of the general purchasing power of sterling at December 31, 1976, in accordance with the bases outlined in the accompanying notes, consistently applied.

Klynveld Kraayenhof & Co., The Hague
Turquands Barton Mayhew & Co., London
Price Waterhouse & Co., New York

March 10, 1977

Problem Areas

Why are more countries not following the Chilean example? The answer is that there are many accounting problems that have yet to be resolved when it comes to effective and comprehensive inflation accounting. Which types of price changes should be accounted for? While Chile has chosen to account for general price level movements, is this really the best way to go? Even if we answer in the affirmative, which statistical price series would we employ—an index of consumer prices, an index of wholesale prices, or some other statistical construct? Then how often should we adjust accounts —annually, semiannually, monthly, weekly? What about gains and losses from holding monetary items? Should these be reflected in current operating income or deferred to future accounting periods? Should financial statements of earlier periods be restated in terms of current period price levels (i.e., rolled forward) when prior statements are presented for comparative purposes? And how should the accounts of foreign subsidiaries and branches be consolidated with those of the parent? Should they first be adjusted for foreign inflation and then translated to their domestic currency equivalents or vice versa?

Many of these issues parallel those discussed in connection with the foreign currency translation problem. For example, both price level restatements and foreign currency translations have a common denominator problem, both have similar difficulties with the methodology of restatement, and both face a dilemma in classifying and disposing of restatement "gains or losses." The similarities, however, are more apparent than real. That is to say, the theoretical accounting considerations involved in the two processes are not the same. Foreign exchange translation is largely a unit-of-account (measurement unit) problem. Price level adjustment is primarily concerned with the distinction between capital and income and, therefore, has predominantly valuation (measurement process) implications. Valuation questions in foreign exchange translation never lose their income statement focus and their *transaction* orientation. On the other hand, price level adjustments are best seen from an *aggregate* value point of view.

Specific effects also differ in the two processes. A cash account translated from one currency to the next is not particularly problematical, whereas a price level adjustment of a cash account is. Accounts properly translated from one currency to another are *not* automatically price level adjusted because foreign exchange rates are seldom perfectly negatively correlated with price level changes and, as we have seen, single accounts in a balance sheet may be successfully adjusted for inflation effects. On the other hand, it makes little sense to have one account expressed in one currency and all others in another.

With these distinctions in mind, let us now examine three inflation accounting issues that have proved especially troublesome to accountants. They are (a) the question of which price level movements to account for, (b) the accounting treatment of inflation "gain or losses," and (c) the translate-restate/restate-translate controversy. To confine our scope somewhat, issue (a) is discussed in conjunction with issue (c).

Consolidating Foreign Accounts in an Inflationary World. All the foreign exchange translation methods described earlier in this chapter have one thing in common. They ignore the effects of inflation in the consolidation process. To remedy this shortcoming, some writers advocate restating foreign account balances to reflect changes in the purchasing power of the foreign currency unit and then translating the adjusted amounts to their domestic currency equivalent. Purported advantages of the "restate-translate" proposal are as follows:

1. It enables statement readers to assess ordinary operating results in terms of the local currency as well as the separate effects of inflation on these results.
2. It enables management to gauge better the performance of a subsidiary after providing for "maintenance" of the subsidiary's assets.
3. It enables management to evaluate the performance of a subsidiary in terms of the environment in which the subsidiary's assets are domiciled.
4. It enables management to ascertain the full effect of any currency devaluation on a subsidiary's operating results if devaluation occurs.

Critics of the restate first and then translate approach argue that this method results in a unit of measure that reflects multiple standards in terms of general purchasing power. For example, a United States parent company consolidating the results of ten foreign subsidiaries (each domiciled in a country experiencing different rates of inflation) would obtain financial statements in United States dollars. These dollar amounts, however, would really reflect the purchasing power of ten different countries. This is criticized as highly undesirable, especially for statement readers in the United States who necessarily have a parent company (i.e., a United States dollar) perspective on the consolidated statements. Restate-translate critics support the adoption of what may be called the *translate-restate approach.* Under this proposal, foreign accounts are first translated to the domestic currency of the parent company and then restated to their domestic general purchasing power equivalents.

The merits of the latter proposal, according to its proponents, are that it not only reveals the financial statement effects of changes in foreign currency exchange rates but also discloses the effect of domestic inflation on the prospective returns to domestic investors. In short, consolidated accounts prepared according to the translate-restate proposal are expressed in terms of a single standard of measure—namely dollars of domestic purchasing power. And that is what counts!

How do we choose between these competing constructs? Debates on the issue thus far have generated more heat than light. Our feeling is that the controversy can only be resolved by addressing it from a decision-oriented framework.

Generally, and in brief, investors are interested in a firm's dividend-generating potential since the value of their securities investment is ultimately related to future dividends. A firm's dividend-generating potential, in turn, is directly related to its capacity to produce goods and services. Unless a firm preserves its productive capacity and thereby its earning power, dividends are a moot consideration.

A direct implication of this argument is that investors are interested in specific rather than general price level-adjusted statements. Why? Because specific price level adjustments [our specific price level or current (cost) value model] determine the maximum amounts of resources that can be paid out as dividends (disposable wealth) without reducing a firm's productive capacity.

What does this conclusion imply about the restate-translate versus translate-restate dilemma? It implies that the dilemma is trivial. The reason is that both processes are based on a valuation framework that has little to recommend it—historical cost. Neither restatement for general price level changes abroad and translation to domestic currency amounts nor translation to domestic currency amounts and restatement for domestic inflation changes that valuation base. In other words, the historical cost model, adjusted for changes in the general purchasing power of the monetary unit, whether it be foreign general purchasing power or domestic general purchasing power, is still the historical cost model!

The price level adjustment procedure that seems appropriate from our point of view is as follows:

1. Restate the financial statements of all subsidiaries, both domestic and foreign, as well as the statements of the parent, to reflect changes in specific price levels (maybe current costs).
2. Translate the accounts of all foreign subsidiaries into domestic currency equivalents using a constant (i.e., the current) foreign exchange rate.

Restating both foreign and domestic accounts to their specific current price equivalents produces information that is decision-relevant. This information encodes the maximum amount of realistic potential dividend flows to investors. It also facilitates predictions of future cash flows. Moreover, comparisons and evaluations of the consolidated results of all firms would be a much easier task than it now is.

Although we have not explicitly considered the decision models of management, the proposal advocated here should also be germane to them. For instance, headquarters management should be in a better position to evaluate the relative performance of its subsidiaries since enterprise results would be comparable not only nationally but internationally as well. And since managers are concerned with the maintenance of productive capacity, our proposal should further facilitate more equitable resource allocations within any national or multinational corporate system—especially when general and specific price levels do not move in parallel.

Inflation Gains and Losses. Although these authors have expressed a decided preference for current (specific) price accounting models over historical cost constructs (adjusted or unadjusted), we are not so *doctrinaire* with regard to practical implementation. There are many variants of current values and prices and we are not prepared to argue over the relative merits of index adjustments versus replacement cost or current value measures.

Indeed, given current practice, it is possible that several of these measures might be appropriate in a given set of financial statements. A very concise and readable study on the problem of implementing "current value" accounting is available in the form of a white paper by Touche Ross & Co., entitled *Economic Reality In Financial Reporting* (1975). This booklet posits the use of a variety of "current value" measures, including present values for monetary assets and obligations, current costs (replacement costs) for inventories and depreciable assets, and net realizable values for all other nonmonetary resources and obligations. Even though we are rather sympathetic with the theme of the Touche Ross booklet, just imagine all of the "gains and losses" that its adoption in practice would produce!

The accounting disposition of holding gains or losses that result from restating balance sheet items for specific price changes is elusive. Should portions of, let us say, inventory gains be "realized" in periods when the respective inventories are turned into finished goods and sold? Are there ever "unrealized" adjustment gains or losses that should be deferred? Or should all such gains and losses simply be lumped together and disclosed in a special new section within stockholders' equity on the balance sheet?

Acknowledging that more practical experimentation and research are needed in this area, our earlier position, stated in regard to the disposition of foreign currency translation gains and losses, seems also applicable here. We feel that holding gains or losses should be disclosed in the income statement and properly labeled as to their nature and source. It is likely that changes in specific asset values may be just as important as operating results for many enterprises.

And what of purchasing power gains or losses from holding monetary items? Again, we feel that debtors and creditors do indeed gain and lose from changes in the purchasing power of the monetary unit. Hence, these gains and losses should receive the same accounting treatment as all other gains or losses discussed thus far. New territories must be charted when it comes to accounting for and disclosure of inflation gains and losses—and your authors are the first to recognize this critical need for developmental efforts in our discipline.

Current Trends

Where will inflation accounting take us? The recent remarks of a prominent American Congressman are perhaps indicative (Haskins & Sells, *The Week in Review,* July 23, 1976, pp. 7–8):

> For some time I have been watching a disturbing development in the accounting profession. There now is a concerted effort by academi-

cians, accounting firms, and regulatory authorities to adopt some radically new model of inflation-based accounting. I am disturbed by this development because it signals that the profession has lost its bearings: it is spending too much time and effort to resolve the transitory problem of inflation while other, more serious problems of the profession go unattended.

The plain fact of the matter is that inflation accounting is a premature, imprecise, and undeveloped method of recording basic business facts. To insist that any system of inflation accounting can afford the accuracy and fairness needed for the efficient operation of our tax system is simply foolish. My years on the Ways and Means Committee have exposed me to the many appeals of business—from corporate tax "reform" to the need for capital formation—which have served as a guise for reducing the tax contribution of American business. In this respect I see inflation accounting as another in a long line of attempts to minimize corporate taxation through backdoor gimmickry.

Remarks such as the foregoing suggest that accounting for the effects of inflation is probably a long way yet from a general solution. Still, some direction seems to be emerging on the international front. At one time, South American experiments with general price level adjustments were expected to become the prototype for inflation accounting elsewhere. These experiments were viewed sympathetically by professional accounting policy-making bodies in both the United Kingdom and the United States—the British in their *Provisional SSAP No. 7:* "Accounting for Changes in the Purchasing Power of Money;" the Americans in *APB Statement No. 3* followed by the FASB exposure draft entitled "Financial Reporting in Units of General Purchasing Power."

Things, however, have suddenly changed. Britain's prestigious government-appointed Sandilands Committee recommended in 1975 a new system of current cost accounting to *replace* existing historical transaction accounting. Purchasing power adjustment methods are rejected on the grounds that use of a single all-inclusive index would give misleading results. The Sandilands recommendations, by and large, were received favorably in the United Kingdom. At the time of this writing, implementation procedures were being formulated by the follow-up Morpeth Committee, although an initial U. K. Institute policy draft in this area met with defeat.

In the United States, the SEC opted for specific price adjustments by requiring larger United States corporations to disclose what it would cost to replace their inventories and production plant at current prices and what their depreciation expenses and cost of sales would be if computed on the basis of replacement costs. Australia joined the chorus by becoming the first country (late in 1976) to issue a formal professional accounting recommendation in favor of current cost measurements. West Germany is reportedly moving in a similar direction.

It is too soon to draw any definite conclusions. But there are now more advocates than ever before of the current cost (value) model. Many are committed to finding a common solution to problems of inflation accounting. All of this suggests that current cost (value) accounting may finally be coming of age.

SELECTED REFERENCES

3.1   ACCOUNTANTS INTERNATIONAL STUDY GROUP, *Consolidated Financial Statements,* New York: Author, 1973, unpaginated.

3.2   AMERICAN INSTITUTE OF CERTIFIED PUBLIC ACCOUNTANTS, COMMITTEE ON ACCOUNTING PROCEDURE, "Restatement and Revision of Accounting Research Bulletins," *Accounting Research Bulletin No. 43,* Chapter 12, "Foreign Operations and Foreign Exchange," New York: Author, 1953, pp. 111–116.

3.3   AMERICAN INSTITUTE OF CERTIFIED PUBLIC ACCOUNTANTS, "Financial Statements Restated for General Price-Level Changes," *Statement of the Accounting Principles Board No. 3,* New York: Author, 1969, 72 pp.

3.4   AMERICAN INSTITUTE OF CERTIFIED PUBLIC ACCOUNTANTS, "Status of Accounting Research Bulletins," *Accounting Principles Board Opinion No. 6,* paragraph 18, New York: Author, 1965, p. 42.

3.5   BARRETT, EDGAR, AND LESLIE SPERO, "Accounting Determinants of Foreign Exchange Gains and Losses," *Financial Analysts Journal,* March–April 1975, pp. 26–30.

3.6   CHOI, FREDERICK D. S., "Price-Level Adjustments and Foreign Currency Translations: Are They Compatible?" *International Journal of Accounting,* Fall 1975, pp. 121–43.

3.7   EVANS, THOMAS G., "Foreign Currency Translation Practices Abroad," *CPA Journal,* June 1974, pp. 47–50.

3.8   FINANCIAL ACCOUNTING STANDARDS BOARD, "Accounting for the Translation of Foreign Currency Transactions and Foreign Currency Financial Statements," *Statement of Financial Accounting Standards No. 8,* Stamford, Conn.: Author, October 1975, 103 pp.

3.9   FINANCIAL ACCOUNTING STANDARDS BOARD, *FASB Discussion Memorandum,* "An Analysis of Issues Related To Accounting For Foreign Currency Translation," Stamford, Conn.: Author, February 21, 1974, 141 pp. plus appendices.

3.10 FINANCIAL ACCOUNTING STANDARDS BOARD, *FASB Discussion Memorandum,* "An Analysis of Issues Related to Reporting the Effects of General Price-Level Changes in Financial Statements," Stamford, Conn.: Author, February 15, 1974, 19 pp.

3.11 HEPWORTH, SAMUEL R., *Reporting Foreign Operations,* Ann Arbor, Mich.: University of Michigan, 1956, 211 pp.

3.12 INTERNATIONAL ACCOUNTING STANDARDS COMMITTEE, "Consolidated Financial Statements," *International Accounting Standard 3,* London, England: Author, June, 1977, unpaginated.

3.13 INTERNATIONAL ACCOUNTING STANDARDS COMMITTEE. "Accounting Responses to Changing Prices," *International Accounting Standard 6,* London, England: June, 1977, unpaginated.

3.14 LORENSEN, LEONARD, AND PAUL ROSENFIELD, "Management Information and Foreign Inflation," *Journal of Accountancy,* December 1974, pp. 98–102.

3.15 MUELLER, GERHARD G., "Accounting for Multinationals," *Accountancy,* July 1975, pp. 69–72.

3.16 NATIONAL ASSOCIATION OF ACCOUNTANTS, "Accounting Problems in Foreign Operations," *Research Report No. 36,* New York: Author, 1960, 71 pp.

3.17 PRICE WATERHOUSE & CO., *Current Foreign Exchange Information,* (Price Waterhouse Information Guide), New York: Author, 1977, 121 pp.

3.18 RADEBAUGH, LEE H., "Accounting for Price-Level and Exchange-Rate Changes for U.S. International Firms: An Empirical Study," *Journal of International Business Studies,* Fall 1974, pp. 41–56.

3.19 SCAPENS, R. W., *The Treatment of Inflation in the Published Accounts of Companies in Overseas Countries,* London: Research Committee of the Institute of Chartered Accountants in England and Wales, 1975, 70 pp.

3.20 SEIDLER, LEE, "An Income Approach to the Translation of Foreign Currency Financial Statements," *CPA Journal,* January 1972, pp. 26–35.

DISCUSSION QUESTIONS

3.1 The practice of consolidating the accounts of foreign subsidiaries, while varying from country to country, is on the increase. Three frequently mentioned rationales for consolidation are geographic location, degree of ownership, and homogeneity of business activities. Comment on the limitations of these consolidation criteria and suggest at least three alternative standards that might better facilitate a parent company's decision to include a foreign subsidiary in the consolidation process.

3.2 In their recent standard "Consolidated Financial Statements and the Equity Method of Accounting," the International Accounting Standards Committee (IASC) recommends consolidation of all subsidiaries except "where control is likely to be temporary or where severe long-term restrictions on the transfer of funds jeopardize the parent's exercise of control." This provision, however, conflicts with the well-established United States practice that permits nonconsolidation of banking, finance, and insurance subsidiaries. Which position do you support? What does the conflict imply about the objectives of consolidated financial statements?

3.3 Despite recent authoritative pronouncements on the subject of accounting for foreign currency translation, little agreement exists regarding the appropriate unit of measure for foreign accounts when consolidated with those of the parent company. Should foreign accounts be expressed in the reporting currency of the parent company or the reporting currency of the foreign entity? Take a position on this controversy and support your answer in a paragraph or two.

3.4 It is often asserted that the traditional monetary-nonmonetary foreign currency translation method is, for all practical purposes, identical in its financial statement effects to the temporal principle of translation prescribed under *FASB Statement No. 8*. Do you agree with this statement? Please explain.

3.5 Should a multinational company with a single partially-owned foreign subsidiary in say, Malaysia, disclose its "foreign exchange gains and losses" in financial reports to its Malaysian shareholders? In answering this question, be careful to distinguish between *conversion* gains and losses and *translation* gains and losses.

3.6 Reactions of the business community to the prescriptions of *FASB Statement No. 8*, especially with regard to the accounting treatment accorded translation gains and losses, has generally been unfavorable. Summarize, in brief fashion, the apparent reasons for these reactions and the extent to which they seem justified.

3.7 On the basis of your readings, identify what you feel are the key issues in the area of accounting for foreign currency translation. What would your recommendations be to the IASC regarding its current effort on the subject?

3.8 Briefly sketch an outline of how you would attempt to measure empirically the capital market effects of *FASB Statement No. 8's* recommended treatment of foreign currency translation gains and loses.

3.9 Leaf through the 1974 *FASB Discussion Memorandum* entitled "An Analysis of Issues Related to Accounting for Foreign Currency Translation," and determine whether the FASB exhausted all the possible issues on the subject. Identify those issues that you feel have been overlooked.

3.10 "In evaluating our business our utmost concern is its health in a stable currency, namely dollars. This is the way most successful independent Brazilian businessmen look at their business also. Sometimes when a business looks very good in cruzeiros but poor in dollars, it is a sign that the business is rapidly heading toward bankruptcy." Evaluate the quote in terms of its policy implications.

3.11 Accounting for the effects of inflation is akin to foreign currency translation. Explain.

3.12 Professional accountancy bodies the world over generally agree that the degree of inflation may become so great that conventional financial statements will lose much of their significance and price level-adjusted statements clearly become more meaningful. Since domestic rates of inflation vary significantly from country to country, at what point do price level-adjusted financial statements become "more meaningful"? How does one determine whether the benefits of price level-adjusted accounting information exceed the costs involved?

3.13 "For accounting purposes, our Italian subsidiary does not revalue its assets to reflect changes in the general level of prices in Italy. Accounting for the financial statement effects of changing prices would mean an increase of about 25–30 people in their accounting department. Besides, they maintain that translating their financial reports into dollars automatically reflects the impact of inflation." Do you agree with the last sentence in this quote?

3.14 As a potential investor in the shares of multinational enterprise, which inflation construct—restate/translate or translate/restate—would provide you with consolidated information most relevant to your decision needs? Which information set is most optimal from the viewpoint of the foreign subsidiary's shareholders?

3.15 Would the information set you recommended in Question 3.14 be equally as useful for purposes of internal management control? Be careful to distinguish between local control and control by headquarters management.

ANNOTATED TEACHING MATERIALS

3.1 *Ramada Inns, Inc.* (ICCH Case 9–176–272). This case consists of the response of Ramada Inns and their objections to the FASB Exposure Draft that eventually became FASB Standard No. 8. Alternative foreign exchange translation methods are discussed. Both conceptual and procedural issues are treated.

3.2 *A Note on Foreign Exchange Rates* (Centre for International Business Studies Note: University of Western Ontario, Canada). This note provides a concise introduction to foreign exchange systems and the underlying economic and market factors influencing the determination of foreign exchange rates. It is divided into five separate parts. The first discusses how foreign exchange rates are interwoven with a country's overall governmental economic policy. Next a historical account is given of foreign exchange rates and systems from 1875 to 1975. Then follows a description of the international financial institutions such as the IMF and the World Bank that are directly involved with foreign currencies. The fourth section identifies the factors that underlie the value of a particular currency. Finally, the note concludes in section five with an outlook on foreign exchange developments for the world in general as well as for selected specific countries.

3.3   The Clifford Company (Case 5, Zenoff and Zwick, *International Financial Management,* pp. 98–104). This Swiss-based company uses a generalized formula approach to measure the degree of risk inherent in any foreign currency at a point in time. The formula uses weighting of five economic factors. These factors are reserves, money supply, cost of living, trade balance, and exchange spread.

Currency risk is scored on a scale from 0 to 100, with a score of 100 signifying overall excellent strength of a currency. The formula allows comparative study of the relative risk quality of different currencies. Included in the case is a table showing 22 applications of the formula.

3.4   *Kibon, S.A.* (ICCH Case 9–110–081). Kibon, S.A. is a 75 percent owned Brazilian subsidiary of the General Foods Corporation. It manufactures and distributes dried egg products, ice cream, and confectionary products. Kibon's internal financial analyses are made by translating cruzeiros into dollars. This policy has been assumed to provide a better evaluation of operations as well as to approximate the actual impact of inflation. Questions have arisen, however, over this policy as well as the underlying translation process.

Should Kibon include both translation and exchange conversion gains and losses in its financial reports to its Brazilian stockholders? How should General Foods report the Brazilian operation to its stockholders? Should internal and external translations employ the same methodology?

3.5   *Imperial Tobacco Company of Canada Limited* (ICCH Case 9–108–001). The 1961 Annual Report of the Imperial Tobacco Company displayed significant departures from previous accounting and reporting practices of the company. Both the presentation of fixed assets and the computation of depreciation charges were based upon replacement costs. Also, a large amount of the intangibles were written off and changes in the format of the financial statements themselves were made.

In view of these changes, questions were raised concerning preferred accounting for inventories of leaf tobacco. Replacement costs for aged tobacco were not available in Canada. Imported aged tobacco had a substantial tariff on it that precluded its use as an acceptable valuation basis. This valuation problem had to be resolved before any further decisions could be made on replacement cost accounting for leaf tobacco inventories.

For additional information and complete restatements of Imperial Tobacco's financial statements from 1962 to 1967 to three different measurement bases other than historical cost, refer to

John R. Hanna, "An Application and Evaluation of Selected Alternative Accounting Income Models," *International Journal of Accounting,* Fall 1972, pp. 135-67.

3.6   *Industrias Brasileria Electrometalurgica, S.A.* (Case 22, Zenoff and Zwick, *International Financial Management,* pp. 513-21). A Brazilian company has requested a loan from a bank for its proposed plant expansion. The bank evaluated the company's performance on the basis of the financial statements submitted. It found problems due to the sharply rising inflation rate that made historical accounting values quite meaningless. To remedy the situation the bank has revised the statements. As a result it was discovered that the cash-generating ability of the company during the period of the loan will produce a cash shortage and additional credit will be required. Should the cash flow projections be price-level adjusted? Should translated financial statements enter into the picture? Close evaluation of both the company's and the bank's analyses is required.

Chapter 4

TRANSNATIONAL FINANCIAL REPORTING AND DISCLOSURE

Transnational financial reporting is most conveniently categorized into four different types. These reporting types are briefly discussed as an introduction to the subject matter of this chapter. The body of the chapter, however, addresses issues beyond different types of financial statements crossing national boundaries.

1. *Internationally Consolidated Financial Statements or Group Accounts.* These are the types of financial statements commonly used by multinational corporations to report to their shareholders and other third parties. In general, these statements and important aspects of their preparation are discussed in Chapter 3. Possible problems with these statements are (a) their high degree of aggregation in the case of the superlarge enterprises and (b) the need to utilize a single national set of accounting standards and principles that renders statements so prepared ineffective and possibly misleading when readers fail to understand the specific accounting bases of their preparation.

2. *Multiple Financial Reporting to International Investors.* To make financial reporting reasonably intelligible to different audiences-of-interest among international investor groups, some Holland- and Japan-based multinational enterprises have begun to report simultaneously on two bases—once according to their home accounting principles for third parties in their respective domicile countries and then again on the basis of United States-type standards and principles for Anglo-Saxon investor groups. The Accountants International Study Group (AISG—see Chapter 5 for details)

has published a recommendation for "primary" and concurrent "secondary" financial statements where a single set of reports to outsiders might cause communications difficulties. This issue is explored beginning on p. 119.

3. *Statutory Financial Reports.* Virtually all countries operating under the so-called code law systems (which is a majority worldwide) require enterprises domiciled within their jurisdictions to present legally specified financial statements irrespective of whether such statements serve the public financial reporting needs of the enterprise in question reasonably well or whether the enterprise concurrently prepares additional sets of statements for nonstatutory purposes. For instance, German, Japanese, and Swiss corporations must publish separate parent company statements in addition to consolidated statements. Since major subsidiary companies must also publish separate statements under this system, there are instances in Germany where as many as five or six separate sets of financial statements are contained within the covers of a single annual report. This topic also receives some attention starting on p. 139.

4. *Special Reports to International Agencies.* Special financial reports are, of course, no strangers to the domestic scene. But in the multinational field they assume special importance and are subject to several specific problems. Examples are the different types of reports required by the international development banks (e.g., the Asian Development Bank or the International Bank for Reconstruction and Development) or the international financial institutions affiliated with the World Bank (e.g., the International Finance Corporation). The International Finance Corporation (IFC) has gone so far as to issue special instruction booklets on the format, underlying accounting standards and principles, and independent auditors' reports for financial statements presented to it. Again, this topic is explored further in subsequent sections of this chapter.

While there are a fair number of issues in the transnational reporting area, three stand out: (a) the entity to be reported upon, (b) standards applicable to transnational reporting, and (c) enforcement of standards and principles appropriate for reporting across national borders. These issues are sketched in the paragraphs immediately following.

The Entity Issue

Accountants distinguish between (a) the so-called entity theory of accounting and (b) the entity concept in accounting. The *entity theory* of accounting seeks to explain how a business unit or enterprise ought to be viewed from the perspective of accountants. The construction of this theory is principally identified with the early writings of Professor William A. Paton. The essential feature of the entity theory of accounting is that it regards the business enterprise as completely separate and distinct from all human beings directly or indirectly associated with it or having an interest in it. Business enterprises operating as proprietorships or partnerships exhibit human types of characteristics since they mirror the rights and responsibilities of the owners. Corporate enterprises have some near-human types of characteristics in that they own property, contract debts, can sue and be sued, and so forth. The entity theory of accounting has proved useful because it has allowed depersonalization of business accounting and reporting processes.

The focus in multinational accounting is on the *entity concept* in accounting. To make a distinction that is not always clear in the literature, the entity concept in accounting asks the question whether something is separate or unique enough on its own to be accounted for and reported upon separately. By way of contrast, the *entity theory* of accounting takes as given distinctness for purposes of separate accountability and postulates how owner and enterprise interests might be segregated within a separately existing entity.

What makes a business enterprise separately distinct? The 1964 American Accounting Association (AAA) Concepts and Standards Research Study Committee on the Business Entity Concept concluded that accountants are concerned only with those entities that

> Represent areas of economic interest to particular individuals or groups—that is, with entities whose activities involve the utilization of scarce resources.

From the AAA statement we conclude that three main characteristics are associated with the entity concept in accounting.

1. Identifiable separate existence of an object or being, i.e., an entity.
2. The entity is economic in nature.
3. Individuals or groups exist who have direct interest in the entity.

Preceding the 1964 AAA Committee's report, Professor Raymond J. Chambers (among others) advanced the following propositions about the existence of an entity concept in accounting.

> Certain organized activities are carried out by entities which exist by the will or with the cooperation of contributing parties;
> These entities are managed rationally; that is, with a view to meeting the demands of the contributing parties efficiently;
> Statements in monetary terms of the transactions and relationships of the entities are one means of facilitating rational management.

It appears that accountants are broadly agreed that there is such a thing as the entity concept in accounting and that it can be applied usefully in practice.

The multinational accounting issue is how inclusively the entity concept in accounting should be applied to multinational enterprises. In general, accounting writers on the subject seem to imply that it is desirable to include as much as possible within the defined limits of an accounting entity. There is much discussion of how much can be included within a single accounting entity rather than what or how much could possibly be excluded. Some discussions about consolidation of financial statements turn on possible exclusion of certain subsidiary companies from consolidation procedures when product or business homogeneity is absent or when significant economic uncertainty prevails. But discussions of this type are usually offered in an apologetic vein. The implication seems clear that the most inclusive accounting entity concept is somehow deemed to be the most desirable. And this is exactly the point where the multinational issue arises. Can or should the often monolithic multinational enterprise be divided into subentities for accounting purposes? In a 1968 study, (*Financial Reporting by Diversified Companies*), Robert Mautz concluded on behalf of the Financial Executives Institute (FEI) that subentity reporting, according to rates of profitability, diverse business risks, and varying business growth opportunities, is desirable.

A. Rappaport and E. Lerner demonstrated in their 1969 National Association of Accountants research study that information on operating results of business segments is essential to investors for analysis of current earnings and estimation of future earnings growth.

Abu-Jabarah came to the following conclusions, among others, in his 1972 doctoral dissertation (see p. 30):

> The interests of the investors are best served when the multinational company segments its financial statements (profit and loss, balance sheets and sources and applications of funds) on the basis of the market's [for company products] category. This does not conflict with the present practice of issuing consolidated statements. Both would be helpful for the investor.

Kubin, also in a 1972 dissertation (University of Washington, *Financial Accounting for Multinational Enterprises—The Problem of Appropriate Reporting Units*), reached a similar conclusion and recommended that "subentity" type of reporting be utilized by multinational enterprises.

Is the multinational company somehow a different entity for accounting purposes than a strictly domestic enterprise? What does *subentity* financial reporting mean? Is multiple reporting, as variously proposed in the multinational realm, compatible with the entity concept in accounting? Questions of this type circumscribe the issues involved.

The Standards Issue

Notwithstanding the nascent work of the International Accounting Standards Committee (IASC), which is prominent among the organizations described in Chapter 5, a reasonably comprehensive set of international accounting standards and principles is not available at this time. Yet multinational enterprises have been reporting to third parties across national boundaries in quite formal fashion for at least 20 years—and even longer in some individual situations. International capital markets like the Eurobond Market have required, at least for the past 15 years or so, that issuers of corporate securities prepare offering circulars and, subsequently, annual financial statements that are broadly understandable to wide cross sections of international investors. International congresses of accountants have been organized periodically since 1904 for the consistently stated purpose of fostering worldwide harmonization of financial accounting standards. Taken altogether, this means that (a) international standards have been advocated for a long time, (b) such standards are still not available in comprehensive fashion, and (c) multinational enterprises and other users of international capital markets have had to resort to ad hoc solutions for their transnational financial reporting problems—which, to them, are both very real and very urgent.

What is the nature of the transnational financial reporting standards that seem to be needed? Generally, they fall into two categories: (a) technical accounting standards and (b) transnational reporting standards. The technical accounting standards must, first of all, address issues unique to multinational accounting, such as foreign exchange translation. They must also tackle subsidiary problems such as the restate-translate versus translate-restate controversy described in Chapter 3. The use of the quality method in accounting for intercorporate investments, the nature and amortization of goodwill, purchase versus pooling of interest accounting in business combinations, the nature and allowable use of contingency reserves—all of these are technical problems that eventually must be covered by appropriate standards if an internationally acceptable form of accounting is to evolve.

The reporting standards needed are more in the nature of implementation standards. For instance, as long as multinational differences in accounting standards and principles exist (particularly if there are social and environmental justifications for such differences), it is not very reasonable to refer to "generally accepted accounting principles" in transnational financial reporting. Consequently, financial reporting across national boundaries should identify financial statements as (a) prepared in conformity with accounting principles generally accepted in country X, (b) restated to conformity with accounting principles generally accepted in country Y, or (c) stated in conformity with accounting principles required by international agency A or in general use in regional economic community B.

Another transnational reporting standard might address the completeness of financial statement restatements or translations for multinational purposes. For instance, partial restatements from one accounting measurement system to another or partial applications of a given currency unit are potentially highly misleading. This is the case especially when owners' equity and earnings per share are restated only and financial analysts begin to calculate return on assets or turnover statistics on the basis of incompatible (i.e., partially restated) financial information.

As a third illustration of needed transnational reporting standards, we pose the problem of reconcilement. In present practice, and certainly under the multiple reporting system referred to on p. 119, there occurs some restatement of financial information from one basis to another. When this happens, complete quantitative reconcilement of the restatement is necessary. The possibility of reconciling financial statements from the application of one set of accounting principles to another is essential to the comparative analysis needed by those who own debt or equity securities in second or third countries. The simple provision of two different results of operations figures—one, let us say, "in observance of all applicable laws in Germany" and the other "for our North American shareholders"—is insufficient by itself. A reasonably informed reader of financial statements should be able to reconcile any two corresponding figures from information directly contained in the respective financial reports.

Of course, many other problems exist in the transnational reporting area. Therefore many other similar standards would have to be evolved before a reasonably comprehensive set of internationally acceptable standards and principles becomes available.

The Enforcement Issue

Even if acceptable standards for multinational accounting and transnational financial reporting come about, so that a complete financial accounting and reporting system could be based on them, there would still be the rather large question as to who would be able to enforce such standards worldwide. Voluntary acceptance by enterprise managements would clearly be ineffective. Managers have an overriding responsibility to protect the interests of their shareholders, and those interests are not always compatible with the application of given accounting standards and principles. Voluntary acceptance might be feasible in economic boom times or periods of high enterprise earnings, but it would surely be a different story when the tables are turned.

National or international institutes or associations of professional accountants are also unlikely to provide effective solutions. The issue of national sovereignty for accounting principles is probably as thorny as most other international agreement questions. One can fairly state that the accounting principles of one country have seldom found willing or unquestioned acceptance in another country. Wilkinson commented in 1969:

> No accountant, no matter how eager a proponent of minimizing differences, willingly accepts the idea that someone else's accounting principles are better than his.

A third possible avenue of enforcement leads via international agencies or supranational councils or commissions. The accounting efforts within the European Common Market discussed in Chapter 6 are probably most illustrative of a movement that might ultimately impose accounting and reporting standards by fiat. The success of this type of approach is, naturally, very much an open question. When extraterritorial enforcement of accounting rules is politically mandated, it probably leads to politicization of accounting itself. This, as amply illustrated by world experience, is quite undesirable from many viewpoints.

The final alternative might be economic sanction through providers of long-term investment capital. If agreement could be reached between all major underwriters of issues of corporate securities and all major banks involved in long-term corporate financing that the financial statements such institutions require must conform to internationally acceptable norms or a certain financing premium must be incurred, compliance would probably be swift and general. An illustration of this is available in the Eurobond Market where underwriters began to demand early that financial statements and financial disclosures be generally comparable to those prevailing in North America, or else a proposed issue might simply not come to market. Today's Eurobond Market-offering circulars bear a remarkable resemblance to United States SEC prospectuses.

The enforcement issue is complex, fraught with nationalistic feelings, void of fixed responsibility, and costly as revealed even in preliminary stages of exploration. It may well be the most critical issue for transnational financial reporting as a whole.

PRESENT PRACTICES

There is always a question as to the extent financial reporting can or should be distinguished from financial disclosure. Without disclosure, effective financial reporting to third parties is impossible. Yet disclosure alone is equally impotent. The two articulate with one another to give modern-day financial communications their substance.

For purposes of this chapter, however, we deem it best to separate reporting and disclosure issues. In the transnational setting, there are a number of reporting issues that cannot be "patched up" somehow by more or different disclosure. Thus, reporting practices are dealt with in the present section of the chapter, whereas disclosure practices are the subject of a later section. Still the interrelationships between the two should not be overlooked.

Before we take a glimpse at existing transnational financial reporting practices, it may be well to reiterate the Chapter 1 observation that international ownership of corporate securities is the generator of this entire issue. Were it not for transnational issuance, trading, and holding of corporate securities, there would not be multiple financial reporting audiences-of-interest and hence really no reporting problems beyond the preparation of multinationally consolidated financial statements.

Yet we do have a world of international capital markets:

1. "Foreign holdings of U.S. stocks and bonds totaled $86 billion at the end of last year, 28 percent higher than a year earlier, a Treasury study said." (*Wall Street Journal,* May 4, 1976, p. 10.)
2. "Sixty-eight United States common stocks are presently admitted for trading on the Zurich Stock Exchange." (*Bulletin Credit Suisse,* Summer 1976, p. 18.)
3. "Mexican Stock Market draws Americans despite risks of insiders and devaluations .... Last year, more than 40 million shares were traded on the Bolsa, a 60 percent increase from 1974 and equal to about 300 million of business. Trading in the first quarter of 1976 was three times heavier than in the comparable period of 1975." (*Wall Street Journal,* July 12, 1976, p. 26.)
4. "At December 31, 1975, the New York Stock Exchange had 182 foreign securities listed: 34 foreign stocks and 148 foreign government and private bonds—with a total market value of approximately $18 billion." (New York Stock Exchange, *1976 Fact Book,* p. 34.)
5. "The New York Stock Exchange said the Securities and Exchange Commission has approved a previously proposed set of standards designed to encourage major foreign companies to list securities on the big board." (*Wall Street Journal,* May 25, 1976. p. 38.)

Questions relating to the issuance of corporate securities in international capital markets and, more generally, international sourcing of long-term corporate capital are discussed in Chapter 7.

Transnational financial reporting as presently practiced (and without benefit of an agreed upon and enforceable set of accounting standards and principles) divides itself into six distinguishable approaches. These are described next.

Convenience Translations

The nationalistic orientation, which so strongly permeates much accounting thinking and many of the rules by which accounting is applied, is probably responsible for the attitude that basically expects investors in other countries to fend for themselves as far as transnational reporting goes. In other words, companies will make copies of annual reports available to investors wherever they happen to reside or have a mailing address, but no special efforts are made to assist such foreign users with understanding and interpreting financial reports prepared on a basis often significantly different from what the reader may be accustomed to.

For instance, quite a few United States corporations have convinced themselves that United States accounting and reporting standards are qualitatively higher than they are elsewhere in the world and that the English language and reports expressed in terms of United States dollars are so universal that any translations or reporting adaptations are simply not needed. Consequently, securities holders the world over simply receive copies of annual reports and other financial information just as United States investors do. French companies are equally nationalistic as a rule. All of their communications are typically in the French language, expressed in French francs and prepared on the customary French basis.

A modest concession to multinational financial reporting audiences-of-interest is made when companies translate at least the language portion of their reports to the national idiom of major groups of addressees. For instance, Proctor & Gamble slipsheets their annual reports mailed to France with French translations of all annual report textual materials. Many Dutch, German, Swedish, and Swiss companies regularly publish their annual reports in as many as six foreign language editions—Dutch, English, French, German, and Spanish, plus the home language (e.g., Swedish or, let us say, Italian in the case of an Italy-based multinational enterprise).

Text translations are, of course, only better than no translations at all, but they often lead to confusion. Where one has, for instance, a Swiss report translated from the original German into an English language text, one is still faced with Swiss francs as the reporting unit and Swiss accounting and reporting practices as the report's frame of reference. This means that foreign currency amounts and foreign accounting principles applications going *into* the consolidated financial statements being reported were all restated and translated to a Swiss basis. But in subsequent reporting to non-Swiss audiences-of-interest, the Swiss reporting foundation is retained, even though language translations are undertaken. This is often frustrating and sometimes misleading to readers outside the domicile country. Many multinational companies have fallen into this unsatisfactory practice—retaining a particular national orientation and basis of preparation for their annual reports, yet giving them a multinational appearance by translating the language portions within them.

Special Information

Recognizing that probably not every multinational portfolio investor can be conversant with all existing national accounting standards and principles, and understand and interpret their respective applications correctly, a small number of multinational companies have made an effort to explain to readers in other countries the particular accounting standards and practices forming the basis for their reporting. For instance the Swedish company Astra makes available to North American readers (a) an English language edition of its annual report published in Sweden and (b) a small booklet, also in English, explaining the accounting and financial reporting principles that characterize their annual report.

Some relevant excerpts from the 1975 (annual report related) Astra information booklet follow:

UNTAXED RESERVES

In accordance with Swedish corporate law, the Company is permitted to make provisions to certain reserves, deductible for tax purposes. These reserves are said to be untaxed because they are not subject to taxation until they are reduced or liquidated through the sale of assets.

Inventory reserve. This item represents the difference between the gross value of the inventory as shown on the asset side of the Balance Sheet and the carrying value (book value) of the inventory. Inventory reserves in Swedish companies may amount to not more than 60% of the inventory's gross value. Gross value is the lowest of cost or replacement cost after deductions for obsolescent goods (goods which are difficult to sell because of damage or age, etc.).

Investment reserve. A certain amount of income may be allocated to a special investment reserve for future investments. The allocation, which is deductible for tax purposes, is actually an appropriation. Of this allocation, 46 percent must be placed on deposit in an interest-free blocked account in the Bank of Sweden.

Appropriations are the adjustments made when the books are closed for the year. These adjustments must be made in accordance with accounting and tax rules. There are two types of appropriations: voluntary and statutory. The voluntary appropriations represent depreciation possibilities that have not been utilized and increases in the inventory and investment reserves. In accordance with an act of the Swedish Parliament in 1974, companies are required to make appropriations to a so-called work environment reserve and a special investment reserve. The appropriations are deductible for tax purposes and are made in conformity with statutory regulations.

BLOCKED ACCOUNTS IN BANK OF SWEDEN

This amount represents funds, deposited in interest-free accounts in the Bank of Sweden. Three types of accounts exist: blocked accounts for investment reserve, work environment reserve and special investment reserve. The funds are to be allocated to investments in property, plant or equipment. The deposit must be made in connection with the tax deductions that the Company obtains when making provision to the above reserves.

IMPACT OF INFLATION

The Group's financial position and earnings have been affected in recent years by inflation and price changes. Prices of raw materials and packaging rose sharply in 1974. Some stabilization occurred during 1975, but labor costs and general expenses increased at a more rapid rate than normal.

In order to evaluate the effects of this development adjustments can be made in the traditional accounts. None of the more fully developed methods have as yet been accepted as general accounting practice, however, and there is no generally accepted method among Swedish companies. We have therefore sought, through partial adjustments, to illustrate the effects of these developments on the earnings, profitability and financing of the Astra Group. It should be noted that the adjustments are not claimed to be complete and precise. The objective is merely to show, in a simple manner, the effects of various partial adjustments.

Consolidated Statement of Earnings

In the Statement of Earnings, below, Group earnings before appropriations and taxes have been adjusted to reflect future higher costs of goods and facilities. This gives some idea of the lowest earnings before tax that should be recorded if the objective is to finance the replacement of goods and services exclusively through internally generated funds. Current tax laws provide other regulations for calculating taxable profit, however, and the adjustments must therefore be brought back into appropriations.

Subentity Reporting. Another minority practice in transnational financial reporting is separate formal issuance of annual reports by major components of a multinational enterprise. For instance, Ford and General Motors publish worldwide consolidated financial reports utilizing United States generally accepted accounting principles. They also permit their major subsidiary companies in Australia, Canada, Germany, and the United Kingdom to report separately, each in its respective country and each using the accounting standards and principles of the domicile country.

In Germany, and sometimes in the United Kingdom, parent companies must report separately from enterprise-wide consolidated totals. As already mentioned, some German annual reports become rather voluminous because they contain not only consolidated financial statements and separate financial statements for the parent company but also separate financial statements for two or three major subsidiary companies. The uninitiated reader of such annual reports surely has problems deciding which applies to what.

Separate subentity reporting is fraught with several problems, as intimated in the introduction to this chapter. Although consolidation of worldwide totals for the giant multinational enterprises may be a reporting basis that is too inclusive, reporting several subentities separately is surely not the answer either. Maybe segmented reporting within single sets of statements is a better approach (see the disclosure discussion beginning on p. 123. If a German investor in General Motors stock receives only the annual report of the GM subsidiary in Germany, transnational financial reporting is ineffective and outright misleading. Your authors are not in sympathy with the subentity approach as described here.

Convenience Statements

When companies translate text portions of their annual reports and mail them to securities holders abroad, we have what was termed earlier the *convenience translations* approach to transnational financial reporting. An extension of the same practice produces so-called "convenience statements." Here, monetary amounts are statistically translated as well (usually at the year-end foreign exchange rate throughout), so that both text portions and monetary amounts appear familiar to the audience-of-interest addressed.

There are, however, several significant problems associated with this type of reporting. First, the statements are still based on the accounting standards and principles of the domicile country of the reporting enterprise—which fact is obscured by the convenience transliteration and therefore often misleads.

The second big problem is that financial analysts and others in the financial community tend to interpret convenience-type statements as comparable to domestically prepared statements for purposes of financial comparisons and securities analysis. Of course, the translated statements cannot be so used, and once again a high potential for misuse is created.

Differences in underlying independent auditing standards and practices also often lead to a misinterpretation of the degree of third-party reliability that may be placed upon these convenience statements.

L. M. Ericsson, the large Swedish telephone company, prepares its United States convenience statements by showing translated United States dollar amounts only and prominently displaying on every page the proviso that "The United States dollar amounts shown in the above statement represent translations from Swedish kroner at the official parity [date] of Skr. [rate] to $1."

Multinational companies based in Japan report monetary amounts in two columns—both United States dollars and Japanese yen. This may "flag" the currency translation practice but it still misleads since, among other things, the text of the independent auditor's report is the same as that used in the United States (whereas the Swedish auditor's report text differs markedly from its United States counterpart).

The authors consider convenience transnational financial reports at best as an evolutionary step in the development of multinational accounting practices. Exhibit 3–1 in the preceding chapter illustrates a convenience statement of a Japan-based multinational company.

Report Restatement

If a financial reporting audience-of-interest is best served with the accounting standards and principles and report formats to which it is accustomed at home, then transnational financial reports should provide corresponding information. This is the philosophy behind the practices of several Netherlands-based multinational enterprises that present not only translations of respective annual reports into the English language but specifically provide a restatement of the owners' equity section of respective balance sheets to the basis of accounting principles generally accepted in the United States. Thus, Dutch readers see statements in full accord with local practices and North American readers have at least owners' equity sections restated to a basis they can understand and use comparatively.

Again, one would wish that this practice would be applied to financial statements in their entirety rather than only to sections thereof. For instance, some financial analysts will apply restated earnings figures to Dutch-basis inventory and fixed-asset measurements. This yields wrong turnover and/or return-on-assets financial ratios.

Audience-of-interest directed restatements of financial statements are probably the most useful form of transnational financial reporting until comprehensive international accounting and reporting standards can be evolved. The following excerpt from the 1976 English language edition of the annual report of the Dutch Philips Company provides a good restatement illustration.

EXHIBIT 4 – 1. N.V. Philips[1] Gloeilampenfabrieken 1976 Annual Report Excerpt

INFORMATION FOR AMERICAN SHAREHOLDERS

In the United States of America net profit attributable to ordinary shares is customarily determined by reducing net profit by profit-sharing with Supervisory Board, Management and Officers, and with employees pursuant to the articles of Association on the subject of Profit Appropriation.

Moreover the accounting principles applied by N.V. Philips' Gloeilampenfabrieken in calculating profit differ in some respects from principles customarily followed in the United States.

An attempt is made below to estimate what adjustment to net profit would be required if those accounting principles customarily followed in the United States were applied that differ substantially from those of N.V. Philips' Gloeilampenfabrieken, viz.:

- Depreciation on property, plant and equipment based on the cost of the assets concerned.
- Cost of sales determined by applying the first-in, first-out method, except to a minor extent, as in the Combined Statements, the last-in, first-out method.
- A write-off period of five years for the amounts paid for the acquisition of participations in so far as the total of such payments in any year exceeds the total net tangible asset value acquired.

The tax effect of the foregoing principles has been taken into account.

	In Millions Of Guilders	In Millions Of United States $[a]
The adjustment is as follows:		
Net profit 1976, shown in the Combined Statement of Results	562.5	229.6
Deduct: Profit-sharing with Supervisory Board, Management and Officers, and employees	– 46.0	– 18.8
Increase of net profit when applying the aforementioned accounting principles customarily followed in the United States	286.6	117.0
Adjusted net profit	803.1	327.8
(including result relating to operations to be discontinued and a provision for estimated losses on disposal aggregating f 40 m)		
Number of ordinary shares of f 10 of N.V. Philips' Gloeilampenfabrieken outstanding at 31 December 1976	170,455,617	
Per ordinary share of f 10 of N.V. Philips' Gloeilampenfabrieken:		
Adjusted net profit	f 4.71	$ 1.92
Adjusted net profit, excluding a loss of f 40 m for operation to be discontinued	f 4.95	$ 2.02
Dividend	f 1.60	$ 0.65

EXHIBIT 4-1. Continued

Assuming conversion of all outstanding convertible debentures, the adjusted net profit per ordinary share would be f 4.40 ($1.80).

If the method of historical cost had been applied in the past it is estimated that the item Revaluation Surplus as shown in the Combined Statement for Financial Position as at 31 December 1976, would have appeared as follows:

	In Millions Of Guilders	In Millions Of United States $[a]
Addition to retained profit	1,809.6	738.6
Deduction from property, plant and equipment, stocks, and provision for deferred taxation (net)	1,179.6	481.5
	2,989.2	1,220.1

[a]converted at the rate of f2.45 per U.S. $

Reach for World Standards

The 1975 annual report of CIBA-GEIGY Ltd., a multinational pharmaceutical enterprise headquartered in Switzerland, illustrates an attempt at innovating what the reporting company must think of as a useful transnational standard of financial reporting. The English language edition of the report in question contains the customary parent company statements denominated in Swiss francs, prepared on the basis of Swiss accounting standards, and circumscribed by a standard short-form Swiss audit certificate.

Worldwide consolidated financial statements presented as an appendix to the annual report reflect a partial application of replacement cost measurements and other reporting standards that the company no doubt believes to be of world class. The underlying accounting standards are clearly different from those employed for the parent-company-only report—in fact, Swiss standards at the present time do not require consolidated financial statements at all.

Regrettably, the CIBA-GEIGY attempt is not very successful. The partial application of replacement cost measurements leads to confusion. North American shareholders were told in a letter accompanying the mailing of the 1975 annual report that consolidated worldwide earnings would have been higher than stated in the report had United States generally accepted accounting principles been applied. Also, the consolidated financial statements are not covered by an independent auditor's report.

Once the IASC (see Chapter 5) produces a comprehensive set of international accounting standards, efforts like CIBA-GEIGY's will probably bear fruit because they can be oriented to a general set of norms, but that time has simply not yet come. Meanwhile, the multiple reporting system discussed in the next section probably represents the optimal alternative available at this time.

THE MULTIPLE REPORTING SYSTEM

In its February 1975 study entitled *International Financial Reporting,* the Accountants International Study Group (AISG) recommends that two kinds of financial statements be recognized as part of formal (or official) generally accepted accounting standards and principles. *Primary* financial statements would be prepared according to financial accounting principles generally accepted in a company's country of domicile and in that country's language and national currency. Independent auditors would express opinions on primary financial statements—again according to both the generally accepted financial accounting principles and the generally accepted auditing standards of the domicile country.

Secondary financial statements would be prepared specifically for financial reporting audiences-of-interest in other countries. Such secondary financial statements would have one or more of the following characteristics:

1. The reporting standards of a foreign country would have been followed.
2. The statements would have been translated into a foreign currency.
3. The statements would have been translated into a language that is not the language of the reporting company's country of domicile.
4. The independent auditor's report would be expressed in a form not commonly used in the reporting company's country of domicile.

If the primary statements include sufficient information to satisfy the information requirements of financial reporting audiences-of-interest in other countries, the primary statements themselves will serve multiple purposes and secondary statements are unnecessary. The AISG recommendation presumes that all companies prepare primary statements and that the majority of companies with financial reporting audiences-of-interest in more than a single country will also prepare secondary statements (at least until greater worldwide harmony of financial accounting standards evolves).

Multiple financial reporting, as proposed by the AISG, is not quite as revolutionary as it appears at first. There has always been multiple reporting between financial accounting and tax accounting in most countries. Also, it is found in many regulated industry situations, required in the United States under some so-called "blue sky" laws, and it quite often creeps into special reporting circumstances like those found in connection with proposed mergers, long-term financing arrangements, bankruptcy, and the like.

Advantages

A primary/secondary system of transnational reporting allows full recognition of national points of view parallel with other national or possibly even international viewpoints. Specific recognition of reader audiences for primary and secondary reports should increase the information content (and therefore quality) of both types of financial statements. The degree of generality of published corporate reports would be reduced by a dual system, and thus the likelihood of more useful relevant information entering economic and decision channels would be greater.

Multiple transnational reporting explicitly recognizes that the nature of multinational business and finance differs in several important respects from strictly uninational business and finance. This difference is not only a matter of degree but of organizational structure, business policy, and nature of business transactions as well. Since the multinational enterprise is a full economic reality in our day and age, institution of a multiple reporting system would be a first step toward more realism in recognizing accounting effects resulting from the multinational business phenomenon.

Furthermore, it seems reasonable to assume that primary/secondary transnational reporting will encourage the growth of broad and active international money capital markets. One of your coauthors, Professor Choi, has demonstrated through his research that increased financial disclosure by firms performing above average in their respective industries lowers their respective capital costs when they source long-term money capital in the relatively unregulated international capital market. These findings permit the assertion that the increased amount of financial disclosure resulting from dual reporting is likely to benefit firms entering, or active in, international financial markets. In turn, the international capital market should be stimulated into further growth and should be able to increase its relative economic efficiency.

Disadvantages

A substantial difficulty with the primary/secondary reporting proposal is that it runs counter to the so-called "single domicile for financial statements" point of view. The substance of this viewpoint is that business managers make a great many business decisions with at least an awareness of how these decisions are later mirrored in their financial statements. Thus corporate mergers, equipment leasing policies, and investments involving foreign exchange exposure (FASB Statement No. 8 implications) are often made with a half an eye to corresponding financial statement effects. If different financial accounting rules would apply, then possibly some business decisions would be made differently. And if this is so, realistic financial reporting results are unobtainable when a set of "alien" accounting rules is imposed upon a set of specific business decisions and their financial consequences.

The single domicile viewpoint, therefore, holds that financial statements can present only a single representation of financial decisions and results of operations—only for a given time, under a given set of rules, and for a given purpose. When business decisions are made under these conditions, they ought to be reported only in terms of the same conditions.

Potential reader confusion is another difficulty. One can probably not refer to "generally accepted accounting principles" when one in fact recognizes several different "generally accepted" sets of rules. Even sophisticated statement readers are likely to be perplexed if they receive different financial statistics for the same company at the same period of time. Most affected would probably be the financial press, which always seems to use its own foreign exchange and accounting "translation" rules when it reports on multinational business occurrences.

The solution to the reader confusion problem must be sought in terms of disclosure. In fact, the AISG study takes it as one of its specific recommendations that "a public company which has significant international ownership or financing interests and presents a summary of its accounting policies should identify the nationality of the accounting principles followed" (Paragraph 65).

To convey the flavor of some of the difficulties an independent auditor might encounter with secondary financial statements, here are three review paragraphs from the May 1975 issue of the (Canadian) *CA Magazine* (p. 4):

> If currency is the only difference between primary and secondary statements, they [the auditors] will express their opinion on the domestic currency figures according to the reporting standards of the company's country of domicile but may have to limit their opinion on the foreign currency figures to the accuracy of the translation.
>
> If language is the only difference, they will again report according to the standards of the company's country of domicile; they must, however, satisfy themselves on the accuracy of the translation.
>
> If both the form and substance differ, they report according to the accounting principles and auditing standards of the foreign country. They should also refer to the primary statements, stating that they have been prepared according to the accounting principles of the company's country of domicile. They should then summarize the main differences between these principles and those of the foreign country, pointing out their effect on net income and/or financial position.

FINANCIAL DISCLOSURE OF MULTINATIONAL OPERATIONS

APB Statement No. 4 stipulates as one of five general objectives for financial statements:

> Disclosure to the extent possible of additional or supplemental information related to the financial statement that is relevant to statement users' needs.

Available disclosure literature leads us to assert that (a) disclosure is not only fundamental to financial reporting but is, at the same time, its most qualitative aspect and (b) the nature and extent of disclosure needed in individual reporting situations is determinable only by expert professional judgment. The qualitative nature of disclosure often renders its format indeterminate. For instance, disclosure can occur directly within financial statements by appropriate statement captions, various parenthetical disclosures, or procedures such as listing items even though monetary amount balances may be zero. As an example, it is customary in Germany to disclose fully all fixed asset movements directly within balance sheets proper.

In Anglo-Saxon countries, disclosure occurs predominantly by means of footnotes to financial statements. This development was probably influenced heavily by requirements established through the various United States Securities Acts and their amendments. Right or wrong, there are many financial reports published in North America and in the United Kingdom in which the total space devoted to footnotes exceeds that devoted to the financial statements themselves. Moreover, the texts of these footnotes sometimes are written in technical jargon that taxes even the experts when it comes to ready comprehension.

Countries that regulate financial reporting through national (or federal) companies legislation tend to put a fair amount of stress on published annual reports of company directors or the chief operating officer of a company. In these countries, the directors and/or top operating management need to be *discharged* from their annual management duties by a formal vote at the annual meeting of shareholders. Such discharge is normally predicated upon the presentation of an annual report and a formal proposal on how earnings should be either distributed or reinvested. The management letter to the shareholders, often printed at the beginning of an annual report, typically becomes the basis for the shareholder motion "to discharge management from further fiduciary obligation to the shareholders for the period just ended." In these circumstances, it is quite natural that the management letter to the shareholders would contain financial disclosures of various types—some of which are not included again in other portions of respective annual reports or the financial statements comprising a part of it.

Finally, there are situations—notably in Germany—where annual reports contain fairly detailed elaborations of major financial statement items in a so-called *"Geschaftsbericht,"* which is separate from and furished in addition to the management letter. Such a business report is very similar to a long-form audit report, as that term is understood in the United States. There can be no question that business reports of this type contain significant amounts of financial disclosure.

Selected Present Practices

Since many enterprises with financial reporting obligations to diverse audiences-of-interest also have significant multinational business operations, *multinational* financial disclosure is often associated with line-of-business reporting as now required by FASB Statement No. 14 in cases where multinational business operations amount to 10 percent or more of total operations. Of course, multinational activities may have to be separately disclosed whether or not there are foreign financial reporting audiences-of-interest. Conversely, an enterprise doing all its business uninationally, but with significant long-term financing from abroad, may have multinational financial disclosure obligations even in the absence of multinational business activities.

Let us first illustrate a few cases of disclosure of multinational business activities.[1] Several studies have shown that such disclosure is a highly variable affair among United States-based companies. (For example, see "Annual Reports Go International," *Journal of Accountancy,* August 1967, pp. 59–64). Present practices range from virtually no disclosure to reasonably satisfactory disclosure. Among the worst examples, from a disclosure point of view, is ITT. Even though widely recognized as one of the largest and most influential United States-based multinational companies, its 1975 annual report makes virtually no disclosure about multinational operations.

Disclosure focusing on international sales and related net earnings is contained, for example, in the 1976 annual report of the General Electric Company (Exhibit 4–2). Even though this is still a severely limited disclosure of multinational operations, it represents a threshold effort.

---

[1] These illustrations all predate the implementation of FASB Statement No. 14.

EXHIBIT 4 – 2. General Electric Company 1976 Annual Report Excerpts

INTERNATIONAL

In millions	1976	1975	1974	1973	1972
Sales	$4,024	$3,745	$3,218	$2,318	$1,830
Net earnings	196	158	174	139	98

FOREIGN OPERATIONS

Foreign currency translation gains, calculated in accordance with Financial Accounting Standards Board Statement No. 8, and after recognizing related income tax effects and minority interest share, were $16.6 million in 1976 and $24.7 million in 1975. Prior to implementation of FASB Statement No. 8, effective January 1976, the Company included in these amount translation gains and losses on certain accounts such as inventories which are now required to be translated at exchange rates in effect when the assets were acquired. This change had no significant effect on operating results, but changed the definition of gains and losses attributed to foreign currency translation. Appropriate amounts, consistent with the definition the Company formerly used, were losses of $24 million and $17 million for 1976 and 1975, respectively.

A summary of certain information, before elimination of intercompany transactions, for all foreign operations of General Electric except for exports from the United States is shown below.

FOREIGN OPERATIONS

(In millions) December 31	1976	1975
OPERATING RESULTS		
Sales	$3,982.9	$3,398.2
Net earnings	339.6	239.5
General Electric share of net earnings	311.5	213.9
FINANCIAL POSITION		
Total assets	$3,250.2	$2,898.4
Total liabilities	$1,831.2	$1,721.8
Minority Interest In equity	118.9	104.4
General Electric interest in equity	1,300.1	1,072.2
Total liabilities and equity	$3,250.2	$2,898.4

Ford Motor Company discloses consolidated sales percentages between the United States and Canada and the rest of the world, as well as respective contributions to consolidated net income. In addition, it reports separately the equity amounts of net investments outside the United States and Canada, as well as the level of reserves for foreign operations—really "provisions" established by periodic charges to profit and loss (Exhibit 4–3).

EXHIBIT 4 – 3. Ford Motor Company 1975 Annual Report Excerpts

FOREIGN OPERATIONS

The contributions to sales and net income by operations outside the United States and Canada were as follows:

	1975		1974	
	Amount	*Percent*	*Amount*	*Percent*
	(in millions)		*(in millions)*	
Sales	$7,880	33	$6,523	28
Net income	161	71[a]	71	20

[a]Before cumulative effect of an accounting change

Net investments outside the United States and Canada included in the consolidated balance sheet were as follows:

	1975	1974
	(in millions)	
Equities of the Company in net assets:		
Europe	$1,345	$1,091
Latin America	319	248
All other, principally Asia-Pacific	455	406
Total equities in net assets	2,119	1,745
Excess of cost of investments over equities in net assets	252	252
Total investments	2,371	1,997
Less reserve for foreign operations	26	26
Net investments outside the United States and Canada	$2,345	$1,971

The reserve for foreign operations was provided by periodic charges to income. There were not changes in the reserve in 1975. During the fourth quarter of 1974, $34 million was charged to the reserve. This charge was principally for the abnormal costs incurred during 1974 in Argentina, where the Company's operations were adversely affected by unsettled political and economic conditions.

In accordance with Statements of Financial Accounting Standards No. 5 and 11, the reserve will be added to retained earnings in the first quarter of 1976 and net income for 1974 will be restated to eliminate the charge to the reserve. This restatement will reduce net income for 1974 by $34 million.

Exxon Corporation probably goes the furthest by providing a breakdown of total assets employed according to geographic or operating areas. These area groupings no doubt reflect economic and political risk assessment factors among other things. They provide fairly comprehensive disclosure as far as worldwide business operations are concerned (Exhibit 4–4).

EXHIBIT 4 – 4. Exxon Corporation 1975 Annual Report Excerpts

SUMMARY OF EARNINGS AND RETURNS ON TOTAL ASSETS
(AMOUNTS IN MILLIONS OF DOLLARS)

	EARNINGS		YEAR-END TOTAL ASSETS EMPLOYED		PERCENT RETURN ON AVERAGE TOTAL ASSETS	
	1975	*1974*	*1975*	*1974*	*1975*	*1974*
Petroleum and Natural Gas Operations						
United States	$1,107	$1,021	$ 8,908	$ 7,988	13.1	13.8
Other Western Hemisphere	237	442	4,950	4,840	4.8	10.2
Eastern Hemisphere	964	1,068	12,038	11,721	8.1	10.0
Chemical Operations						
United States	107	148	718	697	15.1	23.3
Foreign	77	306	1,258	1,229	6.2	29.1
Other[a]	11	45	4,967	4,679	–	–
Consolidated Totals	$2,503	$3,030	$32,839	$31,154	7.8	10.8

[a]Earnings include corporate net interest and administrative expenses, and results of nuclear fuel, coal, minerals and land development operations none of which was material; related assets employed include corporate portfolio investments.

INVESTMENT IN PROPERTY, PLANT, AND EQUIPMENT
(MILLIONS OF DOLLARS)

	ADDITIONS – 1975				INVEST-MENT DEC. 31, 1975	INVEST-MENT DEC 31, 1974
	United States	*Foreign*	*Total*	*Cost*	*Net*	*Net*
Petroleum and Natural Gas						
Producing	$ 675	$ 710	$1,385	$ 8,487	$ 4,898	$ 4,630
Manufacturing	348	324	672	5,779	3,479	3,169
Marketing	46	141	187	4,374	2,759	2,851
Transportation	675	257	932	4,275	3,072	2,454
Other	14	36	50	673	399	392

EXHIBIT 4-4. Continued

Chemicals	88	170	258	1,914	1,046	875
Other	70	4	74	590	499	467
Total	$1,916	$1,642	$3,558	$26,092	$16,152	$14,838
United States			$1,916	$12,627	$ 7,527	$ 6,416
Other Western Hemisphere			354	3,738	2,237	2,726
Eastern Hemisphere			1,288	9,727	6,388	5,696
Consolidated totals			$3,558	$26,092	$16,152	$14,838

In the future, separate disclosure of multinational operations should follow the dictates of FASB Statement No. 14. Any elaboration of such disclosure should have primary regard for (a) geographic dispersion of revenue and income sources as well as asset locations according to broad risk categories (e.g., distinction between developed and developing countries), (b) changes in size of nondomestic investments—on the basis of equity method accounting whenever appropriate, and (c) numerical expressions of important single events and transactions arising out of multinational operations (e.g., expropriation of properties, material foreign exchange gains or losses, and single country events with major financial consequences).

Irrespective of the degree of involvement in multinational business operations, reliance on multinational sources of long-term money capital should lead to some special disclosures. For instance, Sears, Roebuck & Company discloses the financial impact on the corporate group of its international subsidiaries (Exhibit 4–5).

EXHIBIT 4 – 5. Sears, Roebuck & Company 1975 Annual Report Excerpts

INTERNATIONAL OPERATIONS
CANADIAN AFFILIATE

Net sales of Simpsons-Sears Limited increased 16 per cent to $1.549 billion (Can.) from $1.341 billion (Can.) in 1974. Net earnings declined to $32.1 million (Can.) compared with $34.5 million (Can.) in 1974. Sears equity in net earnings after translation loss was $12.7 million (U.S.).

Simpsons-Sears opened five new retail stores in 1975, increasing the number of stores in operation to 56. The new store locations are Capilano in Vancouver; Brossard and Place Vertu in Montreal; Gerrard Square in Toronto and Chilliwack in British Columbia. Our Canadian affiliate also operates four catalog merchandise distribution centers and 646 catalog sales offices.

In November 1975, Sears made an additional investment of $23.5 million in Simpsons-Sears for 2.8 million shares of voting common stock.

EXHIBIT 4-5. Continued

SIMPSONS-SEARS LIMITED

STATEMENT OF EARNINGS CANADIAN $ IN MILLIONS	FOR FISCAL YEAR ENDED	
	January 7, 1976	January 8, 1975
Net revenues	$1,551	$1,343
Expenses	1,493	1,276
Pretax earnings	58	67
Income taxes	29	35
Operating earnings	29	32
Equity earnings	3	2
Net earnings	$ 32	$ 34

STATEMENT OF FINANCIAL POSITION CANADIAN $ IN MILLIONS	AT FISCAL YEAR END	
	January 7, 1976	January 8, 1975
ASSETS		
Current assets	$ 716	$ 655
Fixed assets—net	298	254
Investments and other assets	37	32
TOTAL ASSETS	$1,051	$ 941
LIABILITIES		
Current liabilities	$ 284	$ 312
Long-term debt	403	342
Deferred income taxes	19	18
TOTAL LIABILITIES	$ 706	$ 672
SHAREHOLDERS' EQUITY	$ 345	$ 269

LATIN AMERICAN SUBSIDIARIES

Net sales of subsidiaries in Mexico and South America rose 18 percent to $398.9 million. Net income, after exchange losses, increased $1.9 million to $23.3 million. Sears equity in this income was $20.1 million; however, $2.2 million was not available for remittance under current laws in certain countries. A reserve for this amount is included in the Sears statement of income but is not reflected in the schedule below. Our Brazilian subsidiary added one sales office and our Venezuelan subsidiary opened a new medium size department store in a shopping center in Caracas. Our Mexican subsidiary opened a medium size department store in Mexicali. This store will be sold to a new company owned 49 percent by our Mexican subsidiary and 51 percent by Mexican nationals in accordance with the foreign investment law of Mexico.

Sears is planning for the reduction of its equity from 80 percent to 20 percent in the Venezuelan subsidiary in accordance with a decree of the Venezuelan government. It is still anticipated that no loss will be incurred in this disposition.

EXHIBIT 4-5. Continued

EUROPEAN SUBSIDIARIES

Net sales of the Spanish subsidiary rose 28 percent to $67.3 million in 1975. Net income was $3.1 million compared with a loss of $1.2 million (restated) the previous year. Another complete department store and a sales office were opened in Barcelona. There are three complete department stores and 17 retail sales offices in Spain. Subsequent to the close of the fiscal year Spain's currency depreciated by approximately 11 percent which will result in an exchange loss for the Spanish subsidiary of some $2.6 million which was not included in 1975 results.

Net sales for Galeries Anspach, our Belgian subsidiary, were $96.5 million, up 16 percent. The net loss for 1975 was $11.2 million, after exchange gain of $6 million, compared with a $23.8 million loss (restated) in 1974, which included an exchange loss of $9.1 million. Expenses continued to increase as a result of inflation while profit margins were restricted by price controls, making improvement in operating profits difficult. One small store was reclassified to a retail sales office. At the end of the year Galeries operated three complete department stores, five medium size stores, one small hard lines store and two retail sales offices. It also owns and operates two shopping centers.

During 1975, Sears made an additional equity investment of $18 million in Galeries Anspach.

SUMMARY OF INTERNATIONAL OPERATIONS
$ IN THOUSANDS

	NET SALES	
	1975	*1974*
Canada	$1,521,340	$1,367,681
Latin America	398,905	337,865
Europe	163,808	135,453
TOTAL	$2,084,053	$1,840,999

	NET INCOME (AFTER EXCHANGE ADJUSTMENTS)	
	1975	*1974*
Canada	$ 30,915	$ 35,965
Latin America	23,265	21,410
Europe	(7,760)	(24,516)[a]
TOTAL	$ 46,420	$ 32,859[a]

[a]Restated.

	SEARS EQUITY IN NET INCOME	
	1975	*1974*
Canada	$ 12,716	$ 14,851
Latin America	20,108	18,210
Europe	(7,759)	(24,516)[a]
TOTAL	$ 25,065	$ 8,545[a]

[a]Restated.

Another case of special note is the British Electrical and Musical Instruments Company Limited (EMI), which regularly discloses the number of shareholders and the number of ordinary shares they hold for their "American Register" (Exhibit 4–6).

The argument is sometimes encountered that companies do not know whether there are foreign holders of their securities or in which country such holders might be located. It is also a fact that many banks and investment houses hold securities on accounts of their various clients. Nonetheless, companies are required by law to maintain accurate securities transfer records, if for no other reasons than potential or required interest and dividend payments. Thus, ownership information should be available in most cases. In instances where indirect ownership percentages are large and indeterminate, it seems reasonable to apply some statistical sampling techniques. There is no reason why statistical estimates of nondomestic securities ownership and its location cannot be utilized in disclosure procedures.

Some General Guidelines
for Transnational Disclosure

Review of the applicable literature and present practices suggests some broad guidelines in relation to disclosure needs for transnational financial reporting. These guidelines are as qualitative as the disclosure process itself. Taken together, they might form a "Code of Disclosure in Transnational Financial Reporting" similar to the OECD Code (see Chapter 10).

Adequacy. At present, disclosure is almost the sole tool by which a degree of multinationalization of financial reporting can be achieved. Throughout this book, we are cognizant of the fact that internationally accepted standards of financial accounting and reporting do not yet exist, even though limited and very cautious initial steps are under way toward the establishment of agencies and instrumentalities that hope for a measure of success in formulating and enforcing such standards. Consequently, achievement of a reasonably high quality of transnational financial reporting is highly sensitive to and dependent on substantial amounts of financial disclosure.

General Interest. Since there is a broad awareness of and general public interest in multinational business affairs, disclosure of a company's multinational involvements should become a standard item of financial reporting. As a minimum, each publicly owned company should report regularly (a) all exchanges on which its securities are listed or admitted for trading, (b) an estimate of the number and percentage of ownership holders

EXHIBIT 4-6. EMI Stockholding Analyses (as at 30 September)

BY SIZE OF HOLDING	1975				1974			
	Number of Stockholders	%	Number of Units Held	%	Number of Stockholders	%	Number of Units Held	%
English Register								
1 – 200 units	15,406	23	1,763,038	2	17,873	28	2,148,076	3
201 – 1,000 units	26,922	41	13,296,733	14	25,217	39	12,547,601	17
1,001 – 2,000 units	5,061	8	7,146,488	8	3,689	6	5,345,922	7
2,001 – 10,000 units	2,399	4	8,977,894	9	1,800	3	7,116,929	9
10,001 – 20,000 units	232	—	3,345,443	4	205	—	3,027,827	4
20,001 – 50,000 units	193	—	6,534,395	7	159	—	5,214,534	7
Over 50,000 units	221	—	49,218,792	52	178	—	36,025,009	48
American Register	16,009	24	4,100,112	4	15,568	24	3,751,817	5
	66,443	100	94,382,895	100	64,689	100	75,177,715	100

131

not residing in the company's country of domicile, and (c) the full extent of a company's multinational business involvement—whether it extends only to minor export/import activities, multinational business based on direct foreign investments, or transnational sourcing of capital. Even if a company were not involved at all with any type of multinational activities, it appears that present social and economic climates dictate that investors be so informed explicitly. Disclosure is (at present) the only vehicle by which this can be achieved.

Type of Disclosure. Effective disclosure should relate directly to the financial statements in question. This means that referenced footnotes or elaboration reports tied directly to financial statement items constitute the most desirable type of disclosure. Disclosure is least effective when it occurs in documents or media entirely separate from an annual report or when specific disclosure occurs in a manner that appears to disassociate it from corresponding financial statements.

Several large multinational enterprises have begun to prepare separate brochures containing nothing but an annual financial information package. This package is published and distributed separately from a public relations-oriented annual report. Given a choice, the authors favor this type of approach to financial reporting and regard the financial information package currently distributed by the SONY Company as a desirable prototype.

Nature of Disclosure. APB Statement No. 4 spells out several qualitative objectives for financial statements, including relevance, understandability, verifiability, neutrality, comparability, and completeness. These qualitative standards are directly relevant to disclosure in transnational financial reporting. For instance, verifiability is comparatively more difficult when financial reports cross national borders, and therefore appropriate disclosures may be even more important here than in counterpart domestic reporting. The same applies to neutrality. Accounting neutrality vis-a-vis business transactions and events is not a foregone conclusion or general condition. Relatively more disclosure in international circumstances can help to render financial information more neutral.

Comparability and completeness can never be achieved entirely. Nonetheless, as their accomplishment seems very elusive in most transnational situations, particular attention should be paid to them.

Parenthetically, we might point out why we are relying on qualitative guidelines originally evolved to serve strictly national or domestic financial reporting needs. Davidson and Kohlmeier concluded 12 years ago, after they studied the impact of foreign accounting principles on financial reporting processes, that the application of foreign accounting principles to a given set of transactions and events was not really much different from choosing among alternatives of generally accepted accounting principles in the United States.[2] Since that time, other researchers have reached similar conclusions. Hence, one might argue that financial reporting to transnational audiences is not really all that different from reporting to national audiences—except that it is twice as complex, since available choices are usually much larger. If this viewpoint is accepted, one can extend it to the disclosure problem by observing that the transnational disclosure problem is similar to the domestic disclosure problem, except that the former is more intensive.

Quantification. Any national set of generally accepted accounting standards and principles constitutes a language. And languages are means of communication serving specified information purposes. But different national users of financial statements do not always understand each other's accounting principles language. While disclosure facilitates international financial communications somewhat, resorting to a more commonly understood language may prove desirable. Such a language may be the quantitative expressions that are a part of the general accounting language. Quantification should be used as widely as possible as a tool of disclosure in transnational financial reporting. Of course, not every item of needed disclosure can be given quantitative expression. Thus quantification *whenever practical* is probably the only feasible decision rule in this respect.

Postscript

Securities regulations in different countries easily lead to quirks in transnational financial disclosures. One example is the December 1975 offer by Plessey Company, the British-based telecommunications concern, to its shareholders to sell one new share for the equivalent of about $1.21 for each four shares held. The New York announcement specifically states that warrants to buy the new shares will not be sent to holders with a permanent or temporary address outside the continental United States and Canada or with an APO or FPO address. These holders would receive special instruction forms.

The press release giving the details of this financial operation that would net Plessey some $50 million was circulated carefully in London only to non-United States reporters with a cautionary note that transmitting the announcement to the United States could violate United States securities laws. The problem came about because Plessey officials concluded that

---

[2] "A Measure of the Impact of Some Foreign Accounting Principles," *Journal of Accounting Research,* Autumn 1966, pp. 183–212.

SEC disclosure requirements applied only to the holders of American Depository Receipts (ADR's) and not to the *sterling* shareholders who comprise 98 percent of all the outstanding Plessey common stock.

Thus, American news organizations in London received an announcement saying only that Plessey would be offering one-for-four rights to holders of about 11 percent of its shares called *dollar ordinary* shares. This announcement did not mention that the holders of the sterling shares would be offered the rights as well.

As it turned out, British shareholders with immediate access to the full picture promptly bid down the price of Plessey shares to take advantage of the pending rights issue, but Americans holding Plessey sterling shares were not fully in the picture until later. Mentioning the rights offer to American holders of sterling shares might have been construed as a solicitation for Americans to buy "unregistered" stock—a clear breach of United States securities laws. Would it have been? And who finally suffered from unduly protective disclosure regulations?

INDEPENDENT AUDITS

Independent auditors perform the attest function in financial reporting. As competent outside experts, they review financial information and then attest to its reliability, fairness, and other aspects of quality. This process establishes and maintains the integrity of financial information.

Investors have a big stake in such attestation since they can make decisions with better expected outcomes if they have relatively better information available. The public is also involved. Incomplete, unreliable or even misleading financial information may well have a negative effect on capital formation processes within an economy. Moreover, scarce resources may be misdirected into socially less desirable channels or wasted through excessive rates of bankruptcy. Sensitivity to the attest function is probably higher in multinational settings than it is in single country situations.

Differences in financial information user wants and perceptions have led to variations from country to country in (a) auditing standards and procedures, (b) professional education and qualifications of auditors, (c) degree of independence required to perform the public attest function, and (d) conditions under which a CPA may practice and the scope of activities.

Standards and Procedures

In very general terms, auditing standards the world over are probably less diverse than accounting standards. Most of the highly industrialized countries impose high professional standards for public auditors and developing countries are moving in the same direction. Israel, Korea, Mexico, and the Philippines are good examples of the latter course of development.

One reason why auditing standards are relatively similar the world over is that professional auditors are the only parties involved in setting such standards, rather than all the legislative, judicial, and administrative procedures that come to bear on the establishment of accounting standards. A good comparison of auditing standards from country to country can be made on the basis of the AICPA's book entitled *Professional Accounting in 30 Countries.* From it one can readily determine that auditing standards are pretty much alike in, for example, Australia, Canada, Germany, Japan, Mexico, the Netherlands, Sweden, Switzerland, the United States, and the United Kingdom. For instance, one general principle of the *Statements on Auditing No. 1,* published by the Institute of Chartered Accountants in England and Wales, reads

> To make such tests and inquiries as the auditor considers necessary
> to form an opinion as to the reliability of the records as a basis for the
> preparation of accounts.

This type of standard might well apply to any of the reasonably developed countries of the Western world.

Auditing procedures are somewhat less uniform multinationally in comparison to auditing standards. The extended American procedures of confirming trade accounts receivable and observing physical inventory counts are still not commonly practiced elsewhere, although there seems to be a trend toward greater use of these procedures in several countries. By contrast, trade accounts payable are sometimes confirmed in a number of countries but not in the United States. This is also the case for legal titles to real properties. Although auditing procedures among countries seem to vary more than respective auditing standards, both still do not vary nearly so much as accounting principles.

Certain audit practices also have a multinational dimension. German independent auditors are known for relatively brief audit-working papers and at the same time for rather long-winded formal long-form reports. There is an apparent tendency to show as much as possible of the audit work performed directly in an audit report. On the other hand, typical audit working papers are quite voluminous in North American practice, and audit reports are often held to the so-called short-form report.

Detailed figure checking for all material amounts occurs in some countries, while sampling and different statistical methods are used in others. Professional conduct is regulated by law in some countries, while elsewhere there are only recommendations from professional institutes to which professional auditors must belong in order to achieve professional recognition and acceptance. The latter situation still prevails in the Netherlands, although their Registration Act for Auditors has produced several changes in this respect. Several countries have laws excluding professional auditors from other countries from making their services available for local statutory financial reporting purposes. Professional reciprocity again varies widely from country to country.

Professional Qualifications

A particular difficulty with auditing in the multinational setting lies in recognizing the status of an auditor rendering an opinion. Most countries register or certify several classes of auditors; often only one and, in exceptional cases, two, types of auditors have the professional qualifications and the necessary independence to render meaningful opinions on financial statements that might be used in other countries.

France is an example in point. Several classes of bookkeepers and accountants may obtain government licenses to practice their respective trades and professions. Yet only the French *Expert Comptable* is in a position to render a professional opinion on financial statements.

To make matters even more confusing, some certificates on French financial statements are signed by so-called "Commissaires." These parties are statutory auditors whose appointments are mandatory under French commercial law. They are required to oversee in very general terms a company's bookkeeping and accounting and then to report annually to the stockholders' meeting. The law does not specify any professional qualifications for Commissaires. Often one or several stockholders serve in this capacity. Consequently, a statement of an opinion by a Commissaire has a completely different meaning and premise from a possibly similar statement or opinion by an Expert Comptable.

Educational requirements for professional qualification range from modest in Great Britain to substantial in Germany. On the other hand, practical experience requirements are substantial in Britain and the Netherlands but are no longer required in some jurisdictions in the United States. The type of audit work performed and professional standing of the auditors are simply key variables in assessing audit quality between different countries.

Independence

Professional independence is another variable that differs widely from country to country. It seems generally agreed that CPA's in the United States are subject to the highest order of independence requirements that exist internationally. In some nations, auditors may sit on corporate boards of directors or own small financial interests in companies their firms audit. On the Continent, many large audit firms are owned, at least in part, by large banks. This does not mean that European auditors are necessarily dependent in fact or in appearance. Rather, it means that a thoroughly different organization of the independent auditing profession prevails. While a non-United States person may hold that an audit firm performing management advisory services and tax advocacy for a client cannot possibly be independent, United States auditors would argue that bank equity ownership of an audit firm (though carefully separated from audit operations) impairs independence. Who is right?

The auditor independence question often raises some operational problems in multinational engagements. Auditor independence is a concept not only entrenched in professional ethics codes in the United States but anchored in administrative SEC regulations such as their basic Regulation SX and Accounting Series Release No. 126. Therefore, independent auditors of publicly held United States parent companies have the responsibilities of assuring themselves that foreign subsidiary companies are all audited by persons who meet United States definitions of auditor independence. This is not always a simple matter when audits abroad are conducted by associated or correspondent firms rather than by a firm's own branch offices. The situation may be even more vexing in those countries where local rules require that independent audits be performed only by local nationals.

Audit Conditions

Multinational conditions of independent audits vary in many ways. Such audits may be legally required in some cases and voluntarily submitted to in others. Regulatory agencies may have control over them or stock exchanges may stipulate them as a condition to listing a company's securities or simply admitting given securities for trade on an exchange. Audit fees may be legally prescribed in one country and left to market forces in another. In some places auditors only audit, while in others they engage in executive placement, financial investment management, tax advocacy, and other professional-type services. Thus it is not surprising to find a number of unresolved issues when it comes to the multinational dimensions of the independent audit function.

One such issue is the wording of an independent auditor's opinion (report). Japan, as well as several countries in South America, has adopted a report form which is the same, verbatim, as the corresponding United States form. By simply reading the text, one can no longer be sure where a given auditor's report may have been issued. This may be desirable from a worldwide harmonization point of view, but it is clearly not so informative as the situation in which each country essentially has its own unique wording of auditors' reports.

Canadian and United States auditors' opinions refer to *fair presentation.* British professional auditors refer to a *true and fair view.* Swedish auditors customarily report that nothing has come to their attention to suggest that management has not discharged its administrative functions properly. The Germans state rather legalistically that the books and records and the annual report conform to all applicable legal requirements. Examples of a Dutch, German, and Swedish auditor's opinion are illustrated for comparison purposes in Exhibit 4−7. The AICPA's *Professional Accounting in 30 Countries* may be consulted for the specific wordings of customary auditors' reports in other countries.

EXHIBIT 4 − 7. Examples of Selected Countries Auditors' Reports

1. THE NETHERLANDS

We have examined the consolidated financial statements together with the statutory financial statements of Naamloze Vennootschap DSM for the year ended December 31, 1975, as included in the official Annual Report published in Dutch.

In our opinion, based upon our examination, these financial statements present fairly the financial position of the company at December 31, 1975, and the results of its operations for the year then ended, in conformity with Netherlands accounting principles.

The statutory financial statements have not been included in this abridged English version of the Annual Report.

Heerlen, March 30, 1976   MORET & LIMPERG

2. WEST GERMANY

ALLGEMEINE ELEKTRICITÄTS-GESELLSCHAFT
AEG-TELEFUNKEN
The consolidated Financial Statement and the Annual Report were duly verified and found by us to comply with the law.

Deutsche Warentreuhand-Aktiengesellschaft
Wirtschaftsprufungsgesellschaft. Steuerberatungsgesellschaft
Berlin and Frankfurt (Main), April 8, 1976

Hamann, Wirtschaftsprüfer   Feik, Wirtschaftsprüfer

3. SWEDEN

We the undersigned, being duly commissioned by the shareholders of Stora Kopparbergs Bergslags Aktiebolag at the 1975 Annual General Meeting, have examined the administration of the Company's affairs during 1975 and have drawn up the following report thereon.

In the course of our audit we have examined the Annual Report and Accounts presented by the Board and the Managing Director, studied the Minutes and other documents bearing upon the financial position and management of the Company, and undertaken such other examinations as we deemed necessary.

EXHIBIT 4-7. Continued

The requirements of the Swedish Companies Act relating to the disclosure of intragroup relationships have, in our opinion, been duly observed, as have the requirements regarding disclosure of loans, assets pledged and contingent liabilities involving persons, concerning whom the right to such loans is restricted.

The Board and the Managing Director recommend that Skr 19,300,000 of the available earnings be allocated to the Supplementary Legal Reserve and that Skr 49,290,000 be distributed to the shareholders, that Skr 8,000,000 be allocated to the General reserve, and that Skr 9,959,310 be carried forward to the next Account. In our opinion, this recommendation is not at variance with sound business practice, having regard to the position of the Group and the results of its operations as a whole.

Our audit having given no cause for censure in respect of the Accounts, the bookkeeping, the inventory of the assets or any other aspect of the Company's administration, we recommend

that the Balance Sheet as at December 31, 1975, as signed by us, be adopted

that the Board of Directors and the Managing Director be given a full discharge from liability for their conduct of the Company's affairs during 1975, and

that disposition of the profit be made according to the above recommendation, which takes due account of legal requirements concerning allocations to reserves.

Falun, April 7, 1976

M. von Essen	*S.-H. Leffler*
	Authorized Public Accountant
Sten Nackstad	*Anders Carlehall*
Authorized Public Accountant	

STATUTORY AND SPECIAL REPORTS

Some statutory accounting requirements exist in all industrialized countries, even though the scope and stringency of such requirements vary greatly. Statutory financial statements are those prepared in accordance with all applicable laws, regulations, and administrative rules. These types of statements must normally be filed with public or semipublic agencies such as the Board of Trade in the United Kingdom or the Public Commercial Register in many European and South American countries. Often there is also a legal requirement to publish financial statements once a year in a government journal or some type of official gazette. Statements so published are normally of the statutory type.

Since public laws and rules are the basis for statutory financial statements, the statements are only as good or as comprehensive as the underlying laws are. If applicable legislation is revised frequently and if business and professional groups make effective inputs to successive law revisions, then one can expect statutory statements to be up-to-date and practically useful. This is predominantly the case with British statutory statements. If, on the other hand, statutory statements are allowed to become outdated or otherwise obsolete, then financial statements produced under such statutes are only a matter of formal compliance and have no real significance. This situation is found in several South American countries.

Statutory financial statements make no pretense at being "fair," "useful," or otherwise relevant to business activities or business decisions. These statements are strictly and only compliance statements to satisfy applicable public laws. Public laws are often geared to minimum standards, and consequently statutory statements often reflect only minimum standards. In addition, general laws cannot easily anticipate each and every business situation. Therefore, statutory financial statements are sometimes very general and do not convey information important to any individual statement user.

One specific accounting concern with statutory requirements arises through the direct legal interference in financial reporting processes when model formats are prescribed for financial statements or when specific accounting classifications are legally required—for instance, when the par value of common stock in the United States has to be separated from the total amounts of investments made in a company by the initial purchasers of the stock.

Another illustration occurs in situations where certain non-United States statutory requirements specify establishment of so-called "legal reserves" within the owners' equity section of a balance sheet. In many ways such legal reserves are similar to appropriations of earnings in the United States, even though the latter can typically be created or abolished by Boards of Directors, whereas the former are more in the nature of a legally required reinvestment of a portion of a company's earnings. Still, both an "appropriation" and a "legal reserve" represent earned and undistributed equity capital in an enterprise. Both limit possible dividend distributions. If United States financial statements were to be restated on the basis of West German accounting principles, a retained earnings appropriation would simply become "a reserve for future contingencies" or the like, and a German statutory retained earnings reserve would become a "legal appropriation of retained earnings." Naturally, this type of legal requirement can create confusion and is often treated as a special disclosure situation.

Even if statutory accounting requirements or financial statements are not always the most useful, they are prepared on a common denominator and therefore uniform basis. Statutory statements produce at least minimum levels of record keeping and accounting and also a minimum amount of financial disclosure. Therefore, they do serve a distinct purpose in many countries.

Using arbitrary judgment, one can probably say that for most countries with statutory financial statement requirements, statements prepared according to generally accepted accounting principles or sound business customs will also satisfy the statutory requisites. In these instances, a single set of financial statements is used to satisfy both interested business and financial groups as well as legal authorities. Particularly in the case of the multinational enterprise (as demonstrated on p. 118 with reference to CIBA-GEIGY), one finds more and more situations where local statutory requirements are exceeded because international competition or participation in international capital markets dictate a higher order of financial reporting. From a multinational accounting perspective, statutory accounting requirements of individual countries are likely to decrease in importance, but regional organization statutes (e.g., for EEC countries— see Chapter 6) might well supersede them and eventually become more stringent. The student of multinational accounting should understand the history, present applications, and likely future developments of statutory financial statements whether freestanding or parallel to business/professional type of reporting.

Special Reports

In the transnational reporting sphere, special reports abound. They are not very different from their domestic cousins, but naturally many of them address problems that do not exist on a uninational plane.

Two brief examples will suffice to make the point. The first might be taken from the annals of the Boeing Company when it provides aircraft and various spare parts and training services to the small flag-carrying airlines of the developing countries. Typically, Export–Import Bank financing is sought in these situations. But before such financing can be obtained, the financial statements of the respective airlines have to be restated to a common denominator so that they (a) become comparable to financial statements of other airlines and (b) can serve as a basis for some financial forecasting. The resulting financial statements are clearly special reports.

Another illustration might be taken from the operations of the International Finance Corporation (IFC), which is an international investment institution established to assist industrial development in the third world through investments in productive private enterprises. National governments are agreement members of IFC. The capital base of IFC exists by virtue of quota contributions from all member governments.

IFC investments are spread throughout the economically less developed countries of the free world. Since IFC borrowers normally are independent private industrial or commercial enterprises, they are subject to the laws of the respective countries in which they are domiciled. Hence the accounting and financial reporting of each borrower are subject to applicable local laws.

Notwithstanding locally binding statutes, IFC requires periodic financial reporting from the borrower firms so that the investments can be properly monitored. This means that some form of transnational financial reporting has to be involved for meaningful analysis possibilities at IFC headquarters. IFC has published manuals that specify both its accounting and financial reporting requirements and the independent audit reports it expects. These are best seen as special reports within the larger area of transnational financial reporting.

SELECTED REFERENCES

4.1 ACCOUNTANTS INTERNATIONAL STUDY GROUP, *International Financial Reporting,* Study No. 11. Toronto, Canada: Author, 1975, unpaginated (monograph).

4.2 BALL, ROBERT, "The Declining Art of Concealing the Figures," *Fortune,* September 15, 1967, pp. 136–39, 160, 163, 166, 171.

4.3 BARRETT, M. E., "Financial Reporting Practices: Disclosure and Comprehensiveness in an International Setting," *Journal of Accounting Research*, Spring 1976, pp. 10-26.

4.4 BERG, KENNETH B., GERHARD G. MUELLER, AND LAUREN M. WALKER, "Annual Reports Go International," *Journal of Accountancy,* August 1967, pp. 59–64.

4.5 BREEK, P. C., "Accounting Problems Peculiar to International Enterprises." *New Horizons of Accounting,* Paris: Ninth International Congress of Accountants, 1967, pp. 185–215.

4.6 CHOI, FREDERICK D. S., "European Disclosure: The Competitive Disclosure Hypothesis," *Journal of International Business Studies,* Fall 1974, pp. 15–23.

4.7 CHOI, FREDERICK D. S., "Financial Disclosure and Entry to the European Capital Market," *Journal of Accounting Research,* Autumn 1973, pp. 159–75.

4.8 CHOI, FREDERICK D. S., "Financial Disclosure In Relation to a Firm's Capital Costs," *Accounting and Business Research,* Autumn 1973, pp. 282–92.

4.9 CRAWFORD, JOHN M., "Accounting Considerations for Japanese Issuers in the United States Capital Market," *Haskins & Sells Selected Papers 1974,* New York: Author, 1975, pp. 55–63.

4.10 CUMMINGS, JOSEPH P., "Beware of the Pitfalls in Foreign Financial Statements," *World* (House Journal of Peat, Marwick, Mitchell & Co.), Winter 1972, pp. 45–47.

4.11 DE LEEUW, H. D., "Some Aspects of Auditing in the International Field," *Accountant*, March 30, 1963, pp. 385–91.

4.12 FREDERIKSON, BRUCE, "On the Measurement of Foreign Income," *Journal of Accounting Research,* Autumn 1968, pp. 208-21.

4.13 JUDGE, A. J. N., "Multinational Business Enterprises," *Yearbook of International Organizations,* 12th ed., Brussels: Union of International Associations, 1969, pp. 1189–1214.

4.14 LUDEWIG, R., "Trend Toward More Information in Annual Accounts—A Comparison of Practice in Different Countries," *Journal UEC,* October 1972, pp. 292–99.

4.15 MORRIS, R. C., "The Financial Reporting Problem of Multinational Companies," *Accountant's Magazine,* September 1975, pp. 317–20.

4.16 MUELLER, GERHARD G., "An International View of Accounting and Disclosure," *International Journal of Accounting,* Fall 1972, pp. 117–34.

4.17 MUELLER, GERHARD G., "Accounting for Multinationals," *Accountancy,* July 1975, pp. 70–75.

4.18 MUELLER, GERHARD G., "The Dual System for Transnational Financial Reporting," *The Accounting Forum* (Baruch College of the City University of New York), May 1976, pp. 17–25.

4.19 MUELLER, GERHARD G., and LAUREN M. WALKER, "The Coming of Age of Transnational Financial Reporting," *Journal of Accountancy,* July 1976, pp. 67–74.

4.20 STICH, ROBERT S., "How Well Do Multinational Companies Perform?" *Management International Review,* No. 4/5, 1971, pp. 33–39.

DISCUSSION QUESTIONS

4.1 What are the four different *types* of transnational financial reporting identified in the chapter? Write a definitional sentence for each of them.

4.2 The accounting "entity concept" has been used as a springboard to view all multinational business operations through the "eyes" of the domestic parent company as well as regarding each national unit of a multinational enterprise as a separate and distinct being. How do these two viewpoints affect the choice of foreign exchange translation procedures used in multinational consolidations of financial statements? Which viewpoint underlies the recommendation in Study No. 11 of the Accountants International Study Group?

4.3 Strictly speaking, there is no multinational accounting entity concept found in authoritative accounting pronouncements and regulations. Construct, in your own words, a one-paragraph definition of a *multinational* accounting entity concept.

4.4 Present either an abbreviated illustration or a short descriptive essay to elaborate the notion of "subentity" type of financial reporting usable by multinational enterprises.

4.5 Arguments supporting the establishment and application of international standards for financial accounting and reporting seem to contradict the proposition that different accounting environments are best served by different accounting standards and practices. (Refer particularly to the discussion in Chapter 2.) Can this divergence be reconciled?

4.6 Develop a list of five different ways in which international standards for financial accounting and reporting might be enforced. For each different enforcement mechanism, write a brief description of how it might work.

4.7 What is the link between international financial markets and transnational financial accounting and reporting? Find at least two recent statistics or financial news items (*different* from those cited in the chapter) that illustrate the relative significance of international financial markets.

4.8 What is meant by *convenience translations* in multinational financial reporting? Find an example of this type of reporting either in your Business Administration or University Library or from an appropriate department of a nearby bank or securities brokerage firm.

4.9 List and briefly describe three advantages and three disadvantages of formal "subentity" financial reporting by overseas components of multinational enterprises.

4.10 Assume you are the administrative assistant to a member of the U.S. Securities and Exchange Commission. Write a short executive memorandum to your superiors—either endorsing or rejecting the presently used "convenience" financial statements of multinational companies not based in the United States. Include any recommendations for actions that might logically follow from the position you take.

4.11 Pick three large non-United States-based multinational enterprises, some of whose securities are traded on stock exchanges outside the home country. Determine, to the best of your ability, whether one or more of them should prepare secondary financial statements in the sense of the AISG's 1975 recommendations. If you find a candidate for primary and secondary financial statements, should more than one set of secondary statements be furnished?

4.12 Financial disclosure of multinational operations is akin to "line-of-business" reporting. What is the latest FASB requirement in this area? Does it specifically include multinational operations as a line of business? Taking, as a point of departure, the examples illustrated in the chapter, forecast likely developments in respective United States practices over the next 5 years.

4.13 Compare and contrast the general guidelines for transnational financial disclosure set forth in the chapter with the corresponding points in the 1976 FASB Discussion memorandum on Objectives for Financial Statements. If you see no connection, please say so and state your reasons.

4.14 From references beyond the discussion in the chapter, draw an international comparison among five different countries as to (a) independent audit standards, (b) independent audit procedures, (c) professional qualifications of independent auditors, (d) auditor independence itself, and (e) formats of independent auditors' reports. Do you conclude that independent auditing is more or less uniform between the comparison countries than financial accounting and reporting? Support your answer in specific (possibly arithmetic or statistical) terms.

4.15 Is there a difference between statutory or special reports and secondary financial statements as advocated by AISG? What definition fits financial statements prepared for taxation purposes? Is *multiple* financial reporting tantamount to keeping two, three, or more sets of books? Take and defend a position on whether a single set of financial statements should or could serve *all* practical (i.e., real world) financial reporting purposes and/or objectives.

ANNOTATED TEACHING MATERIALS

4.1 *Strassli Holding AG* (ICCH Case 9–110–038). In December 1964, the executive committee of Strassli Holding AG, of Berne, Switzerland, met to decide how much financial information to disclose in the next annual report and whether any additional information should be rendered to shareholders at the annual meeting in April 1965. The issue was touched off by a resolution submitted by a shareholder who suggested publication of consolidated financial statements.

Also at stake was a new share issue. Strassli's controller concluded that more financial disclosure would reduce rather than increase the demand for the company's new shares. Various financial statements and schedules are included in the case.

4.2 *Dalgety Group* (ICCH Case 9–176–064). The company annual report indicates the breakdown of sales, margins, net income, etc., by country and industry. Using indexes from various published sources, the case contains estimated financial statements for each subsidiary on a number of inflation adjustment bases as well as foreign exchange translation methods. The estimates differ widely. The case permits analysis of the differences derived. Which was right?

4.3 *USIF Real Estate* (ICCH Case 9–192–242). Redemption and sales of shares of the USIF Real Estate Fund, an open-ended mutual fund, were temporarily suspended. This suspension of transactions affected 23,000 non-United States investors who held shares of the Fund. The temporary suspension of activities decreed by the management of the Fund came under heavy criticism to the extent that USIF share sales were banned in the West German market. The case lends itself to an assessment of offshore mutual investment activities. Various exhibits are provided. They include excerpts from the USIF Prospectus to facilitate appropriate analysis.

4.4 *Barclays Bank Limited* (A) (ICCH Case 9–172–207). Barclays was classified as a banking and discount company under the United Kingdom 1967 Companies Act. Even though the Act required certain financial disclosures, it specifically exempted United Kingdom-based banks (and certain other companies) from its financial disclosure requirements.

During 1970 the United Kingdom Board of Trade revoked these exemptions for clearing banks, including Barclays. In response to this action, Barclays provided the required disclosures and also changed the bases of its accounting in several major areas, e.g., bad and doubtful debts and investments. An evaluation of the changes in Barclays' basis of accounting and financial disclosures lies at the core of the case.

4.5 *Analysis of New United States Disclosure Standard.* FASB Statement No. 14 requires, among other items, the line-of-business disclosure of multinational business operations when such operations amount to 10 percent or more of a company's total activity. Select three United States-based multinational companies with which you are somewhat familiar or that interest you. Compare their financial disclosures of multinational operations between the respective 1976 and 1977 annual reports. What differences, if any, did you find? Make specific suggestions for further improvements for each of the three situations you reviewed.

Chapter 5
INTERNATIONAL ACCOUNTING STANDARDS AND ORGANIZATIONS

Throughout Chapters 2, 3, and 4 we have demonstrated the rather substantial degree of diversity that exists among financial accounting standards and principles the world over. We have also observed that there are many multinational similarities in accounting—usually clustered among countries whose socioeconomic systems and general business environments are similar.

WORLD SCENE OF ACCOUNTING PRACTICES

Accounting practices change. Prior to World War II, British accounting influence was dominant throughout the English-speaking world and a Franco-German influence permeated Code Law countries like Belgium, Japan, Sweden, and Switzerland. The latter, for instance, produced a great deal of emphasis on national charts of accounts and uniform accounting in general.

Today the United States is the signal force in accounting worldwide. It leads other countries in such matters as expenditures for accounting research, numbers of accounting publications, and college and university graduates with degree concentrations in accounting. At the same time, and properly so, other nations are not eager to adopt United States-developed accounting standards and principles. In fact, substantial diversity (see especially Chapter 2) still characterizes the world scene of accounting.

What are some of the points that evolve from a review of world accounting practices?

Asset and Liability Measurement. It is abundantly clear that accountants still measure most of the world's business assets in terms of original transaction costs. This measurement concept is not applied in pure form anywhere, however. To greater or lesser degree, original transaction cost applications are mixed with some forms of appraisals or current market valuation techniques, some specific and general price-level change adjustment techniques, some imputed interest calculations, and estimates of future transaction levels—especially in the areas of foreign exchange and future collections of receivables. At the conclusion of Chapter 3 we speculated that current cost measurement applications might soon make additional inroads into the historical cost bulwark of present accounting practices.

The term *asset* does not have a well-established meaning in terms of which resources are included or excluded. Comparatively, it covers various interpretations of intangibles such as goodwill and research and development. In several countries the definition of an asset includes foreign exchange losses arising from liabilities payable in foreign currencies. Assets may or may not include various types of leases, tax loss carry-forwards, or economic interests in affiliated companies.

Similarly, different liability concepts are applied from country to country. Accounting for income taxes provides a specific example. In some countries income tax liabilities are not accrued and are recognized on a cash basis only. In others, periodic accruals take place with or without the recognition of deferred income tax liabilities. In turn, deferral may require one of several different methods of tax allocation. In the Netherlands the amount of deferred income taxes is sometimes a discounted amount.

Other examples of differential definitions of a liability can be discovered readily. In some European and South American countries, provisions are not made for all known liabilities or losses. This may include items like severance pay obligations to workers, pension agreements or death benefits like burial costs, and estimated losses on purchase commitments or other forward contracts. Conversely, the definition of a liability is sometimes stretched to allow for the creation of "secret" reserves. German and Swiss practices, for example, often deliberately overestimate contingent liabilities and the effects of uncertain future events.

Owners' Equity and Periodic Income Determination. The greatest comparative variation in the owners' equity area concerns the question of whether certain enterprise resources or obligations may be written off directly to retained earnings, i.e., the well-known "clean versus adjusted surplus" concept. Because of the difficulty in separating normal business operations from unusual events and the problems of periodicity in past period adjustments, some countries require that all transactions except stockholder investments, capital donations, or capital accretion flow through the income statement. Yet many countries still permit direct owners' equity adjustments for unusual gains or losses.

Another major variation is the concept of periodicity in measuring the results of operations. Generally accepted accounting principles in the United States require sharp annual cutoffs. But in many European and South American countries applicable accounting principles insist that a calendar year is too short a period for reasonable determination of business results. Therefore they allow some smoothing between report periods. In Sweden the length of the business cycle is sometimes considered to be the most appropriate time period over which business results should be measured and reported.

Legal requirements clearly interfere with accounting for investment capital transactions. For instance, some countries have uniform par values for a given class of shares, others have different par value denominations for specific classes of shares, and still others permit no par value shares. Also, many variations exist in the principles that guide accounting for share distributions (in United States North American terminology, stock dividends and stock splits), stock option plans, and treasury stock transactions. Earnings per share is a nonsensical notion in Western Germany because most par value common stocks have different German mark denominations per share. The charging of retained earnings with a market value equivalent of small share distributions is a practice unique to the United States. Undoubtedly, this practice evolved from a concern over potential abuse of the *stock dividend* mechanism since market value charges to retained earnings limit the share distribution possibilities, especially where there are miniscule legal par values in relation to current market values.

Financial statement consolidation practices also vary widely. There is no comparable agreement on the meaning of an accounting entity. Consequently a "full range" of multinational consolidation practices is observable. As we have already pointed out, foreign subsidiaries are normally consolidated in the United States but not in Germany. In some countries, separate parent company statements are considered more important than consolidated financial statements. In other countries, joint ventures are accounted for at cost, in some on the equity basis, and in still others on arithmetic percentages of ownership. Minority interests and the amounts of positive or negative goodwill arising from business combinations are also sources of practice variations. These differences relating to consolidation practices are usually considered important enough to warrant the first (and presumably most important) footnote to published financial statements.

The interrelationship of asset and liability measurements with periodic income determination naturally causes reciprocal effects. Usually, over or understatements of assets or liabilities are accomplished through corresponding income statement inclusions or exclusions. This we have already pointed out. It should also be noted, however, that a great many smaller procedural variations exist as well. For instance, purchased goodwill may be amortized in the United States over a period of 40 years, whereas in Germany the maximum allowable amortization period is 5 years. In Australia, Ireland, New Zealand, Peru, and the United Kingdom, goodwill is generally not amortized at all. Similar procedural accounting variations apply to research and development, oil and mineral exploration costs, sales promotions, education and staff training, and many other accountable transactions or events.

EFFECTS ON BUSINESS DECISIONS

After all the preceding discussion, it is now appropriate to ask what difference, if any, does it make to have variety rather than uniformity in financial accounting and reporting from country to country?

Your authors submit that it does make a difference indeed! A number of enterprise management decisions are affected and thereby the allocation of economic resources. Investment project analysis is affected with the consequence that different goods and services might be produced in different locations under conditions of economic or social suboptimality. The cost of capital of firms sourcing long-term investment funds in international money markets or in nondomicile countries could well suffer because of multinational accounting diversity. Regrettably, though, the foregoing are only speculations. No good research evidence has yet been produced that demonstrates what economic and social costs and benefits flow from the multinational accounting problem.

In an attempt to illustrate some likely consequences for individual companies, we have selected a few problem situations that are briefly described in the following paragraphs.

Merger Activities

Business mergers appear to occur in cyclical patterns. For instance, during the early 1960's, United States-based companies invested very heavily in Continental Europe; by 1975, some divestments occurred—for instance, Singer Company's electronic computing activities and a number of Hertz's car rental agencies.

In contrast, a host of German companies were on an acquisitions spree in the United States during 1975. The big detergent maker, Henkel, bought 10 percent of California's $538 million sales Clorox Company and is continuing to increase its stake. In 1974, the huge German chemical maker, Bayer, purchased Cutter Laboratories; its competitor, Hoechst, bought specialty chemicals maker Foster Grant from United Brands. Boehringer Mannheim, a leading German drug company, has taken over Bio-Dynamics, and the top electronics group of Siemens AG, which already had a strong foothold in the United States, added three high technology companies totaling $20 million in sales in 1975. In still another takeover, the German retailer Hugo Mann Group, with sales of about $430 million in 1974, bought control of the $320 million sales Fed-Mart Corporation—a food and variety retailer in California and the Southwest.[1]

Several reasons are usually advanced for German companies becoming so interested in United States mergers beginning in 1974. Most important was the 30 percent strengthening of the Deutche mark vis-a-vis the dollar since 1971. While the dollar devaluation hurt the German export business, it made direct investments in the United States comparatively very attractive. Cash shortages of recession-plagued North American companies were another factor, as were the general doldrums of stock prices on Wall Street.

But a United States accounting standard was also involved. *Dun's Review* reported in its July 1975 issue (p. 54):

> A recent change in U.S. accounting rules also benefits foreigners. The rules are complex but the change in effect stipulates that when an American company buys less than 100 percent of another company—a division, say—it is normally not classified as a pooling of interest but a "purchase of assets." The buyer must then write off what it paid for goodwill (the excess of purchase price over book value) over a period of 10 years, and the annual write-off is not deductible as a pre-tax expense. But foreign firms are not governed by these rules and this, for example, gave Hoechst a certain (bookkeeping) cost advantage over American Cyanamid in bidding for Foster Grant.

Required amortization of differences between purchase prices and underlying book values in business mergers is an accounting rule unique to the United States (some foreign companies use it—but only if they so desire). It obviously produces differential management decision effects in multinational business.

Translation of Foreign Currencies

The problem of different methodologies for foreign currency translations is explored at some length in Chapter 3. From this prior discussion we recall that under the prevailing Standard No. 8 of the U.S. Financial Accounting

---

[1] "Germany's Business Blitzkrieg," *Dun's Review,* July 1975, pp. 54–56.

Standards Board all translation "gains and losses" must be brought into the income statement for the period during which they occurred. Table 3–4 reflects some of the impacts that this rule evoked on reported earnings per share for 1975 for a number of United States companies.

The current rate translation method usually has a similar effect. It recognizes all current foreign exchange rate movements and, in the absence of special reserves or contingency provisions for foreign exchange fluctuations, brings them directly into current profit or loss.

Differences produced by these varying accounting approaches can also be substantial. The German chemical and pharmaceutical group Hoechst uses the current rate translation method throughout. As a result of the German mark revaluation during 1973, fixed assets of foreign subsidiaries were written down by DM 205 million. Hoechst's major British competitor, Imperial Chemical Industries (ICI), translated foreign currency fixed assets at historical rates during the same time period and therefore shielded its income statement from the consequences of the 1973 deterioration of the exchange value of the United States dollar and the corresponding relative appreciation of other hard currencies like the German mark and the pound sterling. On this one accounting standard alone, therefore, the pretax net income of ICI was not at all comparable with that reported by Hoechst.

Of course, from a high of about $2.50 per pound sterling during mid-1973 to a rate of about $1.70 per pound sterling by mid-1975, enormous translation effects were produced for companies with monetary items denominated in pounds sterling. For example, assume a United States-based company had various liabilities arising from subsidiary operations in the British Isles and amounting to £100 million. These liabilities would have been carried at a United States dollar equivalent of about $250 million in 1973. Three years later the same amount of sterling liabilities would have appeared in a corresponding balance sheet at $170 million. Whether differences of this proportion do or do not enter corresponding income statements seems very likely to produce economic effects on such variables as labor negotiations, cost of new long-term money capital, and medium- and short-term credit availability.

Inclusiveness of Accounting Income

Concepts of what accounting income is or should be have generally developed conventionally (in part for reasons explained in Chapter 2). For instance, in North America the idea is accepted that any gain or loss objectively measurable and resulting primarily from the business activities of the present period should represent part of the accounting income of said period and therefore be included in it. The inclusion of foreign exchange translation gains or losses as discussed in the preceding section is but one manifestation of this convention.

By contrast, in most Commonwealth and Continental European countries, the idea pervades that accounting income should be based strictly upon business operating gains and losses for the present period. Gains and losses arising from transactions in items not usually held for resale or from extraordinary events are not considered a part of periodic accounting income but are instead credited or charged against what are known as *reserve* accounts. (Reserve accounts are shareholders' equity accounts, similar in certain ways to paid-in surplus and retained earnings accounts found in North American balance sheets.)

Comparing financial statements of brewing companies in Canada, the United Kingdom, and the United States for periods in the early 1970's, Derrek W. M. Pretty (unpublished University of Washington MBA research paper) found that restatement of income statements for the large British brewing companies to an all-inclusive (i.e., North American) basis changed their reported net income figure from a plus 18 percent effect to a minus 58 percent effect. In the majority of cases, reported net income would have been lower had the all-inclusive convention been applied.

In the British case, movements through various reserve accounts are disclosed and thus net income restatements are fairly easily accomplished. Scandinavian and Continental European (especially Swiss) companies do not generally disclose movements through respective owners' equity reserves. Consequently their reported net accounting income means something quite different from the counterpart figure in North America. Immediately affected are respective financial ratios produced through securities analysis and many of the resource allocation decisions drawing upon published profitability indexes as one of their analysis variables.

THE DILEMMA OF INTERNATIONAL STANDARDS

As long as the products of the accounting process were used largely within the confines of single countries, a uninational approach to the formulation of accounting standards and principles seemed justified and even desirable. With the advent of the multinational enterprise and its global investment and financing strategies together with the increasing interdependence of nations through trade and economic assistance programs, however, ethnocentric approaches to accounting prescriptions are becoming more and more anachronistic. They produce problems of the type just described—with the likely consequence of at least some misallocation of economic resources and some suboptimization of social welfare—within individual countries and possibly groups of countries (for instance, all countries in which *one* multinational enterprise conducts operations or has decided to refrain from operations or withdraw existing operations).

Yet at the same time we have the arguments posed in Chapter 2. There we observe that different accounting environments ought to spark different accounting responses so as to make accounting processes and their information products as socially useful as possible. The sociological/environmental argument allows for different developmental patterns of accounting and for a dozen or so quite definitive *clusters* of financial accounting standards and principles. Hence the apparent dilemma.

Closer investigation suggests that advocacy of international standards should not be regarded as synonymous with complete international accounting uniformity. In the United States, adherence to "generally accepted accounting principles" has a long and uncompromising history. It has been "built" into elements of SEC requirements, legal contracts and court cases, some federal income tax provisions, and of course the standard opinions of independent CPA's. Yet a movement is now afoot in the United States to recognize different sets of generally accepted accounting principles for the larger, publicly held corporations and for smaller, closely held companies. In Germany there is likewise a difference between the accounting requirements of the large public *Aktiengesellschaft* (AG) and the *Gesellschaft mit beschränkter Haftung* (GmbH).

The size and scope distinction promises to become the resolution of the international standards dilemma. Internationally uniform accounting standards for any and all situations are simply not a reasonable goal for the time being. International standards, as they are slowly emerging through the efforts of the International Accounting Standards Committee (IASC) and the influence of international capital markets as well as other international financial institutions and organizations, are really directed at the large multinational enterprise rather than at the local small-to-medium size, closely held companies.

Your authors are convinced that fairly multinational *clusters* of financial accounting standards and principles will continue to exist in the foreseeable future, recognizing the environmental differences that characterize people, natural resource configurations, geographies, and the like. At the same time and parallel to the clusters of nationally oriented standards and principles, we are likely to see rapid development of international standards appropriate for the financial accounting needs of the giant multinational enterprises whose operations span the globe in every conceivable crisscross pattern. These standards are likely to find acceptance through the competition for new financial capital fostered by Adam Smith's *invisible hand* of the market. No regulatory commission, court of law, or national institute of professional accountants will be able to enforce these standards completely through political power or economic sanction. But the market is altogether likely to succeed where bureaucrats are sure to fail. Availability of new money capital might well depend on the observance of international accounting standards. New international investments might be controlled through the application of such standards. Stock exchanges and consumer groups might have enough boycott potential to make application of such standards quite advisable. In short, we predict for some years to come a state of coexistence between nationally appropriate and internationally relevant accounting standards and principles. These two sets of rules are likely to be quite different in most cases because they will serve quite different purposes and objectives. In some instances, they will have to be met and utilized in financial reporting side by side. This is why the multiple reporting idea (see Chapter 4) of the AISG makes such good sense to your authors.

The Kraayenhof Proposal

Most discussions of the international accounting standards issue that have occurred since World War II can be traced by and large to the highly perceptive article on the subject by the late Jacob Kraayenhof. Kraayenhof was a founding partner of the largest European firm of independent accountants, a past president of the Netherlands Institute of Accountants, and President of the Seventh International Congress of Accountants (Amsterdam, 1957). His paper, which is already a classic in the literature, was presented at the annual meeting of the American Institute of CPA's in San Francisco in 1959.

At that time Jacob Kraayenhof keynoted the urgency of close international accounting cooperation and, ultimately, work on international accounting standards and accounting theory based on global assumptions. He suggested the establishment of standing committees in various countries for the search and study of accounting standards. He also hoped that such national committees might exchange the results of their individual efforts and thus promote widespread discussion of areas of disagreement. He advocated the American Institute of CPA's taking the initiative in accomplishing the international accounting standards objectives he suggested. This was clearly a pioneering effort, especially in the light of 1959 circumstances.

The Fantl Rebuttal

Professor Irving Fantl (Florida International University), among others, has been an outspoken critic of internationally uniform accounting standards and principles. Writing as late as May, 1971 (*Management Accounting*, p. 13), he observes

The growth of multinational business interests and the expansion of governmental and quasi-governmental assistance make the prospect of compatible worldwide accounting most appealing. Unfortunately, the solution is too simple and the problem too complex. However desirable such a monolithic concept appears, practical impediments to such uniformity must be clearly recognized so that accountants and users of financial information will not rely on the prospect of uniformity as a cure-all for the problems accruing from international accounting diversity.

... Traumatic evidence of the practical obstacles to uniformity are the controversies presently rampant on the American accounting scene. If one well-organized professional group cannot reach agreement on basic procedures, how much more difficult will it be to establish world standards? ... As with all social sciences, accounting contains an inherent flexibility which permits it to adapt to diverse financial requirements. This adaptability is at the same time one of the chief values to accounting and one of the chief obstacles to uniformity.

In the same article, Professor Fantl enumerates (a) national accounting traditions, (b) economic and legal circumstances, (c) problems of state sovereignty, and (d) the problems in developing countries as additional serious obstacles to international accounting uniformity. In summary, he concludes that there are three formidable barriers to any international uniform system of accountancy, even if only the industrially advanced countries are considered. The barriers listed are

1. Differences in background and tradition.
2. Differences in the needs of economic environments.
3. The challenge of uniformity to state sovereignty.

Any one of these, in the opinion of Professor Fantl, is sufficient reason for a nation to resist conforming to a universal system. In most cases, all three elements are present simultaneously.

International Accounting Standards Committee

In recent history, active professional discussion of the international standards issue reaches back to the first International Congress of Accountants held in St. Louis in 1904. Many meetings, committees, and reports have been devoted to the subject after that, especially subsequent to the conclusion of World War II. The predecessor to this book, *International Accounting,* Macmillan 1967, carried the following observation:

The Kraayenhof proposal has not met with tangible success. Other similar proposals have suffered the same fate.

But then a real breakthrough was achieved in June 1973 when the International Accounting Standards Committee (IASC) was established (headquartered in London) with joint representation of professional accountancy bodies from the nine following countries: Australia, Canada, France, Germany, Japan, Mexico, the Netherlands, the United Kingdom and Ireland, and the United States. These nine countries became the founder members of IASC and have since admitted a fairly impressive list of associate members to their group. A complete membership listing for the IASC, as of July 1977, is contained in Table 5 – 1.

The objectives of IASC are clearly set out in the Revised Agreement and Constitution:

1. To establish and maintain an International Accounting Standards Committee with a membership and powers set out below whose function will be to formulate and publish, in the public interest, standards to be observed in the presentation of audited financial statements and to promote their worldwide acceptance and observance.
2. To support the standards promulgated by the Committee.
3. To use their best endeavors
   a. To ensure that published financial statements comply with these standards or that there is disclosure of the extent to which they do not and to persuade governments, the authorities controlling securities markets, and the industrial and business community that published financial statements should comply with these standards.
   b. To ensure (1) that the auditors satisfy themselves that the financial statements comply with these standards or, if the financial statements do not comply with these standards, that the fact of non-compliance is disclosed in the financial statements, (2) that in the event of non-disclosure reference to non-compliance is made in the audit report.
   c. To ensure that, as soon as practicable, appropriate action is taken in respect of auditors whose audit reports do not meet the requirements of (b) above.
4. To seek to secure similar general acceptance and observance of these standards internationally.

Definitions of audited accounts and financial statements, the nature and scope of the basic standards, the working procedure, the voting, the language to be used, and the authority attaching to the standards are all discussed in the 1975 IASC booklet entitled *Preface to Statements of International Accounting Standards*. This booklet is readily available from all IASC members and from its Secretariat in London, and therefore its content is not quoted or reproduced here in whole or in part.

The working procedures of the IASC are not unlike those of the U.S. Financial Accounting Standards Board, with the exception that the latter can afford full-time paid board members and a huge research effort (including formally published *Discussion Memoranda* and other procedures). Both bodies receive lists of problems from the profession at large and through special committees and then select topics on which they judge work to be most urgently needed. The following topics are presently under study by IASC.

1. Accounting for Taxes on Income.
2. Accounting for Diversified Operations.
3. Accounting for Leases in the Financial Statements of Lessees.
4. Financial statements of banks.
5. Working capital.
6. Accounting for pension costs and commitments.

TABLE 5 – 1. Founder and Associate Members of IASC (as of July 1, 1977)

FOUNDER MEMBERS:

Australia	The Institute of Chartered Accountants in Australia, Australian Society of Accountants
Canada	The Canadian Institute of Chartered Accountants in conjunction with the General Accountants' Association and The Society of Industrial Accountants of Canada
France	Ordre des Experts Comptables et des Comptables Agrees
Germany	Institut der Wirtschaftsprufer in Deutschland e.V. Wirtschaftspruferkammer
Japan	The Japanese Institute of Certified Public Accountants
Mexico	Instituto Mexicano de Contadores Publicos, A.C.
Netherlands	Nederlands Instituut van Registeraccountants
United Kingdom and Ireland	The Institute of Chartered Accountants in England and Wales, The Institute of Chartered Accountants of Scotland, The Institute of Chartered Accountants in Ireland, The Association of Certified Accountants, The Institute of Cost and Management Accountants, The Chartered Institute of Public Finance and Accountancy
United States	American Institute of Certified Public Accountants

ASSOCIATE MEMBERS:

Bangladesh	The Institute of Chartered Accountants of Bangladesh
Belgium	College National des Experts Comptables de Belgique, Institut des Reviseurs d'Entreprises, Institut Belge des Reviseurs de Banques
Brazil	Instituto dos Auditores Independentes do Brazil
Cyprus	The Institute of Certified Public Accountants of Cyprus
Denmark	Foreningen Af Statsautoriserede Revisorer
Fiji	The Fiji Institute of Accountants
Finland	KHT-Yhdistys—Foreningen CGR

TABLE 5-1. Continued

Ghana	The Institute of Chartered Accountants (Ghana)
Greece	Institute of Certified Public Accountants of Greece
Hong Kong	Hong Kong Society of Accountants
India	The Institute of Chartered Accountants of India, The Institute of Cost and Works Accountants of India
Israel	The Institute of Certified Public Accountants in Israel
Jamaica	The Institute of Chartered Accountants of Jamaica
Korea	Korean Institute of Certified Public Accountants
Luxembourg	Ordre des Experts Comptables Luxembourgeois
Malaysia	The Malaysian Association of Certified Public Accountants
Malta	The Malta Institute of Accountants
New Zealand	New Zealand Society of Accountants
Nigeria	The Institute of Chartered Accountants of Nigeria
Norway	Norges Statsautoriserte Revisorers Forening
Pakistan	The Institute of Cost and Management Accountants of Pakistan, The Institute of Chartered Accountants of Pakistan
Philippines	Philippine Institute of Certified Public Accountants
Rhodesia	The Rhodesia Society of Chartered Accountants
Sierra Leone	The Association of Accountants in Sierra Leone
Singapore	Singapore Society of Accountants
South Africa	The National Council of Chartered Accountants (S.A.)
Spain	Instituto de Censores Jurados de Cuentas de Espana
Sri Lanka	The Institute of Chartered Accountants of Sri Lanka
Sweden	Foreningen Auktoriserade Revisorer
Trinidad and Tobago	The Institute of Chartered Accountants of Trinidad and Tobago
Yugoslavia	Yugoslav Association of Accountants and Financial Experts, Social Accounting Service of Yugoslavia
Zambia	Zambia Association of Accountants

After a topic has had adequate study and discussion, it is released for publication as an exposure draft. IASC exposure drafts presently outstanding are

E-8 The Treatment in the Income Statement of Unusual Items and Changes in Accounting Estimates and Accounting Policies.
E-9 Accounting for Research and Development Costs.
E-10 Contingencies and Events Occurring After the Balance Sheet Date.
E-11 Accounting for Foreign Transactions and Translation of Foreign Financial Statements.
E-12 Accounting for Construction Contracts.

Finally, after exposure periods of approximately 6 months' duration and interim restudy of the subject and feedback thereon, final international accounting standards are issued by IASC. Those already completed include

IAS-1 Disclosure of Accounting Policies.

IAS-2 Valuation and Presentation of Inventories in the Context of the Historical Cost System.

IAS-3 Consolidated Financial Statements.

IAS-4 Depreciation Accounting.

IAS-5 Information to Be Disclosed in Financial Statements. ·

IAS-6 Accounting Responses to Changing Prices.

IAS-7 Statement of Changes in Financial Position.

The work of the IASC is without doubt the most promising development so far with respect to setting and achieving a measure of adoption for international accounting standards. Among other developments, the World Federation of Stock Exchanges has adopted a resolution binding members to require conformance with IASC standards in listing agreements. Part of this resolution reads

> Member exchanges of the Federation Internationale des Bourses de Valeurs situated in countries whose professional accountancy bodies are either founder or associate members of the International Accounting Standards Committee should take steps to include in their listing requirements reference to compliance with standards issued by the International Accounting Standards Committee.[2]

The London Stock Exchange has already issued a statement to the effect that such compliance is expected of all listed companies incorporated within the United Kingdom and the Republic of Ireland as well as any incorporated outside the United Kingdom that do not have to conform to United Kingdom accounting standards.[3]

In the United States, the *CPA Letter* of August 1975 reported the following:

> At its July 24 (1975) meeting, the AICPA's Board of Directors reaffirmed its support for the work of the International Accounting Standards Committee and adopted a revised statement on the Institute's position on implementation of international standards. The statement includes the following points:
>
> 1. In order to achieve acceptance in the U.S., international accounting standards will have to be specifically adopted by the Financial Accounting Standards Board.
> 2. If there is no significant difference between an international standard and U.S. practice on a subject, compliance with U.S. GAAP will constitute compliance with the international standard. If there is a significant difference between the two, the Institute will urge the FASB to give early consideration to harmonizing the differences.

[2] *CA Magazine,* January 1975, p. 52.
[3] *CA Magazine,* December 1974, p. 5.

3. Published pronouncements of the IASC will be included in the appropriate volume of *AICPA Professional Standards* with an indication as to whether there are any significant differences between the international standards and U.S. generally accepted accounting principles.
4. The AICPA will continue to encourage government authorities, stock exchanges and the business community to put forth their views on IASC draft proposals.

By every measure of performance, the IASC has major accomplishments to its credit since its foundation only a few years ago. Support for it, professional visibility and respectability, as well as guarded acceptance by nonaccounting members of the international financial community are all still growing. We consider this a good omen indeed.

In a major address at the annual Accountantsdag of the Netherlands Institute in 1976, Sir Henry Benson, the founding chairman of the IASC (1973 to 1976), came forth with the following penetrating observation:

> *From National to International Standards.* The step from national standards to international standards looks to be a short one, but it has grievous pitfalls. Nationals of every country prefer their own ways just as they prefer their own food, wine and customs. There is an even more formidable obstacle; national government. No government will willingly give up its sovereignty and yield the right to decide what will happen in its own country .... In the last three years, it has begun to be realized the world over that acceptable international standards can be prepared. Those that have been written and those now under exposure are far from perfect. They are sometimes too permissive and they allow for alternatives; sometimes they are not sufficiently penetrating, but they will be improved and tightened as the years go by. The mere fact of preparing them has had the merit of pointing out to all of us in different countries how illogical some of our own existing standards are. The work is likely to be important in another way. The profession in many countries has not got the money or the resources in manpower to write standards. These countries are now able to adopt international standards as their own standards which otherwise would have taken them years of work to achieve.

The foregoing quote provides a particularly enlightening perspective on the policy-making activities surrounding international standards. We urge readers not to overlook the environmental issues involved.

INTERNATIONAL ACCOUNTING ORGANIZATIONS

In Chapter 1 we indicate that the growth of attention to international accounting matters has brought about the seemingly inevitable side effect of institutionalization. One of the major operating divisions of the AICPA is its International Practice Division. Since 1962, the American Accounting Association (AAA) has operated International Accounting Education and Research Committees, and in 1976 a formal International Accounting Section was organized for this Association. The AAA International Accounting Section periodically publishes a newsletter entitled *Forum.*

Universities have also done their share in organizational activities. At the University of Illinois at Urbana, the Center for International Education and Research in Accounting operates. Professor V. K. Zimmerman is its director. The Center hosts an annual seminar, publishes the semiannual *International Journal of Accounting,* and issues a series of research monographs.

At the University of Washington in Seattle, the International Accounting Studies Institute (INTASI) is active. Professor G. G. Mueller serves as its director. INTASI publishes bibliographies and research monographs, and it sponsors other multinational accounting research activities.

Professor Edward Stamp is the director of the International Centre for Research in Accounting at the University of Lancaster in Great Britain. The Centre's activities are similar to those of INTASI. In 1976 a Center for International Accounting Development was established at the University of Texas at Dallas. Professor A. J. H. Enthoven is its director. An activities thrust for the Dallas Center was only just evolving at the time of this writing.

At the SEC in the United States, the Office of International Operations oversees and directs multinational accounting activities. Also, the U.S. Internal Revenue Service (IRS), General Accounting Office (GAO), and the audit agencies of the various larger departments (ministries) operate multinational divisions, have offices in various countries abroad, and are con-ascerned with those aspects of multinational accounting related to their respective spheres of influence.

Financial executives groups and organizations of industrial accountants are similarly involved. Their committees, task forces, and researchers pay more and more attention to multinational accounting. Again in the United States, the National Accountants Association (NAA) was the first one to recognize in 1960 the conceptual appeal of the monetary/nonmonetary foreign exchange translation method. As discussed in Chapter 3, this method is the intellectual parent of the methodology required by FASB Statement No. 8. Similarly, the Financial Executives Institute (FEI) has sponsored, through its Research Foundation, a number of multinational accounting research studies. One of its early studies addressed the question of information systems appropriate for the operations of international subsidiary companies.

Multinational accounting institutionalization through national accounting associations, institutes, and other organizations has really occurred in every country characterized by an organized accounting profession—even though the degree of such institutionalization is typically somewhat less than it happens to be in the United States. This is not to say, though, that corresponding efforts are less intense. The Canadian Institute of Chartered Accountants was the first to come forth with a multinational accounting column in its official monthly journal. The Dutch Institute (NIVRA) has a long and strong history of international activities, as do, of course, the Chartered Accountants Institutes in the British Isles.

Aside from multinational dimensions recognized by national bodies and groups, a real thrust has developed over the years from and through various organizations created and operated specifically for various international purposes of accounting. We have already introduced the IASC. Other international accounting organizations are (a) worldwide in purpose and scope, (b) regional in orientation, or (c) devoted to a specific international purpose or objective. In the sections that follow, two world organizations, three regional organizations, and two special-purpose organizations are identified and briefly discussed.

International Congresses of Accountants

The International Congresses of Accountants are probably the most prestigious and most elaborate of all the international accounting meetings. At present these Congresses are held every 5 years. Nearly 3,000 persons from 48 countries registered for the 1957 Congress. That number almost doubled for the 1977 Congress. Congress registrants come from as many as 60 different countries.

The first International Congress of Accountants was held in St. Louis in 1904, the second in Amsterdam in 1926, the third in New York in 1927, the fourth in London in 1933, the fifth in Berlin in 1937, the sixth in London again in 1952, the seventh in Amsterdam in 1957, the eighth in New York again in 1962, the ninth in Paris in 1967, the tenth in Sydney in 1972, and the eleventh in Munich in 1977.

The program pattern of these Congresses now is that general interest papers are presented at plenary sessions, and international summary reports on specific technical topics are read at technical sessions. Underlying each technical summary report are a number of national position papers officially submitted through the professional accounting institutes that send formal delegates to these Congresses. Additionally, many small concurrent discussion groups on technical topics have become a feature of the International Congresses of Accountants since the 1962 New York Congress. These small groups are limited to about 25 participants each and typically meet in the board rooms of major corporations headquartered at the Congress site. The small discussion groups typically prove valuable to Congress participants and serve as a means for greater personal interaction and follow-up on the part of those who travel long distances to attend these Congresses.

Up to the time of the Sydney Congress in 1972, each International Congress of Accountants was pretty much an individual venture. No permanent technical committees stayed at work; there was no carry-forward in secretariat organizations and no continuing exchange of ideas between Congress organizers and/or participants. The Sydney Congress spawned an International Coordination Committee for the Accountancy Profession (ICCAP), which in turn became the progenitor of the International Federation of Accountants (IFAC). One of the objectives of IFAC is to provide needed continuity for the International Congresses. IFAC and its ICCAP predecessor are discussed in the next section.

As a final note on the International Congresses of Accountants, we would like to point out that the proceedings of these meetings and the technical papers presented at them are some of the more important multinational accounting raw materials. They have not only historical value but high levels of descriptive accuracy as well as occasional conceptual depth and analytic potential. (The latter two characteristics are outside the usual specifications for these papers.)

International Federation of Accountants

At the meeting of heads of delegations held during the Tenth International Congress of Accountants in Sydney in 1972, the final report of the International Working Party (appointed during the 1967 Paris Congress) was approved and the International Coordination Committee for the Accountancy Profession (ICCAP) came into being. The following countries were ICCAP members:

Australia	Mexico
Canada	The Netherlands
Federal Republic of Germany	The Philippines
France	United Kingdom and Ireland
India	United States of America
Japan	

The charge to ICCAP was

1. To consider invitations submitted and to select the host country for the next International Congress (after assessing the facilities available, the financial considerations, and other relevant factors) and to give guid-

ance to the country selected in the planning and conduct of the next Congress—the name of the next country selected to be announced on the occasion of each Congress.

2. To maintain a continuing liaison with all participating bodies.
3. To keep under review progress in the development of regional organizations in the assistance being provided by participating bodies in the more developed countries and in the exchange of information between the participating bodies and to report thereon to the periodic Congresses.
4. To recommend such changes for widening or amending the work of ICCAP as may from time to time appear expedient, taking into account recommendations received from the participating bodies and discussions and recommendations submitted at each Congress.
5. To keep under review the need for an international secretariat and the associated problems referred to earlier.

ICCAP held five meetings between 1973 and 1976. It (a) gave guidance to the organizers on the planning and conduct of the 1977 Munich International Congress, (b) examined its own role objectives and organizational structure, and (c) carried out specific studies on professional ethics, professional education and training, and the structure and constitution of regional organizations. At its fifth meeting in Honolulu (February 12–14, 1976), it recommended its own replacement by the International Federation of Accountants (IFAC). This proposal was accepted by the heads of delegations at the Munich Congress.

IFAC is organized into an assembly (replacing the former International Congresses of Accountants' heads of delegations) and an Executive Committee (replacing the former ICCAP). The initial location of the full-time IFAC Secretariat is in New York.

The basic objectives and purposes for IFAC as stated in its Constitution are that it

1. Initiates, coordinates, and guides efforts that have as their goal the achievement of international, technical, ethical, and educational guidelines for the accounting profession and reciprocal recognition of qualifications for practice, and works toward this purpose by establishing appropriate committees and through cooperative effort with regional organizations for implementation.
2. Encourages and promotes the development of regional organizations with common objectives and develops guidelines for the structure and constitution of such regional organizations.
3. Arranges the holding of International Congresses of Accountants so as to

a. Enable members of the accountancy profession to meet one another in an environment that facilitates discussion and the interchange of ideas on accounting and related matters.

b. Direct attention to and inform accountants of developments in selected fields of accountancy thought and practice.

c. Reach broad conclusions on desired common aims.

In its March 19, 1976 issue (p. 9), *The Wall Street Journal* reported on the proposal to create IFAC by saying that IFAC would promote "a coordinated worldwide accounting profession with harmonized standards." In its June 1976 issue, the (Canadian) *CA Magazine* labeled the IFAC proposals a "prospectus for international accounting harmony." Together with IASC, IFAC seems certain to usher in an era of widespread recognition for multinational accounting and never-before-known worldwide cooperation and harmony in matters of professional accounting.

International Conferences on Accounting Education

Even though the International Congresses of Accountants welcome independent practitioners, industrial accountants, and academic accountants alike, their focus essentially remains with the first group. For this reason, an International Accounting Education Conference now piggybacks each International Congress. The Education Conferences are organized from the viewpoint of accounting academics and have a focus on education and research. About 300 persons now attend these International Education Conferences held in conjunction with the quintennial International Congresses.

In 1962, the University of Illinois at Champaign-Urbana was about to establish its Center for International Accounting Education and Research (mentioned earlier in this chapter) when several accounting educators from various countries were preparing to journey to the New York Congress. So the question was asked: why not have a meeting of interested academics immediately before the New York Congress takes place? Thus, the International Conference on Accounting Education first met in 1962 on the campus of the University of Illinois.

The Second Conference was organized in conjunction with the 1967 Paris Congress by the City of London Polytechnic and met at Guild Hall in London. The Third Conference was cosponsored by Sydney University, the University of New South Wales, and Macquarie University, with portions of it taking place on each of the respective three campuses in the Greater

Sydney area. For convenience, the Third Conference was scheduled after the 1972 Congress. The Fourth Conference was organized in West Berlin, preceding the 1977 Munich Congress. Proceedings containing copies of papers presented are available for all International Conferences on Accounting Education held thus far.

An abbreviated version of the program of the 1977 Berlin Conference appears in Exhibit 5 – 1.

EXHIBIT 5 – 1. **Fourth International Conference in Accounting Education**

PROGRAM FOR CONFERENCE PARTICIPANTS

Wednesday, 5th October 1977

10.00 – 12.15	Opening Session
	The Conference will be opened by Dr. Klaus Schutz, Mayor of Berlin
	Introductory lecture by Prof. Louis Perridon, Universitat Augsburg:
	"Development and State of Conventional Accounting Education Systems"
	Moderators:
	—Prof. Adolf J.H. Enthoven, University of Texas at Dallas/United States
	—Michael N. Chetkovich, Haskins & Sells, New York/United States
12.15 – 14.00	Lunch
14.00 – 15.30	Plenary Session
	Introductory lecture by Maurice Lorton, Expert Comptable, Centre de Formation Professionnelle Superieure de Comptabilite de Gestion, Paris/France:
	"New Demands on Educational Systems in Accountancy"
	Moderators:
	—Prof. Santiago Garcia Echevarria, Universidad Complutense, Madrid/Spain
	—Prof. Andre Zund, Hochschule St. Gallen, St. Gallen/Switzerland
	Maurice Lorton will examine the problems of education from the point of view of professional practice in its widest sense and inform participants of an experimental educational system in France.
15.30 – 16.00	Coffee break
16.00 – 17.30	Panel Discussion
	Chairman:
	—Prof. H.M. Schoenfeld, University of Illinois at Urbana/United States
	Panel members:
	—Prof. A.M. Ansari, Accounting Teachers' Association, Karachi/Pakistan
	—Dr. Heinz Bolsenkotter, WIBERA Wirtschaftsberatung, Wirtschaftsprufungsgesellschaft, Dusseldorf/Germany
	—Johan C.C.Harr, Arthur Anderson & Co., Oslo/Norway
	—Prof. Masaatsu Takada, Kobe University/Japan
	—Pro. Klaus von Wysocki, Universitat Munchen/Germany

EXHIBIT 5-1. Continued

Thursday, 6th October 1977

9.00 – 10.00	Plenary Session

Chairman:
— Prof. Reginald Jagerhorn, Svenska Handelshogskolan, Helsingfors
Finland

*"Recent Demands made on Accounting Education by Accountancy
and Audit which can be demonstrated in the Areas of*
a) *Inflation Accounting*
b) *Forecast Audit*
c) *Social Accounting"*

Speakers—authors of the keynotes:
a) — Prof. R.J. Chambers, University of Sydney/Australia
b) — Prof. J.R. Small, University of Edinburgh/Great Britain
c) — Prof. R. Lee Brummet, University of North Carolina/United States

Moderators:
a) *Inflation Accounting*
— Prof. P.E.M. Standish, London Graduate School of Business
Studies, London/Great Britain
— Prof. Otto Wanik, Deutsche Treuhand Gesellschaft,
Wirtschaftsprufungsgesellschaft, Frankfurt/Germany
b) *Forecast Audit*
— Prof. E. de Lembre, Rijksuniversiteit, Gent/Belgium
— R.P. Zimmermann, Touche Ross International New York/
United States
c) *Social Accounting*
— Prof. G. Sieben, Universitat Koln/Germany
— R. Palim, Price Waterhouse, Bruxelles/Belgium

10.00 – 10.30   Coffee break

10.30 – 12.30   Discussion groups
a) *Inflation Accounting*
— in the Lecture Theatre of the Congress Hall with simultaneous
interpretation led by Prof. R.J. Chambers
b) *Forecast Audit*
— in Conference Room 2 in English led by Prof. J.R. Small
— in Conference Room 5 in German led by Prof. Otto Wanik
— in Conference Room 6 in French led by Prof. E. de Lembre
c) *Social Accounting*
— in Conference Room 1 in English led by Prof. R. Lee Brummet
— in Conference Room 3 in French led by Prof. L. Perridon
— in Conference Room 4 in German led by Prof. G. Sieben

12.30 – 14.00   Lunch

14.00 – 15.30   Panel Discussion
Chairman:
— Prof. G.G.M. Bak, Universiteit Tilburg/Netherlands
Panel members:
— Authors of the keynotes and moderators for sections a), b) and c)
as well as the leaders of the discussion groups

EXHIBIT 5-1. Continued

Friday, 7th October 1977

10.30 – 12.30   Closing Session
Summary reports on the results of the Conference:
— Maurice Lorton
— Prof. R. Jagerhorn
— Prof. J.R. Small
— Prof. R. Lee Brummet
Closing speech:
— Prof. K. von Wysocki, Universitat Munchen/Germany

InterAmerican Accounting Association

This is one of the three major regionally organized accounting groupings in the world. It has a Western Hemisphere orientation and thus is comprised of North and South American accounting bodies. Since most nations in the Western Hemisphere have Spanish as their national language, the proceedings of IAA are normally published in Spanish, as are many of the papers presented at the periodic conferences of this group.

Prior to 1975, IAA was known as the InterAmerican Accounting Conference. The 1975 change was a name change only. Consequently, earlier papers and proceedings are referenced under "InterAmerican Accounting Conference."

The First InterAmerican Accounting Conference took place in San Juan, Puerto Rico, in 1949; the Second, in Mexico City in 1951; the Third, in São Palo in 1954; the Fourth, in Santiago, Chile, in 1957; the Sixth, in New York in 1962, the Seventh in Mar del Plata, Argentina in 1965; the Eighth in Caracas in 1967; the Ninth in Bogota in 1970; the Tenth in Punta de Este, Uruguay, in 1972; the Eleventh, in San Juan again in 1974; and the Twelfth, in Vancouver, B.C., Canada, in 1977. The Fifth Conference in the sequence was planned for Havana but had to be canceled because of the then-prevailing political situation in Cuba.

IAA Conferences have a character all their own. They are sincere and fraternal and in keeping with the relative lightheartedness of South American people in general. Many of the Conference activities and technical program sessions are devoted to problems of accounting development rather than to descriptions of existing circumstances. The IAA Conferences clearly identify themselves with Western Hemisphere accounting problems, particularly as they apply to the South American countries.

IAA operates a secretariat located in New York and works through a structure of integrative and technical committees. The headquarters location revolves among the member countries. The administrative activity is similar to that of the UEC (see next section). Continuing technical committees report at the periodic Conferences, and some committee reports and other technical items are published separately. IAA also publishes a quarterly newsletter entitled *Boletín Interamericano de Contabilidad.*

Union Européenne des Expertes Comptables Economiques et Financiers (UEC)

UEC was founded in Paris in November 1951 and has as charter members 12 professional associations of independent (or certified) accountants from Austria, Belgium, France, West Germany, Italy, Luxembourg, the Netherlands, Portugal, Spain, and Switzerland. About 10 years later, professional organizations from the United Kingdom and the Scandinavian countries also joined UEC, as did a Yugoslav group of professional accountants. Thus, UEC represents European accounting interests as contrasted to the more limited European Economic Community (EEC) interests.

Among the world's regional accounting bodies, UEC is the most active as well as the most effective. It has a permanent secretariat in Munich (formerly in Paris) and engages in a continuous program of professional activity. Essentially, UEC works through 12 permanent committees on which membership revolves. These committees prepare reports and present resolutions through the UEC Executive Committee. They also publish recommendations on accounting and auditing matters. There are UEC committees on Auditing Practices, Accounting Practices, Accounting and Bookkeeping Law, Professional Regulations, Terminology, Tax Systems, and Publications.

With respect to publications, UEC operates an extensive quality program. The mainstay of this program is the *Journal UEC,* a quarterly publication in which articles appear simultaneously in the French, German, and English languages. The UEC's *Accounting Dictionary* now covers eight languages (Danish, Dutch, English, French, German, Italian, Portugese, and Spanish) and is in its second edition (1974). The *Auditing Handbook* of the UEC is in its third edition (1974), and there are other publications (such as a book on the principles of valuing a business firm as a whole). Naturally, there are also various UEC brochures and paperbacks.

UEC members meet at Congresses organized every 3 years. The initial UEC Congress took place in Florence and Rome in 1953; followed by the Second UEC Congress in Brussels in 1955, the Third in Nice in 1958, the Fourth in Zurich in 1961, the Fifth in Vienna in 1964, the Sixth in Copenhagen in 1969 and the Seventh in Madrid in 1973. The *Proceedings* of these Congresses yield valuable multinational accounting descriptive materials.

Earlier *Congress Proceedings* are available in the French and German languages only.

Aside from the more formal membership congresses, UEC also operates study conferences and cross-national seminars. The Third UEC Study Conference was held in 1975 in Belgrade and Dubrovnik in Yugoslavia, covering (a) relations between enterprises and accountants under the conditions of modern economy and society; (b) techniques of accountants in the fields of information services, financial management and social aspects of business; and (c) discussion and suggestions for the improvement of the activities of national organizations.

Annual technical seminars (called *Euro-Seminars*) are held on a binational basis—for instance, between Germany and the United Kingdom, Germany and France, the United Kingdom and Scandinavian countries, and Germany and the Netherlands. The Anglo-German Seminar began in 1972 at Wiesbaden and has continued every year since. The Germany-Netherlands Seminar was initiated in Amsterdam in 1973. Full information on these meetings, as well as other UEC matters, including their technical accounting and auditing recommendations, may be obtained from the UEC Secretariat General, 8 Munich 22, Liebigstrasse 22, West Germany.

UEC is a strong international accounting force. It is recognized by authorities of the European Economic Community and the International Federation of Accountants. If nothing else, it has been an agent in producing significantly higher visibility and social and professional status for independent accountants in Europe.

Confederation of Asian and Pacific Accountants (CAPA)

CAPA was initially known as the Asian and Pacific Accounting Convention and later as the Conference of Asian and Pacific Accountants. It is a relative newcomer to the group of international accounting meetings; yet it has established itself quickly and successfully. The first Asian and Pacific Accounting Convention (at that time called the Far East Conference of Accountants) was held in Manila in 1957. The Second Convention followed in Canberra and Melbourne in 1960. The Third took place in Kyoto and Tokyo in 1962 and the Fourth, in New Delhi in 1965. Other conferences in this series are Wellington and Christchurch in 1968; Singapore and Kuala Lumpur in 1970; and Bangkok in 1973. More recently, the Eighth CAPA Conference occurred in Hong Kong in 1976. The ninth is slated for Manila in October, 1979.

The model of the International Congresses is followed closely by CAPA Conventions and Congresses. A student of the technical papers of the various international accounting meetings will easily recognize the names of certain individuals appearing again and again as formal program participants, contributors to discussions, members of arrangements or executive committees, and so on.

Quite naturally, papers delivered at CAPA Congresses focus on Pacific Rim countries and their particular problems. Since available literature on the Asian and Pacific Region is much more limited than multinational accounting literature in general, the CAPA papers are a useful source of information. Moreover, these papers are available in the English language, whereas much of the native literature in the Asian and Pacific Region is available only in the respective native languages.

The organizational overhead of CAPA is small. A permanent Secretariat was created in 1976 with headquarters in New Zealand (to be moved to Hong Kong in 1978). Present executive committee membership includes Australia, Hong Kong, Japan, New Zealand, The Philippines, Singapore, and the United States. CAPA's aim is to develop a coordinated regional accounting profession. Available evidence indicates that it is doing just that.

Organizations with More Restricted Scope

Earlier in this chapter, we referred to various European study groups and seminars arranged loosely under UEC aegis and typically involving two countries at a time. Of course, many other such groups operate throughout the multinational accounting landscape. For instance, the recent significant integration of companies legislation throughout the Scandinavian countries was accomplished in large measure by the work of cross-Scandinavian commissions and committees of which the group drafting the accounting provisions of the respective new companies acts is just one example.

From among the many internationally oriented accounting groups or organizations whose objectives are less global and generally professional but more specifically related to a country or project, we would like to point to the Accountants International Study Group (AISG) and the International Committee for Accounting Cooperation (ICAC) as examples.

Accountants International Study Group. AISG undertakes studies on accounting and auditing subjects as understood and practiced in Canada, the United Kingdom, and the United States. These comparative studies lead to publication of (a) information as collected or (b) recommendations as deemed appropriate. The charge to AISG stipulates "To institute comparative studies as to accounting thought and practice in participating countries, to make reports from time to time which, subject to the prior approval of the sponsoring institutes, would be issued to members of those institutes."

The studies produced by AISG so far include the following:

1. Accounting and Auditing Approaches to Inventories in Three Nations—1968.
2. The Independent Auditor's Reporting Standards in Three Nations—1969.
3. Using the Work and Report of Another Auditor—1969.
4. Accounting for Corporate Income Taxes—1971.
5. Reporting by Diversified Companies—1972.
6. Consolidated Financial Statements—1972.
7. The Funds Statement—1973.
8. Materiality in Accounting—1974.
9. Extraordinary Items, Prior Period Adjustments, and Changes in Accounting Principle—1974.
10. Published Profit Forecasts—1974.
11. International Financial Reporting—1975.
12. Comparative Glossary of Accounting Terms in Canada, the United Kingdom, and the United States—1975.
13. Accounting for Goodwill—1975.
14. Interim Financial Reporting—1975.
15. Going Concern Problems—1975.
16. Independence of Auditors—1976.
17. Audit Committees—1976.
18. Accounting for Pension Costs—1977.

Among the projects that AISG had in progress in 1977, one finds (a) accountants' responsibilities in connection with public offerings of securities, (b) revenue recognition, and (c) related party transactions.

The AISG studies are quite diverse in nature. *International Financial Reporting,* as already described in Chapter 4, is a truly pioneering piece of work. The recommendations put forward in this particular study are original with AISG. In contrast, the *Glossary* has a technical focus on the specific meaning of 160 different accounting, auditing, and financial reporting terms. Several of the other studies are simply syntheses of existing circumstances and therefore serve primarily informational purposes.

In all, the AISG studies have considerable utility for practitioners and academics alike. They are written in a crisp, professional style and therefore are easy to use in connection with professional accounting services, for instance, to multinational clients. From an academic perspective, these studies represent a surprisingly small group of items devoted specifically to the *comparative* multinational study of accounting. The existence of these studies is probably not so widely known as it deserves to be.

International Committee for Accounting Cooperation. In January 1966, the AICPA prepared a statement on accounting aid for developing countries. This policy statement suggested steps that might be taken to initiate a program of professional accounting assistance for the Third World. The statement was submitted to international finance and lending institutions with a request that they designate a representative to serve on a committee that would formulate and help to implement an accounting assistance program. This was done, and ICAC was established by separate charter with the following membership—AICPA, Canadian Institute of Chartered Accountants, Mexican Institute of CPA's, U.S. Agency for International Development, InterAmerican Development Bank, and International Finance Corporation.

Among the formal objectives that ICAC established for itself at its inception is the following statement:

> The benefits of accounting, which are for the most part lacking in developing countries, are urgently needed if economic growth is to be achieved. Failure to understand accountability and other accounting concepts impedes economic progress, not only in those countries which are in the preliminary stages of development but also in those developing countries which have advanced to the maturity stage of economic growth.
>
> The importance of accounting is illustrated by the fact that aggregate national figures must be supported by accurate economic data recorded at the source by industry and commerce. The absence of such economic data often discourages the granting of credit and reduces the flow of essential loan and equity capital from domestic and foreign sources. The success of many economic development programs is also dependent on the existence of accurate and reliable accounting data and the competency and skills of accounting professions. Without reliable information, development programs cannot be realistically formulated, accurately assessed or successfully carried out.

Early in 1967, ICAC began its work with a major study project and an intensive accounting development in Colombia, South America. A blue ribbon report resulted from this project, but its recommendations were never fully implemented due to a lack of available funds.

Since 1967, ICAC has sponsored a number of less ambitious projects, including exchanges of university professors and students, a blueprint for accounting seminars throughout Central and South America, and some publication efforts. The tangible results of ICAC's work have been disappointing. Nevertheless, its continued existence calls attention to one of the most serious continuing multinational accounting problems—namely effective and efficient accounting development in Third World countries.

We pointed out earlier that much money and time are invested daily by numerous professional accountants and their respective national institutions and international organizations toward the goal of greater multinational accounting harmony. Only 20 years ago many of these efforts seemed like mere straws in the wind. Today they are taken very seriously. They command widespread attention, especially from world bodies like the United Nations (see Chapter 10). Cautious optimism is no longer out of place. The momentum of multinational accounting development seems sure to become a major force in accounting as the 20th century draws to a close.

SELECTED REFERENCES

5.1 ARTHUR ANDERSEN & CO., *Accounting Standards for Business Enterprises Throughout the World,* Chicago: Author, 1974, 168 pp.

5.2 BARR, ANDREW, "The International Harmonization of Accounting Principles," *Federal Accountant,* November 1967, pp. 1–17.

5.3 BENSON, SIR HENRY, "The Story of International Accounting Standards," *Accountancy,* July 1976, pp. 34–39.

5.4 CHOI, FREDERICK D. S., "Multinational Financing and Accounting Harmony," *Management Accounting* (U.S.), March 1974, pp. 14–17.

5.5 CONFEDERATION OF ASIAN AND PACIFIC ACCOUNTANTS, *Proceedings* (latest available volume: Hong Kong, 1976).

5.6 COWPERTHWAITE, GORDON H., "Prospectus for International Accounting Harmony," *CA Magazine,* June 1976, pp. 22–24.

5.7 EVANS, THOMAS G., "Can American Accountants Serve Two Masters: FASB and IASC?" *CPA Journal,* January 1976, pp. 6–7. (Also, see response by Mr. Joseph P. Cummings, *CPA Journal,* June 1976, pp. 5–6.)

5.8 FANTL, IRVING L., "Case Against International Uniformity," *Management Accounting* (U.S.), May 1971, pp. 13–16.

5.9 HAUWORTH, WILLIAM P., II, "International Accounting Organizations," *The Arthur Andersen Chronicle,* July 1974, pp. 92–95.

5.10 INTERAMERICAN ACCOUNTING ASSOCIATION, *Proceedings* (latest available volume: Vancouver, B. C., Canada, 1977).

5.11 INTERNATIONAL CONGRESS OF ACCOUNTANTS, *Proceedings* (latest available volume: Munich, 1977).

5.12 INTERNATIONAL ACCOUNTING STANDARDS COMMITTEE, *Work and Purpose of the International Accounting Standards Committee,* London: Author, most recent edition, unpaginated.

5.13 KEOWN, K. C., "Development of Accounting Standards around the World," *Australian Accountant,* April 1968, pp. 193–202.

5.14 KRAAYENHOF, JACOB, "International Challenges for Accounting," *Journal of Accountancy.* January 1960, pp. 34–38.

5.15 MUELLER, GERHARD G., Review of Studies No. 11, 12, 13, and 14 of the Accountants International Study Group, *Accounting Review,* July 1976, pp. 690-93.

5.16 NEDERLANDS INSTITUT VAN REGISTER ACCOUNTANTS, *Storms about Norms* (Technical Proceedings of the 1976 Accountantsdag of NIVRA), Amsterdam: Author, 1976, 83 pp.

5.17 STAMP, EDWARD, "Uniformity in International Accounting Standards?" *Journal of Accountancy,* April 1972, pp. 64–67.

5.18 UEC, *Proceedings* (latest available volume: Madrid, 1973).

5.19 WATT, GEORGE C., "Toward Worldwide Accounting Principles," *CPA Journal.* August 1972, pp. 651-53.

5.20 WILKINSON, THEODORE L., "International Accounting: Harmony or Disharmony." *Columbia Journal of World Business,* March–April 1969, pp. 29–36.

DISCUSSION QUESTIONS

5.1 Deliberate understatement of assets and/or overstatement of known liabilities leads to the creation of so-called "secret reserves." Why are secret reserves frowned upon in Anglo-American financial accounting practice? Do some library research to determine the current status of the use of secret reserves in Swiss financial reporting.

5.2 Some authoritative requirements for the preparation of consolidated financial statements have recently been introduced in Denmark, Germany, Japan, and Sweden. On the other hand, there is still no formal requirement whatsoever for consolidated financial statements in Switzerland. Write a short essay defending the absence of any consolidation requirements from a national set of authoritative financial accounting standards.

5.3 Write and explain three distinct advantages *and* three distinct disadvantages to the conduct of multinational business operations arising from the existing international diversity of financial accounting standards and practices.

5.4 Write a concise essay in defense of efforts aimed at establishing international financial accounting standards. Within your essay, list as many specific reasons as you can muster.

5.5 Draw a flow chart of the basic working procedures of the International Accounting Standards Committee. On the basis of your chart, can you suggest any improvements as far as IASC procedures are concerned?

5.6 International Accounting Standard No. 3 covers the subject of consolidated financial statements. Compare IAS No. 3 with counterpart generally accepted accounting principles in the United States and list any significant differences between the two.

5.7 From whatever library resources available to you, compile a list of research monographs published by one of the three academic centers of international accounting (at the University of Illinois, the University of Washington, or the University of Lancaster) and comment upon the nature of the research in evidence. Is it multinational in nature? What distinguishes it from other accounting research—e.g., the AICPA or the FASB? Where would you look for titles of recently completed Ph.D. dissertations in the field of multinational accounting?

5.8 Look up the latest published report of the American Accounting Association's Committee on International Accounting. Does this report make a contribution to unresolved multinational accounting issues? Defend yourself adequately—whether in the affirmative or the negative.

5.9 Review a set of papers delivered at a recent International Congress of Accountants. How are these papers organized? Are there any apparent themes? Who should benefit the most from the availability of these papers?

5.10 Write a brief progress and current status report on the International Federation of Accountants (IFAC). You may have to consult current editions of the *Accountants' Index* and the CCH *Accounting Articles* or make inquiry of a national institute of professional accountants— e.g., the AICPA in the United States or the NIVRA in the Netherlands.

5.11 Suppose the International Conference on Accounting Education were to organize itself as a service organization of accounting educators worldwide. What organizational format might be appropriate for such a purpose? How would such a structure relate to national academic accounting organizations—e.g., the American Accounting Association? List five merits and five demerits for a possible worldwide organization of accounting academics.

5.12 CAPA, the InterAmerican Accounting Association, and the UEC are major regional professional organizations in accounting. Compare and contrast their respective forms of organization and scope of activities. Which of the three do you deem the most effective? Why?

5.13 Read and briefly critique a current issue of the *Journal UEC*. How would you compare its quality with a recent issue of the *Journal of Accountancy?* How does it compare to the University of Illinois' *International Journal of Accounting and Research?* Also, list three journals not specifically devoted to accounting in which one is likely to find articles dealing with multinational accounting issues. Can all of the foregoing be considered "authoritative" in the multinational accounting field?

5.14 Some well-informed professional accountants in Canada, the United Kingdom, and the United States are advocating the abandonment of the Accountants' International Study Group—largely on grounds that this group has accomplished its primary mission in drawing widespread attention to multinational accounting issues. Moreover, a number of observers feel that there has been undue proliferation (and therefore, among other things, unwarranted expenditure of resources) in international meetings, conferences, and organizations of accountants. Assume that you are a member of the AICPA's International Practice Executive Committee. How would you vote on the question of continuing support for the AISG? Why?

5.15 For a friend interested in a historical perspective on and current status of international standards for financial accounting and reporting, prepare a briefly annotated list of 10 "basic" references.

ANNOTATED TEACHING MATERIALS

Almost no formally prepared cases or teaching notes are available in the area of international standards and organizations. Hence, it is suggested that the subject matter of this chapter be used as a springboard for the assignment of student (research) papers.

5.1 *Accounting Principles Effects on Business Decisions.* There is some discussion in the chapter about the differential effects of accounting standards and principles upon business decisions. These effects seem particularly pronounced in multinational business operations.

As a term project, one might undertake a listing of 5 to 10 major differences in accounting principles between two or more countries. After identifying these differences, a numerical illustration could be constructed on how they affect a particular financing, merger, or new investment decision. After analysis, the question might be addressed on whether United States-based multinational companies have an advantage or a disadvantage internationally over competitor companies based in other countries when it comes to differential effects of applying national accounting standards and practices.

5.2 *Minimum Threshold for International Accounting Standards.* In the United States, a large number of administrative and professional standards and rules constitute the set of "generally accepted accounting principles." Similar sets of accounting rules and requirements have been established in other countries.

What is the minimum foundation, in terms of accounting standards and principles, upon which a separately distinct set of financial statements might be erected? Taking, as a starting point, all standards issued so far by IASC, identify the additional pronouncements needed before a professional auditor could say, in a report, that the financial statements under audit are in conformity with "international accounting standards promulgated by IASC."

5.3 *Securities Prices and Multinational Business Operations.* Market prices of corporate securities ultimately signal the success or failure of an enterprise in a free or administered market economy. Such market prices dictate a firm's cost of capital, which, in turn, allocates new capital availabilities in money markets and regulates individual firm investments.

If multinational operations tend to strengthen market prices of a firm's securities, international business might expand further, and even greater urgency of international financial accounting standards will arise. On the other hand, the international standards issue is less acute if increasing volumes of multinational business tend to affect securities prices adversely.

Using Ref. 4.18 (Stich) and more recent articles by Koher (*Michigan Business Review,* etc.), analyze the available empirical evidence and reach a conclusion about the effects of multinational business operations upon market prices of a firm's securities.

5.4 *Governmental Role in Setting Accounting Standards.* References appear throughout this book on the fact that political processes have a major influence upon setting accounting standards in Code Law countries. One also observes a growing role of government in the setting of financial accounting policies in the Common Law countries.

Would it be desirable to have governments somehow involved in setting international accounting standards? Would international agencies or organizations be the standard setters? Is the international accounting standards machinery more likely to remain in the private sector than any national accounting policy-making process? Since no literature is available on this issue, premises have to be carefully established, issues identified, and conclusions carefully reasoned.

5.5 *Regional Accounting Developments.* Among the Americas, Asia, and Europe, the chapter identifies three major regional centers of accounting development. Is the regional focus compatible with the international standards movement? Should one be able to expect closer harmonization between the development of regional accounting standards and international accounting standards than between the latter and individual national standards and practices? Is a three-tier system evolving? Careful analysis of (quite recent) regional developments in multinational accounting will contribute significantly to the fuller understanding of the international ramifications of accounting as a whole.

Chapter 6
EEC ACCOUNTING

The present chapter concludes our excursion into the *financial* accounting dimensions of multinational accounting. We have explored technical problems such as consolidation of financial statements, translation of foreign currencies in accounts, inflation accounting, and the many ramifications of transnational financial reporting in Chapters 3 and 4. Chapter 5 is devoted to a cursory description of the existing worldwide diversity of financial accounting standards and practices, the case for international accounting standards, and the institutions and organizations fostering the international standards movement.

Now we wish to provide some insights on a few actual accounting situations in selected countries. Our aim is to give the reader a realistic, albeit abbreviated, appreciation of what goes on in financial accounting in a number of real-world situations.

For this purpose, we chose the EEC countries because they represent several interesting characteristics. On the one hand, accounting in the nine EEC member countries is as diverse as anywhere else; yet, at the same time, strong (and costly) efforts are underway to bring about accounting harmonization within the EEC. This harmonization effort gives the present chapter its institutional focus.

A second element in our choice of the EEC countries was the relatively easy accessibility of descriptive accounting information about all the EEC countries and financial statements and annual reports from companies domiciled in these countries. Moreover a substantial amount of the relevant materials is available in the English language. It should thus be relatively simple to expand the leads provided in this chapter into more comprehensive study and/or research.

Finally, the current economic and political potency of the EEC taken as a whole keeps it in the limelight of current news. Without detracting from the relative importance of developments in Asia, South America, or the OPEC countries, the treatment of multinational accounting would simply be incomplete without separate and specific attention to the EEC situation. Regional harmonization of accounting may be more feasible now than worldwide harmonization. If the EEC experiment works, it may well become a model for other geographic regions or groupings of countries. We can ill afford to overlook this possibility when it comes to multinational accounting.

The organization of the material for this chapter begins with a general description of the EEC accounting environment and then proceeds to short descriptions of the accounting practices prevailing in each of the EEC member countries. The descriptive sections are followed by a discussion of the accounting harmonization efforts under way within the EEC. Finally, some space is devoted to the prospects for creating the so-called "European Company"—a proposal aimed at incorporating companies on a community-wide basis rather than in one or more individual member countries.

THE GENERAL EEC ACCOUNTING ENVIRONMENT

Central Europe is generally regarded as the cradle of the modern world's commercial and industrial business system. The developments that brought about this business system stretch over centuries and have come from many different impulses. But in different ways and at different times, each of the EEC member countries has participated in these developments, and traditions do not change easily. In Chapter 2, we explored a number of the environmental characteristics that tend to influence accounting development and practice. Given historical backgrounds, impediments to changing traditions, and responsiveness of accounting developments to environmental conditions and influences, it is little wonder that the general EEC accounting environment is different from that found in North America, South America, Asia, or elsewhere.

Accounting Policy-Making

In the United States, financial accounting policies are developed and determined in the private sector. Interested parties furnish financial support to the FASB, which, in turn, sets the standards and rules according to which financial accounting is practiced and financial information is conveyed to third parties. Stock exchanges, courts of law, and the accounting profession at large recognize the authority of the independent FASB. The SEC, as the major Federal Governmental agency concerned with financial accounting, has specifically recognized the authority of the FASB in its Accounting Series Release No. 150.

Inside the EEC, the situation differs substantially. While the Dutch establish their accounting policies much as is done in the United States (even though through different instrumentalities—for instance, with direct inputs from their labor movement), the systems in France, Germany, and Italy rely predominantly on political processes. In other words, financial accounting policy-making in these three countries occurs largely in the public sector. Government ministries typically with only modest inputs from the accounting profession, propose laws that specify all needed accounting rules. Typical political processes then modify whatever proposals are at hand, and eventually corresponding national laws are ratified and put into effect. The process is analogous to bringing about and periodically amending Medicare legislation at the Federal level in the United States.

A hybrid system is found in the British Isles. Successive companies acts specify general accounting standards and financial reporting requirements, with some enforcement responsibility vested in the U.K. Board of Trade. The accounting profession makes formal inputs to each new companies act that comes along. In addition, though, the British profession on its own develops specific practice-related accounting standards and principles. This occurs through their Accounting Standards Steering Committee (ASSC), which is empowered to bind the members of all professional British accounting institutes. Hence a private/public mixture of financial accounting policy-making is found in the United Kingdom.

Overall, wide diffusion characterizes accounting policy processes within EEC member countries. The majority of inputs utilized probably comes from nonaccounting sources.

Public Interest in Financial Reporting

The degree of the public's interest in accounting and financial reporting is largely a function of the degree of public ownership of corporate securities. The securities markets in the United Kingdom compare in depth and breadth with those in the United States. While somewhat smaller, the Dutch securities markets are also sufficiently broad to garner sustained public interest in accounting and financial reporting practices of companies domiciled in Holland.

But the situation is fundamentally different in the rest of the EEC. Even in the larger countries like France, Germany, and Italy, there exist only very thin public markets for corporate equities. Companies finance most of their long-term money capital needs through bank credits. Those corporate equities that are outstanding are held largely by banks and other financial institutions, either in trust or for their own accounts. In Germany, for instance, banks are the largest ownership group of corporate securities. In turn, banks typically have access to inside financial information about their clients. This negates most of their interest in public corporate financial reporting.

Public interest is a key driving force behind sound financial accounting and wide open corporate financial disclosure. In the absence of this force, especially when politicians have the responsibility for setting accounting policies, accounting progress often languishes.

Professional Auditors

Because of reasons already cited, the number of professional auditors in relation to the total population base and gross national product is roughly comparable between the United Kingdom and the United States. In Germay and the Netherlands professional auditors number only a few thousand. In France and Italy there are even fewer. If independent audit requirements were significantly increased in the Continental EEC countries, there would still simply not be enough professional auditors to shoulder any significantly larger professional audit activities (at least not in the short run).

What happens in countries like Belgium, France, and Italy is that companies law typically requires only the appointment of statutory auditors (*Commissaires aux Comptes*). These statutory auditors are not necessarily qualified independent accountants—they quite often are shareholders of the companies concerned. Sometimes statutory auditor appointments are honorary. Audits carried out by *Commissaires aux Comptes* are not opinion audits in the Anglo-Saxon sense. They are typically very general reviews, often based for the most part on interviews with company management directed at coincidence between books actually kept and amounts shown in financial statements and observance of a company's charter provisions and bylaws.

Larger companies, and usually those seeking initial listings of their securities on stock exchanges, must submit to opinion audits by professionally qualified independent auditors. But these cases are still relatively rare in Continental Europe. Moreover, the uninitiated often have difficulties distinguishing between statutory and opinion audits and the qualifications of persons or companies respectively engaged.

Another noteworthy differentiation occurs in that firms of auditors in the British Isles and the Netherlands are organized as unlimited partnerships much as is the case in North America. In the rest of the EEC countries, professional service corporations are the normal format of auditor organizations. Beyond that, banks often own the majority interest in professional auditing service corporations (e.g., Germany). This does not mean, however, that German professional auditors belonging to a majority bank-owned auditing service corporation are any less independent than their Anglo-Saxon or Dutch colleagues. Great pains are usually taken to restrict such bank interests to financial aspects only, leaving all operational controls in the hands of a board of directors comprised entirely or largely of Certified Public Accountants. Again, the existence of professional auditing service corporations in Europe has given rise to all manner of unfortunate misunderstandings.

Financial Accounting Orientation

EEC accounting, most notably again in countries other than Ireland, the Netherlands, and the United Kingdom, permit or require some basic accounting approaches that seem strange or antiquated to accountants elsewhere.

One example is the strong reliance on statutory provisions rather than on fair presentation as a basis for evaluation of a financial report. As we have seen in Chapter 4, the typical German short-form auditor's report is anchored upon the "sea of law" rather than fairness of presenting results of business operations and financial position. This legal viewpoint might become buried in details without regard for the overall synergistic effects produced by considerations of fairness aspects. We do not wish to imply any qualitative differences here—we just observe that a different perspective guides the preparation of financial statements.

A similar difference is produced by continued strong orientation of the financial reporting process to *creditor protection* rather than *investor decision-making*. The creditor protection viewpoint favors the financial position statement over the earnings statement, parent company only statements to consolidated group statements, and secret reserves over sharp annual income determination. One of the consequences of the emphasis on creditor protection in some EEC financial reporting practices is a comparatively conservative orientation to all matters involving financial accounting.

Yet another example of a general orientation of EEC accounting is the rather pervasive influence of tax laws. All countries have to contend with this factor to a greater or lesser degree—as illustrated by the U.S. legislative edict that LIFO pricing of inventories is only available for tax purposes as long as it is simultaneously used for financial reporting purposes. In many Continental EEC countries (e.g., Belgium, France, and Germany) the tax law infringement upon financial accounting reaches much further. Most income and expense items in these countries must be treated the same for both book and tax purposes. This naturally creates formidable obstacles to effective decision-related accounting development.

Higher Education and Accounting

In 1977, approximately 50,000 persons received a baccalaureate degree with a major or concentration in accounting from an institution of higher learning in the United States. A contrasting phenomenon is the complete lack of undergraduate accounting majors in EEC countries. Accounting courses are taught in commerce curricula in the United Kingdom, undergraduate auditing courses are taught widely in the Netherlands, and some accounting theory courses creep into undergraduate university curricula in Germany. About the only study concentrations in accounting available are at the M.S. or higher graduate level—and then only in a highly theoretical format.

Large firms of Chartered Accountants in the British Isles hire only university graduates as beginning staff accountants, but these graduates come mostly from liberal arts backgrounds. In Germany, a graduate degree is a prerequisite for public accounting certification, but this usually means degrees in economics, law, or business administration in general. The most frequent way to a professional accounting certificate in most of the EEC countries still is high school graduation followed by a long period of practical training in a public accounting firm concurrent with night school classes and successive examinations administered by the local institute of professional accountants.

As the foregoing implies, full-time faculty appointments in accounting are relatively rare at EEC universities. In turn, this affects the output of academic research, professional development courses and seminars, etc., from institutions of higher learning. The output that does occur, moreover, is often highly theoretical. In fact, academic and professional accounting seem to be clearly on different wavelengths as far as the EEC is concerned (with the notable exception of the Netherlands and the partial exception of the United Kingdom). Less restrictive academic practices would surely benefit the profession at large in the EEC.

Indigenous Problems

Several special conditions and/or situations are present in EEC countries without counterparts elsewhere. Naturally, special accounting solutions are required for them. We have already mentioned, for instance, that quite a number of EEC-based multinational enterprises have very high percentages of their total worldwide sales outside the country of domicile. This means greater attention to multinational accounting problems in everyday accounting and reporting practices.

An even more intriguing problem is created by the so-called *binationality* of several EEC enterprises. Shell and Unilever are both binational between the United Kingdom and the Netherlands. At Shell, binational corporate profits are shared on a 60:40 basis, whereas at Unilever it is a 50:50 basis. In the Shell case, dividend equalization funds have to be created in order to allow for roughly equal dividend payments to stockholders in the two domicile countries.

The Dunlop-Pirelli binational agreement is different again. Each parent company is entitled to a 40 to 49 percent equity stake in the present or future subsidiaries of the other partner. Somewhat similarly, the Belgian-German binational creature, Gevaert-Agfa (from the German viewpoint, it is Agfa-Gevaert), allows each parent to take up to a 50 percent participation in the other's affiliates or subsidiaries. In both the Dunlop-Pirelli and Gevaert-Agfa binational structures, unequal national dividends are possible, as well as peculiar financial statement consolidations, liabilities measurements, and so on.

A 1976 combination brought together the United Kingdom's British Cavenham Foods and France's Générale Alimentaire. This combination is probably the biggest challenge to local and multinational food firms that Europe has ever experienced. Some attendant accounting complications will become clear when the underlying organizational entanglement is considered. Originally, Cavenham had a French subsidiary, FIPP, which was merged with Générale Alimentaire. Subsequent to that, Cavenham attempted to increase its stake in Alimentaire above 50 percent. This was disallowed by the French government.

As it turned out, a Mr. Goldsmith, Cavenham's managing entrepreneur, also owned 30 percent of a French holding company, Générale Occidentale. Occidentale owned, among other things, 19 percent of Cavenham and 68 percent of Anglo-Continental, a London bank, which, in turn, owned 20 percent of Cavenham. Several other companies that were majority-controlled by Occidentale also held interests in Alimentaire.

To settle the combination, Occidentale bought out all remaining individual French investors in Alimentaire. Then it conveyed 52 percent of its Alimentaire equity holding to Cavenham. Cavenham issued new shares to Occidentale (for the Alimentaire equity), which increased Occidentale's percentage stake in Cavenham to 34.8 percent, while Anglo-Continental ended up with 16.2 percent of Cavenham (its former 20 percent stake diluted by the new share issue). In this fashion the French Ministry of Finance was satisfied that Cavenham was French-owned, and Alimentaire, of course, turned into a controlled subsidiary of a United Kingdom firm.[1] Accountants, as the reader can well imagine, are very much a part of these binationality "schemes."

As a final example, we refer to the strong labor union participation in European business affairs. Unions elect representatives to German boards of directors, and they formally occupy seats on accounting policy-making

[1]*Business Europe*, July 2, 1976, pp. 211–12.

councils in the Netherlands. Among many other things, this has led to relatively sophisticated social responsibility accounting in a majority of the EEC countries. As a specific illustration, German companies report revenues on a "value-added" basis, separately disclose additions and retirements for all fixed asset categories, and also disclose research and development costs openly. So there are some instances in which EEC accounting clearly leads the rest of the world.

SPECIFIC EEC ACCOUNTING PRACTICES

We now turn our attention to the bookkeeping, accounting, and financial reporting situations within each individual EEC member country. Greater detail on this subject matter is available from many sources. For instance, the "Big Eight" international accounting firms publish and continuously update booklets on individual countries (up to 100), covering general conditions of doing business there—including descriptions of prevailing accounting practices and requirements. Professional accounting institutes in the member countries are likewise publishing monographs and comparative studies on each other's accounting, auditing, and financial reporting situations. EEC administrative agencies in Brussels are also good information sources on EEC accounting. If one adds to the foregoing the regularly appearing descriptive articles about EEC countries in accounting periodicals, one has no shortage of source materials and a lot of duplication to wade through.[2]

Belgium

Bookkeeping and accounting matters are generally based on the provisions of the *Commercial Code*, which broadly follows the French *Code de Commerce*. A law enacted on July 17, 1975 regulates the form and content of accounting records and provides for the preparation of annual accounts.

In April 1973, the Central Council of the Economy in Belgium issued a proposal for a Belgian National Accounting Plan (*Plan Comptable Général Belge*). This proposal became a binding Royal Decree on October 8, 1976. It is closely patterned after the French National Accounting Plan and is part of a reform movement seeking to upgrade local practices before Community-wide directives take effect. The *Collège National des Experts Comptables* favors the adoption of national uniform accounting for Belgium and, in fact, originally recommended the new Plan in 1964.

[2]The most concise reference available is Price Waterhouse & Co., Europe, *Accounting Principles and Practices in European Countries,* Revised (London: Author, 1976), 104 pp.

Accounting standards and principles in the Anglo-Saxon sense do not exist in Belgium except for the 1975 and 1976 legislation just referred to. Annual financial statements are the sole responsibility of the directors, who can be held liable for overvaluations and, therefore, broadly insist on the most conservative accounting possible. A specific requirement stipulated by company law is that liabilities guaranteed by effective liens must be shown separately from nonguaranteed liabilities.

Since tax laws contain a great many accounting rules and since there are no countervailing generally accepted accounting principles, tax rules have tended to become standard practices. Most companies prepare only one set of financial statements for both financial and taxation purposes, mainly because certain tax provisions are available only if the procedures in question are used all around. The dominance of tax accounting practices in Belgium was referred to earlier.

One special Belgian reporting obligation is to Works Councils (*Conseils d' Entreprises*). These councils were established under a law dated September 20, 1948. Through a Royal Decree dated November 27, 1973, they must regularly receive economic and financial information about companies. This includes financial statements and items relating to the competitive position of the enterprise in its markets, production and productivity, budgeting and cost calculations, expenses relating to personnel programs, costs of scientific research, etc. In actual practice, financial reports to Works Councils are not so encompassing as a reading of the Royal Decree would suggest.

Companies whose securities are publicly traded must appoint a *Reviseur d' Entreprises* as auditor (in contrast to the typical *Commissaire aux Comptes* appointment). Such a reviseur must be selected from the list of members of the respective institute, which only comprises qualified accountants.

Denmark

With its 1973 companies legislation (effective January 1, 1974), Denmark joined the nations that conduct their financial accounting affairs in a modern investor decision-making context. This was done by abandoning the more conservative tax and creditor protection viewpoint that prevailed until then. The new Danish companies law is based largely on the recommendations of a joint committee of representatives from all the Nordic countries (see, for instance, Per V. A. Hanner, "Towards a 'Nordic Companies Act'," *UEC Journal*, January 1971). In December 1973, the Danish Institute (*Foreningen*) established an accounting standards committee charged to make recommendations on "good accounting practices." Hence financial accounting policy-making in Denmark is now similar to the process in force in the Netherlands and the United Kingdom.

The accounting requirements of the June 4, 1973, Danish companies law are numerous and comprehensive. As they apply to corporations and privately listed companies, they include, among others, the following provisions:

1. Annual financial statements shall be prepared in accordance with "good accounting practices" not only as regards the valuation of financial statement amounts but also the disclosure and form and descriptions of financial statements.
2. Lower of cost or market valuation rules shall apply for current assets; write-ups above cost are allowed under special circumstances if consistent with "good accounting practices."
3. Fixed assets are subject to maximum valuation at cost.
4. Treasury shares shall be shown in the balance sheet as an asset with no value. If such shares were acquire legally within the last two fiscal years, they may be shown at amounts not exceeding acquisition cost.
5. Purchased goodwill may be recorded, subject to a minimum 10 percent annual amortization.
6. Research and development costs may be capitalized if they represent significant and realizable values for a company, with a minimum annual amortization of 20 percent.
7. Marketable securities may be valued at bid prices on the balance sheet date.
8. Full disclosure shall be provided in all annual financial statements. This includes tax assessments on fixed assets, nonrecognized deferred tax liabilities, etc.

The Danish *Foreningen* has slightly more than 1,000 members. Their Auditing Standards Committee has achieved significant success with its recommendations on auditing standards and procedures. All companies must have at least one auditor (not necessarily certified), and all quoted companies must have at least two auditors, one of whom must be certified. Special provisions apply to holding companies, court-directed special examinations (e.g., in bankruptcies), and so on.

France

The French Republic is the world's leading advocate of national uniform accounting. The first formal *Plan Comptable* was approved by the Ministry of National Economy in September 1947. A revised *Plan* came into effect in

1957, and yet another revision is pending at this writing in 1977. The existing *Plan* provides

1. A national uniform chart of accounts.
2. Definitions and explanations of terminology.
3. Explanations, where necessary, of the form of entries and which accounts to debit and/or credit in the recording of special events and transactions.
4. Principles of accounting measurements (valuation).
5. Standard forms for financial statements.
6. Acceptable cost accounting methods.

A law dated December 28, 1959 requires the progressive application of the *Plan Comptable*. A further decree dated April 13, 1962 establishes committees for various industries to adapt the *Plan* to the needs of those industries. Specific industry applications of the *Plan Comptable* have meanwhile been made mandatory by the government and cover over 50 trades and industries.

The mandatory use of the National Uniform Chart of Accounts is not really burdensome to French enterprises since the *Plan Comptable* has found wide acceptance in practice and since all academic training in France is based on it. Moreover, various schedules required for income tax returns are also based on the official National Chart of Accounts.

The French Professional Institute (*L'Ordre National des Experts Comptables*) and the National Council of Accountancy (*Conseil National de la Comptabilité*), composed of high public officials and prominent members of the accounting profession, industry, commerce, labor unions, and others chosen for competence in accounting matters, issue opinions and recommendations on accounting principles needed to implement and expand the *Plan Comptable*. These opinions and recommendations, however, are *not* mandatory.[3] They cover issues such as

1. Sources and uses of funds statements.
2. Accounting for research and development costs.
3. Treatment of value-added tax.
4. Income and expenditure allocations.
5. Off-balance sheet agreements.
6. Investment tax credit treatment.
7. EEC agricultural transactions.
8. Leasing.
9. Profit-sharing plans.
10. Accounting for welfare benefits granted to employees.

[3]See especially J.H. Beeny, *European Financial Reporting—France* (London: Institute of Chartered Accountants in England and Wales, 1976), 290 pp. mimeographed.

The French *Code de Commerce* was last revised as of July 24, 1966. This revision did not affect the *Plan Comptable,* but it did require additional financial disclosures from companies and tightened requirements for statutory auditors. Also noteworthy is the 1968 advent of the *Commission des Opérations de Bourse* (COB). Among other things, COB requires initial opinion audits of companies seeking to list their securities on a French stock exchange. The COB's aim is to play a significant role in the improvement of French financial reporting.

Statutory auditors (*Commissaires aux Comptes*) must be appointed for all French companies with capital in excess of F300,000. The *Commissaires* have their own institute and, since April 1, 1975, only listed members may be appointed as statutory auditors. The more highly qualified *Experts Comptables* (numbering about 4,000 in all) may act as *Commissaires* but work primarily on opinion audits like those required by the COB or larger French enterprises seeking capital in the international capital markets. If the present French government is indeed able to expand equity markets in France and make Paris into more of an international financial center, significant growth of the *Expert Comptables'* profession may be expected.

Germany

West German financial accounting is marked by three critical dimensions: (a) principles of proper bookkeeping (*ordnungsmässige Buchführung*) are basically determined by tax laws and regulations, (b) the German Commercial Code sets up requirements for procedures such as the physical count of inventories and other assets and the annual preparation of financial statements, and (c) the Stock Corporation Law of 1965 governs basic accounting principles (e.g., valuation) for incorporated business entities.

Unless kept in accordance with very specific tax accounting principles, accounting records can be rejected by tax authorities as a basis for taxation. The authorities are then entitled to estimate in whole or in part any taxable income to the best of their ability. This is a powerful incentive to keep *all* accounting records on a basis acceptable to tax authorities.

The *Commercial Code* provisions are too general to be of much use in a modern economic system. Their influence on present-day accounting standards and principles is nil.

The regulations embodied in the 1965 Stock Corporation Law are pervasive, however. Among other things,

1. Fixed assets are to be stated at cost less appropriate depreciation.
2. Current assets are to be priced at the lowest of cost, net realizable value, or replacement price.
3. Intangible assets may be capitalized only if acquired from third parties.

4. All liabilities including unrealized losses must be provided for fully.
5. Unrealized profits may not be recognized.

The German Institute (over 3,000 members) makes recommendations (interpretations?) on accounting standards and principles anchored in the corresponding provisions of the Stock Corporation Law. For example, the following apply:

1. Consolidation requirements exclude foreign subsidiaries.
2. Minimum amortization of purchased goodwill is at 20 percent per year.
3. Pension liabilities are not always fully recognized.
4. Some deferred charges must be fully written off against income in the year in which they are incurred.
5. Income tax allocation is not recognized since tax basis amounts are typically reported in published financial statements.
6. Retained earnings are typically carried in some form of disclosed reserve accounts.

Published German financial statements are comparable in scope and disclosure to Anglo-Saxon statements. However, most financial statements of German companies carry only one or two perfunctory "notes" (one of which typically covers the 30-year-old "equalization of burdens act"). The essence of disclosure occurs in the *Management Report* which accompanies each set of financial statements and which is covered by the auditor's opinion insofar as it elaborates the financial statements. Much of the contents of the *Management Report*, as well as the requirement for examinations of financial statements by independent public accountants, is anchored in the August 15, 1969 Corporate Publicity Law. This law covers companies falling under at least two of the following conditions:

1. A German statutory balance sheet total exceeding DM125 million.
2. Annual sales exceeding DM250 million.
3. Average monthly number of employees during the year exceeding 5,000.

In Germany all statutory auditor appointments must go to Certified Public Accountants (*Wirtschaftsprüfer*). Some larger closely held companies also employ independent auditors. Educational requirements to become a CPA in Germany are probably the highest worldwide. Needless to say, entry to the profession is very restricted in Germany.

Italy

The Italian situation is so fluid that general statements about it are very difficult. Hence it seems best to rely on an expert for comment (Michael Lafferty, pp. 194 – 195):

The accounts of Italian companies are prepared primarily for tax purposes and are consequently of little value to investors. This unfortunate state of affairs arises from the mutual distrust between taxpayers and the authorities. The tax authorities have compiled data on expected net profit percentages and these they apply to declared turnover to measure whether declared profits meet their criteria. On the other hand, companies frequently underdeclare their profits in order that in the ensuing negotiation process they are able to concede a certain amount without incurring a disproportionate tax liability .

The lack of sophistication in Italian accounting cannot, however, be attributed entirely to the tax authorities. The absence of any sizable and demanding body of shareholders has resulted in companies regarding annual accounts as primarily fiscal documents and this attitude is enforced by the many accounting rules in tax law which are now standard accounting practice in Italy.

Italian accounting anomalies are many and varied and include the omission of sales, understatement of assets (especially inventories) and the introduction of fictitious liabilities. Secret bank accounts are not unusual. While opinions differ as to whether many Italian companies keep more than two sets of books, an additional set could merely comprise a series of adjustments to the official accounts to eliminate fictitious entries or to incorporate sales or other income not entered therein .

Corresponding figures for the previous year are not required; nor need financial statements be consistent from year to year .

No reference is made to consolidated accounts in the law and very few companies consolidate.

Against this background, a real breakthrough occurred with laws published in June 1974 and March 1975 that provide for the establishment of a committee to control companies quoted on Italian stock exchanges. The committee is known as CONSOB (*Commissione Nazionale per le Societa e la Borsa*).

CONSOB is similar in concept to the U.S. SEC. Its aim is to bring a degree of credibility to financial statements of Italian companies. It proposes to do this through the requirement of opinion audits for publicly held companies. The appointment and eligibility of auditing firms is to be strictly controlled by CONSOB, and each audit appointment is to be submitted to CONSOB for approval. CONSOB also has authority over accounting and auditing standards to be applied. For instance, it may require the preparation of consolidated financial statements.

One interesting feature of the new legislation is that auditors' appointments vary from 1 year for the very large companies (in excess of 50 billion lira of legal capital), to 2 years for companies with a capital between 10 and 50 billion lira, 3 years for all other companies, and 4 years for credit companies and institutions. All appointed auditors may act for no longer than a maximum of 9 years. Thereafter, at least 5 years must elapse before the same auditors can be reappointed. This is the first known statutory system for independent auditor rotation.

The organized Italian accounting bodies are the College of Accountants and Commercial Experts, the Order of Graduates in Economics and Commerce, and the Official Auditors of Accounts (*Sindaci*). The first body offers a high school qualification and the second, a university degree. To become inscribed on the register of the Official Auditors of Accounts, a person must have (a) Italian citizenship and (b) at least 5 years' experience in a recognized professional organization as a lawyer, accountant, etc., functioning as a director, statutory auditor, or administrative manager with a corporation having a legal capital base of at least 50 million lira. For university graduates with degrees in economics and/or commerce, the term is reduced to 3 years. None of the Italian professional bodies have issued pronouncements on accounting or auditing standards.

Aside from the new CONSOB requirements, all limited liability companies with a capital of at least 1 million lira are required by the Civil Code to submit to annual statutory audits.

Republic of Ireland

The Irish Companies Act is rather similar to United Kingdom companies law in that it does not set forth specific matters of accounting principles beyond that "every balance sheet of a company shall give a true and fair view of the state of affairs of the company as at the end of the financial year, and any profit and loss account of a company shall give a true and fair view of the profit or loss of the company for the financial year."

The Institute of Chartered Accountants in Ireland, with a membership of approximately 3,000, is a member of the Accounting Standards Steering Committee for the British Isles. ASSC has issued a string of Statements of Standard Accounting Practice, each of which is effectively binding on all companies in the British Isles.

On occasion, the Irish Institute has issued some notes or statements on specific matters of local interest. For purposes of the present book, readers may assume that accounting, auditing, and financial reporting matters are essentially similar in the Republic of Ireland and the United Kingdom.

The Irish Companies Act requires that proper books of account be kept so as to provide all information necessary to give a true and fair view of a company's affairs and explain its transactions. Thus the books must record

1. All sums of money received and expended by the company and the matters in respect of which the receipts and expenditures take place.
2. All sales and purchases of goods of the company.
3. All assets and liabilities of the company.

Books must be kept at a company's registered office, which must be located in the Republic or at such other place as the directors think fit. If the books are kept outside the Republic, there must be sent to and kept at a place in the Republic such accounts and returns as will disclose with reasonable accuracy the financial position of that business at intervals not exceeding 6 months and that will enable the company's balance sheet and profit and loss account to be prepared in proper form.

Although there is no general statutory requirement that the accounts of a business be audited, companies incorporated under the Companies Act must appoint an independent auditor or auditors. In certain other cases there may be relevant legislation imposing audit requirements. There is no specific requirement under tax law for the protection of audited accounts, but the revenue authorities normally insist on audited accounts where these are required by the Companies Act or other relevant legislation. Depending on the circumstances, failure to have the accounts audited by reputable accountants might prejudice their acceptance by revenue (taxation) authorities.

The Netherlands

The Dutch *Commercial Code* requires the keeping of records that must show a company's financial position and give comprehensive information about its business transactions. In very summary terms, it also specifies the contents of financial statements to be published. Since the statutory provisions of the *Commercial Code* are very general, the Dutch Institute has played an active role in developing recommendations on accounting and auditing standards to supplement *Code* provisions over the years.

A major change came with the 1970 *Act on Annual Accounts*, which became effective for financial years ending on or after May 1, 1971. It contains detailed provisions for financial reporting by Dutch companies but left the development of specific accounting standards and principles to those concerned with them, i.e., companies, professional accountants, labor union representatives, and government officials. The interested parties have combined into an official study group and have begun to make recommendations that eventually might become as binding as those now issued in the United Kingdom and the United States.

The *Act on Annual Accounts* provides, among other things, that

1. Annual financial statements shall show a fair picture of the financial position and results for the year, and all items therein must be appropriately grouped and described.
2. Financial statements must be drawn up in accordance with "sound business practice" (i.e., accounting principles acceptable to the business community).

3. The bases of stating assets and liabilities and determining results of operations must be disclosed.
4. Financial statements shall be prepared on a consistent basis and material effects of changes in accounting principles properly disclosed.
5. Comparative financial information for the preceding period shall be disclosed in the financial statements and accompanying footnotes.

Financial accounting and reporting standards and principles in the Netherlands are highly developed. They take their place with the most sophisticated in the world. The Dutch separate strictly financial accounting from tax accounting. Differences between the two are typically linked through tax allocation procedures.

Consolidated financial statements are the rule, and the equity method of accounting for intercorporate investments is widely applied.

A rather novel feature of generally accepted accounting principles in the Netherlands is the inclusion therein of current replacement value measurements (which has been mentioned and described in earlier chapters). Especially, larger Dutch companies carry certain inventory and depreciable fixed-asset items at their current replacement values, with corresponding replacement value-based depreciation expenses in income statements and replacement valuation "reserves" in the owners' equity sections of balance sheets. The large and well-known Dutch Philips Lamp Company has used replacement value measurements in its published financial statements since 1951.

The Dutch Institute of "Register Accountants" has approximately 3,500 members, half of whom are in public practice. Close to 6,000 individuals are student members of the Dutch Institute. Qualification as a public accountant in the Netherlands occurs predominantly through extension study with the Institute of Register Accountants. The necessary study period is reduced for university graduates with appropriate degree concentrations. Practical experience is necessary in all cases prior to certification.

Statutory audits became obligatory for the first time in 1970 during the introduction of the *Act on Annual Accounts.* Only Register Accountants or other experts (usually professional auditors with foreign qualifications) may act as statutory auditors. The professional and ethical rules governing independent auditors in the Netherlands are as strict as any in the world.

Grand Duchy of Luxembourg

Luxembourg has an antiquated *Code de Commerce* that requires records much the same as is the case in Belgium. No separate authority has attempted to define accounting standards and principles. As a consequence, accounting practice is almost totally dominated by taxation considerations.

The Luxembourg *Code* provides that one or more statutory auditors must be appointed by each company. A statutory auditor need not have professional accounting qualifications and may even be a company employee. As with company directors, each statutory auditor must hold a number of qualification shares. Of course, statutory auditors may employ qualified accountants to carry out opinion audits on their own or the company's behalf.

A decree dated March 5, 1970 began the regulation of Luxembourg's *Experts Comptables* profession. Since only about 20 to 30 individuals are *Experts Comptables* in Luxembourg, the scope of this degree is limited. More professional accounting activity can be expected in Luxembourg, however, if the Grand Duchy continues its rather remarkable growth as a leading European financial center.

United Kingdom

As already pointed out in our discussion of the Irish situation, the United Kingdom *Companies Act* (dating from 1844 and last amended and extended in 1967) does not contain specific accounting standards and principles beyond the general "true and fair" financial reporting requirements. Thus the Institute of Chartered Accountants in England and Wales began to issue recommendations on accounting principles in 1942. These statements were not binding, however. When a number of financial failures occurred in the late 1960's, the British profession had no option other than taking a more definitive approach to accounting principles.

In 1970, the Accounting Standards Steering Committee (ASSC) was organized in association with most other professional accountancy bodies in the British Isles. The ASSC now issues formal Statements of Standard Accounting Practice (SSAP) that are binding upon the members of all the professional bodies making up the ASSC. Much as in the United States, some titles of standards issued are as follows:

1. Accounting for the Results of Associated Companies.
2. Disclosure of Accounting Policies.
3. Earnings per Share.
4. The Accounting Treatment of Government Grants.
5. Accounting for Value-Added Tax.
6. Extraordinary Items and Prior Year Adjustments.
7. Accounting for Changes in the Purchasing Power of Money.
8. The Treatment of Taxation under the Imputation System in the Accounts of Companies.
9. Stocks and Work in Progress.
10. Statements of Source and Application of Funds.

The details of British accounting standards need not be elaborated here since they permeate much of the English language accounting literature and are thus readily available. Suffice it to say that these standards are by and large similar to those prevailing in North America, that published financial statements in Great Britain reflect a fair amount of financial disclosure, and that British accountants of late are innovation-minded, as in their support of the 1975 Sandilands Committee Report that advocates the abandonment of historical cost valuations in accounting in favor of current cost measurements.

The five principal accountancy bodies in the United Kingdom are

1. The Institute of Chartered Accountants in England and Wales.
2. The Association of Certified Accountants.
3. The Institute of Chartered Accountants of Scotland.
4. The Institute of Cost and Management Accountants.
5. The Chartered Institute of Public Finance and Accountancy.

These five bodies are linked and individually and jointly strengthened through the Consultative Committee on Accountancy Bodies which was formed in May 1974 and to which the Institute of Chartered Accountants in Ireland also belongs.

The five United Kingdom professional accountancy bodies referred to above have a combined membership in excess of 80,000, approximately 35,000 of whom are in public practice. As explained before, companies incorporated under the *Companies Act* must appoint independent auditors even though there is no general statutory requirement that financial statements be audited. We have also observed already that audit requirements are imposed by certain special legislation and that taxation authorities normally insist on audited statements where these are already required by the *Companies Acts*. Consequently there is a significant amount of opinion auditing in the British Isles that supports the membership statistics just cited. The relatively heavy incidence of professional auditing in Great Britain prompts the inevitable comparison with other EEC countries and the resulting research question of how much an economy or a social system really benefits from broadly applied professional auditing activities.

EEC HARMONIZATION EFFORTS

When the Treaty of Rome established the EEC on March 25, 1957, a specific objective was cited as "the approximation of their respective national laws to the extent required for the Common Market to function in an orderly manner." Since *Codes of Commerce* and/or *Companies* or *Corporation Laws* were on the books of all member countries, the EEC Commission embarked upon a major program of *EEC Company Law* harmonization almost from the start.

The process by which this is done entails various preliminary work leading to the issuance of a so-called "draft directive" (i.e., exposure draft) by the EEC Commission. Hearings and various other evaluation procedures are then conducted and a given draft directive may be reissued several times over. When the Commission finally feels that a draft directive is broadly acceptable, it submits it to the member states for ratification after approval to do so from the EEC Council of Ministers.

A distinction is necessary here between regulations, directives, decisions, recommendations, and opinions. With regard to the implementation of the Treaty of Rome and with specific respect to the EEC Council and the Commission, regulations are of general application and binding in every respect with the direct force of law in every member state. Directives are binding on member states to which they are addressed with respect to the results to be achieved, but mode and means of implementation are left to the discretion of national authorities. Decisions, whether addressed to governments or companies or private individuals, are binding in every respect on the party or parties named. Recommendations and opinions are not binding.

Since EEC directives (or drafts thereof) cover all aspects of companies law, we propose to single out only those that have a direct bearing on accounting.

The *Draft Fourth Directive* was originally published in November 1971 and reissued in February 1974. It contains detailed requirements concerning the form and content of corporate financial statements. As it presently stands, the 52 sections of the *Draft Fourth Directive* range from broad standards to specific rules. This range covers prescriptions of the valuation bases allowable for certain balance sheet items as well as the format of published financial statements.

Included in the *Draft Fifth Directive* are proposals dealing with the structure, management, and outside audits of larger corporations. This proposal anticipates a two-tier corporate board system based on the German or Dutch models—thereby rejecting the classical management structure prevalent in the United Kingdom. For this and several other reasons raised since the January 1, 1973 admission of Denmark, the Republic of Ireland, and the United Kingdom to EEC membership, the proposed *Fifth Directive* has been withdrawn for the time being. How the resulting vacuum is to be filled cannot yet be determined. Perhaps the directive will be redrafted and perhaps its auditing provisions will become the subject of a separate draft directive. We are unable at this time to forecast the likely outcome of the present holding action.

In May 1976, the text of a *Draft Seventh Directive* was issued by the EEC Commission calling for consolidated financial statements. Despite some controversial aspects of this proposal, we venture the guess that it will be adopted at least by 1980.

We now turn to more specific, even though nonexhaustive, comments on the proposed *Fourth and Seventh EEC Commission Directives.*

(Revised) Draft Fourth Directive

In basic philosophy, the draft directive is similar to the S-X Regulations of the U.S. SEC. The aim of the draft is to achieve financial disclosure to a roughly equivalent degree for all limited liability companies within the EEC. Toward that goal, financial position statements and periodic income statements, together with appropriate notes thereto, are required as the basic financial disclosure "package."

Reflection of a "true and fair view" of a company's assets, liabilities, owners' equities, and periodic results of operations is defined as the essential purpose of the financial statements to be required. Companies must keep proper books and records as support for the information that has to be disclosed.

The "true and fair view" (i.e., essentially Anglo-Saxon) point of view serves as the basic guideline where alternatives of presentation and/or valuation are allowed by the draft directive. If specific provisions of the draft are inadequate for the fair presentation of a company's position and/or its results of operations, then it is compulsory to state this fact in the notes to the financial statements so that interested parties are not misled. A similar disclosure requirement exists for all departures from the specific provisions of the draft directive.

Financial Statement Format. Articles 3 through 6 require that statement format may not be arbitrarily changed from year to year, comparative figures for previous periods must be shown, and additions to and retirements from long-term asset and depreciation accounts must be disclosed separately. Physical layout is optional, as are any subdivisions of prescribed account categories.

Articles 7 through 11 provide for financial position statement format. Articles 12 through 18 contain implementation provisions relating to a number of items specified for balance sheets (e.g., "participating interest").

Both the horizontal and vertical forms of financial position stateents are acceptable. For the main asset, liability and owners' equity sections, account categories are comparable to typical Anglo-Saxon financial reporting practice. For example, secured liabilities must be reported separately, but full details of long-term debt maturities and/or redemption provisions need not be stated directly within the body of balance sheets.

The periodic income statement is dealt with in Articles 19 through 27. Again, both the vertical and horizontal statement forms are allowed, and netting of items, especially between revenue and expense transactions, is prohibited. Line-of-business reporting is required to (a) show the sources of periodic net income and (b) specify the origins of the period's results of operations. With respect to the former, sales have to be segregated according to main lines of business. With respect to the latter, segregation must follow four breakdowns:

1. Ordinary business activities of a company.
2. Results of financial (nontrading) developments during the year.
3. Exceptional operations unconnected with usual operations for the year.
4. Results attributable to another period.

The main income statement captions are (a) results from operations, (b) total financial results, (c) extraordinary gains and losses, and (d) taxes. "Operating results" may be derived according to the (a) total cost method or (b) cost of sales method. The former brings changes of finished and in-process inventory items into a revenue measure typically called *cost of inventory changes.* If, in addition, capitalized costs of self-constructed assets or major repairs are added to the revenue section of an income statement, the resulting total is an item like the one appearing in many German income statements as "total output rendered."

Valuation. The draft directive specifies valuation rules in Articles 28 through 39. These articles are based on the following fundamental accounting concepts:

1. *Going concern*—the assumption that a company will continue to stay in business.
2. *Consistency*—as understood in Anglo-Saxon practice.
3. *Accrual*—again as understood in Anglo-Saxon practice.
4. *Prudence*—which includes things like realization, provision for known losses, and periodic depreciation.

The draft retains as its basic valuation method the historical cost principle. However, it allows member states to authorize, as appropriate, the use of replacement value measurements or other methods based on current or market values. Where departures from historical cost are applied, companies must disclose that fact in the financial statements. Moreover, any differences between historical cost valuations and replacement cost or current market valuations must be aggregated and separately disclosed as an item of "revaluation reserve" in the owners' equity section of financial position statements. The summarized "revaluation reserves" must be broken down according to the main asset categories to which they pertain.

Intangibles must be amortized over a period not to exceed 5 years. Dividends can be paid out only from unrestricted retained earnings, inventories are subject to lower-of-cost-or-market measurements with either FIFO, LIFO or weighted average flow assumptions, provisions for contingencies must be specifically justifiable, and movements in reserves must be separately disclosed.

Supplementary Information and Annual Reports. The remaining articles of the draft specify individual disclosure items, preparation of the annual (management) report, and publication requirements. For instance, one provision states that names and registered offices of every company must be disclosed in which a parent company holds 10 percent or more of the voting capital stock. Furthermore, sufficient financial information must be provided to enable a reader to appraise a parent company's interest in any affiliate or subsidiary undertaking.

The existence of any entitlement on the part of any person or organization to a share in the profits has to be disclosed as must be any convertible debentures or similar rights. Also, the total amount of financial obligations not included in balance sheet sums has to be shown, if material, so as to permit appraisal of the overall financial position of a company. This includes leases, long-term rentals, and purchase commitments. Similarly, personnel costs have to be shown separately if they are not segregated in the income statement.

The "annual report," as contemplated in the draft, elaborates all items in the financial statements that affect an assessment of a company's business and financial position as a whole. In this annual report the board of directors express their personal opinions on the status and future prospects of their company. The type of annual report contemplated in the draft directive is similar to the annual management report currently used in German financial reporting practice (see p. 192).

Draft Seventh Directive

On April 29, 1976, the EEC Commission published its first draft of a proposed directive on consolidated financial statements. This draft of a *Seventh Directive* distinguishes between *dominant* and *dependent* undertakings. Consolidated financial statements have to be prepared if *either* a dominant undertaking *or* a dependent undertaking is a limited liability company. This means that an undertaking other than a limited company needs to consolidate if it has at least one dependent undertaking that is incorporated. Whether a dominant, unincorporated undertaking can be forced into consolidations not otherwise required remains to be seen.

Articles 3 and 4 of this draft directive introduce a concept of consolidation of financial statements of undertakings under central or unified management but not necessarily with a controlling degree of ownership. In this respect, *dominant influence* is defined in Article 2 as presumably existing directly or indirectly when an undertaking

1. Holds the major part of another undertaking's subscribed capital.
2. Controls the majority of votes in another undertaking.
3. Can appoint more than half of the members of another undertaking's administrative, managerial, or supervisory body.

Specific Provisions. Article 6 of the draft directive requires preparation of consolidated financial statements for all subgroups where the head of a subgroup is incorporated. As the draft stands, there is no exemption from this obligation if the head of a subgroup is a wholly owned subsidiary of another limited company that itself prepares consolidated financial statements.

There is also the requirement that where, within the EEC, dependent companies of a group or subgroups independent of each other are dominated by an undertaking outside the EEC, consolidated financial statements must be prepared for the dependent undertakings within the Community. Assume that one company in France and another company in Germany are independent of each other but both are dominated by a United States company. In this case, the draft directive requires that consolidated (or in fact combined) financial statements be prepared for these two companies and any of their own independent undertakings. This provision introduces a whole new consolidation/combination concept not presently found in practice except for a very few unusual cases.

Article 9 specifies the composition of consolidated accounts but makes no provision for group funds statements. This is in keeping with the revised draft of the *Fourth Directive,* which likewise does not provide for funds flow statements.

The consolidation process is dealt with in Article 12. Among other things, it specifies valuation of assets acquired on a fair value basis. Nonattributable amounts (goodwill) are required to be allocated to a "consolidation difference."

Article 14 sets out general consolidation principles. It requires that whenever the financial year of a group undertaking does not correspond with that used in the consolidation of group accounts, the "out-of-phase" undertaking is to be consolidated on the basis of audited interim financial statements prepared as of the date of the group accounts.

Article 15 provides, among other things, that in normal circumstances the same accounting principles must be used in preparing annual accounts later to be included in consolidated financial statements as those that are used in the consolidated statements themselves. According to Article 16, "consolidation differences" have to be written off over a maximum period of 5 years. The equity method of accounting applies to all intercorporate investments over which a "significant influence" is exercised—meaning any ownership interest of 20 percent or more.

An occasional consolidation practice in France is to include in consolidations joint ventures or companies managed by other companies on a line-by-line financial statement basis and at the individual ownership percentage held. This practice is stipulated in Article 18.

Article 20 requires the disclosure of certain specific information in the notes to the consolidated financial statements. In addition to details of undertakings consolidated, accounted for on the equity method, or accounted for on the line-by-line percentage inclusion method, the name, registered office, percentage of capital held, subscribed capital, reserves, and operating results must be given for any other undertaking in which 10 percent or more of the voting capital is held by the group undertaking.

Article 24 deals with publication. As with the proposed draft of the *Fourth Directive,* publication of consolidated financial statements is required in the official gazettes of member countries.

Under the terms of Article 25, it is permissible to calculate goodwill arising from consolidations as of the first time a consolidation would be required under the proposed *Seventh Directive* rather than as of the date of acquisition for the investment in question.

General Observations. The drafts of both the *Fourth* and *Seventh Directives* seem to lean heavily on French and German corporation law concepts. In part, this may be a reflection of the fact that many attorneys and administrators working for the EEC came to Brussels prior to the admission of Denmark, the Republic of Ireland, and the United Kingdom. France and Germany, being the largest members of the founder group of countries, naturally provided proportionately larger shares of EEC staff personnel and administrators. This bias, if it exists, seems certain to correct itself over time.

Both drafts are void of any provisions for professional auditing. As already described earlier in this chapter, in the descriptive sections on individual member countries, professional auditing capabilities vary significantly among the member countries, and therefore the time for finding an "average" approach to outside auditing may not yet have come. It is possible that professional audit requirements for financial statements will be spelled out in a separate draft directive at a later time.

Technically, the draft directives deal with form at least as much as with substance. Again, this is understandable when one considers the strong French predisposition for national uniform accounting. It is hoped that the many form specifications now contained in the drafts will not introduce undue rigidity in both the final directives and the applications that necessarily will flow from it.

Finally, some technical aspects of the drafts are novel, to say the least, from Anglo-Saxon viewpoints. These will have to be evaluated and tested carefully before they are put into practice. But it is entirely possible that several Anglo-Saxon accounting standards and principles will change in response to the technical developments likely to be induced by these directives when they become effective.

THE EUROPEAN COMPANY PROPOSAL

In 1970, the EEC Commission presented to the European Council of Ministers a proposed statute aimed at the creation of a new type of company—the "Societa Europea"—for short, the SE (note that a Latin name was chosen for the proposed creation to avoid offending any one EEC member nation). The creation envisaged would be something new and distinctive in the world of legal persons—namely a company with European citizenship.

The rationale for the SE proposal is rather straightforward:

1. The present legal framework within which European undertakings operate does not correspond to the EEC political and economic framework. Thus the legal framework hinders EEC community development.
2. The basic EEC idea has always included companies or industries operating on an EEC-wide scale. Appropriate legal accommodation of this basic idea is desirable and/or necessary.
3. Companies operating on an EEC-wide basis (i.e., multinationals) ought to be subject to a form of control beyond the legal institutions in any one member country.

Chronology of Background

1959 Concept of the SE first proposed by Professor Pieter Sanders in his inaugural address at the University of Rotterdam.
1960 Conference convened by the Paris Bar on the SE idea meets with enthusiastic response from leading company lawyers. EEC industrial federations, however, regard the concept unnecessary because they fear yet another layer of administrative interference and control.
1965 Concept officially revived by French government—in part as a manifestation of its desire to combat increasing United States investment and control in Europe.

1966 Professor Sanders is commissioned by the EEC to submit preliminary draft proposals of his ideas. The Dutch refuse to discuss the proposals unless non-EEC companies are included.

1967 Limited French national legislation to facilitate international cooperation between companies, especially with respect to marketing and research and development.

1968 French government brings the proposals again to the attention of the EEC.

1969 French withdrawal of support for the SE draft due to internal French political pressures.

1970 Relying on Professor Sanders' preliminary draft proposals and a study of worker participation in company management prepared by Professor Lyon Caen of the University of Paris, a draft statute is presented to the EEC Council of Ministers by the EEC Commission.

1972 EEC Economic and Social Committee reports favorably upon 1970 draft after 2 years of evaluation. Nonetheless, extensive redrafting is suggested before submission to European parliaments.

1977 Draft statute still under consideration by all parties concerned—with apparently some very low priorities.

Contents of Proposed Statute

The complete proposal consists of 284 articles that are contained within 14 titles. The latter embrace

1. General provisions.
2. Formation.
3. Capital, shares and rights of shareholders, debentures.
4. Administrative organs.
5. Representation of employees in the European Company.
6. Preparation of annual accounts.
7. Groups of companies.
8. Alteration of company regulations.
9. Winding-up, liquidations, insolvency, and similar procedures.
10. Conversions.
11. Mergers.
12. Taxation.
13. Offenses.
14. Final provisions.

As proposed, SE's would be commercial or industrial companies with limited liability, showing the suffix "SE" behind their name, and being registered in the European Commercial Register and the Court of Justice of the EEC. As the proposal stands, an SE could be created *only* by

1. Merger of companies existing within the EEC.
2. Formation as a holding company for existing companies within the EEC.
3. Formation as a joint subsidiary.

The legal capital of an SE shall be no less than

1. 500,000 European currency units of account—in the case of a merger or a holding company.
2. 250,000 European currency units of account—in the case of a joint subsidiary.
3. 100,000 European currency units of account—in the case of a subsidiary of an SE.

Further, with respect to legal capital, (a) it must be fully paid up in cash or in kind, (b) an SE cannot reacquire its own shares or engage in reciprocal shareholdings with other SE's, (c) nonvoting shares may be issued for up to 50 percent of legal capital, and (d) bearer or registered shares may be issued with the provision that, in the bearer share's case, public notification must occur when more than 10 percent of the shares of an SE are owned by any one party.

Accounting and Financial Reporting Requirements

In general, the proposed articles follow the (original) draft of the proposed *Fourth Directive*—even though possibly in somewhat greater detail. They also contain some regulations about the preparation of consolidated financial statements, but these are minor when compared with the provisions of the draft of the proposed *Seventh Directive* just discussed.

If the *SE* proposal becomes current again, and if the *Fourth* and *Seventh Directives* are issued at that time (which would seem likely), it seems fairly certain that a full integration of these three sets of regulations can and should be expected as far as accounting, auditing, and financial reporting are concerned.

Other Items of Note

An SE is to be administrated by two-tier control devices—a board of management and a board of directors. The board of management would be appointed by the board of directors—with a majority of the members nationals of EEC member states. The board of management would be responsible for running the day-to-day affairs of an SE. Members of the board of management may not also serve as members of the board of directors.

The board of directors would function pretty much as customarily understood in Anglo-Saxon practices with the exception that at least one-third of its members must be representatives of the employees. The two-tier board idea is adapted from present Dutch and German practices.

The European idea of works councils is also represented in the proposed statute. Works councils are created to ensure that employees' interests are considered in all respects of company management, conditions of work, and other conditions or events affecting the welfare of employees.

With respect to taxation, an SE would have a domicile in one member country where SE corporate income would then become taxable. An option is provided, however, for the possibility of taxation on a worldwide basis. Thus, there are provisions for loss relief and protection from double taxation. Essentially, though, tax regulations presently prevailing in the EEC member countries would apply to an SE.

Brief Commentary

Two of the most serious criticisms leveled against the proposed SE statute is that it would make it impossible for an existing individual firm to become an SE or for any business organization other than a corporation to take part in settng up an SE. Moreover, it would be impossible for a national company in a single EEC country to set up an SE by itself. The minimum capital requirements for organizing an SE are also considered to be on the high side.

A third difficulty, of particular concern to the Dutch, is that the proposal does not allow SE status or development to firms based in non-EEC countries. In today's world of multinational enterprises, this is considered unduly restrictive.

Last, the idea of two-tier boards for companies is still considered by many to be experimental and not necessarily optimal. Many fear that adoption of the two-tiered board idea for purposes of SE's would directly carry over into national companies legislation in the individual member states. This possibility is not welcome everywhere in the EEC.

EEC watchers are only cautiously optimistic about the eventual creation of SE's. Despite many setbacks though, the idea appears to have staying power and thus continues as a significant element on the map of the EEC accounting territory.

SELECTED REFERENCES

6.1 BEENY, J. H., *European Financial Reporting—France,* London: Institute of Chartered Accountants in England and Wales, 1976, 290 pp. (mimeographed).

6.2 BENSTON, GEORGE J., "Public (U.S.) Compared to Private (U.K.) Regulation of Corporate Financial Disclosure," *Accounting Review,* July 1976, pp. 483–98.

6.3　*BUSINESS EUROPE,* "European Mergers: Playing Binationality for All That It's Worth," July 2, 1976, pp. 211-12; "Italian Firms Turn to Independent Auditing," October 10, 1976, p. 327.

6.4　DIETERICH, WILHELM, "The European Parliament Discusses the EEC Commission's Directive Relating to the Right of Professional Accountants to Establish a Practice and Render Services Freely." *Journal UEC,* January 1972, pp. 14–17.

6.5　*THE ECONOMIST* (London), Intelligence Unit, "In Depth: Financial Disclosure in Europe—Differences in Accountancy Plague Harmonization Efforts," *Multinational Business,* May 1972, pp. 35–43.

6.6　KAMINSKI, HORST, "Recommendations of the EEC Commission for the Fourth Directive on the Harmonization of Accounting Regulations," *Journal UEC,* April 1972, pp. 122-30.

6.7　KRAMER, RICHARD L., "Status Report on Auditing in the European Community," *Auditing Symposium III,* University of Kansas, May 13–14, 1976 (mimeographed).

6.8　LAFFERTY, MICHAEL, *Accounting in Europe.* Cambridge, England: Woodhead, Faulkner, Ltd., 1975, 425 pp. (Published in association with National Westminster Bank.)

6.9　LOUWERS, PIETER C., "The European Public Accountant: A Different View," *Management Accounting* (U.S.), September 1975, pp. 43–46. (Response to an earlier article on the same subject in the same journal by Professor William S. Crum, March 1975, pp. 41–44, 54.)

6.10　MARRIAN, IAN, and HUGH CHRISTIE, "Italian Accounting Renaissance," *Accountant's Magazine,* May 1976, pp. 173-75.

6.11　MCDOUGAL, E. H. V., "Professional Qualifications and the EEC," *Accountant's Magazine,* October 1972, pp. 479-83.

6.12　MCLEAN, ALASDAIR D., "Societas Europea—A Consideration of the Proposals for the European Company," *Accountant's Magazine,* December 1971, pp. 631-40.

6.13　MCLEAN, ALASDAIR D., *Business and Accounting in Europe.* Westmead, U.K.: Saxon House, 1973, 269 pp.

6.14　MCLEAN, ALASDAIR D., "Group Accounts in the EEC: A Look at Some of the Proposals of the Draft Seventh Directive," *Accountant's Magazine,* June 1976, pp. 211-12.

6.15　MORRIS, RICHARD, *Corporate Standards and the Fourth Directive* (Research Committee Occasional Paper No. 2), London: Institute of Chartered Accountants in England and Wales, 1974, 107 pp.

6.16　PRICE WATERHOUSE & CO., *EEC Bulletin No. 23,* Brussels: Author, May 1976, pp. 1–4.

6.17　PRICE WATERHOUSE & CO., *Doing Business In ...* (Denmark, France, Germany, Italy, Republic of Ireland, Grand Duchy of Luxembourg, The Netherlands, and the United Kingdom) New York, Author, most recent edition, various paginations.

6.18 TYRA, ANITA I., "Financial Disclosure Patterns in Four European Countries," *International Journal of Accounting,* Spring 1970, pp. 89–99.

6.19 VOLPI, EDOARDO, "Accounting and Financial Reporting Aspects of the EEC Company Law Harmonization Program and the Proposed European Company Structure," *Proceedings,* Accounting and Finance in Europe Conference, London: The City University, Graduate Business Centre, 1976, pp. 3–23.

6.20 WATTS, TOM, "Company Accounts in Europe: Revising the Fourth Directive," *Accountant,* May 9, 1974, pp. 590-94.

DISCUSSION QUESTIONS

6.1 Does regional harmonization of financial accounting and reporting standards (discussed in Chapter 6) conflict with or produce counter-productivity as regards worldwide international standards (discussed Chapter 5)?

6.2 Discuss the environmental factors—by drawing upon materials presented in Chapter 2—that characterize the nine EEC countries. Name the three factors (or parameters/characteristics) that are most similar and the three that are most dissimilar when it comes to the EEC member countries.

6.3 Write a concise, descriptive paragraph on financial accounting policy-making in each of the following countries: (a) France, (b) West Germany, (c) the Netherlands, and (d) the United Kingdom.

6.4 What are the essential differences in qualifications and work performed by (a) statutory auditors and (b) independent professional auditors? If you were the chief executive officer of a large multinational corporation based in France, how would you justify a professional independent opinion audit to your shareholders?

6.5 Write a short essay on the system of higher education for accounting as it exists in the EEC countries.

6.6 Early in this chapter, the so-called *binationality* of several EEC-based enterprises was referred to. Identify one such enterprise by name and briefly describe what binationality means in this case.

6.7 Compile a list of the 10 most salient features of financial accounting and reporting in Belgium.

6.8 By going to supplementary sources (i.e., material beyond that contained in the chapter), identify major similarities and dissimilarities between Danish and United States financial accounting and reporting.

6.9 In France, financial accounting standards and practices originate primarily from three authoritative sources: (a) companies legislation (Plan Comptable), (b) professional opinions and recommendations

(L'Ordre National des Experts Comptables and Conseil National de la Comptabilité), and (c) stock exchange regulations (Commission des Opérations de Bourse). Which of these three has the greatest influence on day-to-day French accounting practice? Can you identify a specific instance of French accounting influence upon actual or proposed EEC accounting regulations?

6.10 Review 10 published German corporate annual reports. From this review, list 20 items or characteristics that a North American reader of such reports might misunderstand or misinterpret.

6.11 In this text, there is a lengthy quote on accounting in Italy from Michael Lafferty's *Accounting in Europe*. Also in the text, the new Italian regulatory committee CONSOB is referred to. In light of the quote from Lafferty, what are the major obstacles that CONSOB is likely to encounter? Do you agree with CONSOB's announced independent auditor rotation plan?

6.12 On the basis of library research, determine the contents and meaning of the accounting-related "schedules" that attach to the Companies Acts found in the British Isles.

6.13 Devise an informal system for measuring the quality of financial disclosure in corporate annual reports. Then apply your system to five companies each from the Netherlands and the United States, *but* in the same industry. Present your findings in the form of a short essay.

6.14 From a North American point of view, write a brief critical analysis of the philosophy behind and the contents of the EEC proposed Draft Fourth and Seventh Directives. Do these documents augur well for the future of EEC accounting development? Can you suggest any improvements concerning these drafts?

6.15 As chief financial executive of a United States-based multinational enterprise with substantial operations in the EEC, what steps (if any) would you undertake now to prepare for the advent of the *SE*? Why?

ANNOTATED TEACHING MATERIALS

6.1 *Dunlop Holdings Limited* (ICCH Case A, 9–173–124). Dunlop Holdings Ltd. is involved in a major transnational merger between United Kingdom-based Dunlop and Italy-based Pirelli. The formal union of these two companies came into being January 1, 1971. Two years have passed since this union, and Pirelli has experienced substantial financial losses. Some rather significant accounting decisions must be made in light of these developments. The entire range of EEC financial accounting problems is touched by this case. A complete update to the present is possible since actual data are utilized in the presentation.

6.2 *French Financial Reporting and the Standard Code of Accounts* (ICCH Case 9–175–200). This technical note provides an introduction to financial reporting practices in France. Subjects surveyed include historic and legal foundations of French accounting practice, general presentation of accounts, asset valuation, depreciation, accounting "provisions," capital gains and losses, financial statement consolidation, and operating income. Appendices provide information on uniform financial statement format and a glossary of French accounting terms.

6.3 *Audit Standards in the EEC* (ICCH Case 9–175–207). Auditing standards and practices within the EEC are described and compared. Specific commentary is focused on (a) the size and scope of the respective auditing profession in each EEC member country, (b) audit responsibilities and procedures, and (c) auditing standards in relation to European capital markets. Exhibits summarizing major auditing differences and case illustrations of independent auditor's reports are also provided.

6.4 *The EEC and Company Law Harmonization* (ICCH Case 9–175–193). This case deals with the formal EEC *Draft Fourth Directive,* which addresses directly the problem of financial reporting harmonization within EEC countries. Underlying the directive's issuance is the belief that more uniform accounting systems facilitate corporate regulation and operation within the member states. Excerpts of individual provisions of the draft directive are presented for critical analysis and evaluation in light of these objectives.

6.5 *The British Companies Act of 1967* (ICCH Case 8–172–120). The 1967 (most recent) amendments to the United Kingdom *Companies Act* are described and their effects on British reporting practices noted. This is followed by a comparison of the revised United Kingdom reporting norms with those in the United States. In view of 1967 dateline, the case lends itself to further analysis. Students, for example, may be asked to gauge the changes in United Kingdom financial reporting practices that have occurred since the 1967 revision. This may be accomplished by comparing the contents of a recent British annual report with that of the same company 10 years earlier. Extension of the original case can be used as a vehicle for (a) forecasting what the next revision of the *Companies Act* is likely to entail, as well as (b) developing an appreciation for the merits and possible limitations of the legislative approach to accounting development.

6.6 *Dividend Declaration and Balance Sheet Terminology in Europe and the United States* (ICCH Case 9–110–062). This case note examines differences in balance sheet terminology and presentation between the United States and Europe. Institutional considerations that shape these financial reporting differences are also explained. Specific topics include (a) legal forms of business organization, (b) rights and duties of shareholders and directors, (c) dividend and earnings appropriations, (d) classes of capital stock, (e) cash and stock dividends, (f) assets and liabilities, (g) balance sheet formats, (h) net profit and retained earnings, and (i) free reserves. Valuation issues are not discussed. Several changes have occurred since this case note was prepared in the early 1960's.

Chapter 7

FINANCIAL PLANNING FOR MULTINATIONAL OPERATIONS

Previous chapters dwelled on financial reporting for external users of enterprise data. We now shift our attention to accounting for managerial decisions, particularly as it relates to the multinational enterprise.

The concept of managerial accounting entertained here does not incorporate the traditional notions of accounting for enterprise costs. While the origins of managerial accounting are found in cost accounting, the latter, today, encompasses little beyond the determination of inventory values for financial reporting purposes. Moreover, cost accounting concepts are, to a large extent, the same both domestically and internationally. Attention is therefore focused on the newer strategic area of managerial planning and control systems. It is here that significant international challenges are making themselves felt.

The foregoing implies that managerial accounting exists to provide information inputs to managerial decision processes. Accordingly, accounting issues are examined from the perspective of a management decision framework.

International Financial Management

The spread of business internationally has fostered mutations of domestic management specialties. This development has been necessitated by additional variables and constraints that typify the multinational dimension. Foreign currency exchange risks, restrictions on fund remittances across national borders, diverse national tax laws, interest rate differentials between various national financial markets, the global shortage of money capital, and the effects of worldwide inflation on enterprise assets, earnings, and capital costs are just examples of variables calling for specialized knowledge among multinational financial executives.

A direct response to such environmental complexities is the emergence of the international financial management function. One Conference Board study reveals that more than half of the companies queried reported having a specially designated executive in charge of arranging the financial decisions of its international operations. The trend in this direction, furthermore, is on the increase.[1]

In view of the emergence of this managerial specialty, a description of some of the major international financial management issues along with their accounting implications is provided in this and the following chapter. Needless to say, a viable set of financial decisions and policies cannot be produced nor the attainment of enterprise objectives properly gauged without adequate and timely information. Managerial accounting thus commands a strategic role in the development of information support systems for financial decisions within the multinational entity.

For purposes of discussion, multinational managerial finance is divided into two broad areas: financial planning and financial control. Financial planning for multinational operations is examined in the remainder of this chapter. Specific subtopics include (a) foreign investment analysis, (b) international financial sourcing, and (c) multinational risk management. Financial control and information systems constitute the subject matter of Chapter 8.

FOREIGN INVESTMENT ANALYSIS

The decision to invest abroad is a principal means of implementing the global strategy of a multinational company. Direct investment beyond national boundaries, however, typically involves an enterprise in a commitment of enormous sums of capital to an uncertain future. In this respect, risk is inevitable. The added risk dimension is compounded by an unfamiliar international environment that is distant and complex and in a constant state of change. Under these circumstances, formal planning becomes highly desirable and is normally performed within a capital budgeting framework, i.e., a framework that compares both the benefits and costs of any contemplated activity.

Owing to significant advances in domestic capital budgeting theory, sophisticated approaches to investment decisions are now available. Pro-

[1] Irene W. Meister, *Managing the International Financial Function* (New York: The Conference Board, 1970), pp. 1–2.

cedures exist for determining a firm's optimum capital structure, measuring a firm's cost of capital, and evaluating investment alternatives under conditions of uncertainty. Normative decision rules for investment choice typically call for the discounting of an investment's risk-adjusted cash flows at an appropriate interest rate, namely, the firm's weighted average cost of capital. In the absence of capital rationing, a firm increases the wealth of its owners if it accepts independent investment projects promising positive net present values. When considering mutually exclusive options, rational behavior dictates selection of alternatives promising the maximum net present value.

When we enter the international arena, investment planning quickly becomes a "mission impossible." Different tax laws, differential rates of inflation, risks of expropriation, fluctuating exchange rates, exchange controls, restrictions on the transferability of foreign earnings, and language and intercultural differences all introduce a degree of complexity not usually found under more homogeneous and stable domestic conditions. Add to this the difficulty of quantifying such data, and the problem is quickly magnified. Modifications of domestic capital budgeting theory that accommodate these additional environmental complexities are thus called for.

Multinational adaptations of traditional investment planning models have taken place in at least three major areas and are discussed below. These include (a) determination of the relevant return from a multinational investment, (b) identification of project cash flows, and (c) calculation of the multinational cost of capital. Modification of domestic decision models for foreign political and exchange risks is discussed later in the chapter.

Financial Rates of Return

In considering the feasibility of a foreign investment opportunity, we must address the question of what constitutes the *relevant rate of return,* that is, should the international financial manager evaluate expected investment returns from the perspective of the host country or the home country? One might argue that, ultimately, return and risk considerations of a foreign investment should be for the parent company's stockholders. This, of course, is consistent with domestic capital budgeting doctrine. On the other hand, arguments can be made that such an ethnocentric posture is now outmoded. To begin with, investors in the parent company are increasingly drawn from a worldwide community. Thus, investment objectives must reflect a much more cosmopolitan outlook than before. Observation also suggests that many companies, in true multinational fashion, possess long-run as opposed to short-run investment horizons. Funds generated abroad tend to be reinvested there rather than repatriated to the parent company. Under these circumstances, a host country perspective seems appropriate.

Another response to the original question of appropriate return standards might be, "it all depends." Planned reinvestment of funds in the original host country would justify a local country perspective; planned deployment of the funds elsewhere would justify a parent country perspective. In short, consideration of the financial returns should vary depending on how a given foreign investment fits into a multinational company's foreign investment portfolio now and in the future. Rita M. Rodriguez and E. Eugene Carter express this viewpoint.

A more appealing solution is offered by Eiteman and Stonehill.[2] Drawing on a behavioral theory of the firm, they posit that there is a multiplicity of goals that financial managers must satisfy, depending on the aspiration levels of both investor and noninvestor groups comprising the organization and its environment. In the case of a foreign investment, the host country government is one such group. To assure some congruity between the goals of the multinational investor and the host government, at least two financial return calculations are proposed: one from the host country perspective and the other from the parent country perspective. Calculation of the former is based on the assumption that if a foreign investment promises to be profitable, the foreign investor would not be misallocating the host country's scarce resources. For example, a country enjoying full employment of its resources would probably not look favorably on a proposed foreign investment promising a 12 percent return on assets employed when investments of comparable risk elsewhere in the country are yielding 18 percent.

At first glance, the accounting implications of multiple rate of return calculations appear straightforward. After all, dual rate of return calculations would simply involve a doubling of data requirements, would they not? Nothing could be further from the truth. In the earlier discussion, project rate of return calculations were assumed to be a proxy for host country evaluations of a foreign investment. In practice, the analysis is much more complicated. For example, proposals submitted to host country officials probably have to reflect various *macro* considerations. Thus, would project rate of return calculations really reflect a host country's opportunity costs? Are the expected returns from a foreign investment limited to projected cash flows or are there additional social externalities to be considered? If there are additional benefits, how are these measured? Does a foreign investment require any special overhead expenditures by the host government? What is risk from a host country viewpoint and how can this aspect of a foreign investment be measured? Questions such as these indicate a geometric as compared to an arithmetic expansion in the information requirements associated with this aspect of foreign investment analysis.

[2] David K. Eiteman, and Arthur I. Stonehill, *Multinational Business Finance* (Reading, Massachusetts: Addison-Wesley Publishing Company, 1973), pp. 198–200.

Measuring Cash Flows

Measuring the expected cash flows associated with a foreign investment is also more complex than the corresponding domestic case. As noted earlier, international considerations that account for this increased complexity are examined first from a local country perspective and then from a parent country perspective. Assume, for purposes of discussion, that a United States multinational corporation is considering acquisition of 100 percent ownership of a foreign manufacturing company in Israel. Let us also simplify matters by disregarding cash flow effects associated with alternative financing modes.

The projected cash flows of the Israeli operation are determined much as those for a domestic company. Expected receipts are based on sales projections and anticipated collection experiences. Operating expenses, converted to their cash equivalents, and local taxes are similarly forecast. Additional elements of return have to be accounted for, however. They include (Paul O. Gaddis, pp. 115–122)

1. The additional operating income of the overseas unit resulting from the merger of its own capabilities with those of the investing corporation.
2. Additional income from increased export sales resulting from the proposed investment action, including (a) additional export income at each United States operating unit which manufactures products related to those which will be produced overseas and (b) additional earnings from new export activity at the overseas operating unit resulting from its increased capabilities to sell beyond the boundaries of its traditional national markets.
3. Additional income from increased licensing opportunities shown on both the books of the affected United States units and the books of the overseas unit.
4. Additional income from the importation to United States operating units of technology, product design, or hardware from the overseas operating unit.

An even more distinguishing feature of this process is that the behavior of foreign exchange rates has to be projected for all transactions affected by exchange rate changes, e.g., export and import transactions. Since many countries, as noted in Chapter 3, employ different exchange rates for different transactions, separate exchange rate projections for each class of activity as well as their cumulative effects on projected cash flows are also necessary.

Once a parent country perspective is employed, we find that cash flows to the United States parent company need not parallel those of the Israeli subsidiary. This seems strange indeed, as cash generated from, say, a Hawaiian subsidiary is immediately available to its California parent. The explanation for this phenomenon lies in the various constraints that foreign governments can impose on the flow of funds across national boundaries. As a result, cash flows that can be repatriated to the parent company must be identified and estimated, taking into account current and anticipated changes in foreign exchange rate behavior, restrictions on fund transfers, and other government constraints. In addition, while tax assessments under any given national jurisdiction tend to be uniform, this is not the case internationally. Consequently, differential tax levies between Israel and the United States as well as other costs of transferring funds to the United States parent have to be accounted for.

Multinational Cost of Capital

If foreign investments are evaluated in the context of the discounted cash flow model, then an appropriate discount rate must be developed. Capital budgeting theory typically employs a firm's cost of capital as this discount rate; i.e., a project must yield a return at least equal to a firm's cost of capital to be acceptable. This "hurdle rate" is, in turn, functionally related to the proportions of debt and equity in a firm's financial structure.

The response of a firm's cost of capital in relation to increased leverage is manifested in the familiar U-shaped cost of capital curve. This behavior pattern implies that firms should confine their debt-equity mix within a range that minimizes its capital costs.

While both financial theorists and practitioners disagree over certain aspects of this deduction, evidence suggests that firms do seem to seek optimum capital structures within any given industry. For example, financial ratios published by Dun and Bradstreet, Robert Morris Associates, and the Securities and Exchange Commission reveal rather striking similarities in financing patterns among firms in similar industry groupings.

But are these considerations equally applicable to the multinational case? The temptation to answer this question in the affirmative is great. And yet, once again we cannot or should not ignore the modifying influences of environmental variables peculiar to international operations. An examination by Stonehill and Stitzel of the financial structure of 463 companies from 9 industry groupings in 11 countries suggests rather conclusively that financial structures of firms in the same industry do not adhere to any worldwide industry norm. The disparity in international debt ratios is illustrated in Table 7-1.

Higher relative debt ratios for Germany, Italy, Japan, and Sweden, for example, are explained by their rather thin equity markets vis-à-vis those in the United States or the United Kingdom. The absence of widespread interest by individuals in security ownership, perhaps due in part to the rela-

TABLE 7 – 1. Debt Ratios in Selected Industries and Countries[a]

	ALCOHOLIC BEVERAGES	AUTO-MOBILES	CHEMICALS	ELECTRICAL	FOODS	IRON AND STEEL	NON-FERROUS METALS	PAPER	TEXTILES	TOTAL
Benelux	45.7	—	44.6	37.5	56.2	50.0	59.2	35.9	54.2	47.9
France	35.8	36.0	34.3	59.1	24.7	33.7	55.0	35.5	20.9	37.2
W. Germany	59.2	55.1	54.8	67.5	42.5	63.8	68.1	71.8	44.9	58.6
Italy	64.9	77.3	68.2	73.6	66.4	77.9	67.5	—	66.6	70.3
Japan	60.9	70.3	73.2	71.1	78.3	74.5	74.5	77.7	72.2	72.5
Sweden	—	76.4	45.6	60.1	46.8	70.0	68.7	60.7	—	61.2
Switzerland	—	—	59.7	50.8	29.2	—	26.3	—	—	41.5
United Kingdom	43.8	56.5	38.7	46.9	47.6	44.9	41.7	46.6	42.4	45.5
United States	31.1	39.2	43.3	50.3	34.2	35.8	36.7	33.9	44.2	38.7
Total	48.8	58.7	51.4	57.4	47.3	56.3	55.3	51.7	49.4	

[a]The number in the matrix represents average total debt as a percent of total assets based on book value. Each company is weighted equally; i.e., the individual company debt ratios are summed and divided by the number of companies in each sample.

Source: Stonehill, Arthur and Thomas Stitzel, "Financial Structure and Multinational Corporation." *California Management Review,* Fall 1969. Vol. 12, No. 1, pp. 91 – 96. United States corporations are the 10 largest in each industry [four only for automobiles, ranked by 1965 sales and reported in *Moody's Industrial Manual* (New York: Moody's Investor Service, Inc., June 1966]. Japanese corporations are the largest publicly owned corporations in each industry as reported in *Kaisha Shikiho* (Quarterly Reports on Corporations) (Tokyo: Toyo Keizai Shinpo Sha, July 1967). European corporations are all the publicly owned corporations reported in *Beerman's Financial Yearbook of Europe* (London: R. Beerman Publishers, 1967).

tively lower financial disclosure levels existing in those countries and a shortage of large financial intermediaries, including mutual funds, insurance companies, and private pension funds, undoubtedly account for this state of affairs. In addition, banks in these countries are permitted to acquire a substantial equity position in creditor companies, thus reducing the perceived risks of default on what are in effect loans to "captive" companies. Under these circumstances, increased leverage appears highly desirable.

Our discussion suggests that the multinational cost of capital issue for the individual firm is a rather nebulous one. Considerations of whose cost of capital to use in evaluating a foreign investment opportunity are just as confusing. Thus, should the financial manager employ a company-wide cost of capital estimate in discounting promised cash flows to their present value equivalents? Or, should he employ the cost of capital appropriate to local firms operating in the same industry?

Arguments favoring one approach over the other have proven less than satisfactory. For example, in countries where the local cost of capital is high relative to a multinational company's cost of funds, use of the local cost of capital to evaluate foreign investments causes profitable opportunities to be foregone. On the other hand, it seems foolish for a multinational company to ignore the fact that some of its subsidiaries abroad may have access to lower cost funds than the parent.

A way out of this dilemma seems possible if we again introduce the notion of dual or multiple audiences-of-interest. A parent company perspective calls for use of a company-wide discount rate that reflects the effects of both parent and subsidiary financing costs. A local project perspective, on the other hand, calls for the use of a discount rate that reflects what the subsidiary has to earn in its own operating environment. This, of course, is dictated to a large extent by a financial structure that is adapted to local realities and local norms.

Management Accounting Considerations

Despite the improvements and modifications undertaken to internationalize capital budgeting theory, the fact remains that little progress has taken place in the actual implementation of these conceptual refinements. One study of the methods used by multinational firms to evaluate foreign investments discloses that, in most cases examined, firms employ the same tools of analysis internationally as they do domestically.[3] A somewhat more recent study of a similar nature concludes that not only do firms not modify

---

[3] Arthur Stonehill, and Leonard Nathanson, "Capital Budgeting and the Multinational Corporation," *California Management Review,* Summer 1966, pp. 39–54.

existing tools when evaluating foreign investment opportunities but that the overall approach to foreign investment decision-making is actually *less* sophisticated than that employed at home.[4] What accounts for such a phenomenon? The answer should come as no surprise to accountants. All the capital budgeting constructs that we have examined naively assume that the required information is readily available. Thus, given this happy state of affairs, all that remains to be done is for the financial manager simply to input the required numbers into some mechanical decision process and "crank out" the answers. Unfortunately, obtaining accurate and timely information is the most difficult and critical dimension of the entire capital budgeting decision, more so in the international sphere where different climates, culture, languages, and information technology complicate the generation of required intelligence. Until information systems are designed that promise to capture these extranational considerations, the present gap between investment theory and practice will continue.

FINANCIAL SOURCING FOR THE MNC

"Last week was an exciting week around here," comments the Vice President of Finance at International Utilities (IU), a billion dollar conglomerate. The reason: within a week's time, $100 million in financing and refinancing had fallen into place all at one time:

1. A $25 million Eurobond issue that, among several innovative features, amounts to a second mortgage on ships already being operated by IU's Gotaas-Larsen Shipping Corp. and four of its subsidiaries;
2. A $5 million mortgage financing, on trucking equipment, of the more conventional sort that IU gets into periodically;
3. A $45 million line of trucking credits for the Ryder and P-I-E systems that is one of the largest "evergreen"—loans without specific maturities—credits ever arranged for the trucking industry;
4. A $25 million conversion of a West German domestic Deutsch mark obligation into a Euro-Deutsch mark loan—in effect, a refinancing that results in a lower cost of the money to IU.[5]

While hardly reminiscent of a typical week, this brief scenario does provide an idea of the diversity of financial markets and instruments that international financial managers increasingly contend with. For, much to the chagrin of corporate treasurers, traditional sources of long-term financing have been drying up. Double-digit inflation, the after effects of global recession, and depressed share prices have dampened investor's enthusiasm for corporate equities and commitments to long-term debt in many coun-

[4] James R. Piper, "How U.S. Firms Evaluate Foreign Investment Opportunities" *MSU Business Topics,* Summer 1971, pp. 11–20.

[5] Adapted from "The Week They Broke the Bank at IU Corp." *Finance,* June 1972.

tries. Massive government borrowing to finance social services and other public expenditure programs, balance of payments deficits caused by soaring energy costs, and increasingly tight monetary policy to cope with domestic inflation are also contributing to the shortage. As a result, forward planning for financial sources is becoming a strategic variable in the competitive calculus of the multinational enterprise.

Effective financial planning in the multinational company, in turn, requires a data base on extant sources of funds both internal and external to the firm. In this regard we can distinguish a larger spectrum of financing possibilities than that available to any single country operation.

Internal Sources of Funds

Internal financing consists of funds that are generated within the parent-affiliate network. It assumes such familiar forms as capital contributions from the parent, retention of subsidiary earnings, intersubsidiary fund transfers, and borrowing under parent company guarantees. Such internal financing modes are not unlike those employed in a strictly uninational setting. Additional considerations must be entertained, however, once foreign operations are involved. For example, parent loans to foreign subsidiaries are generally preferred to equity contributions for a number of strategic as opposed to purely business reasons. A common rationale for this is the flexibility afforded by loans in remitting cash back to the parent company. As one financial executive puts it:

> In almost every part of the world, it's legally more difficult to return funds to shareholders through a reduction of capital stock than it is to pay off a loan; so if you have any prospects of converting the operations from a "cash requirer" to a "cash generator" over time, it's very handy to have on the books of the subsidiary some debt that it can repay as a means of getting funds into the parent country.[6]

Tax considerations are another reason favoring loan financing. In most cases, interest on subsidiary loans is tax deductible in the host country whereas dividends are not. Furthermore, repayment of a subsidiary loan, unlike the repayment of dividends, does not ordinarily constitute taxable income to the parent. Still another reason relates to management motivation. Foreign managers often operate more effectively under the pressure of required loan repayments than if equity capital were more amply supplied.

The provision of loans to overseas subsidiaries is, however, complicated by a number of considerations. To begin with, host governments may

[6]Sidney M. Robbins and Robert B. Stobaugh, *Money in the Multinational Enterprise: A Study in Financial Policy* (New York: Basic Books, Inc., © 1973), pp. 50–51.

insist on specified equity levels in relation to debt. Parent country controls over capital outflows, due to balance of payments considerations, also restrict direct parent company financing of foreign operations. Fluctuating exchange rates, in turn, add a unique risk dimension to lending abroad. For these and other reasons, variations in parent company lending patterns have evolved.

Parent guarantees of subsidiary debts, for example, are a means of indirectly financing overseas operations. A more recent innovation is the use of "currency swaps" or parallel loans among sister locations. A simple swap transaction involves a loan by a parent company to a domestic-based subsidiary of a foreign corporation. This subsidiary, in turn, makes a corresponding loan to the foreign subsidiary of the original parent company. This possibility is illustrated in Exhibit 7–1.

EXHIBIT 7-1. Illustration of a Simple Swap

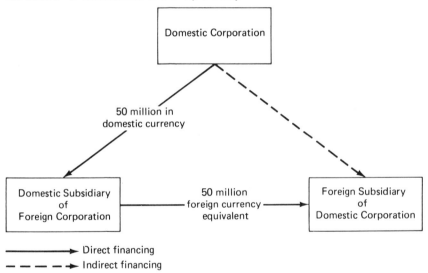

Another version of the swap is the parallel loan arrangement. For example, say a French firm decides to establish a subsidiary in Canada. The Central Bank of France, however, has restricted the transfer of capital from France. On the other hand, a Canadian parent company is reluctant to transfer Canadian dollars to its French subsidiary for fear of a possible French franc devaluation. Under these circumstances, two parallel loans could be arranged: one from the French company to the French subsidiary of the Canadian company; the other, of like amount, from the Canadian company to the Canadian subsidiary of the French company. This is illustrated in Exhibit 7–2.

EXHIBIT 7-2. Illustration of a Parallel Loan

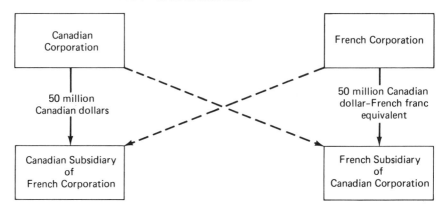

External Sourcing

Other financing patterns are discernable within the international enterprise; however, these internal sourcing patterns are largely variations of common domestic themes. Once external financing is entertained, the multinational alternatives that comprise a financial manager's decision set are quickly expanded both in number and scope.

External financing may be sought not only from financial institutions in the parent country but increasingly from a variety of sources abroad as well. Foreign financing can take the form of joint business ventures with local owners and/or borrowing from lending institutions in the country of an affiliate. It can also take the form of financing in the international financial markets. These external sourcing possibilities are summarized in Exhibit 7-3.

EXHIBIT 7-3. External Sources of Funds for the Multinational Company (MNC)

Foreign Financial Markets. Raising funds in foreign financial markets requires an awareness of a number of financing instruments and institutions not typically found at home. For example, an American financial manager operating in Europe will find overdraft financing a commonly employed credit tool. An overdraft is essentially a short-term line of credit arrangement that allows a borrower to write checks in excess of existing deposit balances up to some predetermined limit. The borrower usually agrees to make good the amount overdrawn together with financing charges within a stipulated period of time, normally a year. In countries where medium-term credit facilities are not available, these overdraft facilities are often renewed from year to year, thus filling a financing void.

The international financial manager also finds that financial institutions assume different roles in foreign financial markets. While a sharp distinction is drawn between commercial and investment banking functions in both the United States and the United Kingdom, this is not the case on the European Continent. Banks there typically perform both services and more.

Additional financing patterns evolve once cross-country borrowing is contemplated. As an example, interest arbitrage loans (arbi-loans) are available to firms wishing to augment relatively scarce local short-term financing with cheaper funds elsewhere. Thus, an Italian subsidiary desiring short-term funds might arrange a short-term loan from Switzerland where money is more readily available. Upon converting the proceeds of the Swiss franc loan to Italian lira, the Italian subsidiary simultaneously arranges a forward exchange contract to provide for the reconversion of lira to Swiss francs at the time the loan is repaid. Under this arrangement, the cost of the arbi-loan includes the nominal interest on the foreign loan plus the cost of hedging in the forward exchange market.

At times, however, the cost of obtaining a forward exchange contract may turn out to be negative. This would occur in our example whenever the Swiss franc sold at a discount in the forward market relative to the lira; i.e., the Italian subsidiary could purchase Swiss francs for repayment of the loan at a rate below the original conversion rate. Under these circumstances, borrowing Swiss francs, when interest rates in Switzerland exceeded those in Italy, could turn out to be the cheaper option. Profits realized on the forward exchange transaction could more than offset the unfavorable interest rate differential.

Provision by management accountants of timely and accurate information on the availability, relative costs, and currency implications of inter-country credit would no doubt enable financial managers to exploit favorable financing opportunities. When seeking longer-term funds, financial managers also need to be informed on the state and functioning of national capital markets as well as government policies and controls that typically vary from country to country.

A very concise and useful management reporting format on credit conditions abroad is reproduced in Exhibit 7–4 for a number of selected countries. Exhibit 7–4, adopted from Coopers & Lybrand's July–August 1976 *Newsletter* (International Supplement) is merely suggestive. More detailed breakdowns and specific geographical orientations would be dictated by a company's particular overseas financing strategy.

EXHIBIT 7 – 4. A Summary of Credit Conditions in Selected Countries

	CREDIT			PUBLIC ISSUES	
	Short Term	Medium Term	Long Term	Bonds	Stocks
CANADA (1976)					
Facilities	Well developed	Well developed	Well developed	Well developed	Well developed
Availability	Available	Available	Available	Available	Available
Sources	Commercial banks, Investment banks, Brokerage houses, Loan companies	Commercial banks, Finance companies, Insurance companies	Trust companies, Commercial banks, Development banks and companies, Insurance companies, Public funds	Investment banks, Brokerage houses	Stock exchange, Brokerage houses, Investment banks
Restrictions	None	None	None	Permission of provincial securities commission must be obtained.	
Costs	9.375% to 9.75%	9.75% to 10.5%	10% to 10.5%	9.5% to 11.75% Generally 1.5% higher than in U.S. Cost of issue, 1.5% to 2.75%	3% to 4% cost of issue for well-known company 8% to 10% cost of issue for smaller company
FRANCE (1976)					
Facilities	Well developed	Well developed	Well developed	Very limited for foreign-controlled enterprises	
Availability	Available	Available	Available	Tight	Tight
Sources	Commercial banks, Banque de France				Chamber of brokers
Restrictions	French residents may borrow foreign currencies up to the equivalent of 10 million francs per borrower without prior Ministry approval. French residents, including registered banks in France, may not grant loans in FF to nonresidents. Authorized banks are permitted to grant loans to importers in any currency. The authorized bank must remit the funds lent directly to the foreign supplier. The importer may repay such loans only after the funds have been remitted abroad. Limits of advances: 30% (capital goods), 10% others. Importers may not cover the above foreign currency loans by forward exchange contracts.			Stock listing generally required as well as government authorization.	Stock exchange commission approval required as well as Finance Ministry approval for foreign-controlled firms
Costs	11.5% to 14.2% Exports from 9.7% up	11.7% to 12.9%	12% to 15%	Interest 9% to 10% Issuing costs are approximately 2% to 3% Eurodollars 7.5% to 8% for 5 to 7 years	5%

EXHIBIT 7 – 4. Continued

	CREDIT			PUBLIC ISSUES	
	Short Term	Medium Term	Long Term	Bonds	Stocks
	JAPAN (1976)				
Facilities	Well developed	Adequate	Limited	Limited	Well developed
Availability	Ample	Ample	Ample	Tight	Tight
Sources	Commercial banks	Commercial banks, Long-term credit banks, Insurance companies	Long-term credit banks, Development banks, Insurance companies. Commercial banks	Stock exchange. Private placement, Commercial banks. Insurance companies, Securities companies	Stock exchange. Private placement
Restrictions	Compensatory deposit required (usually 5% to 40% of principal amount, depending on industry practice)	Government consent required in majority of cases. Compensatory deposits are also required, depending on the availability of funds and the customer's credit standing.		Stock exchange committee or government permission required	
Costs	6.75%	9.2% to 10%	9.2% to 10%	Cost of 10-year bond yields 8.894% to 9.195%	Cost, 4.5% to 5% (based on par value of stock)
	LEBANON (1975)				
Facilities	Well developed	Adequate	Limited	Available	Very limited
Availability	Ample	Available	Available	Available	Thin market
Sources	Commercial banks	Government-controlled development banks, Investment banks, Finance companies	Government-controlled development banks, Finance companies	Placement through commercial banks and finance companies	Stock exchange
Restrictions	Legal maximum interest charges: a) Commercial—12% b) Maximum imposed by courts—9%	Available with parent company's guarantee, or if company is involved in processing surplus agricultural production.		None	Stock exchange committee and government permission required
Costs	9% to 11% to prime customers plus 0.5% to 1.5% of other charges	9% to 10%	9% mortgage rate	Interest, 9% to 10%	Yield, 5% to 7%

International Financial markets. In addition to domestic and foreign capital sources, multinational enterprises can also look to a number of international institutions for external financing. Companies able to secure approval for projects in the developing nations have access to a variety of international as well as private and public regional lending agencies whose purposes are to support economic development programs around the world.[7] Examples of international lending agencies include the World Bank, the International Development Association (IDA), and the International Finance Corporation (IFC). These agencies, collectively referred to as the *World Bank Group,* provide debt and equity financing on both conventional (hard) and more lenient (soft) terms to governments, financial institutions, and private corporations that undertake economic projects of high priority in member countries. The Inter-American Development Bank (IDB) and the Atlantic Development Group for Latin America (ADELA) are examples of public and private regional development banks, respectively. Like the World Bank Group, these institutions offer a variety of credit programs within the context of economic development.

Of all the post-World War II developments that have occurred in international lending, perhaps none compare with the phenomena of the Eurocurrency markets. These financial markets owe their existence primarily to the innovative activities of private banks in responding to the credit needs of multinational enterprises.

Eurocurrencies are foreign currencies that are owned and deposited in banks outside the country of issue. Thus, British sterling deposits in Frankfurt are called *Eurosterling*; German deutsch mark deposits in Geneva are called *Euromarks*; and United States dollars deposited in Belgium are called *Eurodollars.* Because of the preponderance of dollars in Eurocurrency transactions, the market is often referred to as the *Eurodollar market.*

The short-term segment of the market started when dollar deposits in Europe, primarily owned by Eastern Europeans, were used to satisfy the credit needs of various international borrowers, both public and private. Since that time, the financial base of the market has expanded. It now includes funds from (a) foreign central banks who prefer to hold portions of their dollar reserves in higher yielding dollar deposits, (b) wealthy individuals around the world, (c) multinational corporations with excess cash balances, and (more recently) (d) the growing dollar reserves of the oil-producing nations. The market currently offers most of the short-term credit services available in sophisticated money market centers *with the exception that it is unregulated, international in scope, and multicurrency in nature!*

---

[7] It should be noted that public agencies able to assist in financing international business transactions also exist at the national level. The limited scope of the present discussion does not permit a detailed treatment of these agencies.

A more recent development is the longer-term segment of the Euro-currency market, often referred to as the *Eurobond market.* A Eurobond, unlike a domestic bond, can be denominated in any currency. The bonds are typically issued through an international syndicate of banks and securities dealers from many countries. The syndicate for any one issue is generally outside the country whose currency is being used. A typical Eurobond transaction, for example, might involve the issue of corporate bonds by a Swedish multinational firm, denominated in dollars, and managed by a consortium of European and, perhaps, American bankers. A portion of the issue might then be placed with wealthy Italian investors who maintain investment accounts with Swiss banks.

The Eurobond market owes its existence to a number of governmental restrictions barring the access of foreign borrowers to national capital markets. In the United States, such a restriction was manifested in the 1963 Interest Equalization Tax (IET). This measure had the effect of closing the New York market to foreign borrowers causing them to rely more heavily on the Eurocurrency market. Multinational corporations in the United States began to enter the Eurobond market in 1965 to finance their foreign operations when the United States government instituted a series of voluntary (later mandatory) foreign credit restraint programs.

The Eurobond market has accommodated both large and small debt issues with varying maturities and currencies. Both straight and convertible bonds have also been well received in the market. A summary of credit conditions in both the Eurobond and shorter-term Eurocurrency markets is illustrated in Exhibit 7-5.

EXHIBIT 7 – 5. A Summary of Credit Conditions in the Eurocurrency Financial Markets (Euromarkets)

	EUROCURRENCIES			
	Dollars	*Sterling*	*Deutsche Marks*	*Guilders*
Facilities	Well developed	Developed	Developed	Developed
Availability	Ample	Adequate	Available	Limited
Sources	The main centers for Eurocurrency deposits and borrowings are London and Zurich and, to a lesser extent, Paris, Frankfurt, and Amsterdam. Commercial banks (foreign banks and branches of United States banks) keep deposits denominated in foreign currencies and lend these same deposits for periods of up to five years.			
Restrictions	The use of Eurocurrencies, as alternate sources of credit, is sometimes limited by various restrictions on capital inflows. The restrictions are either in the form of controls on nonbank borrowings abroad or negative interest charges on nonresident accounts that are considered "speculative." Various restrictions exist in many countries.			
Costs	6% to 7.75%[b]	12% to 13.375%[b]	3.625% to 5%[b]	6% to 8%[b]

EXHIBIT 7 – 5 (Continued)

		EUROBONDS			
		Dollar		Deutsche Mark	Guilder
	Straights	Convertibles	Notes	(Notes)	(Notes)
Facilities		Well developed		Developed	Developed
Availability	Limited[d]	Limited[d]	Adequate[d]	Tight[d]	Limited[c,d]
Sources	Commercial banks, Investment banks, Consortia of banks and investment houses				
Restrictions	There are some restrictions on the use of borrowed dollars. The markets are generally unregulated.			Volume and timing of DM borrowings in Germany for external use are limited by the Capital Market Committee. The proceeds must be converted into a currency and immediately transferred out of Germany.	The Netherlands bank must approve issues made by foreign borrower and denominated in guilders. Private placements require no approval. External guilder issues not privately placed are restricted to sale outside the Netherlands.
Costs	9%[e]	6.8%[e]	8.85%[e]	Interest, 8.25% to 9%	8% to 8.25%
		Cost of issue, approximately 0.25% to 0.5% per year		Cost of issue, 3.3%	Cost of issue, approximately 0.6% per year

[a]Information subject to change at any time.

[b]Eurocurrency interest charges are for periods of from three months to one year.

[c]The Euroguilder market is mainly a note market (under seven years). It is not a large market, but Euroguilders are currently the third most important internationally syndicated bond issue.

[d]In some countries, such as Switzerland, funds in the Eurobond market are more available.

[e]Costs reflect a recent issue.

[f]Source: *Coopers & Lybrand Newsletter*, July–August 1976, p. 20.

Future Scenarios. The spectrum of financing options, identified in this or any other textbook on the subject, can never be exhaustive. The reason is that international financial markets are in a constant state of flux. Indeed, while the Eurobond market has yet to celebrate its fifteenth birthday, many of the conditions that gave rise to its inception have ceased to exist. The United States Interest Equalization Tax, mentioned earlier, has been officially removed. This action was recently accompanied by the dismantling of other controls on outward capital flows administered by the United States

Office of Foreign Direct Investment. In addition, the failure to reform the international monetary system and the resultant state of floating exchange rates have magnified the risks associated with Eurocurrency financing.

Do these developments spell an end to the long-term viability of this vital source of multinational financing? We think not, for the simple reason that there will never be a shortage of borrowers seeking to raise funds on any capital market. For example, trade and investment among the industrialized countries, both East and West, will increase rather than decrease. This must be financed somehow. The efforts of the less developed nations to accelerate their industrialization timetables also show no signs of abatement. Then there is the energy crisis that will, no doubt, continue to focus attention on the creation of new and improved energy sources around the world. This seems sure to create substantial new demands upon *all* elements of the international financial markets.

While the Eurobond market seems certain to prosper, however, it will undoubtedly undergo major structural changes in the years ahead. In fact, this is what multinational finance is all about. As new developments in the international environment create new capital demands, financial market innovations take place to meet those demands. A good illustration of this is the recent successful flotation of SDR-denominated bonds in the Euromarket. An SDR (Special Drawing Right) is a basket of 16 currencies created as a central bank reserve asset. Like other currency constructs, the SDR is an attempt to provide borrowers and investors alike with a store of value that is more stable than any single currency in today's world of floating exchange rates. As a new financing vehicle, SDR bonds promise to restore some of the Eurobond market's resiliency.

In addition, newer developments are also occurring on the international financial scene. The massive cash payments flowing to the oil-producing nations, as well as the recent emergence of the "Asia dollar" market in Singapore and Hong Kong, suggest that the Middle East and the Pacific Basin are assuming importance as new financial centers to be reckoned with.

While the future is never easy to foresee, we are certain of one thing. Financial markets, both national and international, will continue to adapt to whatever new economic and political forces emerge. Our time of "future shock" relentlessly places a burden on management accountants to monitor new developments on the international financial scene constantly.

MULTINATIONAL RISK MANAGEMENT

International financial managers are exposed to a variety of risks not encountered by their domestic-only counterparts. Environmental adversities that account for these added risks internationally include such phenomena as fluctuating currency values, restrictions on fund transfers beyond national boundaries, differential rates of price inflation, and expropriatory actions by host governments. These added considerations introduce yet another dimension to financial planning for multinational operations.

In a general sense, the subject of risk management is all-encompassing as it affects virtually every facet of an entity's affairs. To limit the scope of the present discussion, we emphasize the nature and accounting implications of those risks that are most prevalent and significant financially for multinational companies, namely foreign exchange and political risk.

Foreign Exchange Risk

Foreign exchange risk refers to the risk of loss due to changes in the international exchange value of national currencies. Thus, a British parent company operating a wholly owned subsidiary in Sweden, whose monetary assets are denominated in Swedish kronor, experiences a foreign currency translation gain or loss in terms of British pounds whenever the exchange value of the krona appreciates or depreciates relative to the pound. Since foreign currency amounts typically are translated to their domestic currency equivalents, either for management review or external financial reporting purposes (see Chapter 3), the translation gain or loss in this case is reflected on the financial statements of the British parent.

Fluctuations in currency values have been quite pronounced in the past. For example, De Vries reports that during the 20-year period from 1948 to 1968, 96 countries devalued their currencies. Of these, 62 countries devalued by more than 40 percent and 24 countries devalued by more than 75 percent. In terms of frequency of devaluations, about half of the countries examined devalued their currencies three or more times during the same period.[8]

Now that foreign currencies are relatively free to find their own value levels in the international marketplace, the frequency of exchange rate changes has become almost a daily occurrence. And contrary to what one might expect, the magnitude of these exchange rate changes has been far from insignificant. As examples, in 1975, the South African rand was devalued by 18 percent. That same year the Argentine peso was devalued by 82 percent. More recently, the Italian lira depreciated 30 percent within a 2-month interval, and the British pound lost 25 percent of its value within a year.

---

[8] Margaret G. DeVries, "The Magnitude of Exchange Devaluation" *Finance and Development,* No. 2, 1968, pp. 10–11.

In view of such currency instability, a major objective of international financial management is to minimize financial losses caused by this phenomenon. Risk management techniques in this regard include (a) forecasting exchange rate movements, (b) measuring a firm's exposure to the risks of loss occasioned by such currency movements, and (c) designing strategies to hedge such exchange risks.

Forecasting Exchange Rate Movements. In developing an exchange risk management program, the financial manager must have an idea of the potential direction and magnitude of exchange rate changes. Great disagreement, however, exists about the feasibility of predicting such movements.

Those supporting exchange rate forecasting as a valid risk management tool operate on the premise that decision-makers in the firm have the capability of outperforming the market as a whole when it comes to predicting exchange rate behavior. This capacity is, in turn, premised on the existence of timely and comprehensive information on which to base such predictions. Required data to facilitate currency forecasts might include, as a minimum, information as to

1. A country's balance of payments position.
2. A country's monetary reserves or external debt paying ability.
3. The rate of domestic inflation relative to that of its major trading partners.
4. The level of confidence in a country's currency as measured by
   a. Changes in the forward exchange premium or discount quoted on its currency for future delivery.
   b. the presence of a black market rate (for countries still adhering to fixed exchange rates) that differs significantly from the official rate.
5. Changes in a country's monetary and/or fiscal policies.
6. The behavior of currencies of other countries with which a country has close economic ties.
7. The past history of local currency stability.

While the foregoing items of economic intelligence are necessary inputs for any predictions, they are not sufficient. For changes in currency parities have been and still are, to some extent, a function of political sentiments. Political responses to devaluation or revaluation pressures in the past have frequently manifested themselves in a number of temporary alternatives other than exchange rate changes. Included here are selective taxes, import controls, export incentives, and exchange controls. (Mexico, in 1976, is a case in point.) Thus, indicants of the political frame of mind of a country whose currency is under pressure may enable financial managers to discern whether a particular government will lean toward market intervention or rely on free-market solutions to remedy its currency disequilibria. With the advent of floating exchange rates, such political "guestimates" are somewhat reduced but not entirely eliminated.

To others, however, exchange rate forecasting is a futile exercise. Foreign exchange markets, in a world where exchange rates are free to fluctuate, are said to be "efficient" markets.[9] Thus, current market rates can be thought of as representing the consensus of all market participants about future rates of exchange. All the opinions are based on interpretation of what currently available information means for future rates. If a significant number of market participants were to receive information that would lead them to expect a decline in the exchange rate in the future, they would reduce their holdings of that currency by selling it in the exchange markets. This action, in itself, would drive the price of the currency down until the market reflected the new opinions of all market participants, given the latest set of information. In short, information that is generally available would immediately be impounded in current exchange rates by the market and thus have little value for predicting future exchange rate behavior.

What does all this imply for management accountants? For one thing, subscription to exchange rate forecasting as a valid risk reduction technique means that accountants must develop information systems that are privy to the firm. These systems must be capable of gathering and processing timely and accurate information that is not generally available to the market. Only by so doing can accountants ensure financial managers of a "superior" source of information on which to base currency forecasts. If this is not possible or is economically unfeasible, then both financial managers and accountants should devote more attention to arranging a multinational company's affairs in such a fashion that, regardless of exchange rate behavior, the detrimental effects of rate changes are minimized. This process is referred to as *exposure management.*

The Management of Foreign Exchange Exposure. A firm's resources are considered to be exposed to foreign exchange risk whenever a change in exchange rates alters their value. A firm's net exposure is often defined by accountants as the difference between its exposed assets and exposed liabilities. Accountants are not generally agreed, however, as to how a firm's net exposure should be measured. As we saw in Table 3–3, at least six different measures of exposure can be distinguished. These range from a firm's

---

[9]For example, see Ian H. Giddey and Gunter Dufey, "The Random Behavior of Flexible Exchange Rates: Implications for Forecasting," *Journal of International Business Studies,* Spring 1975, pp. 1–31.

net working capital position, under the current-noncurrent foreign currency translation method, to a firm's net asset position, under the current rate method.

To illustrate, let us assume that a United States parent company has a single wholly owned subsidiary overseas. Under United States generally accepted accounting principles, the parent company's foreign exchange exposure measured by the net monetary asset position of its foreign subsidiary. If the rate of exchange between the foreign currency (FC) and the United States dollar were to decline from FC 4 = $1 to FC 5 = $1, the potential foreign exchange loss on a firm's exposed net monetary assets of FC 300 million would be $15 million. This is illustrated below:

Monetary assets	FC 600 million
Monetary liabilities	300
Net exposure	FC 300 million

Predepreciation rate (FC 4 = $1)	FC 300 = $75 million
Postdepreciation rate (FC 5 = $1)	FC 300 = 60
Potential foreign exchange loss	$15 million

In short, exposure identification for many firms has traditionally been a function of the specific accounting conventions adopted by a company. Under this framework, the measurement of foreign exchange risk at any point requires the collation of detailed reports from each entity within the multinational network of companies in a form that allows analysis of exposure on a continual basis. This presupposes a centralized control function, typically administered from corporate or perhaps regional headquarters, as the logical approach to analyzing both individual and aggregate exposure positions of the group.

To implement such a system, local balance sheets must distinguish among assets and liabilities according to the currencies in which they are denominated. A receivable denominated in Norwegian kroner is unlikely to have the same future value as a receivable in Portuguese escudos, even if both have the same face values at the time of sale. An exposure report along these lines is illustrated in Exhibit 7–6. The report is assumed to be that of a Philippine subsidiary of a United States parent company that manufactures a durable good for the local, Australian, and American markets. Factor supplies are imported from South Korea.

While similar in appearance in many respects to a conventional balance sheet, the exposure report contains a number of distinguishing features. In

EXHIBIT 7 – 6. Foreign Exchange Exposure Report for a United States' Philippine Subsidiary[a] (000's omitted)

	Philippine pesos[b]	Australian dollars[b]	Korean won[b]	United States dollars	Consolidated Results[b]
EXPOSED ASSETS					
Cash/marketable securities	$2,700				$ 2,700
Accounts receivable	4,000	$3,000		$ 5,000	12,000
Other exposed assets	900				900
Foreign exchange purchase contracts			$6,000		6,000
Future sales commitments		1,000			1,000
Total	$7,600	$4,000	$6,000	$ 5,000	$22,600
EXPOSED LIABILITIES					
Short-term payables	$3,800	$ 400	$1,000	$ 900	$ 6,100
Long-term debt			4,000	20,000	24,000
Foreign exchange sales contracts					
Future purchase commitments and Long-term leases		5,400			5,400
Total	$3,800	$5,800	$5,000	$20,900	$35,500
NET EXPOSURE	$3,800	$(1,800)	$1,000	$(15,900)	$(12,900)

[a]Adapted from a white paper published by First National City Bank, entitled "Corporate Foreign Exposure Management."

[b]Stated in United States dollars at the spot rate effective on the date of the report.

addition to disaggregating balance sheet items by currency, it also omits from consideration items that are not considered exposed in an accounting sense. These might be inventories, plant and equipment, owners' equity, and other nonmonetary items. It also includes items which typically do not appear in the body of financial statements but which have a definite effect on a firm's currency exposure. This includes items such as foreign exchange contracts, future purchase and sales commitments, and long-term leases.

A financial manager looking at an exposure report should be able to gauge the potential effect of a Philippine peso revaluation or devaluation on the consolidated results. Given this information, hedging policies then can be undertaking to offset any potential losses. One such policy would be to enter into specific contractual arrangements to ensure against a given amount of loss, i.e., hedge foreign currency risks in the forward exchange market.[10] Another policy would be to reduce a firm's exposure to as close to zero as possible by adjusting both the levels and monetary denomination of

[10] A forward exchange contract refers to the sale or purchase of a specified amount of a foreign currency at a fixed exchange rate for delivery or settlement on an agreed date in the future.

a firm's exposed assets and liabilities. Falling under the rubric of multi-national working capital management, specific methods of reducing a firm's exposure in a subsidiary located in a devaluation-prone country include

1. Keeping cash balances at the minimum level required to support current operations.
2. Removing excess cash to a central location, preferably in a strong (hard) currency country.
3. Invoicing sales in hard currencies.
4. Speeding up the collection of outstanding local currency receivables.
5. Using excess cash that cannot be removed from the devaluation prone environment to acquire inventories and other assets whose values are less subject to loss by a devaluation.
6. Liquidating foreign currency debts.
7. Maximizing both short- and long-term local currency borrowing.
8. Deferring payment of local currency payables.
9. Speeding up the payment of foreign currency payables.
10. Prepaying expenses denominated in strong currencies.

Accounting versus Economic Exposure. The reporting framework described above enables a financial manager to identify his company's consolidated exposure position in an accounting sense. But does it really measure exposure in an economic sense? We think not, for although the previous framework highlights a firm's exposure to foreign exchange risk as of a given time, it does little to identify the temporal dimensions of that risk. That is to say, it does not measure the effects of currency value changes on the operating performance of the firm. In many instances, the economic effects of exchange rate changes on the operations of a foreign subsidiary simply dwarf any accounting effects reported in the consolidated financial statements.

For example, assume that our Philippine subsidiary, described in connection with Exhibit 7–6, obtains all its labor and materials in its domestic economy. Assume also that it sells its entire output abroad. In this instance, depreciation of the Phillipine peso relative to all other foreign currencies (FC) might very well improve rather than worsen the subsidiary's position. A depreciated peso could increase the subsidiary's FC revenues by making its goods cheaper in terms of other foreign currencies. The subsidiary either could maintain its product prices in terms of the foreign currency, thereby increasing its FC receipts by the devaluation percentage, or could lower the FC price and, presumably, increase its sales volume. In turn, the devaluation would have no appreciable effect on the cost of its factor inputs as they are locally sourced. Thus, the profitability of the Philippine subsidiary conceivably would increase rather than decrease because of the currency depreciation. Under these circumstances, there would be little economic justification in booking a translation loss as called for under most present accounting standards and practices.

As another example, Exhibit 7–6 indicates that the Philippine subsidiary is short on Australian dollars ($A); i.e., exposed liabilities exceed exposed assets. On the basis of this report, a financial manager might decide to hedge this exposed position by purchasing $1.8 million worth of $A's in the forward exchange market. Would this be the right decision? Probably not. Although the Philippine subsidiary is short on $A's, not all the items appearing in the exposure report necessitate an immediate inflow or outflow of the Australian currency. Thus, the future purchase commitment of $5.4 million will probably not require a cash outflow until a subsequent accounting period. In addition, not all $A receipts or disbursements are included in the exposure report since future sales denominated in $A have not been considered. And, while $A receivables currently total $3 million, this figure will not remain stationary for long. From an *external* reporting perspective, these future cash flows should not be considered. From an *internal* reporting perspective, however, these future scenarios cannot be ignored.

Required—An Expanded Information Base. The concept of economic exposure necessitates reporting modes that, for most multinational companies, do not yet exist. Much more experimentation, such as that undertaken by First National City Bank (Exhibit 7–6), is needed if this developmental effort is to be sustained. While your authors do not have a specific exposure format to offer, we are in a position to suggest areas in which further development efforts need to be directed.

One such area is the formulation of a reporting system capable of differentiating between exposures which are static from those which are fluid in nature. Balance sheet items, which are considered adequately hedged in terms of the consolidated statements but which promise to affect the operations of the subsidiary or future income flows to the consolidated group, need to be identified and their effects measured and communicated. Similarly, currency receipts and disbursements should be monitored in terms of their behavior over time, such as the ensuing 12 months. This "flow of funds" reporting format would emphasize the significance of exposure generated by the currency movements of a going concern.

Accounting responses alone are not sufficient, however. Hedging decisions are often rendered difficult by the variety of legal and political complications that exist internationally. Envision, for instance, a situation where a Canadian parent corporation with several subsidiaries in Spain expects a devaluation of the Spanish peseta. Under these circumstances, an ideal hedging policy would be to have the Spanish subsidiaries remit their excess liquid funds to company headquarters. In practice, unfortunately, such transfers are usually difficult, especially if the currency concerned is already under pressure. Penalty taxes on fund remissions above a certain percentage of a subsidiary's earnings, withholding taxes on dividend payments, and objections to fund repatriations by local partners in joint venture arrangements are just a few examples of the obstacles that might constrain a company's hedging tactics.

Consequently, information with respect to both external constraints likely to affect defensive currency postures should also be an integral feature of the expanded information base. In a similar vein, internal constraints on exposure management, such as the availability of credit facilities, fund transfer mechanisms, local money market conditions, and budgeted cash requirements of the corporate system, should also be considered and reported upon.

Since foreign exchange losses on currency translation are very conspicuous in published financial reports, there is an incentive to pursue the "safe" path to eliminating accounting exposure, regardless of the costs involved. This would appear to be a highly undesirable state of affairs. For example, a common hedging technique against depreciating foreign currencies is for the firm concerned (say, a United States company) to invoice all exports in dollars and invoice imports in the foreign currency of the respective seller. In this case the risk of exchange loss is shifted to the foreign importer or exporter. While potential exchange losses to the United States company are thereby minimized, however, valuable sales may be sacrificed. The United States sales manager could very well increase his sales to the foreign importer by invoicing sales in a currency less prone to devaluation but softer than the dollar. The converse situation would apply to the United States purchasing executive. A likely result is that the increased profits, generated from added sales and/or more favorable purchasing terms, could more than offset any potential exchange losses involved.

One more example should suffice. Whenever the threat of devaluation is imminent, foreign subsidiaries in the country concerned are urged to minimize their local currency working capital balances—cash and receivables in particular. The subsidiaries are also encouraged to increase holdings of local currency debt. In many instances such policies prove to be short-sighted. Increased export potential, made possible by more favorable international terms of trade, might call for an increased investment in working capital rather than a decrease. The opportunity cost suffered in terms of lost sales could far exceed any translation loss shown for the year. In addition, local currency borrowing prior to an expected fall in local currency values usually prove extremely costly. Since other foreign companies have the same idea concurrently, the local banking system may be able to accommodate such credit demands only at an exorbitant cost. Furthermore, bank credit during these periods is usually scarce, since the economy is under severe credit restraint to counter the problems causing the devaluation pressures in the first place. The cost of borrowing under these circumstances often exceeds any protection provided.

These examples illustrate that hedging policies designed to reduce foreign exchange risks are not costless. Financial managers need to be kept informed of whether the benefits of a hedging policy exceed the cost of the hedge in terms of out-of-pocket costs and/or profitable opportunities forgone. We would argue that, in most cases, much of the required data for such an analysis can be garnered from existing accounting systems within the multinational corporate network. The challenge to accountants lies in their ability to reroute and recast such data to a form readily suitable for international financial decisions.

Political Risk

At one time, foreign business strategies of multinational enterprise were assessed primarily in terms of a country's economic climate. Today, the global political climate, as well as the political stability of a nation, must be considered in any international planning framework. Increased operating risks attending such recent developments as the fall of Indochina to communism, the socialist victory in Portugal, the fall of Angola to the Marxist MPLA, Peru's leftist coup, India's move toward totalitarianism, the OPEC boycott, and selective acts of terrorism, all bear witness to this state of affairs.

Political risk generally refers to the risk of loss occasioned by actions of governments that interfere with the profitable conduct of international business. Included here are (a) actions that limit the freedom of a foreign investor to operate in a given host environment and (b) actions that result in the actual takeover of enterprise assets. The former category includes such things as government restrictions on the transfer of funds out of a country; the imposition of discriminatory taxes of one form or another; quotas for local nationals in management positions; limitations on visas, work permits, and procurement of factor supplies; and breaches or revisions of contracts and agreements between the foreign investor and the host government.

The second category is financially more significant. Here, changing political and economic fortunes produce situations in which business assets are required to be sold to local shareholders (localizing ownership schemes); sold to local, state, or federal government units (nationalization schemes); or confiscated with or without compensation (expropriation or deliberate wealth deprivation schemes). Recent multinational petroleum divestments fall into the nationalization category, whereas certain multinational business properties located in Indochina were expropriated outright.

A recent study examining the characteristics of foreign takeovers of 170 American firms during the postwar period is illuminating.[11] A categorization of such takeovers, extracted from this same study, appears in Table 7–2.

TABLE 7 – 2. Summary Distribution of the Sample Foreign Takeovers of U.S. Firms, by Type of Characteristics and by Subperiod.

	ENTIRE POSTWAR PERIOD					
	Number	*Percent*	*1946-60*	*1961-66*	*1967-71*	*1972-73*
Total—All Industries and Regions	170	100	12	22	79	57
		(percent of the total for the period indicated)				
By Industry:						
Extractive	69	41	50	50	39	37
Financial	32	19	—	5	28	18
Manufacturing	51	30	—	27	27	40
Utilities	18	10	50	18	6	5
By Region:						
Latin America	93	55	83	59	44	61
Africa	51	30	17	—	51	16
Middle East	14	8	—	32	4	7
Asia	12	7	—	9	1	16
By Form of Takeover:						
Expropriation	103	60	67	95	63	42
Intervention/Requisition	25	15	—	—	14	25
Renegotiation of Contract	20	12	—	—	8	25
Forced Sale	22	13	33	5	15	8
By Selectivity of Takeover:						
Entire Industry: Mixed	21	12	33	—	8	19
Entire Industry: Foreign	68	40	42	68	38	28
Selected Firms: No Industry Specificiation	25	15	8	—	21	16
Selected Firms within a Specific Industry	56	33	17	32	33	37
By Political-Economic Circumstances:						
Leftist Change in Government	81	48	17	41	65	33
Right or Center Nationalist	7	4	17	—	6	2
Natural Resource Sovereignty	35	20	33	41	4	32
Mature and Standardized Product	47	28	33	18	25	33

The table reveals that takeovers of United States foreign affiliates by host governments have been on the rise. Moreover, this trend promises to continue. Increasing nationalism, together with the new sophistication in policy-making by host governments, suggests that expropriation is becoming a behavior mode with which multinational enterprises must increasingly contend.

[11]Robert G. Hawkins, Norman Mintz, and Michael Provissiero, "Government Takeovers of U.S. Foreign Affiliates," *Journal of International Business Studies,* Spring 1976, pp. 3–16.

For a time it was believed that firms in the extractive and service industries (including utilities) were the prime candidates for foreign takeovers. While this may have been true in the past, Table 7–2 indicates that is no longer the case. Expropriations in the extractive and utility sectors have declined (although expropriation in an absolute sense is still quite frequent in the extractive sector). In contrast, takeovers in the manufacturing sector, once thought to be least vulnerable to political risk, have increased significantly.

A large share of foreign confiscations appears to be concentrated in a few developing countries. These tend to be nations with a relatively high degree of political instability. While the form of asset takeovers includes all the categories mentioned earlier, expropriation, with or without compensation, is the predominant form. Finally, with respect to the selectivity of the takeovers as between foreign and local enterprises, the data suggest that assets taken over by host governments have been increasingly discriminatory (biased against foreign investors) of late.

Forecasting the Propensity to Expropriate. Research findings, such as those just enumerated, highlight the critical importance of rationally assessing the dimension of political risk. It is indeed surprising, therefore, to find that accountants have devoted scant attention to this growing area of management concern. A search of available handbooks, authoritative pronouncements, or even the literature in general, yields little guidance on this complex subject. This lack of attention on the part of accountants may very well explain why multinational firms have been slow to formalize their appraisal of political risk in each potential host country.

Recently, a number of attempts have been made to explain systematically the national propensity to expropriate foreign enterprises as a basis for subsequent prediction. To quickly sketch the role of accountants in this evolving area of prediction, we draw on one such construct.

The model described here was developed by Harald Knudsen.[12] It essentially involves gathering socioeconomic data to describe the "ecological structures" of a particular foreign environment. From this data, political behavior, with respect to foreign enterprises operating within the national confines of a given country, is predicted for some future period. There is, thus, an expected time lag between observation of "ecological structure" and the occurrence of expropriation or other political action.

The model draws its theoretical rationale from the observed tendency for acts of frustration—revolutionary political activity or political aggression—to occur where societal aspiration levels exceed existing welfare or want-satisfaction levels. The model postulates that when frustration is com-

[12]Harald Knudsen, "Explaining the National Propensity to Expropriate: An Ecological Approach," *Journal of International Business Studies,* Spring 1974, pp. 51–71.

bined with significant and visible foreign investments, foreign entities acquire a "scapegoat role." National leaders release their frustrations by taking expropriatory or similar actions against the foreign entities.

The model is depicted graphically in Exhibit 7−7.

EXHIBIT 7-7. The National Propensity to Expropriate Model

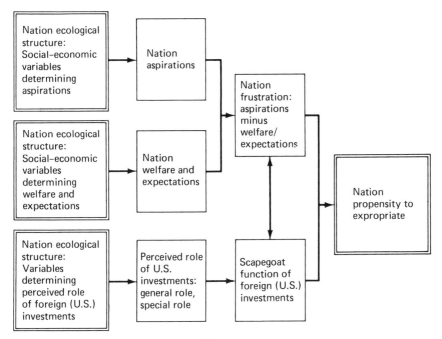

Note: Double line denotes measurable entities.

How does an accountant fit into this scheme of things? This question may be answered most simply by asking another. How is the variable "aspiration" or "welfare" measured? Can we find the answers to this question in some corporate manual or other financial publication? If not, who in the organization would be best qualified to quantify these variables in terms of a common scale of merit? If we conclude that accountants, as information specialists, are best suited to the task, how might they proceed?

Obviously, neither the aspirations nor perceived welfare of a given society can be directly observed. Surrogate measures of these underlying factors have to be used. As an illustration, several proxy indicators of the variable *aspirations* might include the distribution of population by urban/rural residence, the literacy rate among the population above a certain mean age, newspaper circulation per 1,000 inhabitants, the ratio of trade union membership to the total working force, the number of refrigerators per 1,000 inhabitants, and the country's endowment of natural resources. Proxy indicators of societal *welfare* might include the infant mortality rate, caloric consumption relative to estimated requirements, ratio of physicians per 10,000 population, gross national product per capita, and percent of total population living in housing with piped water.

Since the data listed above are expressed in terms of different measurement scales, they could be reduced to a common denominator by quantitative techniques such as factor analysis. As a result of this statistical manipulation, subject nations could be numerically scored on a given variable. By subtracting the "welfare score" from the "aspirations score," a measure of the general level of frustration could be found. A positive score would indicate a high level of frustration, and vice versa. When related to surrogate measures of the visibility of foreign investments, i.e., the level and political sensitivity of foreign investments, these scores would provide a basis for predicting national propensities to expropriate.

General models, such as the one described, are crude attempts at predicting a highly complex phenomenon. Nevertheless, they do provide a framework for gathering information so that financial managers may be better able to identify the possible outcomes of political actions and to estimate the probability of their occurrence. All the data for the model, described above, were readily available from a variety of public secondary sources. These data, which may help to forecast future change, should be monitored and included in the international financial manager's overall intelligence system.

Responses to Political Risks. Having appraised the likelihood of political interference in a given host environment, a multinational affiliate located there can adopt a number of responses to these perceived risks and their economic consequences. The accounting dimensions of some of these strategems are relatively straightforward. They are less clear for others.

Governments today are increasing their surveillance of foreign operations within their national confines. To minimize negative evaluations in any government cost-benefit calculus of its contributions, foreign affiliates often seek to harmonize their policies with the goals and priorities of their national hosts. Sharing ownership with local nationals, utilizing local sources of supply, grooming locals for technical and managerial positions, and exporting locally produced goods to bolster host country reserves of foreign exchange are examples of policy actions in this respect.

Internal accounting systems have two rather obvious roles to play here. First, accounting controls need to be instituted to assure that these "good citizen" policies are, in fact, complied with. Second, accounting systems can provide management with an idea of the benefits and costs associated with these policies. For example, while the practice of local sourcing is usually adopted to minimize the likelihood of expropriatory actions by host governments, it could very well increase the magnitude of loss should expropriation actually take place. Local manufacture of the required inputs by a foreign subsidiary necessitates a larger investment in productive capacity. This, in turn, produces higher losses than if the supplies are imported instead. Similarly, procurement from local suppliers leads to increases in operating costs because of lower quality workmanship and materials, unreliable delivery schedules, and higher invoice prices due to lack of economies of scale. Under these circumstances, the affiliate in question might be trading off a lower political risk exposure for a higher financial and commercial risk.

Another risk reduction tactic is to arrange an affiliate's affairs in such fashion that expropriatory actions are rendered difficult or unfeasible. A number of these arrangements, collectively referred to as *working capital management,* are already described earlier in the chapter. Examples of other techniques include (a) integrating foreign affiliates into a worldwide production and logistical system so that a subsidiary would not be able to operate or compete successfully on its own, as is done in the petroleum industry; (b) controlling key export markets for a subsidiary's output; (c) maintaining control over strategic patents and processes; and (d) entering into joint-venture arrangements with local companies. Identification as well as quantification of the benefits and costs associated with each of these actions is again an accounting concern.

There are many other techniques for minimizing political risk. Concession agreements with foreign governments that specify the rights and responsibilities of both the foreign affiliate and host government are quite common. Strategies employing a limited investment horizon are a more recent development. Insurance against a variety of political risks is also available internationally.[13]

Accounting issues associated with expropriation are similarly troublesome. When foreign assets are forced into ownership changes, it is normally difficult to determine the amount of the resulting economic effect. Book values, whether conventionally determined or, let us say, price level adjusted, are notoriously poor indicators of current economic values. Since forced divestment is generally accompanied by a politically unstable situation, market or liquidation values are difficult to estimate. Discounted future earnings are similarly precarious in these situations and, of course, comparisons with recent similar investments or replacement investments cannot be made since comparison situations are likely to be completely unavailable (forced divestment prospects eliminate or sharply reduce new direct foreign investments in the country concerned).

[13]For an extended discussion of these techniques, see Eiteman and Stonehill, *Multinational Business Finance,* Chapter 10.

So how does one measure the amount or value of an expropriation? Most often, it has to occur on the basis of adjusted book values simply because of the very limited availability of any alternatives. Since book values of assets are a consequence of particular financial accounting policies selected and taxation methods applied, they may bear little or no relationship to the actual economic significance of the event. Estimates of expropriation losses are usually highly subjective.

An additional complication is introduced if it can be established that current economic values, at the time of the expropriation, were in excess of net book values. In such situations, should a gain be recognized on the premise that expropriation constituted a form of "realization"? If the real economic impact of an expropriation event is to be measured and financially reported, a prior adjustment of book values is quite likely to be needed and, therefore, a gain or loss recognition unavoidable.

Forced divestments or expropriations seldom have a "record date." Sometimes they can be linked to a political revolution, an election, or some other definite event. But take-over control over enterprise assets may come gradually or step by step. Should parent company managements have discretion about when to recognize an expropriation? Could such divestments be recognized piecemeal? How might one time recognition of loss if, for instance, a newly established foreign government issues its own long-term bonds in exchange for certain business assets and these bonds have zero current market value? These and other questions must be resolved in timing the accounting recognition of expropriation events.

Finally, determination of the accounting impact of expropriations represents an unsettled issue. On the one hand, one can argue that wealth deprivations in other countries are a normal risk of multinational business and, therefore, should be anticipated with contingency reserves or similar other provisions regularly charged against multinational operations. On the other hand, one might argue that risk assessment in connection with future forced divestments is impossible and that their occurrence should be viewed more as a natural disaster or other outright loss. The latter view suggests treatment of such events as extraordinary gain or loss situations in the period of recognition. Hybrid treatments are often found in actual practice.

SELECTED REFERENCES

7.1 BURNS, JOSEPH M., *Accounting Standards and International Finance,* Washington D.C.: American Enterprise Institute for Public Policy Research, 1976, 59 pp.

7.2 CHOI, FREDERICK D. S., "Multinational Challenges for Management Accountants," *Management Accounting* (USA), October 1976, pp. 45–48, 54.

7.3 DUFEY, GUNTER, "Corporate Finance and Exchange Rate Variations," *Financial Management,* Summer 1972, pp. 51–57.

7.4 EITEMAN, DAVID K., and ARTHUR I. STONEHILL, *Multinational Business Finance,* Reading, Mass.: Addison-Wesley Publishing Company, 1973, 399 pp.

7.5 First National City Bank, *Corporate Foreign Exposure Management,* New York: Author, 1975, 49 pp.

7.6 GADDIS, PAUL O., "Analysing Overseas Investments," *Harvard Business Review,* May-June 1966, pp. 115-22.

7.7 GIDDY, IAN H., and GUNTER DUFEY, "The Random Behavior of Flexible Exchange Rates: Implications for Forecasting," *Journal of International Business Studies,* Spring 1975, pp. 1–31.

7.8 HAWKINS, ROBERT G., NORMAN MINTZ, and MICHAEL PROVISSIERO, "Government Takeovers of U.S. Foreign Affiliates," *Journal of International Business Studies,* Spring 1976, pp. 3–16.

7.9 KNUDSEN, HARALD, "Explaining the National Propensity to Expropriate," *Journal of International Business Studies,* Spring 1974, pp. 51–71.

7.10 LEES, FRANCIS A., and MAXIMO ENG, *International Financial Markets,* New York: Praeger Publishers, Inc., 1975, 538 pp.

7.11 MUELLER, GERHARD G., "A New Breed of Accounting Innovators: Multinationals Flex Their Muscles," *Proceedings,* Accounting and Finance in Europe Conference, London: The City University, Graduate Business Centre, 1976, pp. 93–109.

7.12 PRINDL, ANDREAS R., "Managing Exchange Exposure in a Floating World," *Euromoney,* March 1974, pp. 23–27.

7.13 ROBBINS, SIDNEY M., and ROBERT B. STOBAUGH, *Money in the Multinational Enterprise,* New York: Basic Books, Inc., 1973, 231 pp.

7.14 ROBOCK, STEFAN, "Political Risk: Identification and Assessment," *Columbia Journal of World Business,* July–August 1971, pp. 6–20.

7.15 RODRIGUEZ, RITA M., and E. EUGENE CARTER, *International Financial Management,* Englewood Cliffs, N.J.: Prentice-Hall, Inc., 1976, 619 pp.

7.16 SHAPIRO, ALAN, "Exchange Rate Changes, Inflation, and the Value of the Multinational Enterprise," *Journal of Finance,* May 1975, pp. 485–502.

7.17 SHAPIRO, ALAN, "Optimal Inventory and Credit-Granting Strategies Under Inflation and Devaluation," *Journal of Financial and Quantitative Analysis,* January 1973, pp. 37–46.

7.18 STONEHILL, ARTHUR, and LEONARD NATHANSON, "Capital Budgeting and the Multinational Corporation," *California Management Review,* Summer 1966, pp. 39–54.

7.19 STONEHILL, ARTHUR, and THOMAS STITZEL, "Financial Structure and Multinational Corporations," *California Management Review,* Fall 1969, pp. 92–95.

7.20 ZENOFF, DAVID, "International Cash Management: Why It Is Important and How To Make It Work," *Worldwide Projects and Installations,* July–August 1973, pp. 22–29.

DISCUSSION QUESTIONS

7.1 List 10 environmental considerations that might necessitate adaptations of domestic capital budgeting methodology when applied to transnational investment opportunities and briefly explain the accounting implications of each adaptation cited.

7.2 Consonant with the "multiple audiences-of-interest" focus in Chapter 4 is the question of "whose" rate of return to consider when evaluating foreign direct investment opportunities, e.g., local versus parent currency returns. Describe, in a paragraph or two, the internal reporting dimensions of this issue.

7.3 Obtain a recent annual report of a Japanese company and, using the information provided therein, calculate the following financial ratios: (a) debt to equity, (b) times fixed charges earned, and (c) total debt to tangible fixed assets. Repeat the exercise for an American company preferably (but not necessarily) of similar size and in the same industry. Explain any differences discerned.

7.4 As head accountant of a medium-sized multinational company, you have been asked to prepare a formal proposal evaluating the investment merits of establishing a manufacturing operation in Bangladesh. Assuming that the contents of your report is positive, would you then issue the same prospectus to the Minister of Development in the host country? If not, in what respects would your proposal to the latter differ?

7.5 Enumerate all the parameters that you would consider in measuring a multinational company's cost of capital.

7.6 A recent external financing transaction of a Swedish-based multinational company involved the issue of convertible bonds, denominated in United States dollars, and managed by a consortium of European and American investment bankers with a portion of the issue being placed with Italian investors who maintain investment accounts with Swiss banks. What do transactions of this nature impose by way of transnational financial reporting obligations on the Swedish borrower?

7.7 Is there a relationship between a multinational company's financial disclosure policy and its cost of capital? If you answer in the affirmative, specify as concisely as possible the dimensions of that relationship.

7.8 Critically evaluate the information content of the *Summary on Credit Conditions Abroad* reproduced in Exhibit 7–4. What suggestions would you make to improve the usefulness of that report to financial managers of multinational enterprises?

7.9 How might accounting for a Eurobond issue differ from that of a traditional bond flotation in a strictly uninational capital market?

7.10 Secure the annual report of a foreign corporation ("your" wholly owned subsidiary in this exercise) and measure foreign exchange exposure in at least six different ways (review Chapter 3 for specific methods). Which measure of exchange risk do you feel is superior and why?

7.11 Compare and contrast the terms *accounting exposure* and *economic exposure*. Are these exposure concepts different for most enterprises? Frame your answers in the form of a short essay.

7.12 List 10 ways of reducing a firm's foreign exchange exposure in a devaluation-prone subsidiary. In each instance, identify the cost-benefit tradeoffs that need to be measured and communicated to financial managers attempting to hedge such risks.

7.13 Utilizing references beyond the material in this chapter, devise a numerical rating system that would allow a company to dimension the political risk inherent in a given host environment. In constructing your "environmental risk index," specify at least 15 environmental risk factors about which businesses should be apprised.

7.14 Outline the valuation norms that you would follow in asserting your right to compensation following confiscation of your company's assets by a host government.

7.15 Your company has just learned, from unofficial sources, that the "Zonolian" government is planning to confiscate its assets. Management has given top priority to drafting a formal position paper to dissuade the Zonalian government from its intended action. Management has turned to you for the required intelligence. Suggest the major points that should be covered in your firm's initial communique.

ANNOTATED TEACHING MATERIALS

7.1 *Compagnie Generale Comestible* (Case 8, Zenoff and Zwick, *International Financial Management,* pp. 171–78). The treasurer of a Belgium-based multinational company is considering a field proposal to establish a fish processing and cannery operation in Gelibolu, Turkey. Questions, however, are raised by a young headquarters staff assistant regarding the analytical rigor of the original proposal. More specifically, the application of modern capital budgeting techniques suggests that the Turkish project should not be undertaken. Disagreement over the staff assistant's methodological and accounting assumptions ensues. Policy decisions to resolve the many issues raised are thus called for.

7.2 *INCO* (ICCH Cases A–E, 9–211–017 through 021). This five-part case presents a series of vignettes highlighting financial decision problems faced by a Swiss-based international firm. Case A involves evaluating foreign investment opportunities. Case B involves analyzing the merits of various means of financing foreign subsidiaries. Case C involves measuring the cost of capital for foreign subsidiaries. Case D involves considering changes in the method of evaluating return on investment for subsidiaries in various countries. Case E is concerned with evaluating foreign credit terms.

7.3 *Albo Enterprises, S.A.* (Case 12, Zenoff and Zwick, *International Financial Management,* pp. 250–58). In this case, a Swiss-based holding company for a United States multinational capital goods manufacturer must evolve a portfolio investment strategy in light of excess funds (available for differing time periods) generated by three of its European subsidiaries. Money market instruments under consideration include those of Switzerland, Italy, England, Germany, and the short-term Eurodollar market. Investment choice is further complicated by differing (a) types of debt instruments available, (b) yields, (c) short-term interest rate movements, (d) currency devaluation possibilities, and (e) national income and withholding tax provisions. The case offers a variety of insights regarding the deployment of a firm's liquid funds internationally.

7.4 *Marwick Home Products, Inc.* (Rodriguez and Carter, *International Financial Management,* pp. 228–43). The treasurer of the International Division of Marwick Home Products (MHP) has 4 days left to reach a decision regarding the company's foreign exchange exposure in pounds sterling. The decision to hedge MHP's pound exposure the previous year had proved expensive. On the basis of information regarding the state of the international monetary system and the British economy, MHP's treasurer must decide whether to (a) buy forward contracts to deliver pounds in 1 year, (b) leave the exposure situation uncovered through next year, or (c) do nothing now but sell pounds forward when and if the risks of a pound devaluation increase.

7.5 *K-Mart Australia* (Cases A and B, Graduate School of Business Administration, University of Michigan, 22 pp.). In Case A, the management of S. S. Kresge, a leading United States retailer, is reviewing future strategy regarding its first foreign joint venture in Australia. The current problem facing Kresge is that its Australian subsidiary's ambitious plans are in jeopardy unless long-term funds can be secured. Local sourcing is difficult in view of Australia's relatively thin capital market and a tight network of foreign exchange controls. Consequently, the company must decide whether or not to seek financing in international capital markets. Case B describes the contents of K-mart Australia's Eurobond-offering circular. It also illustrates how a firm desiring to expand abroad can use international financial sources in an imaginative way to solve its specific financing needs.

7.6 *Zweiss Associates* (Zenoff and Zwick, *International Financial Management,* pp. 205–13). Zweiss Associates, a joint venture of three United States-based companies, originally contracts with the Government of Sebacca to construct a fully integrated steel mill in that country. A recent coup, however, has placed a new political faction in power. While agreeing to several provisions of the original contract, the new regime now insists on a controlling ownership interest as well as a revised financing package for the undertaking. This unexpected development alters significantly the risk-return complexion of the construction project. Attention focuses on the nature and content of subsequent negotiation between Zweiss and the new provisional government of Sebacca.

Chapter 8

MANAGEMENT INFORMATION SYSTEMS AND CONTROL

Chapter 7 highlights some of the strategic planning issues faced by financial managers of multinational enterprises. Once questions of strategy have been decided, attention generally focuses on the equally important areas of financial control and performance evaluation. These considerations are especially important as they enable financial managers to

1. Implement the global financial strategy of the multinational enterprise.
2. Evaluate the degree to which the chosen strategies contribute to the attainment of enterprise objectives.
3. Motivate management and employees to achieve the financial goals of the enterprise as effectively and efficiently as possible.

Financial control systems are treated here as a special subset of the broader topic of management information systems. Accordingly, policy issues related to multinational business intelligence systems are examined first as a prelude to the more specialized topics of financial control in the multinational company.

INFORMATION AND INFORMATION SYSTEMS

In the complex world of international business, executives manage largely on the basis of information. Here, as elsewhere, information may simply be defined as data relevant to managerial decisions. As intimated throughout Chapter 7, however, multinational managers typically require an expanded and more sophisticated information set than their domestic

counterparts. For one thing, business decisions of the former are undertaken in a multinational as opposed to a single country framework. Super-
imposed on this framework are a number of environmental complexities
that impede simple and effective business information flows. This is portrayed graphically in Exhibit 8−1.

EXHIBIT 8-1. Decision Cells for International Managers

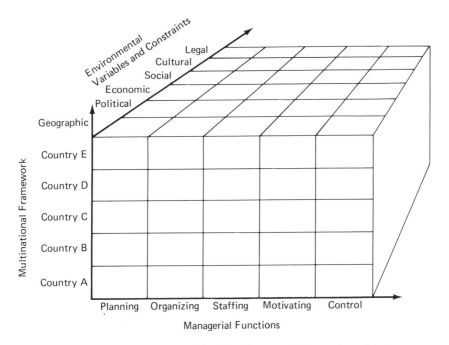

Distance is one of the complicating factors. Informal and instantan-
eous communication between a parent company and its subsidiaries is much
more difficult when they are thousands of miles apart. Due to geographic
circumstances, formal information flows in the form of written
communications generally substitute for relatively frequent personal
contacts between operating managers in local environments and headquarters management. The provision of timely information also becomes a
challenge of no small proportion.

Another factor is the great diversity of external conditions that must be
considered in multinational decision-making. Included here are various
legal, political, social, and cultural factors that bear upon financial decisions. For example, secrecy is much more prevalent in business dealings
abroad than in the United States. Consequently, United States headquarters
management must often rely on the use of internal auditors to monitor the

affairs of its foreign subsidiaries (to be discussed in more detail later). Economic considerations, such as competitive conditions abroad, international tax developments, transnational financing possibilities, foreign inflation, and fluctuating currency values, also need to be acknowledged in this regard.

Then there are information feedback requirements. An operation located halfway round the globe is more easily neglected than one closer to the domestic parent. It is especially important that all components of a multinational system be systematically provided with timely and relevant information. Failing this, coordination of group activities is well nigh impossible.

Business information flows have traditionally assumed a vertical mode in organizational hierarchies; i.e., information moves from lower to higher management echelons and conversely. Such information vectors are indeed appropriate where interorganizational dependence and cooperation is minimal. When organizational interaction is prevalent, as is often the case internationally, lateral information flows, such as between Far Eastern subsidiaries of a European multinational company, may be potentially as important as information flowing to and from company headquarters.

For all of these reasons, international managers are concerned (a) with the type and quantity of information they receive and (b) with the systems through which such information is created or collected and then transmitted to information users. It is important that the information itself not be confused with any particular information system through which it might flow.

Information Issues

Let us first think briefly about business information as such. Cross-cultural studies have established rather convincingly that managers in different environments have not only different ways of analyzing and resolving problems but also different information needs on which they base business decisions. Hence, we have a fundamental dilemma for the multinational enterprise. Local managers in host countries are likely to want different decision information than headquarters management is likely to want in the home country, e.g., local currency versus home currency rate of return statistics. Under these circumstances, deliberate redundancy is often the only way in which different but parallel information needs can be met. We shall return to this point shortly.

A second major information problem is the question of translation, transliteration, or transposition from one information code (language) to another. For example, in appraising the status of their overseas operations, United States managers generally express a preference for management reports stated in terms of United States dollars. Foreign investments are said to be originally sourced in dollars. Accordingly, foreign operations are typically translated to their domestic currency equivalents in order for United States headquarters managers to evaluate the returns produced by these "dollar investments." In translating foreign currency amounts for managerial review purposes, however, do we generally retain the same monetary relations after the translation process is completed as before?

A special feature of consolidated reports is that financial statements prepared according to foreign accounting principles are usually restated first to accounting principles of the parent country before being aggregated with other intracorporate accounts. In transliterating accounting effects from one set of accounting principles to the next, however, do we somehow alter the information content of the various components of a group consolidation?

Finally, can we simply transpose information such as, for instance, the word-for-word translation of a management report from English into French or the straight arithmetic restatement of United States dollar amounts in French franc amounts? Would a French manager receiving a report so transposed receive the same message (information content) as a financial manager in the United States on the basis of the original report? The recent experiences of several Japanese companies are suggestive in this regard. According to the Japan Overseas Enterprise Association (a trade group), a number of Japanese companies are using English as their official business language. One Japanese executive explains, "We have to use an international language because our operations often involve local staff who don't speak Japanese."[1] While such a policy boasts a number of advantages, problems also arise. Messages sent by wire are encoded in the Latin alphabet. The same sounds, however, often have different meanings. For example, the japanese word for *debentures* and for *credits* sounds the same—*saiken*—which often leads to confusion. *Tani* is another problem word that, in phonetic spelling in a financial report, could mean either a unit of money or the word *besides*. In financial affairs, this could make a lot of difference in the information content of transmitted messages. Furthermore, the Japanese language contains many words for which there are no English equivalents. As a result, technical communication in English is often an extremely difficult and precarious affair for Japanese managers.

Even if problems associated with encoding and decoding of internal messages could be solved, there would still be problems of coping with the phenomenon of information overload. The three-dimensional information matrix illustrated in Exhibit 8–1 displays the diversity of external variables that are brought to bear on financial decision-making within the firm.

[1] "Global Report," *The Wall Street Journal,* August 16, 1976, p. 6.

Consider the information load if one were to operate in 20 or 25 different countries! Human information specialists tell us that there are definite limits to an individual's information-processing capabilities. Once such limits are reached, information filtering, sequencing, sampling, or even discarding are resorted to. Because of this, multinational companies, attempting to optimize the use of information within the major constraints of human-processing capabilities and time, must increasingly weigh the benefits and costs of additional intelligence. A promising technique already implemented by some firms is Planned Information Acquisition Analysis (PIAA).[2] This method attempts to measure the incremental value of a new information source. Each new document or information service the firm uses for information is reevaluated after a 2-year interval. The number of times these sources have been used and found relevant as an information input is compared to existing documents in a similar category. Based on the results of this comparison, the information source is either dropped or retained. In this fashion, acquisition of new data may be limited to those items deemed most useful to the firm.

Systems Issues

Quite apart from the issue of information per se, there is the question of the type of system needed to facilitate multinational business information flows. Opinions are divided on this issue. Some business experts argue that information systems employed abroad should be no different from those used in a predominantly uninational setting. Others, however, argue for tailor-made information systems that are developed to accommodate the enlarged perspective of the multinational enterprise. Some would extend this to its logical extreme and adopt a "fresh start" approach that would develop systems with truly global orientations (systems not oriented to decentralized parent country operations) almost from the ground up.

Your authors would approach this issue in a somewhat different way. Rather than treat systems design as mutually exclusive options, we would adopt a more fluid posture. That is to say, information systems need to be responsive to the organizational framework and the particular policies that are implemented by managements of multinational business concerns. One writer has discerningly classified multinational organization policies as (a) ethnocentric, (b) geocentric, or (c) polycentric.[3] This classification scheme seems appropriate for the purposes at hand.

[2] J. Alex Murray, "Intelligence Systems of the MNC's," *Columbia Journal of World Business,* September–October 1972, pp. 63–77.

[3] Howard Perlmutter, "The Tortuous Evolution of the Multinational Corporation," *Columbia Journal of World Business,* January–February 1969, pp. 9–18.

An ethnocentric or home country orientation is one in which home country standards and attitudes are applied to all overseas business. Foreign operations typically do not enjoy independent existence and are tightly controlled from corporate headquarters. From an accounting point of view, business events and transactions abroad are measured and communicated from the perspective of the home country. Management and control occur through home country standards and procedures, by means of home country measurement rules, and on the basis of the home country currency. Overseas activities might be characterized here as *foreign* as opposed to *multinational.* Under these circumstances, it would appear appropriate simply to transplant domestic information and control systems abroad. This would be a good starting point for firms just venturing into the international arena. It makes good sense from a financial consolidation perspective and is, no doubt, cheaper to install than an entirely new system.

A geocentric or world orientation is a second category into which a multinational company might fall. Here, global thinking and organization supplants a purely domestic point of view. From this enlarged perspective, foreign subsidiaries are not viewed as mere appendages or interdependent satellites of the parent company but as parts of an integrated network whose aims are to optimize global objectives. Productive resources are generally secured wherever in the world they are least expensive and employed where their productivity is greatest. This organizational philosophy, in turn, necessitates coordinative decisions and the design of information systems that support the global decision mode. Tailor-made or "from the ground up" approaches to systems design seem called for here.

Despite the conceptual appeal of the geocentric philosophy, the fact remains that this organizational state is still largely an ideal to be achieved. At present, polycentric or host country-oriented companies are becoming the most dominant form of international business. These organizations recognize and thrive on international diversity. Their policies permit substantial degrees of local autonomy for foreign affiliates, with communications being largely of the two-way variety. In these circumstances, local managers in host countries need different decision information than headquarters management is likely to require for control purposes. Therefore, what is needed are expanded accounting systems capable of satisfying different but parallel information needs.

Management accountants can aid in designing information systems that incorporate data retaining their local characteristics (e.g., inflation-adjusted foreign currency reports) and, at the same time can be aggregated (translated) to satisfy more global points of view. Practices instituted by some multinational companies permit information diversity at the subsidiary level but also require that such data and accompanying analyses be remitted to centralized data banks. Such "parallel" systems appear to be far better than the single, centralized global information configurations that are strange to everyone, particularly those at the subsidiary level.

The multiple transnational financial reporting scheme discussed and advocated in Chapter 4 is really an outgrowth of the polycentric viewpoint and a parallel financial information system of a fairly high order.

ISSUES IN FINANCIAL CONTROL

Management control systems may be defined as processes aimed at the accomplishment of enterprise objectives in the most effective and efficient manner. Financial control systems, in turn, are quantitative measurement and communication schemes (information systems) that facilitate control processes. This is typically achieved by (a) communicating financial goals to appropriate responsibility levels within the organizational hierarchy, (b) evaluating the degree to which established objectives are being achieved, and (c) taking corrective action when actual performance deviates from expectations.

A sound control system is a welcome management tool in any business organization. To begin with, it enables top management to arrange the objectives of its various subsidiary units toward a common end. Suboptimal behavior, which typically occurs when each subunit strives to achieve its own ends at the expense of the combined entity, is thereby minimized. A timely reporting system that constantly monitors the activities of each subentity is helpful here. A good control system also enables headquarters management to evaluate the strategic plans of the company and to revise them when environmental conditions warrant changes in their underlying premises. This is facilitated by an information system which keeps management apprised of any environmental changes which might significantly impact on a company's operations. Finally, a good control system enables top management to evaluate the performance of its subordinates at each responsibility level of the firm. This is accomplished by assuring that subordinates are held accountable only for those events within their control.

If a well-designed control system is useful to a uninational company, it is invaluable to its multinational counterpart. As we have repeatedly observed, conditions that impact on management decisions abroad are not only different but are in a continual state of change.

The importance of a well-functioning control system can perhaps be illustrated best by chronicling the recent experience of a multinational company that apparently lacked such a system. According to *Business Week* (January 12, 1976), France's Rhone-Poulenc, the world's ninth largest chemical company, closed its 1975 operations with a hefty $200 million loss. While a recession was partly to blame for the loss, a major contributory cause was a management squabble that frequently pitted chiefs of some of the company's scattered and newly acquired divisions against Paris headquarters.

For example, in an effort to streamline its financial controls, Rhone-Poulenc's 112 major subsidiaries, spread throughout 23 countries, were consolidated under eight central divisions. These plans, however, were resisted from the start. Independent-minded executives in charge of Rhone-Poulenc's far-flung operations reportedly ignored requests for information, engaged in transactions without proper authorization, and even furnished company headquarters with false reports. One company executive explained, "Managers feel more loyalty to their original companies than to the group, and each one still belongs to a local Mafia."

With recession eating into sales, an attempt was also made to lay off some of Rhone-Poulenc's 120,000 workers. French law, however, constrained the company from doing so. Hence its solution was to cut the hours of both its blue and white collar workers. The result was a mini-revolt among Rhone-Poulenc's middle managers who complained that they were actually working just as long as before but for less money. The company's control system simply did not function properly.

Domestic versus Multinational Control Systems

Given the importance of a well-functioning financial control system, questions remain with regard to its implementation; that is, should a parent company use the same control system that it employs domestically for its foreign operations? This issue parallels in many respects the one we encountered on p. 256 in connection with the design of management information systems in general. That discussion, however, was necessarily broad in scope. The strategic importance of financial control in international financial management systems warrants further examination at this point.

Studies have revealed that the systems employed by a number of multinational enterprises to control their foreign operations are identical in many respects to those used domestically by the same enterprises.[4] Moreover, the similarity does not appear to have been the result of an oversight but rather the result of a conscious management choice.

A number of reasons might account for the reported findings. For example, in addition to reasons of expediency, there are obvious cost advantages to transplanting as much of the domestic control system abroad as

---

[4] See Edward C. Bursk, John Dearden, David F. Hawkins, and Victor M. Longstreet, *Financial Control of Multinational Operations* (New York: Financial Executive Research Foundation, 1971) and J. M. McInnes, "Financial Control Systems for Multinational Operations: An Empirical Investigation," *Journal of International Business Studies,* Fall 1971, pp. 11–28.

possible. Then, too, financial control considerations are usually not a critical problem in the early stages of establishing a foreign operation. Indeed, in those instances where the overseas situation is similar to domestic operations, "home country transplants" are probably desirable. But the reason most often cited for the use of identical control systems internationally is that domestic managers assigned to head up new overseas operations are likely to feel more comfortable operating with a familiar control system.

The aforementioned research results have led some writers to posit that financial control systems abroad should be no different from those employed at home. We do not concur with this view. For one thing, while there is some support for the similarity thesis for financial control systems, this does not necessarily negate the "ought to" viewpoint supporting *different* systems. Furthermore, it is unreasonable to believe that a central controller's staff could design a single, uniform worldwide control system, if for no other reason than that the overseas environment is so diverse. A simple transformation of Exhibit 8–1, replacing the horizontal vector with one that emphasizes a control dimension, illustrates this point. (See Exhibit 8–2.)

EXHIBIT 8-2. Decision Framework for Financial Control

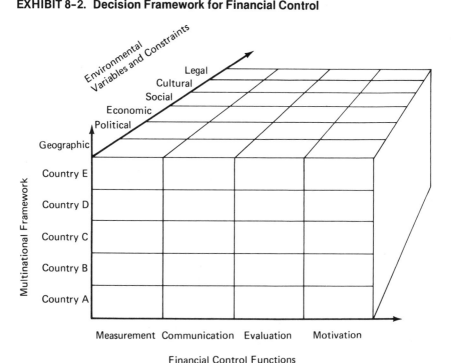

The potential impact of environmental diversity, depicted in Exhibit 8–2, on the financial control process is briefly described in the paragraphs to follow.[5]

Earlier we observed that geographical distance often creates an impediment to traditional methods of communicating business directives and performance results between affiliates and company headquarters. While improved technology promises to ameliorate many of the negative effects of geographic distance on interorganizational communications, there exists a more subtle kind of distance whose effects on cross-national communications are less easily remedied. We are referring to cultural distance, which inevitably accompanies the widespread use of foreign nationals in managing overseas affiliates. Language difficulties, cross-cultural differences in attitudes toward risk and authority, differences in need-achievement levels, and other cultural attributes often result in a number of dysfunctional consequences. These may include (a) misunderstood directives, (b) lower tolerance to criticism, (c) unwillingness to discuss business problems openly or to seek assistance, (d) loss of confidence among foreign managers, (e) unwillingness to delegate authority, and (f) reluctance to assume responsibility.

Under these constraints, managers of multinational companies are confronted with a number of dilemmas. Therefore, should a separate and distinct communications system by implemented for foreign nationals only? Should foreign nationals be evaluated in terms of performance standards that differ from those for their domestic counterparts? Should motivational techniques applied overseas differ from those applied domestically? Answers to these questions necessarily entail modifications to extant control mechanisms.

Distribution channels, credit terms, industrial policies, financial institutions, and business etiquette (including in certain instances expectations of gratuities to secure favorable business treatment), all vary from country to country. These actually diverse business practices call for adaptive behavior on the part of international financial managers.

Consider, for the moment, the subject of business gratuities. Bribes to secure business favors have long been illegal in the United States. In many parts of the world, however, under-the-table payments are a fact of everyday business affairs. Subsidiaries of United States agribusiness corporations with large-scale growing operations in the so-called "banana republics" report that such payments are necessary to assure that containers of fruit waiting for export are placed in "active" positions in the loading queues for outbound shipping vessels. One executive comments, "If these payments

---

[5]For an extended discussion of these environmental effects, see David Zenoff and Jack Zwick, *International Financial Management* (Englewood Cliffs, New Jersey: Prentice-Hall, Inc., 1969), Chapter 12.

were to be stopped, my bananas would just sit there on the docks and rot!'' Another example is local mail delivery. Unofficial payments to mail carriers is quite often a prerequisite for timely delivery of inbound mail. Apart from any ethical issues, the question of business gratuities overseas confronts financial managers of United States multinational enterprises with a very real additional dilemma. If such payments are monitored and acknowledged in the formal financial control system, a United States parent company may open itself to legal action at home. If, however, such payments are kept outside the control system through bogus documentation and contrived accounting transactions, the entire control system is soon rendered ineffective. This problem promises to command the attention of the accounting and legal professions for some time to come.

Companies with operating activities abroad must also adapt to a larger number of governmental regulations and restrictions. Exchange controls, restrictions on capital flows, joint ownership requirements, and a myriad of other specific business regulations are examples of this.

Hawkins offers a useful example of how governmental regulations and restrictions thwarted the application of unadulterated domestic control systems overseas in the case of one multinational company.[6] In this scenario, a business characterized by frequent and dramatic changes in production levels made it crucial for a farm equipment manufacturer to maintain a flexible manpower policy. Closely related to these production requirements was a need for the company to maintain tight control over the levels of its raw material inventories. Accordingly, the entire management control system was geared to communicating to plant managers the need to control labor costs and inventory levels and to motivate managers to exercise this control. Overseas, however, this same control system proved useless.

As it turned out, foreign managers could not and would not lay off labor every time there was a lull in production. Local laws and customs in many countries either prohibited or discouraged laying off workers. Similarly, since many of the raw materials used in the production process abroad were imported, inventory levels were, in large measure, determined by the availability of foreign exchange. In those countries where foreign exchange was restricted, inventory policy was, in effect, controlled not by management decision but by government balance of payments policies. The control system simply did not recognize this operating reality, resulting, not surprisingly, in poor profit performance on the part of the manufacturer's overseas operations.

Of all the environmental considerations enumerated in Exhibit 8−2, perhaps the most influential on the design of overseas control systems are those related to the strength of a nation's currency. Internal rates of inflation and fluctuating currency values are the prime considerations here.

---

[6] David F. Hawkins, ''Controlling Foreign Operations,'' *Financial Executive*, February 1965, p. 31.

Fluctuating currency values, for example, make budgetary goal setting an extremely difficult process overseas. Just imagine the frustration budgetary analysts experience every time sales and profit plans are carefully and painstakingly drawn and laid only to find such projections invalidated by overnight currency exchange rate chages (1976 examples in Germany, Mexico, and the United Kingdom come to mind readily). To keep financial managers apprised of such developments, more frequent and comprehensive data on such environmental trends are needed. And yet, there is the rub! Such data are often unavailable or difficult to gather in many countries that host subsidiaries of multinational enterprises.

Chapter 7 identifies a number of working capital management techniques designed to minimize the adverse effects of fluctuating exchange rates and inflation. Often these practices deviate from asset management policies called for in more stable environments. Corporate control systems need to acknowledge these differences. Failing this, system inadequacies will again surface as a result of applying financial controls designed for a more stable environment to a less stable one.

Considerations identified in the preceding section suggest that financial control systems of a multinational company need to be adapted to the environmental constraints of its national hosts. Three related issues whose resolutions ultimately influence the particular design of any financial control system are discussed in the remaining sections of this chapter. They are

1. The control philosophy of headquarters management.
2. The methodology to employ in evaluating the results of foreign operations.
3. The role of internal auditors in controlling overseas operations.

Administration of the Financial Control Function

Whether or not multinational companies modify their financial control systems when operating in foreign environments, one thing is clear. Most companies differ in their administration of financial controls. Financial control policy is, in turn, related in large measure to management's organizational philosophy, particularly as it relates to the international financial function. Here, as elsewhere, opinions are divided as to a *best* organizational approach. Examine, for example, the remarks of a group treasurer of a medium-sized multinational company headquartered in San Francisco:

> We work very closely with our [local] financial managers and we expect them to follow very closely our policies and procedures. We consult with them, but when something critical comes up, we'll send out a cable directing them that immediately they are to hedge and such and such. But generally speaking, we have an opportunity to review the sub-

ject with them, suggest what we propose to do, and then give them a chance to react to it. I mean as a matter of courtesy, if nothing else. And many times, they can contribute in a very worthwhile way to whatever our plans may be. I don't like to say that our companies don't have any leeway. They are part of our team and we like to use their brains just like they were sitting right here; and we try to operate on this basis. But someone along the line has to say 'this is what we do' and that's San Francisco.[7]

This viewpoint obviously favors *centralization* of the international financial function. Financial policy decisions are located at a high enough level in the organization so that sufficient perspective is gained to appreciate which courses of action best serve company-wide objectives.

Consider now another point of view expressed by the financial vice president of a large industrial goods manufacturer:

> The decision-making levels for particular types of matters are identical in the international and domestic divisions. This, I believe, is a mistake. I think that the local managers abroad are more than just plant managers or sales managers for a particular country. They are the men who in the eyes of the public and their employees are our company. They are executives who run a complete operation. I believe we usually have higher caliber men in these positions than we normally have domestically. If we do have that kind of man overseas, we should give him more freedom to make decisions.[8]

The viewpoint just expressed favors a *decentralized* international financial framework. Financial decisions are delegated to subsidiary managers who have a better "feel" for their operating environments.

How then do we choose between these opposing viewpoints? Does theory provide us with any answers? Unfortunately, No! Management scientists, for example, extol the many virtues of organizational patterns premised on a decentralized profit center orientation. We are also told, on the other hand, that the basic rationale for the multinational corporation is the many economic advantages that accrue from seeking out the most efficient combination of resources worldwide. The global planning and logistical coordination that this entails implies centralized administration and direction for the entire enterprise management system.

Where does this leave us? In the absence of viable theoretical norms, a pragmatic approach to the issue seems best. If we observe the behavior of multinational enterprises in this regard, we find that many are breaking their own ground on the matter. For example, a study analyzing the func-

[7]Sidney M. Robbins and Robert B. Stobaugh, *Money in the Multinational Enterprise: A Study in Financial Policy* (New York: Basic Books, Inc., ©1973), p. 41.

[8]Zenoff and Zwick, p. 463.

tional organization patterns of 300 United States based multinational companies suggests that several basic patterns are beginning to emerge, namely[9]

1. Centralization of the international financial function at corporate headquarters.
2. Centralization of the international financial function at international headquarters.
3. Division of the international financial function between corporate and international headquarters.

One interpretation of these findings is that there is no optimal pattern to the organization of the international financial function. A more plausible explanation is offered by Robbins and Stobaugh who conclude that the patterns observed are not random occurrences. Instead they tend to develop and evolve in a predictable fashion. Moreover, companies' sizes and degrees of international involvement are important determinants of organizational patterns and the resultant financial effects.[10]

Thus, empirical observations suggest that small firms typically run decentralized financial operations. With a small financial staff and a limited involvement in overseas pursuits, company headquarters typically has neither the time nor the required expertise to manage closely the financial affairs of its foreign subsidiaries. Key decisions are generally made by financial managers overseas, with little direction, if any, provided by parent company management.

As a company's foreign involvement grows, several developments occur. Increased company size is normally accompanied by a larger and more experienced financial staff, better attuned to the needs of the total system. The increased importance of overseas operations also encourages closer control by headquarters' personnel. Under these conditions, financial decision-making becomes an increasingly centralized affair. Headquarters staff make strategic financial decisions for the entire system, and implementing decisions are made at the local level. The emphasis now shifts from a policy of "every tub on its own bottom" to one of systems optimization. Often, a stage is reached later on when a company becomes so large and complex that centralized decision-making becomes extremely difficult. Whereas headquarters management would like to maintain tight control over financial decisions abroad, the greater number of financial options, resulting from an increased network of foreign subsidiaries, makes an overall systems approach well nigh impossible to achieve. Adaptations to evolving organizational constraints are thus effected by decentralizing

[9] Irene W. Meister, *Managing the International Financial Function* (New York: National Industrial Conference Board, 1970).

[10] Robbins and Stobaugh, *Money in the Multinational Enterprise*, pp. 37–44.

financial decision-making but within a framework of policy guidelines issued by central headquarters staff.

Where does this leave us? The organizational patterns just described can be seen as representing different stages of evolution along the path toward a more global organizational philosophy. Other patterns are likely to unfold as organizational philosophies attain the heights of geocentrism. The direct implication here is that financial control systems need to assume a chameleonic posture overseas. Financial control systems, in short, are not static concepts. Rather, they must remain ever responsive to changes in the organizational structure of the multinational enterprise, recognizing all the variables and constraints under which its units operate.

Performance Evaluation

The evaluation of enterprise performance is an essential ingredient of an effective control system. As financial strategems are implemented and executed, periodic surveillance is necessary to ensure that enterprise objectives are being accomplished to the fullest. This, in turn, requires an effective reporting system for gathering intelligence on results of actual operations and disclosing deviations from specified standards so that corrective action may be taken.

While these requirements are applicable to enterprise operations both at home or abroad, a number of considerations complicate performance evaluation methodology when applied overseas. Accounting measurements of subsidiary results and the specification of appropriate performance standards are especially troublesome.

Measurement Systems. Return on investment is a generally accepted indicant of the long-run profitability of a business entity. It is reportedly one of the principal measures employed by United States multinationals to gauge the performance of their foreign subsidiaries.[11] The measurement of this performance concept, however, raises a number of vexing questions:

1. What income numbers should be used in return on investment calculations and how should they be measured?
2. What should be included in the investment base and how should these items be measured?
3. What currency construct should be employed in intercountry (comparative) performance reports?

[11] James R. Basche, Jr., *Measuring Profitability of Foreign Operations* (New York: The Conference Board, 1970).

Let us first consider the numerator of any rate of return calculation. Whose income numbers should we include here; i.e., should it be income to the foreign subsidiary or income to the parent? If it is the former, should the subsidiary's operating income be calculated before or after local taxes and other deductions such as parent company overhead or research and development allocations? Similar considerations apply to income flows to the parent company except that now home country tax rates must be considered. The question of international taxation is pursued further in Chapter 9.

The measurement of enterprise income for rate of return calculations is complicated by a number of additional considerations. Since foreign subsidiaries often engage in intracompany transactions, the influence of a given subsidiary on the return streams of other units in the system need to be accounted for; however, such assessments are exceedingly difficult. Imagine the problem of trying to measure the spillover effects of an intersubsidiary sale where merchandise, for tax or other environmental considerations, is channeled through a maze of sister subsidiaries located in different national jurisdictions. Such determinations become unwieldy when the number of products and subsidiaries involved is large. Determining what to include in parent company income streams from abroad is just as troublesome. As an example, which combinations of foreign earnings, royalties, fees, dividends, rentals, interest, commissions, and export profits should we include? Should all these be considered or only profits actually repatriated to the home country?

Now consider the denominator of the rate of return construct. What is the appropriate investment base? Should it be sales, owners' equity, or total assets? If the last, should fixed assets included in the investment base be measured at original acquisition cost or at cost less accumulated depreciation? The behavioral effects of either measurement are not trivial. Assets included in the investment base at gross book value may often lead to suboptimal replacement actions on the part of subsidiary managers. Since their performance is assessed in terms of return on investment statistics, it is possible for a manager to increase his performance indicators by disposing of perfectly useful assets that are not contributing to specified profit targets. While favorable to the subsidiary's return on investment, such action may be detrimental to the enterprise as a whole.

Closely related to the question of the investment base is the problem of asset valuation. In countries where inflation is a significant force, financial managers must face the issue of whether or not to restate asset values for changing price levels. Such restatements directly affect measures of enterprise earnings as well as the investment base in rate of return calculations. Failure to account for inflation generally results in an overstatement of return on investment measures. As a result, enterprise resources may not be channeled to their most promising use within the multinational network, and overall company goals fail to be optimized. Solutions to these problems are not readily formulated. As mentioned in Chapter 3, accountants and enterprise managers are still not agreed on whether financial statement effects of inflation should be accounted for. Even if they were, there still would not be agreement as to the best method of accounting for inflation.

In measuring the profitability of its foreign subsidiaries, headquarters management must also decide whether to hold subsidiary managers responsible for foreign exchange losses. As we learned in Chapter 3, foreign exchange gains or losses can have a significant effect on the results of foreign operations. Favorable operating results, measured in terms of local currency, may become losses when translated to their domestic currency equivalents.

At the present time, firms appear to be equally divided on the issue of a reporting currency for performance evaluation purposes. Those judging subsidiary performance in terms of local currency generally feel that local managers should not be held responsible for hedging foreign exchange risk. They feel that the objective of a performance appraisal is to evaluate the operating efficiency of the subsidiary manager rather than his ability to protect a firm's assets from fluctuating currency values. One company official holding such a view states:

> The management of the subsidiary is not responsible for devaluation losses. The treasury office here [in headquarters] is very much concerned with what happens from a devaluation point of view, and in this sense we're quite centralized. We sit here trying to figure out at all times how to minimize the exchange loss that we have on whatever devaluation occurs. All sorts of analyses are made to figure out how we did. Did we gain, did we lose, did we do all the things that could have been done in hindsight to minimize or eliminate the exchange loss? But as far as the subsidiary performance is concerned, devaluation is excluded.[12]

There are, on the other hand, enterprises that evaluate all foreign subsidiaries strictly on the basis of domestic currency reports. Since many foreign investments are originally financed with domestic currency, they are expected to generate domestic currency returns. Says one official, "when you make a consolidated statement, you have to have a prominent currency, and if you're a U.S. company, it has to be dollars." With respect to top management's viewpoint, he states, "They're interested just in dollars. They don't even want to know how many pesos are in a dollar, what's an Australian dollar worth compared to the U.S. dollar, or what's sterling worth. They don't give a damn. It's strictly dollars."[13]

[12] Robbins and Stobaugh, *Money in the Multinational Enterprise,* pp. 154–55.
[13] *Ibid.*

But then, even if dollars were a better yardstick of performance than local currency, problems would still remain. Currency exchange value changes that lag behind foreign rates of inflation due to local government intervention in the exchange markets could still distort performance measures. In a period of excessive inflation, local currency earnings and their dollar equivalents would increase. In the subsequent period in which the foreign currency depreciates, the dollar value of local earnings would fall despite any increase in local currency earnings. Under these circumstances, dollar measurements introduce a random element to foreign performance measures despite possible stable earnings patterns overseas.

Performance Standards. The use of return on investment criteria in evaluating a firm's domestic subsidiaries predates its use overseas. In the United States, for example, activities organized as independent profit centers have proven to be one of the most successful organizational innovations of the postwar era. Under a decentralized system, subsidiary managers are accorded the necessary authority to engage in decisions directly affecting their spheres of activity. Numerical measures of performance, such as rate of return statistics, have also proven both useful and appropriate at all levels of a decentralized financial control system.

In view of its success on the domestic front, it is not hard to see why the same performance criterion has been employed overseas as well. But are domestic performance standards really useful in evaluating multinational operations? Are the conditions underlying their use at home and abroad the same? The following paragraphs argue that this is seldom the case.

Subsidiaries are established abroad for a number of strategic reasons. For example, companies whose existence is critically dependent on a steady supply of factor inputs, such as in the petroleum and steel industries, generally expand overseas to secure sources of raw materials. Others invest abroad to lower production costs. This is accomplished by gaining access to sources of less costly labor, power, or auxiliary services. When a company can no longer profitably service a market by exporting to it because of increased tariffs, it will often establish a local operation within the country concerned to circumvent such barriers. Other reasons for expanding abroad include (a) the search for new and enlarged markets, (b) the bandwagon or follow-the-leader effect, (c) the desire to spread overhead costs among a larger number of producing units, (d) the utilization of old but still functional equipment, and (e) the creation of markets for components and other products. Despite such strategic considerations, headquarters management often overlooks this fact when subsequently evaluating the performance of their foreign subsidiaries. In many cases, a year or more may elapse between the time the foreign investment is approved and the commencement of its operations. By this time, many executives associated with the original investent decision may (a) be preoccupied with some other strategic problem, (b) have accepted a new assignment elsewhere in the corporate system, or (c) have simply forgotten the strategy of the original decision.[14]

When this occurs, performance evaluations based on company-wide performance criteria are generally unsatisfactory. A couple of examples may help to illustrate this point. In their bid to tap the resources of the multibillion dollar Eurobond market, many United States multinationals established special offshore financing subsidiaries under appropriate enabling legislation. A major purpose of these subsidiaries was to secure funds for profitable deployment elsewhere in the corporate international system. Evaluating the profitability of these subsidiaries by using company-wide performance criteria necessarily proves misleading. Although a foreign financing subsidiary may not be profitable on its own, this cannot be taken at face value since its operations obviously contribute to profits elsewhere in the system.

Used or outmoded equipment with little resale value in the domestic market is often shipped, usually at prices above net book values, to newly established operations in less developed countries. Since production modes are generally unsophisticated in the early stages of an operation, such used equipment transfers make good sense. Once operations are in full swing, however, they are often expected to earn a return consistent with target rates established for all subsidiaries. Whether this produces meaningful results when the investment base bears little or no relation to the opportunity cost of the resources employed (either in the host or the parent countries) is for the reader to decide.

In addition to the strategic nature of many multinational investments, actions affecting the profitability of activities abroad are frequently beyond the control of foreign managers. In attempts to optimize system objectives, decisions affecting subsidiary operations are generally centralized at company headquarters. The management of foreign exchange risk is one such operation calling for centralized control. To protect the value of assets located in devaluation-prone countries, headquarters management will often instruct subsidiaries located there to transfer excess funds to subsidiaries located in countries with stronger currencies. This may be accomplished (at least in part) by increasing the transfer prices that subsidiaries in the devaluation-prone country must pay for imported goods from sister subsidiaries. Such policies are undoubtedly beneficial from a company-wide standpoint. They can, however, lead to serious motivational problems if management performance is gauged by profits allocated to them rather than by those they actually earned.

---

[14] Sidney M. Robbins and Robert B. Stobaugh, "The Bent Measuring Stick for Foreign Subsidiaries," *Harvard Business Review*, September–October 1973, p. 87.

Actions and policies of host governments can also directly affect the reported results of a foreign subsidiary for better or worse. Required minimum capitalization ratios in various countries often bias subsidiary rate of return calculations by inflating the investment base against which earnings are compared. Foreign exchange controls that ration the availability of foreign currency to pay for needed imports will often have a depressing effect on a subsidiary's performance. Such policies generally necessitate the stockpiling of imported inventories and other supplies when foreign exchange is readily available, thus inflating storage and holding costs as well as the investment base for return on investment calculations. Government controls over wages and prices, which has become increasingly popular of late, is another policy variable that could prejudice the reported performance of local managers. As a final example, fluctuating exchange rates may also impact unfavorably on a subsidiary's profit picture. As we have seen, fluctuating currency values and the resultant exchange gains or losses, whether realized or not, can mar what would have otherwise been a satisfactory performance by subsidiary managers.

What is needed, then, are performance evaluation systems that are directly suited to the specific role that each subsidiary plays in a multinational enterprise's global scheme. Moreover, performance indicators need to be sensitive to the specific environmental conditions that affect an entity's performance. Only in this way will headquarters management be able to separate the results for which subsidiary managers can be held responsible from those that are the result of decisions or actions beyond their control.

The previous discussion enables us to list a number of caveats that, while subject to change, may serve as useful guidelines for those interested in appraising the results of foreign operations. They are

1. Foreign subsidiaries should not be evaluated as independent profit centers when they are really strategic components of a multinational system.
2. Company-wide return on investment criteria should be replaced by performance measures more attuned to the specific objectives and environments of each foreign subsidiary being evaluated.

More specifically;

3. A set of specific goals should be targeted for each foreign subsidiary that takes into consideration each subsidiary's internal and external environment.
4. A subsidiary's performance should be evaluated in terms of departures from these objectives; e.g., if a subsidiary's objective is to produce

component parts for other units in the system, it should be evaluated in terms of price as well as production and delivery timetables relative to alternate sources of supply.

5. Subsidiary managers should not be held responsible for results that are beyond their control (at home and abroad).

6. Subsidiary managers whose performance is being measured should participate fully in the establishment of subsidiary objectives (at home and abroad).

7. Multiple measures of performance, both financial and nonfinancial, should probably be employed in most cases for the evaluation of multinational subsidiary performance.

INTERNAL AUDITING

Financial control prescriptions, including those we just enumerated, look fine on paper. The acid test, of course, lies in their actual implementation and use in overseas operations. Even the best laid plans are ineffectual if they are merely honored in the breach. Therefore, an essential ingredient of any multinational enterprise list of policy guidelines is control over the control system itself. Someone in the organization needs to oversee the multinational control system to ensure that its prescriptions are carried out to the fullest.

Who should assume such a major responsibility? Headquarters management is without doubt the obvious choice. Despite its vital interest in management control, however, considerations such as geographical and/or cultural distances make it difficult for headquarters managers to monitor effectively the internal workings of the control system from their "domestic suite." A popular means of overcoming distance problems has been for interested management units personally to visit their foreign operations. Such visits are hailed as a way of allowing headquarters management to become personally acquainted with overseas personnel and their particular problems. But there are limitations. For one thing, the duration of most visits is not long enough to enable headquarters managers to develop an adequate overall feel for the offshore operations. Equally important, such junkets distract top management from attending to other important tasks.

For these and other reasons, more and more firms are turning to internal auditors as a means of maintaining control over far-flung multinational operations. Internal auditors have proved useful in safeguarding enterprise assets, checking on the accuracy and reliability of performance data, and, in general, providing company headquarters with ways of keeping local managers on their toes.

Role of Internal Auditors

The use of internal audit teams abroad is a relatively recent phenomenon. Despite the short historical experience available, several issues present themselves with regard to the role of the internal audit function in the multinational control process.

One issue concerns the proper scope of internal auditing activities overseas. In the past, internal auditors have served as independent checks on the accuracy of internal reporting systems. In this respect, internal auditors mirror the verification activities of their external counterparts. While the importance of the "checking" activity cannot be denied, your authors feel that this role is too limited. Internal auditors can and should assume an expanded role in multinational financial control systems. This view is diagrammed in Exhibit 8–3.

Seen in its broadest sense, internal auditing is a communication channel that reinforces the formal control system. This channel, furthermore, is open-ended in that information flows are mostly two-way affairs. Stated alternatively, the internal auditing function enhances the process of financial control by improving both the timeliness and quality of communications within the multinational entity.

In the upper left-hand portion of Exhibit 8–3, the internal audit function is portrayed as a vehicle for communicating top management goals and priorities to foreign managers. While this communication process is initially activated through formal budgeting systems, face-to-face follow-up explanations of corporate objectives, and the underlying reasns for them, are usually highly desirable. Personal encounters abroad also enable the audit staff to gain a better appreciation of the environmental constraints with which local managers must contend. When the resulting information is communicated back to corporate headquarters, needed modifications of original performance targets to actual operating conditions abroad are much more likely.

The lower right-hand portion of Exhibit 8–3 diagrams the internal audit function as a vital link in the multinational enterprise's feedback system. Apraisal of actual operating performance in relation to specified standards, and the communication of such information to corporate and/or

EXHIBIT 8-3. Control Dimensions of Internal Auditing in Multinational Operations

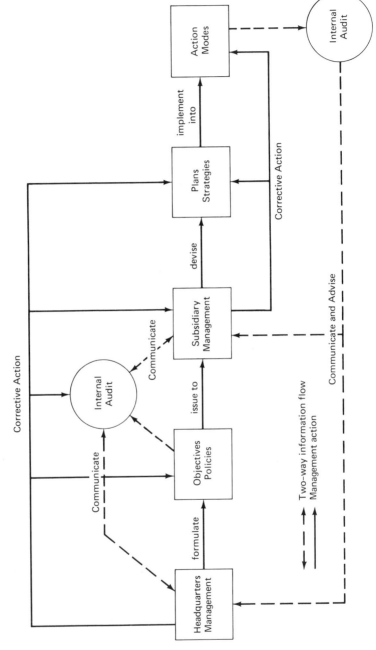

subsidiary headquarters, enables enterprise managers to take corrective actions where necessary. Such actions might include revision of overall corporate objectives and policies, modification of operating plans and stategies of a subsidiary, replacement of subsidiary managers, or possibly even replacement of the internal auditor himself. In given instances, an unqualified or overzealous auditor can be the prime source of multinational control problems. Managers at all levels generally resent an individual whose actions imitate those of a CIA agent.

Finally, by virtue of their widespread travels and exposure to various operations abroad, internal auditors can serve as helpful resource people to local managers. Solutions to similar or identical problems in other operations that have been successful, as well as new methods of accomplishing given tasks, can be suggested. The external perspective offered by the audit staff can also help to identify problems to which local managers may have become myopic. Management services of this nature can play a significant part in persuading overseas managers to identify with the worldwide organization and its control system.

Local Versus Headquarters Audit Personnel

Internal auditors can thus play a significant role in multinational financial control systems. But should this function necessarily be performed by headquarters staff or can another group do as well or better? While the use of parent company audit teams seems logical, worldwide auditor travel is generally expensive. It is probably no exaggeration to state that stationing a United States national abroad generally costs a company twice as much as if a local national were employed instead, especially in light of recent U.S. tax legislation. The high cost of domestic audit teams is compounded by the difficulty of attracting qualified personnel for the task, except at a premium, because of extensive travel and long absences from home. Another consideration is that domestic auditors with a limited foreign language capacity are frequently handicapped when auditing foreign subsidiaries.

A likely solution to this problem lies in using some combination of both domestic and foreign nationals in the control process. One variant is to deploy a small team of internal auditors from domestic headquarters as a supplement to auditing personnel in the field. Another is to employ audit teams that specialize in servicing subsidiaries domiciled in a particular geographic region. One large chemical company reportedly maintains a separate international audit staff in Europe. This regional unit reports directly to regional headquarters in Europe, subject to guidelines framed by the parent company's corporate internal auditing department.[15] Other arrangements are possible. In any case, various possible tradeoffs merit careful consideration.

Hierarchial Relationships

The organizational relationship between the internal audit staff and enterprise management is another issue in financial control systems. Specifically, should the internal audit specialist report directly to (a) headquarters management of the parent company or (b) managers of the foreign subsidiaries whose performance is being reported upon?

Reporting to top management of the parent company, say the group controller, offers a number of advantages. To begin with, it strengthens the position and credibility of the internal auditor vis-a-vis local management. Advice and counsel of the audit specialist is less likely to be ignored by local personnel. Under these circumstances, the auditor becomes an important channel for the communication and enforcement of headquarters policy. A policy of reporting directly to top management also reduces the likelihood of incongruent behavior on the part of local managers. Knowing that independent audit procedures will eventually test their financial representations, local managers are less prone to mask the effects of suboptimal behavior than might otherwise be the case. Finally, reporting to headquarters management achieves greater uniformity and consistency in internal reporting formats.

A major disadvantage of having audit reports bypass local managers is the possible ill will created at the subsidiary level. Internal auditors are easily cast as agents or spies of upper management by local personnel and therefore seen collectively as external threats. Resultant perceptions, deserved or not, contribute to communications barriers already made difficult by distance and culture.

Reporting directly to local managers also has its pluses and minuses. On the plus side, local reporting enables issues and performance deviations to be settled quickly and "on the spot." Moreover, internal auditors are then seen as part of the local management team rather than as some external threat to be guarded against. In this kind of atmosphere, communications are likely to be freer, making it easier for the internal audit staff to identify potential trouble spots in financial control sooner than otherwise.

The major disadvantage of this reporting scheme is self-evident. In the absence of reliable feedback on the status of its foreign operations, the

---

[15] "Internal Auditing Goes International," *Business International,* January 13, 1967, pp. 15–16.

whole concept of financial control becomes academic. Data submitted to headquarters could easily be colored by the internal auditor's allegiance to local management groups. Local managers might also exhibit more reluctance to solicit help from headquarter's staff in view of their quasi-independence. In short, headquarter's management could quickly lose control of its foreign operations—as in the Rhone-Poulenc example on pp. 258–259.

How then might one proceed? Reexamination of the limitations identified with either of the two reporting modes just discussed suggest that the limitations probably are more apparent than real. Properly administered, internal reporting to both headquarters and local managers is a normal and, indeed, essential feature of a multinational control system. The paradigm of financial control illustrated in Exhibit 8–3 suggests that internal audit communiques to both headquarters and local management personnel are part of a closed-loop information system that rejuvenates the entire control process. In short, continual feedback at both the enterprise and subsidiary levels is the critical ingredient that allows the total organization to adapt readily to its ever-changing environment.

SELECTED REFERENCES

8.1 BURSK, EDWARD C., *et al., Financial Control of Multinational Operations,* New York: Financial Executives Research Foundation, 1971, 229 pp.

8.2 DICKIE, PAUL M., and NIRANJAN S. ARYA, "MIS and International Business," *Journal of Systems Management,* June 1970, pp. 8–12.

8.3 DUERR, MICHAEL G., and JOHN M. ROACH, *Organization and Control of International Operations,* New York: Conference Board, 1973, 151 pp.

8.4 FANTL, IRVING L., "Control and the Internal Audit in the Multinational Firm," *International Journal of Accounting,* Fall 1975, pp. 57–65.

8.5 GORAB, ROBERT S., "Effective Management Controls and Reporting Policies for the Multinational Company," *Selected Papers 1970* (Haskins & Sells), pp. 390–400.

8.6 HAWKINS, DAVID F., "Controlling Foreign Operations," *Financial Executive,* February 1965, pp. 25–56.

8.7 "Internal Auditing Goes International," *Business International,* January 13, 1967, pp. 15–16.

8.8 KNORTZ, HERBERT C., "Controllership in International Corporations," *Financial Executive,* June 1969, pp. 54–60.

8.9 LOFTUS, JOSEPH X., "Putting the Brakes on Your Foreign Audit Fees," *Price Waterhouse Review,* No. 3, 1976, pp. 16–19.

8.10 MAURIEL, JOHN J., "Evaluation and Control of Overseas Operations," *Management Accounting* (USA), May 1969, pp. 35–38.

8.11 McINNES, J. M., "Financial Control Systems for Multinational Operations: An Empirical Investigation," *Journal of International Business Studies,* Fall 1971, pp. 11–28.

8.12 MEISTER, IRENE W., *Managing the International Financial Function,* New York: National Industrial Conference Board, SBP #133, 1970, 122 pp.

8.13 MURRAY, J. ALEX, "Intelligence Systems of the MNC's," *Columbia Journal of World Business,* September–October 1972, pp. 63–71.

8.14 ROBBINS, SIDNEY M., and ROBERT B. STOBAUGH, "The Bent Measuring Stick for Foreign Subsidiaries," *Harvard Business Review,* September–October 1973, pp. 80–88.

8.15 RUESCHHOFF, NORLIN G., *International Accounting and Financial Reporting,* New York: Praeger Publishers, 1976, 172 pp.

8.16 SCOTT, GEORGE M., "Financial Control in Multinational Enterprise—The New Challenge to Accountants," *International Journal of Accounting,* Spring 1972, pp. 55–68.

8.17 WATT, GEORGE C., *Accounting for the Multinational Corporation,* New York: Financial Executives Research Foundation, to be published in 1977.

8.18 WHITT, JOHN D., "Multinationals in Latin America: An Accent on Control," *Management Accounting* (USA), February 1977, pp. 49–51.

8.19 WOO, JOHN C. H., "Management Control Systems for International Operations," *Tempo* (Touche Ross & Co.), Summer/Fall 1970, p. 39.

8.20 ZENOFF, DAVID B., and JACK ZWICK, *International Financial Management,* Englewood Cliffs, N.J.: Prentice-Hall, Inc., 1969, Chapter 12.

DISCUSSION QUESTIONS

8.1 Refer to Exhibit 8–1 and describe, by way of an example, a single cell of the three-dimensional decision matrix illustrated there.

8.2 Enumerate and explain what you judge to be the major information issues surrounding the "primary-secondary" reporting construct introduced in Chapter 4.

8.3 "The standard of measurement for overall management of all operations, domestic and foreign, must be the same and must be the standard of measurement in reports to outsiders on the company as a whole." Critically evaluate this statement in light of the information concepts imparted in this chapter.

8.4 Briefly distinguish the information systems implications of the ethnocentric versus geocentric organizational philosophies of multinational enterprises.

8.5 Present an abbreviated illustration of an information system that allows data to retain their local characteristics and yet be aggregated to satisfy more global points of view.

8.6 List six arguments supporting a parent company's use of its domestic control systems for its foreign operations. List six arguments against such a practice.

8.7 If you were charged with the responsibility of designing an organizational pattern for the international financial function of a high-growth, medium-size, technology-oriented company, which pattern would you opt for and why?

8.8 In light of the continuing controversy over illegal corporate payments, state in a paragraph whether or not such payments should be monitored and acknowledged in the formal financial control system of the parent company. Draw on case histories, such as the Lockheed affair, to support your position.

8.9 At present, the Financial Vice-President of your company's overseas operations is held responsible for achieving a dollar profit before taxes, but after foreign currency translation and conversion gains and losses. In your capacity as an independent outside director of the company, draft a short discussion memorandum to the Chairman of the Board evaluating the merits of this policy.

8.10 Identify a company in your immediate vicinity whose activities are multinational in scope. Then, on the basis of a 5- to 10-minute personal interview (or telephone conversation) with the company's treasurer or chief financial officer, ascertain whether the organization of the company's international financial function corresponds with the patterns observed by Professors Robbins and Stobaugh. On the basis of your interview, what conclusions do you draw with regard to the validity of the Robbins and Stobaugh hypothesis?

8.11 Suggest a rating or evaluation scheme that allows an overall judgment concerning the efficiency of a multinational enterprise's international financial function.

8.12 The chapter text cites a number of examples of dysfunctional performance evaluation practies by multinational companies. Take two of examples cited or, alternatively, offer two of your own, and following the caveats suggested for appraising the results of foreign operations, suggest ways of improving the performance evaluation procedures employed.

8.13 "Evaluating profit-center and management performance abroad is no more difficult than at home." Support or refute this hypothesis in the form of a short essay.

8.14 The U.S. Institute of Internal Auditors explicitly defines the role of internal auditors domestically. It has not, as yet, addressed the international dimensions of that role. Help to fill this void by delineating a set of international objectives for the internal audit function.

8.15 A policy dilemma facing international financial managers is the question of whether to employ home country or host country internal audit teams to control their foreign operations. What are the major trade-offs involved?

ANNOTATED TEACHING MATERIALS

8.1 *Sola Chemical Company* (Case 12, Vernon, *Manager in the International Economy*, 2nd ed., pp. 379–92). In this case, a rapidly growing multinational chemical producer, the Sola Chemical Company, is beginning to experience the strains of increased size. The company's international financial function, in particular, has become too complex and diffuse to be managed effectively from central headquarters. A solution to the problem is sought by engaging a prominent international consulting firm to advise Sola on the reorganization of its international division. The consulting firm proposes a remedy only to find everyone on the foreign side of the Sola organization reacting to the proposal with some degree of hostility!

8.2 *The Galvor Company* (ICCH Case 9–313–035). A small French electronics concern that has been managed quite successfully by its original founder/owner is acquired by a large United States-based conglomerate. To facilitate control over its newly acquired subsidiary, the parent company immediately installs an extensive and sophisticated management information system in the subsidiary. Attention focuses on the implementation of the "transplanted system" and the dysfunctional symptoms that begin to surface.

8.3 *General Foods Corporation—International Division* (ICCH Cases A–C, 9–310–104 through 106). Case A introduces the worldwide operations of General Foods Corporation. Case B describes the planning and control reports received by International Division headquarters from its foreign subsidiaries. Case C focuses on the suitability of General Foods' performance evaluation measures and askes the question: What was the net after-tax profit of International Division for the fiscal year ended March 31?

8.4 *Eurochem N. V.* (ICCH Case 9–174–035). A new internal reporting format is designed and installed at Eurochem by its Manager of Finance and Group Controller. Managerial performance is to be measured via a contribution analysis while business performance is to be measured via a partial full cost analysis. Questions immediately arise regarding the system's design. Despite these objections, the original drafters of the plan are firm in their belief that further adjustments to their simple but effective internal reporting scheme will only compromise its flexibility in the future.

8.5 *Chesebrough-Pond's Uruguay* (Case 3, Vernon, *Manager in the International Economy,* 2nd ed., pp. 272–89). The Western Hemisphere Area Controller of Chesebrough-Pond's Inc. is reviewing the operations of its Uruguayan branch. Performance measures continue to reflect a negative trend. On the basis of this information, serious consideration is being given to terminating the Central American operation. Factors contributing to the unfavorable subsidiary performance statistics are (a) an excessive rate of domestic inflation, (b) endless currency devaluations, (c) control by the Uruguayan Central Bank over all fund transfers outside the country, and (d) an economy-wide price freeze.

8.6 *Observations on Multinational Financial Control Systems.* In his article "Financial Control Systems for Multinational Operations: An Empirical Investigation," (*Journal of International Business Studies,* Fall 1971, pp. 11–28), Professor J. M. McInnes concludes

...there is very little fundamental difference in the design and use of [internal] financial reporting systems for foreign operations and domestic operations. Moreover, the similarity does not appear to be the result of an oversight but instead results from a conscious choice on the part of management.

Examine the article from which this quote was taken and critically evaluate the author's research methodology. Does your critique reveal any other considerations that might explain the original findings?

Chapter 9

MULTINATIONAL TAXATION AND TRANSFER PRICING

A treatise on multinational accounting would not be complete without some attention to international taxation. Of all the environmental variables considered thus far, none, with the possible exception of foreign exchange, has such a pervasive influence on all aspects of multinational operations as taxation. Where to invest, how to market, what form of business organization to employ, when and where to remit liquid funds, how to finance, and what transfer prices to charge are examples of management actions colored by tax implications.

Despite substantial effects on business decisions, international taxation remains somewhat of a mystery for many executives because of the enormous complexity involved. To begin with, countries possess fundamentally different tax systems. Being an instrument of national economic policy, tax systems worldwide are understandably as diverse as the nations that create them.

In addition to the bewildering array of tax laws internationally, financial executives must also contend with a number of special rules, formulated at home, with respect to the taxation of foreign corporations and profits earned abroad. For example, financial managers need to be aware that

1. Shareholders of foreign corporations may be subject to different rules than shareholders of domestic corporations.
2. Accounting for domestic taxes on domestic operations may differ from that on foreign operations.
3. Credits against domestic taxes may be secured for taxes paid to host countries.
4. Bilateral tax treaties exist to avoid double taxation.

5. Both home and host countries may offer tax incentives to encourage certain business activities abroad.

6. Tax savings achieved in low tax countries may be lost by taxes on undistributed earnings.

Finally international tax agreements, laws, and regulations applicable to individual countries are constantly changing. This increases the aforementioned complexity since changes in one country's tax provisions often effect relative advantages in a multinational tax network overall.

It is not possible to provide, in a single chapter, a working acquaintance with major tax provisions in all the economically important countries of the world. We have, therefore, limited our scope to a general introduction to taxation on the multinational level and descriptions of selected cases and policy issues. A wide range of international tax literature is available, including professional reference services. Pamphlets dealing with general individual country situations are published by the U.S. Department of Commerce, the major international banks, and the major CPA firms. Much literature is readily available in public, college, and university libraries.

NATIONAL TAX SYSTEMS

Every country boasts its own special array of taxes. Differences among national tax systems range from assessment and collection philosophies to tax computations and procedures. The sections that follow describe various manifestations of these differences generally, including (a) tax philosophies, (b) types of taxes, (c) tax burdens, and (d) special taxes on international operations.

Taxation Philosophies

Under the principles of national sovereignty, every nation claims the right to tax income that originates within its borders. Those adhering to the "territorial" principle confine their collection efforts to this income. Countries holding such philosophies include Hong Kong, Panama, Switzerland, Argentina, Venezuela, and many Central American and Caribbean lands.[1] Business enterprises headquartered or domiciled in these jurisdictions pay no taxes on dividends and other income earned outside the territory.

Most countries, by contrast, adopt what may be called the *worldwide* principle of taxation primarily because of the greater revenue possibilities. This philosophy holds that countries have the right to tap income arising

[1] Frederic K. Howard, "Overview of International Taxation," *Columbia Journal of World Business*, Summer 1975, pp. 8 – 9.

outside their national boundaries when that income is earned by an entity domiciled, incorporated, or otherwise headquartered within their borders. Under this system, income earned overseas could be taxed twice. An American subsidiary of a Dutch parent company, for example, would have to pay both United States and Dutch taxes on income earned in the United States. Fortunately, most countries adhering to the worldwide principle grant some relief from double taxation. With some exceptions, these countries generally tax foreign subsidiary earnings only when repatriated to the parent country. The major exception under United States law is so-called "Subpart F" income, which is taxed even though not repatriated. We return to this topic shortly.

Types of Taxes

A company operating abroad encounters a variety of direct and indirect taxes. Direct taxes typically include income and capital gains taxes. Indirect taxes are more numerous and include, among the major ones, turnover taxes, value-added taxes, border taxes, excise taxes, net worth taxes, and withholding taxes.

Corporate Income Taxes. Internationally, the income tax is probably more widely used than any other major tax, with the possible exception of customs duties. In the United States this direct tax on both corporate and personal income is the major source of government revenue. Owing to low per capita income in the developing countries, individual income taxes or general sales taxes are not very appropriate. In these countries the corporate income tax provides a larger share of government revenues than in industrial countries. Most other countries rely heavily on indirect taxes.

Turnover Taxes. These indirect taxes are assessed on total sales at one or more stages in the production process. In Canada, for example, the turnover tax is assessed when production is complete; in England, when merchandise is wholesaled; in the United States, when merchandise is retailed (sales tax); and in Germany, at all stages in the cycle. In the last instance, since credit is not received for turnover taxes previously paid, the final sales price usually includes all prior taxes.

Value-Added Tax. To remedy the compounding effect of turnover taxes, many countries, notably in Central Europe and Scandinavia, have turned to the value-added tax. This tax is levied at each stage of production or distribution, but only on the value added during that particular stage.

This is done by applying the given tax rate to total sales less purchases from any intermediate sales unit. Thus, if a Norwegian merchant purchased 500,000 kroner of merchandise from a Norwegian wholesaler and then sold it for 600,000 kroner, the value added would be 100,000 kroner and the tax assessed on this increment.

Border Taxes. Value-added taxes often serve as a basis for border taxes. Like import duties, border taxes generally aim at keeping domestic goods competitive with imports. Accordingly, taxes assessed on imports typically parallel excise and other indirect taxes paid by domestic producers of similar goods.

Net Worth and Withholding Taxes. Two other taxes, generally met in international business affairs, are net worth and withholding taxes. The former are those taxes assessed on the undistributed earnings of a company. They are designed to encourage firms to source finances for investment projects externally. Development of domestic capital markets is thus fostered. Under these circumstances, net worth taxes are often substantial. Until recently, for example, undistributed earnings of German companies were taxed at a rate of 51 percent. This has now been increased to 56 percent (Haskins and Sells, *The Week in Review*, July 9, 1976, p. 10).

Withholding taxes are those imposed by host governments on dividend and interest payments to foreign investors. Thus, a foreign purchaser of Malaysian corporate bonds would receive only 85 percent of any interest return expected from his investment, given a 15 percent Malay withholding tax. As the name indicates, these taxes, while legally imposed on the foreign recipient, are typically withheld at the source by the issuing corporation, which, in turn, remits the proceeds to its government. Since withholding taxes often retard the international flow of long-term investment capital, they are usually modified by bilateral tax treaties, which will be described shortly.

Tax Burdens

Differences in overall tax burdens are another feature of the international business scene. Varying statutory rates of income tax are an obvious source of these differences. For example, while the corporate income tax rate is close to 50 percent in the United States, it may range anywhere from as low as zero in Bermuda and other tax haven countries to as high as 60 percent in Libya. Statutory tax rates in countries accounting for over 80 percent of the recent overseas earnings of United States companies are listed in Table 9-1.

TABLE 9 – 1. Statutory Tax Rates in Selected Foreign Countries

COUNTRY		STATUTORY PROFITS TAX RATE	DIVIDEND WITHHOLDING RATE
Argentina		33.0%	29.5%
Australia		42.5	30.0
Belgium		48.0	20.0
Brazil		30.0	25.0
Canada		46.0	25.0
Chile		23.0	40.0
Columbia		40.0	20.0
France		50.0	25.0
Germany	undistributed	56.0	25.0
	distributed	36.0	
India		55.0	25.0
Iran		13.4	60.0
Iraq		55.0	–0–
Italy		25.0	30.0
Japan	undistributed	40.0	20.0
	distributed	30.0	
Kuwait		55.0	–0–
Lebanon		42.0	–0–
Libya		60.0	–0–
Luxembourg		40.0	15
Mexico		42.0	21.0
Netherlands		48.0	25.0
New Zealand		45.0	15.0
Norway	undistributed	50.8	25
	distributed	23.0	
Philippines		35.0	35.0
Saudi Arabia		45.0	–0–
South Africa		43.0	15.0
Spain		36.0	16.5
Sweden		40.0	30.0
Switzerland		3.64–40.0	35.0
United Kingdom		52.0	–0–
Venezuela		50.0	15.0

Note: The rates listed for entities incorporated in the foreign jurisdictions. For those countries with graduated income tax rates, the rates shown are those for the highest levels of income. The dividend withholding data does not reflect United States treaties.

Source: Data extracted from Ernst & Ernst, Ref. 9.7 *Foreign and U.S. Corporate Income and Withholding Tax Rates,* January 1977.

Differential tax rates, however, tell only part of the story. A number of other considerations weigh just as heavily on relative tax burdens for multinational enterprises. Differences in definitions of taxable income are a major consideration. "What is income?" is likely to elicit as many answers as there are sovereign nations. Even if there were some consensus regarding the concept of income, little agreement would exist as to allocation between countries. The United States, for example, generally has its own views as to what constitutes an appropriate transfer price on transactions between related affiliates of the multinational company (discussed in some detail later in this chapter).

Foreign governments also have their own views on the matter and these seldom conform to those of the United States tax authorities. Opinions as to what constitutes appropriate charges by a parent company for research and development, promotion, administration, and various technical services also differ internationally, so much so that domestic operations are often charged for such expenditures to avoid debates over the issue with foreign tax authorities.

Investment allowances and credits, special reserves to stabilize employment, the timing of depreciation deductions and other expense recognition, as well as asset valuations also vary from country to country. For example, business firms in England are allowed to write off immediately up to 100 percent of the total acquisition cost of machinery and equipment during the year of acquisition. In Australia, the figure is 40 percent; in India, 25 percent.[2] Other countries depreciate an asset after its estimated useful life. Rather than granting a tax deduction, some countries allow a direct credit against taxes payable equal to some percentage of an investment's initial cost, such as the 10 percent investment tax credit in the United States. In Sweden, firms are allowed to establish reserves from profits which may subsequently be used for investments in industries or areas which are economically depressed. And, as pointed out in Chapter 3, countries in South America and elsewhere increasingly adjust their assets for changing price levels. These adjustments often significantly affect reported income for tax purposes.

Tax administration systems also affect relative tax burdens internationally. We can identify at least three major systems now in use: (a) the classical system, (b) the split rate system, and (c) the imputation or tax credit system.

Under the classical system, corporate income taxes are levied at a single rate. Dividends are then taxed as income to shareholders at their personal income tax rates. Examples of countries that use this system include Italy, Luxembourg, and Netherlands, Spain, Sweden, most Commonwealth countries except the United Kingdom (which switched to the tax credit system in 1973), and the United States.

Under the split rate system, taxes are levied at two different rates depending on whether profits are distributed or retained. In Norway, for example, profit distributions are taxed at a rate of 23.0 percent, whereas retained earnings are taxed at 50.8 percent. Table 9 – 1 identifies other countries employing the split-rate system.

[2]Coopers & Lybrand, *Newsletter*, International Supplement, July–August 1976, p. 9.

Under the tax credit or imputation system, a tax is levied on corporate income at a given rate; however, part of the tax paid can be treated as a credit against the personal income tax on dividends. Belgium, the United Kingdom, France, and (most recently) Germany have adopted this system. According to the *Financial Times* (London, July 24, 1975) the European Economic Community, as a part of its effort to harmonize taxes among its member countries, is seriously proposing the uniform adoption of the imputation system.

The administration systems just identified are not mutually exclusive, nor are their effects on differential tax burdens minimal. For example, Germany is included under both the split-rate system and the imputation system. While corporate income taxes on distributed earnings are currently 36 percent, German shareholders are permitted to deduct the dividend tax from their personal income tax. Thus shareholders in effect pay no tax on dividends. United States-owned companies in Germany, however, are not allowed to participate in this scheme. For example, while they would have to pay the current tax on corporate earnings in Germany, shareholders—in this case, United States-based parent companies—would not benefit from the dividend exclusion. The result is that income taxes on United States and other foreign-owned subsidiaries in Germany are raised by almost 10 percent.[3]

Dufey identifies a final item that accounts for intercountry differences in effective tax burdens.[4] This relates to social overhead in any host country. Many less developed countries charge lower corporate tax rates than developed countries. Designed to attract investment capital, these incentives, however, rarely fulfill their promise. These countries need to finance government and other social services just as any other country. Lower corporate tax rates, therefore, generally result in higher rates of indirect taxation and/or a reduction in the quantity and quality of public servies provided. In the first case, one form of tax is simply replaced by another. More importantly, the purchasing power of the market place is reduced. This, in a general sense, "taxes" the potential earnings streams of a multinational investor. In the second case, reduced corporate taxes may also mean a higher cost structure, which a deficient social overhead system imposes on multinational operations. Examples would include poor transportation, inadequate postal services, nonfunctioning telephone systems, and power shortages.

These and other variations among countries suggest that effective tax rates seldom equal nominal rates. Intercountry comparisons based on statu-

[3] "U.S. Subsidiaries Get Caught By Tax Reform," *Business Week*, June 7, 1976, pp. 42–43.

[4] Gunter Dufey, "Myths About Multinational Corporations," *Michigan Business Review*, May 1974, p. 15.

tory tax rates are therefore insufficient. Tax burdens internationally should always be determined by examining *effective* tax rates.

Special Tax Provisions[5]

At the local level, tax compliance involves familiarity with local taxes and their administration. At the multinational level, considerations of overlapping tax jurisdictions and the possibility of double taxation come into play. Additional considerations that warrant management attention are various tax incentives and other provisions that either help or hinder multinational operations. These provisions are initially examined from the United States perspective.

Foreign Tax Credit. The purpose of the foreign tax credit is to ensure that profits earned abroad are not subjected to the full tax levies of two or more countries. Taxes paid to a foreign country on income earned there are credited against the United States parent's tax liability to the United States Government. The foreign government, in effect, takes the first bite of income earned in its jurisdiction. Assuming that the income is remitted, the United States Government then taxes the balance.

Taxes subject to these credit provisions are generally income taxes or withholding taxes on dividends, interest, or other income paid to a United States entity by a foreign corporation. Two examples of foreign tax credit computations follow. The first assumes a corporate income tax rate of 30 and 50 percent in the foreign country and the United States respectively. The second assumes a foreign withholding tax on dividends of 15 percent.

	EXAMPLE 1	
Taxable income of foreign branch		$1,000
Foreign income tax at 30 percent		$ 300
Included in United States income		$1,000
United States tax at 50 percent		$ 500
Less foreign tax credit		300
Net United States tax payable		$ 200

	EXAMPLE 2	
Foreign dividends		$1,000
Less foreign withholding tax of 15 percent		150
Net dividend received		$ 850
Included in United States income		$1,000
United States tax at 50 percent		500
Less foreign tax credit		150
Net United States tax payable		$ 350

[5] Based on *Information Guide for U.S. Corporations Doing Business Abroad* (New York: Price Waterhouse Company, March 1976). This publication is revised periodically.

As these examples illustrate, the intended effect of the foreign tax credit is to limit the total foreign income tax paid to the higher tax rate of the two countries. If the foreign tax is lower than the United States rate, the United States Government receives tax revenues on the foreign income. If the opposite occurs, no United States taxes are paid.[6]

Tax Treaties. While foreign tax credits shield, to some extent, foreign source income from double taxation, tax treaties go further than this. Signatories to such a treaty generally agree on how taxes will be imposed, shared, or otherwise eliminated on business income earned in one taxing jurisdiction by nationals of another. Thus, most tax treaties between the United States and other countries provide that profits earned by a United States enterprise in the other country shall not be subject to its taxes unless the United States enterprise maintains a permanent establishment there. Tax treaties also affect withholding taxes on dividends, interest, and royalties paid by enterprises of one country to foreign shareholders. They usually grant reciprocal reductions in withholding taxes on dividends and they often exempt royalties and interest from withholding entirely.

Table 9 – 2 sets forth, in general fashion, various rates of withholding taxes imposed by countries with which the United States has an income tax treaty. Note that these withholding rates are substantially lower than the statutory tax rates depicted in Table 9 – 1.

Foreign Tax Incentives. Countries eager to accelerate their economic development have been aware of the positive influences of the multinational company. To attract multinational enterprises, many countries offer a number of tax incentives. These are often nontaxable cash grants applied toward the cost of fixed assets of new industrial undertakings, or relief from paying taxes for certain periods (tax holidays). Other forms of temporary tax relief include reduced income tax rates, tax deferrals, and reduction or elimination of various indirect taxes.

Some countries, particularly those with few natural resources, offer permanent tax inducements. These so-called "tax havens," include

1. The Bahamas, Burmuda, and the Cayman Islands, which have no taxes at all.
2. The British Virgin Islands, and Gibraltar, which assess very low tax rates.
3. Hong Kong, Liberia, and Panama, which tax locally generated income but exempt income from foreign sources.
4. Countries that allow special privileges that are suitable as tax havens for very limited purposes.[7]

---

[6] Effective November 1976, the foreign tax credit is denied to a taxpayer who participates in, or cooperates with, an international boycott.

[7] Jean Doucet and Kenneth J. Good, "What Makes a Good Tax Haven?" *Banker*, May 1973, p. 493.

TABLE 9 – 2. Foreign Withholding Rates Under United States Income Tax Treaties as of January 1977

-COUNTRY	DIVIDENDS (%)	INTEREST (%)	ROYALTIES (%)
Australia	15	a	a
Austria	10[b]	–0–	–0–
Belgium	15	15	–0–
Canada	15	15	15
Denmark	15[b]	–0–	–0–
France	15[b]	10	5
Germany	15	–0–	–0–
Greece	a	–0–	–0–
Ireland	a	–0–	–0–
Italy	15[b]	a	–0–
Japan	15[b]	10	10
Luxembourg	7.5[b]	–0–	–0–
Netherlands	15[b]	–0–	–0–
New Zealand	a	a	a
Norway	15[b]	–0–	–0–
South Africa	a	a	a
Sweden	15[b]	–0–	–0–
Switzerland	15[b]	5	–0–
United Kingdom	c	–0–	–0–

Notes:
[a] The treaty does not apply to this type of income.
[b] The treaty withholding tax rate is reduced to 5 percent (10 percent in the case of Japan and Norway) if the recipient is a corporation owning a specified percentage of the voting power of the distributing corporation.
[c] Currently under negotiation.

Source: Ernst & Ernst, *Foreign and United States Corporate Income and Withholding Tax Rates* January 1976, pp. 49-50.

Normally, parent companies are not taxed on their foreign earnings until these are received as a dividend. This tax deferral privilege was originally granted by the United States Government to allow United States firms to expand abroad and compete on an equal footing with foreign competitors enjoying similar tax breaks. Unfortunately, it often proved all to easy for some firms to circumvent the intent if not the letter of the tax code. Tax avoidance rather than tax deferral was frequently achieved. This was typically accomplished by establishing a foreign holding company, preferably with a tax haven domicile. The major purpose of such a "shell" corporation was to receive tax-free the profits earned by its operating subsidiaries. These holding companies, for example, would be granted exclusive agency to export the products of the parent company. A portion of the profits that would otherwise accrue to the parent company would thus be shifted to the foreign holding company. Similarly, parent company patents would often be assigned to the foreign holding company, thus entitling it to collect royalties from sister subsidiaries that benefited therefrom. These and other devices thus allowed profits earned abroad to be accumulated and later redeployed for financing other foreign investments without ever being repatriated to the United States where they would be taxed.

Taxation of Controlled Foreign Corporations. To remedy this situation, the Revenue Act of 1962 added an amendment (Subpart F) to that part of the Internal Revenue Code governing the taxation of foreign-source income. Under this novel and complex provision (amended again in 1976), shareholders of controlled foreign corporations are taxable on certain undistributed income of that corporation. A controlled foreign corporation (CFC) is one in which more than 50 percent of the voting shares are owned by United States stockholders. In determining the 50 percent level, only stockholders holding more than a 10 percent interest are counted. The Subpart F provision applies to so-called passive income, including dividends, interest, rents, sales commissions from agency relationships, and fees received for a variety of servies performed by the controlled company for its sister subsidiaries.

There are, however, several exceptions to the general rule. To begin with, if less than 10 percent of the controlled foreign company's gross income comes from sources such as those listed above, the provisions of Subpart F do not apply. Subpart F income above 70 percent is taxed in full; income greater than 10 percent but less than 70 percent is taxed according to a series of graduated rates. Second, if the combined income tax, both United States and foreign, paid on any income distributed by the foreign controlled corporation, approximates the United States tax rate, Subpart F provisions again do not apply. Finally, income earned by controlled foreign corporations domiciled in less developed countries is not subject to Subpart F treatment if reinvested in these countries.

All in all, Subpart F provisions have reduced some of the attractiveness of tax haven corporations. Still, many firms have reportedly uncovered new loopholes in existing tax laws enabling them to continue to siphon profits into remote tax shelters. Said on New York lawyer: "Before 1962, we had a license to steal. The '62 law, by its sheer complexity, stopped some of that. But there hasn't really been much change—we just work harder to achieve the same thing."[8]

United States Tax Incentives. To encourage certain business activities and perhaps counter the balance of payments effects of foreign tax inducements, the United States has legislated its own special set of international tax incentives. These incentives, recently modified by the 1976 Tax Reform Act, involve a number of foreign operations described below.

[8] William M. Carley, "International Concerns Use Variety of Means to Cut U.S. Tax Bills," *Wall Street Journal*, October 16, 1972, p. 1.

A business conducted exclusively in the Western Hemisphere can, until December 31, 1979, be organized and taxed as a United States Western Hemisphere Trade Corporation (WHTC) rather than as a foreign corporation. A United States corporation that meets the Western Hemisphere criterion and derives at least 95 percent of its gross income from sources outside the United States and at least 90 percent of its gross income from the active conduct of a trade or business is taxed at a lower rate than other domestic corporations.

A business conducted primarily in a United States possession can be carried on as a separate United States "possessions corporation." It is entitled to a special foreign tax credit equal to the United States tax on its income in the United States possession and from qualified possessions source investment income. The possessions corporation can remit dividends to its parent company with the latter claiming a 100 percent dividends-received deduction, thereby avoiding United States taxes on the remittance. To qualify for this special treatment, a domestic United States corporation must derive at least 80 percent of its gross income within a United States possession and at least 50 percent from the active conduct of a trade or business.

A United States company engaged in the export business can also organize itself as a Domestic International Sales Corporation (DISC). Enacted in 1971, this provision currently provides a 50 percent deferral of the taxable income of the DISC in excess of that attributable to a base period of export receipts. Companies just entering the export business benefit the most because their exports in the base period are zero.

To qualify as a DISC;

1. At least 95 percent of its gross receipts must be attributed to qualified exports.
2. At least 95 percent of its assets must be "qualified export assets."
3. A capitalization of at least $2,500 throughout the taxable year must be maintained.
4. DISC status must be elected specifically (with the Internal Revenue Service).

To encourage investment in economically less developed countries (LDC's), special tax provisions are permitted for firms doing business there. LDC's include all countries other than those of Western Europe, Australia, Canada, Japan, New Zealand, South Africa, the Soviet Block, and China. To qualify as a Less Developed Country Corporation (LDCC), a firm must be a foreign corporation actively engaged in the conduct of a trade or business. It must secure at least 80 percent of its gross income from LDC's and have 80 percent of its assets located there. A principal advantage of operating as an LDCC is that dividends and interest received by a controlled foreign corporation (CFC) from an LDCC are excluded from that CFC's Subpart F income if reinvested in the less developed countries.

COMPARATIVE ILLUSTRATIONS OF
SPECIAL NATIONAL TAX PROVISIONS

We now turn to some specific countries for tax illustrations. For purposes of comparison, with the United States, we shall examine non-United States taxation of unremitted foreign earnings and how other countries afford relief from international double taxation. Countries examined include Belgium, France, Germany, Italy, Japan, the Netherlands, and the United Kingdom. Information for this section is based on expert testimony presented before the U.S. Senate Committee on Finance by Arthur Andersen & Company in April of 1976.

Taxation on Unremitted Foreign Earnings

Recall that, in the case of foreign subsidiaries, the United States generally taxes foreign source earnings only when remitted to the United States. Under Subpart F provisions, however, certain undistributed income is taxed even though not remitted. Like the United States, Germany, Italy, Japan, and the United Kingdom tax dividends from their companies' foreign subsidiaries. They do not, however, tax unremitted earnings. Belgium and France tax foreign subsidiary dividend remissions but only on a limited basis. They, too, do not assess taxes on unremitted earnings. The Netherlands stands alone in taxing either foreign subsidiary dividends or retained earnings of those subsidiaries.

Of the countries that tax foreign dividends, Germany, Japan, and the United Kingdom allow a foreign tax credit equivalent to that granted by the United States. While Italy does not grant such a credit, it only subjects such dividends to partial taxation and permits a credit for withholding taxes subject to some special limitations.

Existing legislation, as well as government attitudes in many of these countries, encourages the use of tax haven holding companies (referred to earlier) as a means of minimizing or eliminating the taxation of foreign dividends. The large Japanese trading companies use such vehicles on a regular basis. Attitudes in Italy toward the use of foreign tax shelters are so favorable that government-owned industrial enterprises such as Instituto

Ricostruzione Industriale, Ente Nazionale Idrocarburi, and Instituto Mobiliare Italiano use such tax haven vehicles in their corporate groups. The United Kingdom permits setting up offshore nonresident corporations. Although legal entities of the United Kingdom, they are free from United Kingdom taxation on their foreign income. United Kingdom multinational enterprises are also able to utilize tax haven holding companies to own and control foreign subsidiaries.

Foreign branch operations of United States multinational companies are taxed just as if they were United States operations. This is in keeping with the United States philosophy of taxing United States company income wherever earned. United States taxes on income earned abroad are reduced by foreign income taxes paid under the foreign tax credit rules described earlier.

Japan, the Netherlands, and the United Kingdom tax branch operations in a manner similar to the United States. The Dutch credit for taxes incurred in the country of operations, however, is determined to be at the rate of the Dutch corporate income tax, regardless of the rate actually paid. In effect, then, no tax is applied by the Dutch government on branch income.

Belgium and Germany do not tax branches of their corporations in other treaty countries. France, as a matter of tax policy, does not tax foreign branch income at all. Under a new tax system initiated in 1974, Italy does not tax branch income for local income tax purposes providing that the branch has separate management and accounting systems. Italy does tax branch income for national income tax purposes with a foreign tax credit allowed, subject to certain limitations.

Relief from Double Taxation

Foreign tax credit arrangements differ among the United States and the countries under consideration due to basic underlying differences in their taxation systems. To illustrate, since Belgium, Germany, and France do not tax foreign branch income, they do not allow a foreign tax credit for taxes paid by those branches. The Netherlands, in effect, does not tax branch income at all. Belgium, France, and the Netherlands do not tax foreign subsidiary dividends and therefore do not allow a deemed foreign tax credit.

The United States generally limits the amount of foreign taxes creditable in any one year. This limitation is computed on an overall basis that combines foreign-source income and losses from all countries. Under this method, the combined foreign-source taxable income is expressed as a percentage of United States taxable income to determine the limitations on the credit. An example follows.

EXAMPLE 3

	Country 1	Country 2
Taxable income received abroad	$1,000	$1,000
Foreign creditable taxes	500	600

United States tax computation:

Foreign taxable income (Countries 1 and 2)	$2,000
United States-source income (assumed)	3,000
Total United States taxable income	$5,000
United States tax at 50 percent	$2,500
Less foreign tax credit[a]	1,000
United States taxes payable	$1,500

[a]Foreign tax credit (overall limitation):

Taxable income (Countries 1 and 2)	$2,000
Total foreign taxes (Countries 1 and 2)	1,100

$$\frac{\text{Total foreign taxable income}}{\text{Total taxable income}} \times \text{U.S. tax} = \frac{\$2,000}{\$5,000} \times \$2,500 = \$1,000$$

$1,000 is less than foreign taxes paid (i.e. $1,100) so only $1,000 can be allowed; the excess $100 is carried to other years.

Belgium, France, Germany, Italy, and the United Kingdom differ in their limits on allowable foreign tax credits. They generally employ a per country limitation. While the United Kingdom has a rather restrictive limitation, United Kingdom companies are able to minimize the problem. This is accomplished by using foreign holding companies to receive dividends and averaging the foreign tax credits involved so as to achieve an effective overall limitation. Japan and the Netherlands have an overall limitation similar to that of the United States. Japan, however, exempts losses from overseas branches in determining the overall limitation, thus offering Japanese investors a higher limitation on foreign tax credits than their American counterparts.

In the United States, important indirect costs (such as general and administrative expenses of corporate headquarters) are allocated against all foreign income in determining the allowable foreign tax credit. The countries under discussion are generally more liberal in determining the amount of the limitations. Of the seven, only the Netherlands requires an allocation of indirect expenses to all foreign income in determining the allowable credit. Japan requires an allocation of certain indirect expenses but only to income from foreign branches. The other countries have no such allocation requirements.

ISSUES IN INTERNATIONAL TAXATION

Tax Planning: A Mission Impossible?

A well-known professor of corporate tax law, James Eustice, once described United States tax legislation as a "congressional viper's tangle of words," a "four-star example of Byzantine architecture in a statue not noted for its economy of line." The previous sections on taxation in relation to the multinational enterprise demonstrate that the complexity of foreign tax laws is rapidly approaching the intricacy of the United States law. Kalish and Casey, speaking again from a United States perspective, summarize the problems that this complexity poses for the international business executive.[9] These problems

> ... stem from the fact that he (the international executive) must be a combination of an administrator, tax attorney, tax accountant, computer expert, and a human being. He must work within the framework of a society he had very little to do with creating. The complications and intricacies of the U.S. tax laws are monumental. In addition, he is faced with sophisticated tax treaties superimposed over U.S. law which frequently negate its clear implication. The pyramid of levels of tax law priorities is further compounded by the invariable differences in local tax laws which continually exert their influence in eroding the "bottom line" of international business. The dilemma is further enlarged by the fact that internal U.S. law and foreign tax laws are in a continual flux of change.

In view of the complexities involved, business executives are divided in their attitudes toward tax planning for international business operations. One viewpoint holds that taxes are an inevitable feature of the international business scene. Thus, managers should not expend a large effort on an activity that they are ill-equipped to handle. Managers should, instead, devote their energies to what they do best; namely produce and distribute goods and services to the consuming public. It is also observed that the narrowing gap among world tax rates makes it less possible to effect significant tax savings. Thus, the cost of not having a comprehensive tax planning function is continually becoming less significant.

"Not so!" say proponents of an opposing viewpoint. Careful and systematic tax planning, effectuated by international tax specialists, in concert with headquarters management, is said to promise tangible benefits that more than offset any costs involved. When most corporate taxes consume 40 to 50 cents of every dollar earned (this figure could be higher for profits earned abroad), any propensity to neglect the effects of taxation is sheer foolishness. Thus, any company taking advantage of an increase in

[9]Richard H. Kalish, and John P. Casey, "The Dilemma of the International Tax Executive," *Columbia Journal of World Business*, Summer 1975, p. 62.

the investment tax credit from 7 to 10 percent or bringing profits back from overseas operations with only a 15 percent instead of a 30 percent withholding tax enjoys an immediate increase in its return on investment. Tax planning is also said to be good internal discipline, especially for companies that are rapidly expanding abroad. The concepts embodied in tax law, which cover every imaginable phase of corporate existence, are said to form a more precise and comprehensive theory of business than either corporate finance or accounting. In addition, greater knowledge of the public policy aspects of taxation on the part of business executives could contribute to more unified and acceptable approaches to improving tax laws and to reducing double taxation and uncertainty in the international sphere.[10]

As pointed out earlier, the tax variable is just one of many considerations affecting operating and investment decisions of the multinational enterprise. It is often a critical variable, however, because of the differential tax burdens that are imposed on various segments of international business income. Therefore, what seem called for are tax planning systems that incorporate procedures such as these:[11]

1. Explicit statement of the objectives of tax planning in international operations.
2. Assignment of definite responsibilities, at both headquarters and the subsidiaries, for various aspects of the planning.
3. Determination of what decisions and operating procedures are affected by tax considerations, and how they are affected, and dissemination of this information to the decision-makers.
4. Definition of the procedures that will ensure the interaction of the tax planners with the decision-makers.
5. Education about the impact of tax considerations on international operating and investment decisions and on operating procedures.

A necessary ingredient of such a successful tax planning framework is an information system that is capable of keeping financial managers apprised of all relevant international tax variables that impact on their decisions. This is especially important in the international sphere because tax laws and regulations of individual countries are not static. Since tax minimization policies of one subsidiary can often produce unintended sequences elsewhere in the corporate network, the effects of such policies need to be traced throughout the entire system before final decisions are

---

[10] Frederick Howard, "Overview of International Taxation," p. 5.

[11] Russel M. Moore, and George M. Scott (Ed.), *An Introduction to Financial Control and Reporting in Multinational Enterprises* (Austin, Texas: Bureau of Business Research, the University of Texas at Austin, 1973), p. 56.

made. Computerized tax simulation models designed to optimize a company's global tax bill are promising innovations in this regard.

As a minimum, tax planning information systems should enable financial managers to access information on variables such as features of the various domestic and foreign tax systems, tax base definitions employed internationally, tax treaties and incentives, legal structure of the parent and subsidiaries, policies on the movement of resources within the corporate enterprise, and risks of currency inconvertibility. Without such support systems, it is little wonder that many view the complexities of international tax planning as overwhelming. Until this situation is corrected, effective international tax planning will continue to be a major bottleneck for many multinational companies.

When in Rome ...

Carried to its logical extreme, tax planning implies a conscientious policy of tax avoidance. Underlying this policy is an attitude shared by many that tax avoidance is not just a management prerogative but a fundamental responsibility that must be carried out to the fullest if management is to fulfill its fiduciary mandate to existing shareholders. This mode of thinking raises an ethical question for international tax executives.

It is well known that deliberate tax evasion is commonplace in many parts of the world—notably in Africa, Asia, Latin America, and some parts of Continental Europe. In Italy, for example, tax legislation is generally honored only in the breach. Even then, actual tax settlements are usually subject to negotiation between the individual taxpayer and the tax collector. Under these conditions, should mutinational corporations operating in such environments adopt a policy of "when in Rome do as the Romans do" or should they adhere to taxation norms generally subscribed to in their domestic environments?

You might argue, and convincingly so, that multinational operations abroad are merely guests of their national hosts. In view of the visibility and political sensitivity of their positions, therefore, these firms should fully disclose their earnings picture to local tax authorities and pay whatever taxes are called for. Others, however, would surely argue with equal force that it would only jeopardize the competitive position of the multinational corporation if it did not emulate the tax evasion practices of its local corporate peers. Furthermore, since business ethics are colored by the cultural and social fabric of each individual nation, why should multinational enterprises impose their domestic mores in a context in which they may not be deemed appropriate? How would you resolve this dilemma?

Burke-Hartke versus the MNC

The tax morality of the multinational corporation has become a popular topic of debate among American and foreign politicians, businessmen, economists, labor leaders, academicians, and journalists. Opinions range from complete support of the multinational corporation to accusations that it is one of the most exploitative institutions of capitalism ever created. In addition to exporting jobs, adversely affecting a country's balance of payments, and hurting domestic investment, multinationals are accused of not paying their fair share of taxes to either host or home country governments. Calling the foreign tax credit and foreign income deferral policy "the biggest loopholes in the whole tax law," two United States Senators recently introduced legislation to end these international tax provisions for United States multinationals. More specifically, the Burke-Hartke proposal would eliminate the deferral of taxes on profits held abroad and eliminate the United States tax credit on taxes paid to foreign governments. The latter payments would be treated as expenses or reductions in taxable income rather than reductions in the amount of federal taxes owed.

Such proposals, if passed, would surely increase substantially the initial tax take of the United States Government. Substantive evidence, unfortunately, is not yet at hand to ascertain empirically the long-run effects of these changes on United States businesses and the United States economy, if enacted. It may not be too early to speculate, however, as to the possible ripple effects of such proposed legislation.

Earlier in the chapter, an examination of the taxation policies of seven countries revealed more favorable treatment of foreign-source income outside the United States than in the United States. Similar findings were revealed with respect to the foreign tax credit. Thus, in relation to these and other countries possessing similar tax legislation, enactment of the Burke-Hartke provisions could have a significant negative effect on the relative competitive position of United States multinationals. The potential effects of the proposed changes on the competitive position of United States companies is illustrated in Exhibit 9 – 1. The example compares the effective tax rates and rates of return on equity investments when made by United States, German, and Japanese multinational companies doing business in Mexico. It is assumed that the investment shown is in a 100 percent owned foreign subsidiary with identical operations to that of the acquirer. All profits after tax are reinvested in the business. Both Japan and Germany, with tax rates of 56 and 40 percent, repectively, do not tax unremitted earnings. Book value of the investment is $3,000,000.

As can be seen, elimination of the foreign tax credit, in addition to taxing unremitted earnings, increases the total tax burden of the United States company by almost 45 percent. It would also be about 70 percent

EXHIBIT 9-1. Potential Performance Effects on United States Business of Burke-Hartke Proposal

	INVESTMENT BY COMPANY INCORPORATED IN		
	United States	*Japan*	*Germany*
1. Annual income in Mexico	$900,000	$900,000	$900,000
2. Mexican tax—42%	(378,000)	(378,000)	(378,000)
3. Net income in Mexico	$522,000	$522,000	$522,000
Tax on unremitted earnings			
4. Taxable income	522,000	–0–	–0–
5. United States tax on unremitted earnings—48%	(250,560)	–0–	–0–
6. Total taxes: (2) + (5)	(628,560)	(378,000)	(378,000)
7. Net income after all taxes: (1)–(6)	271,440	522,000	522,000
8. Effective tax rate: (6) ÷ (1)	69.8%	42%	42%
9. Rate of return on equity investment	9.0%	17.4%	17.4%

greater than the tax load of a Japanese or German competitor. Furthermore, the rate of return on the United States investment would be reduced to about one-half that of the Japanese and German investors.

Given such a compctititve handicap, a likely result would be the withdrawal of the United States business from the Mexican market. Companies desiring to continue their international operations would also probably remove their operations from the United States taxing jurisdiction by either selling part of the operation or relocating their corporate headquarters outside the United States. The potential reduction this may cause in United States employment, as well as tax revenues, could eventually offset any initial taxes gained from the Burke-Hartke proposal.

Proponents of legislation to tax all undistributed earnings for foreign subsidiaries also base their arguments on the principle of equity in taxation. This principle holds that taxpayers in similar situtations should bear the same tax burden. Applied internationally, this principle implies equal treatment for American firms investing abroad as well as their foreign competitors. This concept, in turn, explains the United States rule that domestic corporations be taxed on all income whether earned at home or abroad. But, in a philosophical vein, are United States foreign subsidiaries simply United States companies that happen to be operating abroad? Or, are they really foreign companies that just happen to be owned by United States residents? Arguments on this score can go either way with regard to the principle of equity. And one can go a step further and question whether this is the real issue. To quote a passage from Arthur Andersen & Company's recent statement on *U.S. Companies in International Markets* before the Committee on Finance of the U.S. Senate,

> The real issue is not, 'Is the current taxation of unremitted earnings of foreign subsidiaries necessary to achieve equity among the United States taxpayers?' Instead, the issue is, 'Is the United States willing to risk driving many U.S.-based companies out of a number of foreign markets and further to risk subsequent major foreign inroads into U.S. markets in pursuit of a theoretical and unrealistic concept of equity in taxation?'

MULTINATIONAL TRANSFER PRICING

The successful conduct of business operations abroad entails coping with a myriad of environmental considerations, including, as we have just observed, the phenomenon of global taxation. Of all the adaptive mechanisms employed by the multinational company, none have proved as flexible nor as troublesome as the technique of pricing resource, service, and technology transfers between affiliates of the multinational enterprise. The dimensions of the problem become readily apparent when we recognize that transfer pricing (a) is conducted on a relatively larger scale internationally than it is domestically; (b) is affected by a larger number of variables than is true in a strictly domestic setting; (c) varies from company to company, industry to industry, and country to country; (d) lacks any theoretical or operationally optimum solutions; and (e) affects social, economic, and political relationships in entire countries.

The remaining sections of this chapter examine the features that characterize and compound the problem of transfer pricing in an international milieu. Emphasis is placed on creating an awareness of the many issues that exist in this vital yet traditionally secretive area of multinational corporate policy.

Complicating Variables

Transfer pricing, as a corporate stratagem, is of relatively recent origin. Shara (*Journal of Accountancy,* April 1974, p. 56) tells us that transfer pricing in the United States developed as a corollary to the decentralization movement that took place in many American business organizations during the first half of the present century. Complex manufacturing and selling organizations began to decentralize their formerly centralized operations into numerous profit centers as a means of spurring productivity. Under conditions of increased local autonomy, the need arose for a system of internal pricing that would (a) assure that resources would be allocated within the corporate system in an optimal fashion, (b) motivate subunit managers to operate their profit centers as efficiently as possible and promote the welfare of the corporate group as a whole, and (c) serve as a monitoring device in the evaluation of subunit performance.

Despite some limited literature on the subject, or perhaps owing to it, the actual creation and implementation of a firm's transfer pricing policy has remained a difficult task. Conceptual approaches that function well under stated assumptions often prove nonoperational when applied to specific business situations. Given its present state, transfer pricing may be characterized as an area where ad hoc solutions generally prevail in the everyday conduct of business affairs.

Once a company expands into the international business sphere, the problem quickly magnifies. To begin with, multinational companies typically transfer greater proportions of their total output between related companies than between strictly domestic counterparts. It is estimated that about 40 percent of all international trade consists of transfers between related business entities.

Cross-country transactions also expose the multinational company to a host of environmental influences that both create and negate opportunities for increasing enterprise profits through the medium of internal price adjustments. Variables, such as differential taxes, tariffs, competition, inflation rates, currency values, restrictions on fund transfers, and political risks, complicate transfer pricing decisions tremendously. On top of all this, transfer pricing decisions generally give rise to numerous tradeoffs, unforeseen and seldom accounted for.

Tax Considerations. Consider the influence of the corporate income tax. Other things being the same, profits accruing to the corporate system as a whole can be increased by setting high transfer prices to siphon profits from subsidiaries domiciled in high tax countries and low transfer prices to move profits to subsidiaries located in low tax countries. As an example, an Australian subsidiary, Roadmaster Inc. (Japan), might purchase a fleet of used Toyota limousines from Hertz Rent-A-Car in Japan for, say, $1,000 each. It might then resell the used Toyotas to Roadmaster Inc. (Hong Kong)—to take advantage of the low profits tax there, currently 15%—for $1,100, a profit of 10 percent. Roadmaster (Hong Kong) might then resell the automobiles to its Australian parent for $2,000 each. In this manner, the Hong Kong subsidiary would book a profit of $900 ($2,000 − $1,100) on each Toyota simply as a result of a paper transaction. The Australian parent company, in turn, might then lease the fleet for a discounted sum close to its cost, thus minimizing its taxable revenues, yet allowing it to depreciate its fleet of Toyotas for Australian tax purposes. In this example, taxes are lowered in high tax jurisdictions relative to those in low tax jurisdictions, resulting in a lower overall tax burden and higher profits for the multinational system as a whole.

Such actions, unfortunately, often create problems that are not anticipated when the pricing decisions are first made. Governments faced with potential losses of tax revenues, owing to the tax avoidance policies of corporate taxpayers, often take steps to counteract such measures. In the previous example, an irate Australian and/or Japanese government might decide to emulate the actions taken by the United States and other governments in asserting their right to reallocate gross income, deductions, credits, or other allowances among related corporations "in order to prevent tax evasion or to reflect more clearly a proper allocation of income." *Business Europe* (June 18, 1976, pp. 193 – 4) reports that the British have recently adopted such a posture. The 1975 Finance Act now empowers British tax authorities to scrutinize closely cross-border pricing and they are doing just that. As its first major test case, British tax authorities have reportedly taken on the giant Swiss pharmaceutical firm, Hoffmann-LaRoche. Having recast the income statements of Hoffmann LaRoche's British operations over a 7-year period, the British government has reportedly made the Swiss giant acquiesce to a settlement for back taxes of 1.85 billion pounds!

Internally, transfer pricing schemes designed to minimize global taxes often produce aberrations in the multinational control system. When each subsidiary is evaluated as a separate profit center, pricing policies that result in inequitable performance measures generally lead to conflicts between subsidiary and enterprise goals. Returning to our earlier example, Roadmaster Inc. (Japan) would report a lower profit than its sister affiliate in Hong Kong. Despite this result (due largely to factors beyond its control) the management of the Japanese subsidiary may be far more productive and efficient than the management team in Hong Kong. Under these circumstances, concluding that one subsidiary, on the basis of its accounting statements, is a better or poorer performer than the other would be a gross injustice. What seem called for at this point are accounting reports that allow management to discriminate between performance measures for tax purposes and those for control purposes. Dual sets of accounts are a possibility in this regard. Alternatively, the transfer price adjustments could be programmed in subsidiary budgets, and their performance measured according to these targets even if a loss was intended. And yet, one could cite numerous accounts in which headquarters management overlooks the facts of the case or, if it remembers, often makes adjustments that are less than satisfactory. Unless some provision is made to correct the inequities in the measurment and evaluation of subsidiary performance, Roadmaster Inc. (Japan) would be motivated to increase its reported profits (a dysfunctional decision) or experience a morale problem, the effects of which could far outweigh any tax savings achieved.

Tariffs on imported goods are another tax consideration affecting the transfer pricing policies of multinational companies. A company exporting goods to a subsidiary domiciled in a high tariff country, for example, could reduce the tariff assessment by lowering the prices of merchandise sent there. Conversely, it could also be advantageous for the exporting company to transfer goods at high prices to subsidiaries domiciled in low tariff countries.

In addition to the tradeoffs identified earlier in this section, the multi-national company would also have to consider additional costs and benefits both external and internal. Externally, it would have now two taxing authorities to contend with—the customs officials of the importing country as well as the income tax administrators of both exporting and importing countries. A high tariff paid by the importer would necessarily result in a lower base with respect to income taxes. Internally, the enterprise would have to evaluate the benefits of a lower (higher) income tax in the importing country against a higher (lower) import tariff as well as the potentially higher (lower) income tax paid by the company in the exporting country.

Competitive Factors.   To facilitate the establishment of a foreign sub-sidiary abroad, a parent company could supply the subsidiary with imputs invoiced at very low prices. These price subsidies could gradually be re-moved as the foreign affiliate strengthened its competitive foothold in the foreign market. In similar fashion, lowered transfer prices could be used to shield an existing operation from the deleterious effects of increased foreign competition. Indirect competitive effects are also possible. To improve a foreign subsidiary's access to local capital markets, its reported earnings and financial position could be bolstered by setting low transfer prices on the subsidiary's inputs and high transfer prices on its outputs. In some instances, transfer prices could be used to weaken a subsidiary's com-petitors. Strategies of this nature would more likely be employed by com-panies possessing control over raw material supplies in a given industry.

Again, competitive considerations such as those just discussed would have to be balanced against a number of offsetting disadvantages. Externally, transfer prices with competitive designs may call forth antitrust actions by host governments or other retaliatory actions by local competitors. Inter-nally, pricing subsidies do little to instill a competitive mode of thinking in the minds of managers who presumably benefit from such actions. The obvious danger here is that what started out as a temporary management aid may all too easily evolve into a permanent management crutch. Thus, the long-run implications of a competitive transfer pricing policy need to be thoughtfully considered.

Environmental Risks. Whereas competitive considerations abroad might warrant the setting of low transfer prices to foreign subsidiaries, the risks of severe price inflation might necessitate just the reverse action. Because inflation erodes the purchasing power of a firm's monetary assets, high transfer prices on goods or servies provided to a subsidiary located in an inflationary environment are designed to remove as much cash from the subsidiary as possible.

Balance of payments problems, related in many cases to the inflationary problems just discussed, often prompt foreign governments to devalue their currencies and/or impose a number of restrictions on the repatriation of profits from foreign-owned companies. Again, currency exchange restrictions may be sidestepped and losses from currency devaluations avoided by shifting funds to the parent or related affiliates through inflated transfer prices. If transfer prices can be set high enough, some margin of cash may be returned to the parent company each time a transaction with the foreign subsidiary is made.

As a final example, high transfer prices are also employed as a means of minimizing a firm's exposure to expropriatory actions by host governments. Whereas high transfer prices on subsidiary imports may remove excess cash to safer havens, low transfer prices on subsidiary exports may allow a subsidiary to export physical inventories otherwise subject to confiscation.

What are some of the tradeoffs that must be considered under conditions of risk? High transfer prices charged on exports to subsidiaries domiciled in high risk environments naturally produce an increased income tax base in the parent country. A question which, therefore, needs to be addressed is, "Do the benefits of the transfer pricing decision more than offset the increased tax burden of the entity as a whole?" Another equally vexing question is, "What are the costs of strategic transfer pricing policies in terms of the company's relationship with host governments?" Drastic changes in transfer prices seldom go unnoticed nowadays. Thus, the firm must increasingly assess the effective costs of compensating strategies, not to mention the costs of deterioration of firm government relationships.

Accounting Contributions. Accountants, as measurement and communications specialists, can play a very significant role in quantifying the various tradeoffs necessitated by transfer pricing strategy. The challenge to accountants in this regard lies not so much in the measurement process per se as it is in the acquisition and maintenance of a global perspective when mapping out the benefits and costs associated with any given intracorporate pricing decision. The effects of a specific transfer pricing policy on the multinational system as a whole must now take precedence over more orthodox managerial accounting and reporting modes.

This enlarged role of accountants is far from easy, however. Quantifying the numerous tradeoffs is rendered difficult by the fact that environmental influences must be considered not individually but in concert. Consider, for example, the dilemma faced by accountants in attempting to measure the tradeoffs surrounding transfer pricing policies applicable to a subsidiary located in a country with high income taxes, high import tariffs, government price controls, a thin capital market, a chronic rate of inflation, foreign exchange controls, and an unstable government. Based on our previous analysis, a high transfer price would result in lowering the subsidiary's income taxes and removing excess cash to the parent country. It might also, however, result in higher import duties, impair the subsidiary's competitive position due to higher input prices, exacerbate the rate of inflation, raise the subsidiary's capital costs, and possibly evoke retaliatory actions by the host government to protect its balance of payments position, made worse by the loss of foreign exchange. The problem is compounded by the fact that all the variables hypothesized above are constantly changing.

The complexity of the cost-benefit calculus associated with multinational transfer pricing is thus a challenge of no small proportion. Despite the magnitude of the problem, however, one thing is clear. Naive calculations of the effects of transfer pricing policy on individual units within a multinational system are no longer sufficient nor acceptable.

Transfer Pricing Methodology

The simultaneous effects of environmental influences on transfer prices also raises questions of pricing methodology. How are transfer prices established? Are standard market prices generally preferred to those based on some measure of cost? Or, are negotiated prices the only feasible alternative? Assuming some conclusions can be reached on this score, do multinational enterprises the world over employ similar transfer pricing methodologies or do cultural factors have a bearing here? Can a single transfer pricing methodology serve all purposes equally well? The following sections are intended to shed some light on these troublesome questions.

Cost versus Market versus ? In a world of perfectly competitive markets, the determination of prices for intercompany resource and service transfers would not pose much of a problem. To the extent that transferred production could be purchased or sold in such markets, transfer prices could be based on either incremental costs or market prices and neither system would necessarily conflict with the other. Competitive markets, unfortunately, seldom exist externally for products transferred between related entities. Accordingly, cost- and market-based transfer prices no longer remain neutral with respect to their business effects. Mention should thus be made of the some of the major features associated with either pricing method.[12]

The use of market-oriented transfer prices offers several advantages. Since market prices represent an opportunity cost to the transferring entity of not satisfying external demand, their employment will usually encourage efficient use of the firm's scarce resources. Their use is also said to be consistent with a decentralized profit-center orientation. In providing meaningful criteria for evaluating performance, market prices help differentiate profitable from unprofitable operations. Market prices are also easier to defend as "arms-length" prices to host governments sensitive to anticompetitive practices associated with arbitrary transfer prices.

These advantages must be weighed against a number of shortcomings. One problem with using market prices is the frequent absence of an intermediate market for the product or service in question. Even if such markets were available, they would seldom be perfectly competitive. Adherence to market prices may also lead to neglect in gathering important cost data that would eventually become lost in the shuffle. Finally, market prices do not afford a firm much room for maneuvering prices for competitive purposes.

Cost-based transfer pricing systems overcome many of the limitations just cited. Moreover, cost-based systems are (a) simple to use, (b) based on data that are readily available, (c) easy to justify before tax authorities, and (d) easily routinized, thus helping to avoid internal frictions that often accompany more arbitrarily determined systems.

As one might suspect, cost-based transfer pricing systems are not flawless either. Transferring goods or servies at actual cost, for example, is said to provide little incentive for transferring units to control their costs. Production inefficiencies may simply be passed on to the buying unit in the form of inflated prices. And, although the substitution of standard or budgeted costs could remedy the situation somewhat, it still would not avoid the more serious problem of suboptimal decision-making. For example, assume that subsidiary X supplies certain parts to its sister subsidiary Y at a standard cost of $15 a unit, including a charge of $6 for fixed overhead. Both X and Y are currently operating at less than full capacity. The additional cost incurred by Y to process and market the final product is $5 a unit. An external supplier, Z, offers to sell Y the same component part for $13 a unit. Assuming that Y can retail the product for no more than $19 a piece, it would purchase the component from Z rather than X as its performance would be improved at the rate of $2 per unit:

[12]Two excellent references in this regard are Charles T. Horngren, *Cost Accounting, A Managerial Emphasis,* 3rd ed. (Englewood Cliffs, NJ.: Prentice-Hall, Inc. 1972; and Gordon Shillinglaw, *Cost Accounting: Analysis and Control* (Homewood, Ill.: Richard D. Irwin, Inc., 1967).

SUBSIDIARY Y PERFORMANCE

	Buy from X		Buy from Z	
Additional revenue		$19		$19
Additional cost:				
Transfer price from X	$15			
Price from Z			$13	
Additional costs in Y	5	20	5	18
		($1)		$ 1

The firm as a whole would benefit, however, if Y purchased from X rather than Z, by $4 a unit:

FIRM AS A WHOLE

	Buy from X		Buy from Z	
Additional revenue		$19		$19
Additional costs:				
X	$ 9			
Z			$13	
Y	5	14	5	18
		$ 5		$ 1

In this example, transfer prices based on costs (actual or budgeted) would lead Y to treat X's fixed costs as variable, thus leading to a dysfunctional decision for the firm as a whole.

Current Practices. While the pros and cons associated with both cost- and market-based transfer pricing models reveal something of their nature, they do not enable us to say a priori which method is preferred in practice. Empirical evidence on this score unfortunately remains somwhat spotty. Still, intermittent studies sponsored by such organziations as the National Industrial Conference Board (NICB), the Financial Executives Research Foundation (FERF), and a few interested scholars enable us to draw a number of interesting observations.

Domestically, transfer pricing practices have not conformed to any single approach, either cost- or market-based, no matter how conceptually superior it may have been professed to be. Rather, company objectives and their related transfer pricing strategies have determined the pricing methodology employed. An NICB study entitled "Interdivisional Transfer Pricing" (1967), reveals that two-thirds of the companies queried use some form of cost-based transfer prices. At the same time, over 50 percent of these same firms also use market-based systems. In vertically integrated operations, transfers from one stage of production to the next have generally been at cost when the transferring unit is a cost center, and at cost plus a profit markup when the transferer is a profit center. Lateral transfers between units engaged in the same stage of production or distribution are usually executed at cost plus handling charges.

Practical compromises seemingly determine just what constitutes cost and market in many instances. Thus, most companies employing cost-based transfer prices prefer to use actual cost data derived from production and cost records. Standard costs, while preferable in many instances to actual cost information, are used but only when standard cost information is available. Interestingly, marginal costs, generally supported in cost accounting literature as the theoretically preferable choice, were used least frequently among firms responding to the NICB study.

Most firms employing a market-based methodology utilize actual market prices obtained from intermediate markets for the transferred item. When direct market quotes are not available, several alternatives are resorted to. For those units enjoying a high degree of local autonomy, competitive bidding and negotiation between subsidiary managers constitute a basis of arriving at "acceptable" market prices. Components or other patented items, which also lack any outside price equivalent, are typically priced on a cost-plus basis. But just what consitutes "cost-plus" is an open question. Should it include selling and administrative expenses? What about research and development costs? Should costs be stated in terms of actual or budgeted amounts? In practice, all of these variations and more were found to be employed as pricing bases.

Due in large measure to the absence of any outside equivalents, transfer prices for services rendered, such as management fees and royalties, are even more difficult to establish. Many companies in these instances reportedly "play it by ear." If tax officials or others with an interest in the transfer price do not complain too severely, the general presumption is that the price established must have been "reasonable."

Some Causal Variables. In addition to the various gyrations that characterize transfer pricing methodology, several variables seem to be clearly associated with any given pricing construct. Acknowledging at the outset that much more research of the empirical variety is warranted on this subject, transfer pricing methods, whether market- or cost-oriented, appear related to a firm's organizational philosphy, its size, its degree of international involvement, and its cultural milieu.

Take a firm's organizational pattern. Highly decentralized operations are characterized by subunit managers with maximum autonomy to establish transfer prices and to compare alternatives outside the organziation. Moreover, interdependencies among subunits organized as variable profit centers tend to be minimal. Under these circumstances, market-based transfer prices, being the antithesis of centrally-administered price systems, would appear appropriate. In contrast, actual cost systems, or some variant thereof, are appropriate where transfer pricing decisions are "manufactured" higher up the corporate ladder. The reason is that cost-based prices, as opposed to external market prices, tend to be more permeable in nature.

Size and Degree of International Involvement. Size is another variable that has a bearing here. Despite variations of the two basic transfer pricing themes under consideration, large firms tend to gravitate toward cost-based systems. This is attributed to the fact that large firms tend to operate in more oligopolisic markets. As a result, their pricing policies tend to be shielded from competitve pressures that would otherwise influence the choice of a transfer price orientation. In addition, since larger firms tend to do more income maneuvering, they are much more concerned with transfer price determination and its subsequent effects.[13] Smaller firms, in contrast, are generally not in a position to justify departures from prevailing market prices for their products. Consequently they generally have no choice but to accept maket prices as given.

Closely allied with the factor of size is the degree of a company's international involvement. We have already examined the many environmental considerations that impinge on transfer pricing policy internationally. Exposed to a broader spectrum of risks and problems than their domestic counterparts, the greater pricing flexibility afforded by cost-based pricing systems becomes a genuine advantage, if not a necessity.

Cultural Influences. And what of culture? Does the nationality of a parent company's management have anything to do with the determination of internal pricing practices? "Yes, indeed!" would be the response of Professor Jeffrey S. Arpan, whose widely recognized work on the subject has been previously cited. His main findings, based on an analysis of the transfer pricing policies of some 60 non-United States multinational firms and their United States subsidiaries, are

1. Multinational transfer pricing systems fall into distinct groupings or patterns (note the parallel line of thought in the Chapter 2 discussion on worldwide patterns of accounting development in general).
2. Non-United States transfer pricing systems are generally less complex and more market-oriented than American Systems. United States, French, British and Japanese managements seem to prefer cost-oriented transfer pricing systems, while the Canadians, Italians, and Scandinavians seem to prefer market price-oriented systems. No particular orientation or preference in this respect was discernible for German, Belgian, Swiss, or Dutch managers.
3. The setting of transfer price policy is the absolute prerogative of parent company executives (whatever a company's nationality may be). In no company does the person responsible for setting transfer prices have a rank lower than treasurer, and, in most cases, he or she is the financial vice-president or the controller.

[13] Jeffrey S. Arpan, "International Intracorporate Pricing: Non-American Systems and Views," *Journal of International Business Studies*, Spring 1972, p. 17.

4. Although non-United States companies generally consider the same environmental variables when formulating guidelines for transfer prices (especially among the larger companies), there are distinguishable national differences in the relative importance attached to each of these considerations. These differences are summarized in Exhibit 9 – 2.

EXHIBIT 9 – 2. **National differences in relative importance given to variables in transfer price determination**

VARIABLES	PARENT'S NATIONALITY						
	U.S.	Canada	France	Germany	Italy	Scandi-navia	U.K.
Income tax	1	1	1	3	1	3	3
Customs duties	2	2	2	3	3	3	3
Inflation	1	2	2	2	2	3	2
Changes in currency exchange rates	3	3	2	2	3	3	2
Exchange controls	2	3	5	5	5	5	5
Improving financial appearance of subsidiary	3	3	3	4	4	4	1
Expropriation	3	3	5	5	5	5	5
Export subsidies and tax credits	4	2	2	4	2	4	2
Level of competition	4	2	2	3	2	3	3

Weighting scale: 1 = high importance, 2 = medium importance, 3 = low importance, 4 = not mentioned, 5 = mentioned only with respect to non-American operations.
Sources: U.S.: Interviews with International Accounting Firm partners.
Non-U.S.: Correspondence and interviews with subsidiary executives and International Accounting Firm partners.
Jeffrey S. Arpan, "Intracorporate Pricing." p. 9.

According to the exhibit, American, Canadian, French, and Italian companies considered income taxes to be the most important variable affecting transfer pricing policy. British companies considered improvement of the financial appearance of their United States subsidiaries as most important. With the exception of Scandinavia, inflation was also identified as a variable receiving attention in transfer pricing policy deliberations.

In contrast to external influences such as those just mentioned, non-United States multinationals reportedly consider only about half as many internal parameters as their American counterparts. With the exception of the British most firms under consideration view transfer pricing more as a means of controlling subsidiary operations than as a technique for motivating and evaluating subsidiary performance. This is largely explained by the fact that the profitcenter concept is not very widespread among non-United States firms. Aside from control, the other major consideration deemed important by all firms is the acceptability of transfer prices to both host and parent country governments alike.

Transfer Pricing and Government Relations

International differences notwithstanding, a major concern shared by multinational companies the world over is the acceptability of their transfer prices to governments hosting cross-country transfers. This concern has been discussed throughout the chapter and for good reason. Aware of the usefulness of these devices to the multinational enterprise in effecting income shifts and worried by the economic and social consequences of such actions, governments are increasing their scrutiny of multinational operations. In 1972, for example, the U.N. Secretary General appointed 20 prominent individuals to form a "Group of Eminent Persons" to examine the role of multinational corporations and their effects on host countries. Multinational transfer pricing systems and procedures are among the subjects studied by this group. Its change also includes evaluation of the feasibility of reaching international agreement on rules concerning transfer pricing policy, especially for purposes of taxation. The work of the Group of Eminent Persons is further elaborated in Chapter 10.

In the meantime, governments are not standing idly by to await the outcome of such deliberations. Governmental concerns, once confined to verbal criticisms, are now taking action. As examples;[14]

1. Members of the Tokyo High Prosecutor's Office recently confiscated some 1500 sets of files from Shell Oil's subsidiary headquarters in Japan to begin an investigation of its oil prices there.
2. In West Germany, members of the Berlin Cartel Office are investigating paper and drug prices that multinationals currently charge their subsidiaries in Germany.
3. The British government (as part of the 1975 Finance Act, mentioned previously) has just issued a new set of tax regulations regarding transfer prices being set in connection with the sale of North Sea oil.
4. In the United States, the Federal Energy Administration has started administrative preceding against Gulf Oil Corporation. Gulf is alleged to have overcharged itself for oil purchased from certain of its foreign subsidiaries to keep profits out of the United States and thus cut its United States tax bill.
5. The developing countries are also getting in on the act. IBM's transfer pricing practices are reportedly under investigation in a number of such nations.

[14] William M. Carley, "Profit Probes: Investigations Beset Multinational Firms with Stress on Pricing" (*The Wall Street Journal*, December 19, 1974), p. 1.

What does all of this portend for the future? Will governments so severely constrain transfer prices as to bring on the demise of such a critical management policy tool? We think not, at least not in the foreseeable future. Granted, both home and host governments are desirous of enforcing "arms-length" and, therefore, "fair" pricing between related affiliates of multinational companies. The problem here is determining what is arms-length or fair. Does fair refer to market-based or cost-based prices, or both? In addition, which variant of cost or market would be the appropriate one? Add to this puzzle the myriad of products to which such pricing decisions apply, not to mention currency fluctuations, language barriers, and other qualitative considerations, and presto we have a problem of gargantuan proportions! And what of enforcement? Given the limited size of most governmental policing staffs relative to the large number of transfer price "setters," this problem also becomes a nightmare.

Even if these problems could be overcome, however, we feel that governments will sooner or later have to face the question of whether the gains accruing from such policing activities really warrant the effort involved. As it currently stands, increased governmental revenues from transfer pricing "reforms" would probably pale in relation to the benefits that multinational enterprises provide host countries in the form of employment, technology transfers, indirect taxes, exports, and the like. It is doubtful whether host governments would willingly give these benefits up in the quest for a theoretical "arms-length price." What we do envision is a new set of limits on transfer pricing policy based on practical compromises by both host countries and multinational enterprises. The range of these limits, furthermore, will be functionally related to the macro benefits that the multinational company's presence will contribute to the welfare of its national host. Within these limits, multinational enterprises will still be able to maneuver their transfer prices to enable the firm to adapt to the complex set of tax, competition, and risks that characterize its ever-changing environment. Transfer pricing, in short, will continue to challenge the ingenuity of accounting and financial managers in the years to come.

SELECTED REFERENCES

9.1 ARPAN, JEFFREY S., "International Intracorporate Pricing: Non-American Systems and Views," *Journal of International Business Studies,* Spring 1972, pp. 1 – 18.

9.2 BAWLEY, DAN, "The Multinational in Search of a Tax Haven," LKHH *Accountant,* **52**, No. 4, 1972, pp. 32 - 42

9.3 BRANTNER, PAUL F., "Taxation and the Multinational Firm," *Management Accounting* (U.S.A.), October 1973, pp. 11–16, 26.

9.4 BRINER, ERNST K., "International Tax Management," *Management Accounting* (U.S.A.), February 1973, pp. 47–50.

9.5 CARLEY, WILLIAM M., "International Concerns Use Variety of Means to Cut U.S. Tax Bills," *Wall Street Journal*, October 16, 1972, p. 1.

9.6 CHOWN, JOHN, *Taxation and Multinational Enterprises*, London: Longman Group, Ltd., 1974, 283 pp.

9.7 ERNST & ERNST, *Foreign and U.S. Corporate Income and Withholding Tax Rates*, New York: Author, January 1976, 45 pp. (updated periodically).

9.8 GREENE, JAMES, and MICHAEL G. DUERR, *Intercompany Transactions in the Multinational Firm*, New York: National Industrial Conference Board, 1970, 55 pp.

9.9 HOLDSTOCK, PETER, "Some Thoughts on International Tax Planning," *Price Waterhouse International Tax News*, December 1975, pp. 1–4.

9.10 HOWARD, FREDERIC K., "Overview of International Taxation," *Columbia Journal of World Business*, Summer 1975, pp. 8–9.

9.11 *(An) Introduction to Financial Control and Reporting in Multinational Enterprises*, Russel M. Moore and George M. Scott (Ed.), Austin, Texas: Bureau of Business Research, The University of Texas at Austin, 1973, pp. 52–57.

9.12 KALISH, RICHARD H., and JOHN P. CASEY, "The Dilemma of the International Tax Executive," *Columbia Journal of World Business*, Summer 1975, pp. 52–57.

9.13 MILBURN, ALEX J., "International Transfer Transactions: What Price?" *CA Magazine* (Canada), December 1976, pp. 22–27.

9.14 National Association of Accountants, *Management Accounting for Multinational Corporations*, Vol. I and II. New York: Author, 1974, 383 pp. and 317 pp. (This is a collection of selected readings—several of which address the subject matter of Chapter 9.)

9.15 Price Waterhouse & Co., *Corporate Taxes in 80 Countries*, New York: Author, July 1976, 308 pp. (updated periodically).

9.16 Price Waterhouse & Co., *Information Guide for U.S. Corporations Doing Business Abroad*, New York: Author, March 1976, 59 pp. (updated periodically).

9.17 SHARAV, ITZHAK, "Transfer Pricing—Diversity of Goals and Practices," *Journal of Accountancy*, April 1974, pp. 56–62.

9.18 SHULMAN, J. S., "Transfer Pricing in the Multinational Firm," *European Business*, January 1969, pp. 46–54.

9.19 STOBAUGH, ROBERT B., *et al.*, *U.S. Taxation of United States Manufacturing Abroad: Likely Effects of Taxing Unremitted Profits*, New York: Financial Executives Research Foundation, 1976, 87 pp.

9.20 "Tax Reform—Foreign Income," *Journal of Accountancy*, November 1975, pp. 34, 36, 38, 40, 42, 44, 46, 48.

DISCUSSION QUESTIONS

9.1 Briefly distinguish, by way of examples, the (a) classical, (b) split-rate, and (c) imputation tax systems. Then describe what you feel are the major advantages and disadvantages of each from the perspective of a multinational corporate taxpayer.

9.2 National differences in statutory tax rates are the most obvious and yet least significant determinants of a company's effective tax burden. Do you agree with this statement? Explain.

9.3 IB Enterprises (USA) receives a $20 million dividend from its majority-owned subsidiary in Belgium. The foreign subsidiary's pretax income was $100 million. Based on the information provided in this chapter, what would IB Enterprises' United States tax liability be?

9.4 Tax policies of national governments change often and at times abruptly. Should a multinational enterprise adjust its policy and planning to every major tax change in countries in which it is operating?

9.5 What are tax credits and what role do they play in international taxation? What considerations might cause the operation of tax credits to fall short of their intended results?

9.6 Assume the role of a director of a medium-sized multinational company. Your fellow directors are divided on the merits of tax planning. Owing to the complexities of international taxes, some feel that the company should pursue a policy of maximizing pretax profits. Others feel that operating managers should strive to minimize taxes whenever possible. Critically evaluate these arguments and offer a solution to the dilemma.

9.7 The cost of new equipment with an estimated useful life of 15 years can be written off 100 percent in the year of purchase in the country of Zonalia. This practice, of course, is not in conformity with United States "Generally Accepted Accounting Principles." As head accountant of the United States parent company, how would you instruct your Zonolian subsidiary to account for any new equipment purchases and related depreciation treatment? What issues are involved here?

9.8 During 1976, Representative Charles Vanik (D-Ohio) released the results of his Fifth Annual Corporate Tax Policy Survey and observed that United States multinational companies on the whole are (a) paying twice as much in foreign taxes as United States federal income taxes and (b) paying a smaller share of the cost of running the country. Assuming that you disagree with these observations, outline (not write) a research proposal that might provide some hard evidence to the contrary.

9.9 Summarize your reactions to a proposal that foreign tax credits be abolished and replaced by a system of tax deductions similar to state and local taxes in the United States. What would be the likely costs and benefits of adopting such a proposal?

9.10 Compare and contrast the role of transfer pricing in national versus multinational operations.

9.11 A principal constraint on transfer pricing policies of multinational enterprises is the popularity of the profit-center concept as a means of monitoring and evaluating the performance of foreign units. Comment on the merits of this statement by means of an illustrative example. What suggestions can you offer in the way of possible remedies?

9.12 Explain the difference between administered and negotiated transfer prices. Who should have ultimate decision power over individual product transfer prices in a multinational company?

9.13 Briefly dimension the role of managerial accountants in the multinational transfer pricing decision.

9.14 Identify the major bases for pricing intercompany transfers and comment briefly on their relative merits. Which measurement construct seems most optimal from the viewpoint of the multinational executive suite?

9.15 What identifiable interrelationships do you perceive (if any) between a multinational company's transfer price system and management's

    a. Master operating budget.
    b. Accounting treatment of foreign exchange gains and losses.
    c. Inventory valuation methodology.
    d. Financial statement consolidation practices.
    e. Divisional operating budgets.
    f. Understanding of international accounting problems.

Prepare a brief commentary on each of the foregoing six points of reference.

ANNOTATED TEACHING MATERIALS

9.1 *Harbison-Walker Refractories Company* (ICCH Case 9-309-104). Harbison Walker Refractories Company (U.S.A.), a leader in the worldwide manufacture and distribution of refractory materials, is confronted with a series of adverse tax measures in Canada. In an attempt to reduce foreign control of Canadian companies, Canada's Finance Minister has introduced (a) a "takeover tax" of 30 percent on certain large sales to foreigners of stocks and assets of Canadian companies, (b) an increase of 33 1/3 percent in the withholding tax on dividends paid by companies that are less than 25 percent Canadian owned, and (c) generous accelerated depreciation allowances only to companies qualifying as having "a degree of Canadian ownership and control." As parent company of a wholly owned Canadian subsidiary, HWR must decide whether it should take any action with respect to the new situation and, if so, what the action should be.

9.2 *Exercises on Taxation of Foreign Income* (Rodriguez and Carter, *International Financial Management,* pp. 592–96). Drawing on materials presented with respect to United States taxation of foreign source income (pp. 581–92), the authors present a series of exercises that clarify and elaborate topics previously discussed. The student is provided data on foreign earnings, taxes, and dividends and is asked to calculate the tax liabilities of a United States parent corporation accruing from foreign investments in six differently situated subsidiaries.

9.3 *"Congress Giveth and Congress Taketh."* In September of 1976, the U.S. Congress enacted one of the most comprehensive tax acts in the past 20 years. The Act, a product of numerous legislative compromises, significantly affects the taxation of foreign income. Many tax incentives formerly granted to encourage international business activities of United States entities have now been either rescinded or substantially modified.

As a term project, secure one or more different booklets summarizing the major provisions of the 1976 Tax Reform Act (available from most large international CPA firms) and describe what you feel are the six most significant *foreign* income tax provisions and their probable effects, both internal and external, on United States multinational enterprises. As part of your analysis, be sure to include the long-run effects of the Act on the international competitive position of United States companies and the implications of your findings for the United States economy.

9.4 *DAAG Europe S.A.* (ICCH Case B, 9-174-019). The Managing Director of DAAG's Regional Headquarters in Europe must evaluate the potential effects of a new and imaginative transfer pricing policy on the reported profits and operations of the company's French subsidiary. Concern is expressed over the use of an administered transfer pricing system that might not only prove difficult to administer but also invite closer scrutiny by French tax and customs officials. The effects of the transfer pricing scheme on employee morale must also be considered.

9.5 *Thorsten A.B.* (ICCH Case D, 9-414-038). The management of Swedish-based Thorsten A.B. has spend the past 14 months trying to convince its Belgian superiors to increase their investment in Sweden. The field proposal is flatly rejected. To counter this decision, the president of the Swedish subsidiary demands the adoption of a novel transfer pricing scheme that "ruffles the feathers" of headquarters management. Attention focuses on the attitudes and political behavior occasioned by the transfer pricing issue.

9.6 *The International Manufacturing Company* (ICCH Case 9-309-252). As a means of improving control over its international operations, the International Manufacturing Company has decided to decentralize its organization structure. In implementing the change, profit centers have been established at various levels including divisional (regional), national, and local within each country, down to the individual factory or sales agency. These profit centers are expected to deal with each other on an arm's-length basis primarily through the mechanism of negotiated transfer prices on intracorporate transfers. Problems attending the transition from the old to the new system are presented.

Chapter 10

CURRENT ISSUES AND DEVELOPMENTS

The scope of multinational accounting does not stop at the technical and conceptual issues involved. It extends to public interest considerations much the same as national accounting standards and practices do. But the applicable dimensions of this public interest are still rather fuzzy and either technically underdeveloped or even undeveloped altogether. Hence Chapter 10 is more speculative and less anchored in existing practices than the preceding materials.

The underlying theme of the present chapter is the growing worldwide trend of holding corporations accountable to the public at large for both their policies and actions. At one time, corporations were thought to be accountable primarily to their stockholders and creditors. This accountability is shifting significantly toward the public at large as the present century draws to a close.

In 1976, the American Management Association published a survey entitled *Business and Society, 1976—2000*: "There is a fundamental change coming in the relationship between business and the society it serves," the report concludes. "The corporation will either transform itself or be transformed by the agents of the public into a unit that formally and continuously considers the desires, needs, and concerns of the individual and forms its policies accordingly." The transformation process, the report stated, is already underway. In 1976, 86 percent of the companies surveyed not only undertook social responsibility programs mandated by government but initiated voluntary and anticipatory programs as well.

The same message is sounded over and over. At the annual meeting of the American Assembly of Collegiate Schools of Business in Las Vegas,

Nevada, in April 1975, Thomas A. Murphy, then Chairman and Chief Executive Officer of General Motors Corporation, said

> If we stand back and look at events, not only in America but elsewhere—in France and Germany and England, for example—we can see a marked change in the governance of large corporations. Government has reached beyond regulations to active direction. In many places, representatives of labor or government or other interests sit on boards of directors. The corporate structure is in transition with the trend everywhere away from private control and toward public control.

THE CONTROL OF MULTINATIONAL ENTERPRISES

The multinational enterprise, as pointed out briefly in Chapter 1, is the object of vehement controversy among the world's economic, political, and social policy makers. Professors Negandhi and Prasad, in their 1976 Study of U.S. Multinationals in Developing Nations, called them "the frightening angels." As the title indicates, these two authors see the multinationals as both angelic and frightening to their host countries. While the multinationals are certainly more effective than many local firms, there is little spillover to the wider interests of local society. Multinationals tend to aggregate and concentrate rather than diffuse training and development. While they help the economy of their national host, important decisions are mostly made back at the home office. Local subsidiaries play small roles in such areas as product research and development or personnel training. Well-intentioned home office decisions are often diluted by local conditions, and these frustrations add to the many tensions already present between different cultures and traditions.

Professor Rosegger goes a step further in his essay contributed to the 1975 University of Michigan anthology entitled *The Economic Effects of Multinational Corporations.* His thesis is that "the heyday of multinationals as agents in the rapid leveling of technology around the globe may already be past." In the same anthology, Harry Magdoff finds severe inherent limitations to the benefits of multinationals in emerging economies. "Multinationals invest in areas which are not necessarily advantageous to the welfare of the host country, ignoring key needs for development."

Equally strong voices argue the opposite point of view. Professor Stobaugh (Harvard University) time and again has extolled the "hidden pluses" of multinationals. His studies have convinced him that the economic health of United States-based multinational enterprises. In his judgment, expansion of production facilites abroad has produced a positive effect on United States employment. Similarly, positive effects, he asserts, have been produced on the United States balance of international payments as well as technological and managerial know-how.

Ray Vicker, in the *Wall Street Journal* (March 18, 1975), provides long lists of examples on how multinational firms have helped poorer nations to boost food output.

> A few years ago, the government of Kenya decided that it wanted to establish a sugar cane plantation here, 200 miles northwest of Nairobi. But the government realized that it didn't know anything about such undertaking, so it approached Booker McConnell, Ltd., a big British foods company, for help.
>
> 'We want you to make this plantation as efficient as if it were 100 percent privately owned,' one of the Kenya officials told the McConnell executives. 'We are a developing country, and we cannot afford to subsidize a state enterprise as you in Britain subsidize, year after year, the coal industry and the railways.'
>
> Today broad fields of green cane stretch along the Nzoia River. Sun glitters on the galvanized steel roofs of a new refinery which went into production on schedule July 1, 1973. Output totaled 4,500 tons last year and is due to rise to 7,000 tons a year by 1976. The estate employs 2,500, practically all local Africans. Many were unemployed before the plantation was built. Some 5,000 small farmers in the area earn about $3 million a year selling cane to the plantation refinery. Booker McConnell manages the plantation for Kenya, and it says the operation already is profitable.

The philosophical pros and cons on the benefits and/or detriments of multinational operations are exacerbated by (a) a corporate public relations blitz that tends to be rather one-sided, e.g., "Multinationals under Seige: A Threat to the World Economy" (David Rockefeller, The Chase Manhattan Corporation), or "Multinational Companies at Bay" (Jacques G. Maisonrouge, IBM World Trade Corporation); (b) growing attitudinal inconsistency, e.g., one attitude toward business and the economic system at home and an entirely different one toward business operations abroad ("The Attacks on the Multinational," George C. McGhee, U.S. Ambassador Emeritus to Turkey and Germany and Undersecretary of State for Political Affairs, *Wall Street Journal*, March 16, 1976); and (c) recent revelations of various bribes and payoffs by United States-based corporations abroad that conform to local mores and expectations but would have been illegal had they been made in the United States (referred to earlier throughout the book, for example, in Chapter 8).

How does the controversy over the existence and activities of multinational enterprises affect accounting? The answer is simple—most of the information used on *all* sides of the arguments is directly or indirectly coming from accounting information systems. Thus, like it or not, accountants found themselves suddenly (and without much preparation, one might add) in the midst of all the scuffles between the accusers and the accused.

The three response avenues in which accountants have had a hand are (a) factualization of arguments and information, (b) support for movements toward "codes of conduct" for multinational enterprises, and (c) addition of an accounting dimension to the recently established United Nations Center on Transnational Corporations. Each of these three responses is sketched briefly in the paragraphs to follow.

Factualizations

In many of the arguments and assertions surrounding the issue of effective international control over the multinational enterprise, much of the data utilized is wrong, inapplicable, or inconsistent. An AICPA Professional Accounting Career brochure refers to accountants as "designers of order." Nowhere is this more applicable than in the total environment of the multinational enterprise.

First the power question has to be put in focus (*Accountancy*, March, 1976, p. 28):

> Even the smallest and most recent newcomer to nationhood (with or without a seat at U.N.) has absolute, unquestioned authority over the largest MNE [multinational enterprise]. It can and does monitor and control new investment. It determines levels and distributions and expatriation of funds. It imposes production quotas and controls prices at levels which may well be uneconomic and therefore unprofitable from the company's point of view. It can and often does rule and legislate on every aspect of the company's activities and in such a way as to put the company at a trading disadvantage vis-a-vis local business.

The analysis of expropriations of business assets and their various effects is one way in which accountants can shed more light on the real seats of power in international economic affairs. This topic is treated at some length in Chapter 7. Let us be reminded here that Unilever had companies taken over or nationalized in 17 different countries between 1945 and 1973. Between 1961 and 1974, expropriations of Shell Companies occurred in Algeria, Ceylon, Cuba, Egypt, Guinea, Libya, Somalia, Syria, and South Yemen.

Another control example occurs with respect to the world currency system. Freely floating foreign exchange rates would certainly not be the choice of multinational enterprises. The virtual lack of control over the world monetary system was one element that prompted the United States FASB to require in its Standard No. 8 that all translation adjustments be currently recognized in income statements. If the multinationals had some control over exchange rate changes other than managing foreign exchange risks at the micro level, an argument for deferrals or even capitalization of translation adjustments would be much more cogent than it is under present circumstances.

There is a myriad of direct ways in which accountants foster factualization of multinational business information. Most of the world's multinationals regularly publish annual reports that exceed national statutory requirements in both scope and quality and do so by a hefty margin of difference. Many of the transnational financial reporting efforts described in Chapter 4 contribute to improved multinational financial information bases.

Finally, many of the research studies on international investments and returns therefrom helped to establish a more realistic picture. The work of Professors Robbins and Stobaugh is particularly noteworthy in this connection and has been referred to in earlier chapters (e.g., *Money in the Multinational Enterprise*, 1973).

Codes Of Conduct

As a partial response to the many pressures for greater control over multinational enterprise activities, international agencies, national governments, and individual multinationals are all involved in the active development of codes of conduct for international business operations. The first such code was adopted in May 1972 by the Pacific Basin Economic Council. It is entitled "Charter on International Investments." Also in 1972, the Economic and Social Council of the United Nations appointed a "Group of Eminent Persons" to hold public hearings and then make recommendations aimed at "some form of accountability to the international community" as far as the multinationals are concerned (see prior mention of this action on p. 313). One outcome of the report of the "Eminent Persons" group was the establishment, on December 4, 1974, of the U.N. Commission on Transnational Corporations. This commission has speedily proceeded to set up an information center, which is discussed later in this chapter.

Besides U.N. efforts, the 24-member Organization for Economic Cooperation and Development (OECD) promulgated a Code of Conduct for Multinational Enterprises in June, 1976. The OECD action represents the first time Western governments have acted in concert to express an opinion on corporate behavior. The OECD Code is voluntary, but considerable political and moral suasion supports it. It seems almost certain that multinationals departing from this Code will find it difficult to operate in certain countries. Many professional accountants served as advisors to the governmental representatives involved in the negotiations leading to the adoption of the OECD Code. Among many other provisions, the Code contains specific financial disclosure guidelines. Exhibit 10–1 shows the pertinent details.

EXHIBIT 10 – 1. Annex to the Declaration of 21st June 1976 by Governments of OECD Member Countries on International Investment and Multinational Enterprises

---

GUIDELINES FOR MULTINATIONAL ENTERPRISES

Disclosure of Information

Enterprises should, having due regard to their nature and relative size in the economic context of their operations and to requirements of business confidentiality and to cost, publish in a form suited to improve public understanding a sufficient body of factual information on the structure, activities and policies of the enterprise as a whole, as a supplement, in so far as necessary for this purpose, to information to be disclosed under the national law of the individual countries in which they operate. To this end, they should publish within reasonable time limits, on a regular basis, but at least annually, financial statements and other pertinent information relating to the enterprise as a whole, comprising in particular:

  i. The structure of the enterprise, showing the name and location of the parent company, its main affiliates, its percentage ownership, direct and indirect, in these affiliates, including shareholdings, between them;

  ii. the geographical areas where operations are carried out and the principal activities carried on therein by the parent company and main affiliates;

  iii. the operating results and sales by geographical area and the sales in the major lines of business for the enterprise as a whole;

  iv. significant new capital investment by geographical area and, as far as practicable, by major lines of business for the enterprise as a whole;

  v. a statement of the sources and uses of funds by the enterprise as a whole;

  vi. the average number of employees in each geographical area;

  vii. research and development expenditure for the enterprise as a whole;

  viii. the policies followed in respect of intra-group pricing;

  ix. the accounting policies including those on consolidation, observed in compiling the published information.

Source: Adolf J.H. Enthoven, *Social and Political Impact of Multinationals on Third World Countries (and Its Accounting Implications)*, American Accounting Association 60th Annual Meeting, Aug. 23–25, 1976, Plenary Session, p. 33.

Not to be outdone, a number of multinational enterprises have moved to establish their own multinational operations codes. For example, Caterpillar Tractor Company, in 1974, published a comprehensive statement of worldwide activities." Topics covered include ownership and investment, [Caterpillar Tractor Co.] in a broad and ethical sense in all aspects of our worldwide activities." Topics covered include ownership and investment, corporate facilities, relationship with employees, observance of local laws, business ethics, and public responsibility. With regard to ethics, the following statement is made; "The law is a floor. Ethical business conduct should normally exist at a level above the minimum required by law."

A score of other multinational enterprises have followed the Caterpillar lead. A good overview of the entire "code" development is available from two booklets published by Stanford Research Institute in Menlo Park,

California. Their 1975 publication is entitled "International Business Principles—Codes" and the 1976 follow-up volume carries the heading "International Business Principles—Company Codes."

How likely is it that this plethora of recent international business codes will make any difference? The jury is not in yet on this question! But the authors speculate that some significant effects are very likely to be produced—and relatively soon. A small illustration of this is a 1976 German-United States executive agreement on antitrust cooperation.[1] This agreement is a first attempt, as far as we know, by national governments to put some teeth into the OECD Code referred to above, which urges, among other things, that companies voluntarily provide information to relevant authorities on competitive issues. Specifically, the German-United States agreement stipulates that "each party ... will provide the other party with any significant information which comes to the attention of its antitrust authorities and which involves restrictive business practices which, regardless of origins, have a substantial effect on the domestic or international trade of such other parties."

This means that United States antitrust authorities, for example, would be obliged to pass on to their German counterparts any evidence uncovered that shows that a company (whatever its nationality) has engaged in illegal restrictive practices with effects in Germany—even though such company may not have violated any United States laws or regulations. Furthermore, the agreement commits one government to act as a kind of mailman for the other. Each must endorse the other's request for information from a locally based company stating to the suspected offender that it is free to comply with the request. Of course, compliance cannot be enforced. Companies are protected by national laws on confidentiality; however, moral pressure to respond will certainly be great.

As far as the developing countries are concerned, the OECD Code (or at least portions thereof) seems certain to become a component of both project and general investment contracts with multinational enterprises.

United Nations Center

As mentioned above, the 1974 establishment of the United Nations Commission on Transnational Corporations also spawned that Commission's creation of the Center on Transnational Corporations. This Center is an information-gathering agency charged with building a comprehensive system of information on transnational corporations. There are, however, some difficulties.

[1] "Antitrusters Build Bridge between Germany and U.S.," *Business Europe,* July 16, 1976, pp. 228–229.

At the organizational conference of the U.N. Commission on Transnational Corporations held in the spring of 1975 in Lima, Peru, the Developing Countries, with support from the Warsaw Pact Affiliates, argued that the Commission's jurisdiction should extend only to multinational corporate entities operating in the private sector. On the other hand, the industrial countries contended that government agencies and state-owned trading groups should be included as well. This dispute remains unsettled at the date of this writing.

The difference of opinion that surfaced at the Lima conference has obvious accounting ramifications. Among many other things, the conference recommended the establishment of an expert group on international standards of accounting and reporting. The work of this group is to be supported by a comprehensive information bank. The Third World plus the Warsaw Pact Affiliates contend that any information gathering from public sector agencies or organizations would be contrary to national sovereignty. The free enterprise bloc, on the other hand, fears that a politically appointed group of expert accountants would seek to impose more drastic accounting and disclosure requirements for multinational enterprise than exists on any present domestic scale.

Notwithstanding the individual merits of the foregoing views, the U.N. Center on Transnational Corporations has begun operations and is actively collecting data on the operations of multinational enterprises. The classification system used for this data collection effort is shown in Exhibit 10 – 2. Many of the data classifications clearly rely on output from accounting information systems. Thus, a rather direct relationship exists between the work of the U.N. Center and accounting systems of multinational enterprises.

EXHIBIT 10 – 2. United Nations Center on Transnational Corporations Classification for Bibliography on Transnational Corporations (TNC's)

1 Conceptual and definitional questions and general
    10 Conceptual questions
    11 Definitions
    12 Disclosure and reporting procedures and regulations
    13 Reference sources (including bibliographies, sources of research)
    14 General studies on TNC's
    15 Evaluation, history of TNC's
    19 Other
2 Explanations of foreign direct investment and management and organization
    20 Explanations of foreign direct investment
    21 Management and organization
        210 Strategies
        211 Organization and structures (including relationships between headquarters and foreign affiliates)
        212 Functions
        213 Teaching case studies
        214 Business in selected countries
        219 Other

EXHIBIT 10-2. Continued

3 Data and information on individual enterprises
    30 Individual enterprises
    31 Directories
    39 Other

4 Aggregate data and information on TNC activities: size, growth, distribution, characteristics, trends
    40 Inward investment
    41 Outward investment
    49 Other

5 The role of TNC's in individual economic sectors
    50 Industrial structure
    51 Agriculture, forestry, fishing
    52 Mining and petroleum
    53 Manufacturing
    54 Construction
    55 Wholesale and retail trade and restaurants and hotels
    56 Transport, storage, and communications
    57 Financing, insurance, real estate, and business services (including accounting, engineering, advertising)
    58 Community, social, and personal services
    59 Other

6 The role of TNC's in individual countries, regions, and the international system
    60 Developing countries
    61 Developed countries
    62 Centrally planned economies
    63 Regional groups
    64 International system

7 The impact of transnational corporations
    70 Economic impact
        700 Transfer of technology
        701 Industrial and economic development
        702 Employment, training, wages, and working conditions
        703 Finance and balance of payments
        704 Ownership and control
        705 Market structure and restrictive business practices
        706 Transfer pricing
        707 Consumption pattern
        708 Environment
        709 Other
    71 Political impact
        710 Government-business relationship
        711 Incentives, guarantee programs, investment climate, political risk
        712 Bargaining power
        713 International relations
        719 Other
    72 Sociocultural impact
    73 Legal implications
        730 Regulation and control of TNC's
        731 Nationalization and compensation
        732 Extraterritorial application of laws and regulations and antitrust
        733 Corrupt practices
        734 Contracts and agreements

EXHIBIT 10-2. Continued

Among the earliest reports published by the Center is one entitled "Information on Transnational Corporations." It not only specifies sources of information on multinationals, but addresses problems of disclosure and comparability together with possible steps toward the development of a globally comprehensive information system on multinational business operations.

ACCOUNTING FOR MULTINATIONAL CORPORATE SOCIAL RESPONSIBILITY

The many pressures for greater control of multinationals are the same pressures felt by multinational companies for assuming greater amounts of social responsibility in each of the countries in which they operate and then measuring and reporting their social responsibility performance to third parties. This type of reporting may well help to defend them against pressures for massive regulation, not only by national governments and international governmental agreements but also by various international agencies and organizations.

Harvey Kapnick, Chairman of Arthur Andersen & Co., advocates formal business statements of economic and social goals (see his *The Challenge for International Business,* California State University, San Jose, October 25, 1972). Such statements would address a company's expected rate of growth, its priorities, and its part in solving social problems of the day. It would also report on new jobs created, in which countries, and at what costs. It would furnish details on employee training costs and worker productivity, on research and development expenditures, and on planned product changes. It would list taxes paid to given units of government and interest and dividends paid to providers of long-term money capital. It would also attempt to estimate costs of various regulations imposed from various sources. Says Mr. Kapnick

Information of this type would provide a realistic basis for the public to evaluate the progress of a particular business in helping to solve the social problems in each country in which it operates, the priority it has given to those social goals, and the clear indication of the social liabilities under which it is operating in each country and the cost of those liabilities. Such information would also supply the fact to those who believe that multinational businesses are insensitive to the business practices and social needs of the countries in which they operate.

Few will dispute the imperatives set by Mr. Kapnick and many others. Yet at this time we have little idea as to *who* might set the goals to be measured and reported and *what* types of measurement standards and procedures might be appropriate for the necessary reporting system. Many books and papers have been written on the subject, many professional conferences held regarding it, and official policy statements produced by organizations such as the AICPA and the National Association of Accountants in the United States. Accounting scholars have produced some textbooks directed at the problems involved and book-length collections of readings are available as background materials. Yet the fundamental questions of what, how, who, and when are still substantially unanswered.

Social responsibility (SR) concerns are no doubt more pronounced in Europe than in North America. Public policy in Europe has moved further in this direction than elsewhere. Consequently, more private and institutional research on this topic, as well as more practical experimentation with it, is available on the Continent than in the Anglo-Saxon countries, but the results are roughly the same. As far as your authors are able to determine, only very few comprehensive social responsibility financial statements have been published in France, Germany, and the Netherlands, despite the relatively large amount of research backing up this particular effort. A few such statements are available in North America as well—with no comparative advantage or differential development levels evident at this time.

In the absence of a conceptually sound or pragmatically supportable system of social responsibility measurement and reporting, most companies have resorted to disclosure as the vehicle for publicizing their increasingly higher levels of discharging perceived social responsibilities. The disclosure techniques employed are simply appendages to the conventional financial accounting and reporting system.

One of the more informative surveys in this respect is published annually by the international CPA firm of Whinney, Murray, Ernst & Ernst (E & E) regarding "Fortune 500" companies making social responsibility (SR) disclosures. The growing incidence of this disclosure is portrayed in Table 10−1 and makes interesting reading. Usually, SR disclosure appears in various sections throughout the respective corporate annual reports and covers a wide array of issues.

TABLE 10 – 1. Number of Companies Providing SR Disclosures

	1975	1974	1973	1972	1971
Companies making SR disclosures	425	346	298	286	239
Companies with no SR disclosures	N.A.*	151	198	206	226
Reports not readily available	N.A.*	3	4	8	35
		500	500	500	500

*N.A. = Not available.

The E & E survey catalogs disclosures under six general headings—each broken down by further subheadings. A condensed listing of the categories used is as follows:

A. Environment
   1. Pollution control
   2. Product development to reduce the pollutive effects arising from its use
   3. Repair of the environment
   4. Recycling of waste material
   5. Other disclosures relating to the environment
B. Equal opportunity
   1. Minority employment
   2. Advancement of minorities
   3. Employment of women
   4. Advancement of women
   5. Minority business
   6. Other disadvantaged groups
   7. Other statements on equal opportunity
C. Personnel
   1. Employee health and safety
   2. Training
   3. Other disclosures concerning responsibility to personnel
D. Community involvement
   1. Community activities
   2. Public health
   3. Education or the arts
   4. Other community activity disclosure
E. Products
   1. Safety
   2. Quality
   3. Other product-related disclosures

F. Other social responsibility disclosures
1. Special items
   a. General disclosure of corporate objectives with regard to social responsibility
   b. Disclosure of compliance with applicable governmental regulations
   c. Disclosures of code of business ethics or acknowledgment of corporate social responsibility
   d. Participation in self-regulatory trade associations
2. Additional information provided
   a. Offer to send additional material relating to social responsibility

One of the more critical problems with SR measurement, reporting and auditing relates to monetary expression. Table 10 – 2 yields some indication of the quantitative versus nonquantitative disclosure mode utilized by the survey companies.

TABLE 10 – 2. Topics of Quantification of SR Disclosures (as of 1975)

GENERAL SR CATEGORY	NUMBER OF COMPANIES PROVIDING	
	MONETARY QUANTIFICATION	NONMONETARY QUANTIFICATION
A. Environment	117	103
B. Equal opportunity	11	66
C. Personnel	7	59
D. Community involvement	52	54
E. Products	2	10
F. Other SR disclosures	0	1

Multinational enterprises have much to gain from being leaders in the corporate social responsibility game. Even though no appropriate survey statistics are available, your authors hazard the guess that the multinationals among the "Fortune 500" were the leaders in SR disclosures. Moreover, we are convinced that the multinationals stand ready to experiment with full-fledged social responsibility financial statements and reports as soon as the needed technology has been developed. This is an area in which the multinationals are likely to become accounting innovators and practice leaders. The first indications of this likelihood are already at hand.

INTERNATIONAL BALANCE OF PAYMENTS ACCOUNTING

Accounting for a country's international balance of payments is a subject that traditionally has fallen into the preserve of economics. It is considered a part of macroaccounting and therefore, like national income accounting, separated from the microaccounting concerns (both in the private and public sectors) that have occupied accounting departments in business schools.

Both macroaccounting and microaccounting are still accounting! Recognizing the many interrelationships between the two, beginning as well as advanced accounting texts have recently started to include materials on national income accounting. Similarly, a book on multinational accounting would be remiss if it did not at least raise the issue of accounting for international balances of payments. Moreover, many multinational enterprises now routinely monitor the effects of their investment and operating decisions on the balances of payments of the countries in which they operate. In fact, full social responsibility disclosures would dictate periodic reporting of balance of payments effects caused by various economic movements of the reporting multinational company. Financial executives operating multinationally and their independent CPA's must certainly have a good grasp of international balance of payments accounting if they are to budget, control, and subsequently report upon the balance of payments ramifications of their actions.

Definition. A nation's international balance of payments statement can be compared to a statement of a family's household finances. In the latter, deficits in a checking account must be financed by withdrawals from savings accounts or with new loans. Conversely, newly available funds that are not spent currently may be added to savings or used to retire outstanding loans. Exactly the same holds true for the international balance of payments of a country. If there is a deficit, withdrawals from stockpiles of gold or foreign currency (i.e., savings) must take place, or new liabilities must be negotiated with foreigners (new loans).

An official U.S. State Department pamphlet states

> The U.S. international balance of payments is the record of financial transactions which take place between the United States and the rest of the world during a particular period of time. The balance of payments statement covers receipts and payments for both private and governmental transactions, whether they are settled in cash or financed by credit.

The Federal Reserve Bank of New York explains

> A nation's balance of payments is the result of countless private and public decisions to buy or sell, lend or borrow abroad. The total of all our receipts from exports of goods and services, including investment income, is not sufficient to cover the amounts spent in imports, travel, military aid, and investments. The result is an overall deficit in our balance of payments.

In short, then, all financial transactions that a country, any of its resident organizations, or any of its citizens has with foreigners enter international balance of payments accounting. Simply by subscribing to a foreign newspaper or by purchasing a foreign book for its library, your university made a decision that affects the country's international balance of payments!

Accounting Procedures. Balance of payments accounting is similar to conventional financial accounting. Receipts or exports or inflows are increases (credits), and payments or imports or outflows are decreases (debits). The object of recording classified receipts and payments is to arrive at a "balance" between the two. Hence the name *balance of payments* statement.

Just as in any other double entry system, *the payments balance always balances by definition.* The accounting equation involved is simply defined to be an identity just as in conventional accounting. So-called balance of payments "surpluses" or "deficits" are merely items needed to produce equality between the inflows and the outflows (or the debits and the credits).

Not all international financial transactions involve two-way considerations. Examples of unilateral items are gifts, grants, and other types of transfer payments. Moreover, the debit and the credit for the same event may sometimes have to be taken from different source documents. For instance, an export item in the United States is recorded as a receipt on the basis of Bureau of the Census statistics. The corresponding increase in the foreign exchange holdings of the exporter's bank, however, is likely to be recorded on the basis of a Federal Reserve Bank statistic. The two cannot be matched precisely. Therefore, a number of items may be double counted or omitted altogether since no automatic check and balance system exists for completeness. Hence, an asymmetry arises that produces the so-called "errors and omissions" items in any formal international balance of payments statement.

Overall, balance of payments accounting in nonsocialist countries is guided by the International Monetary Fund's *Balance of Payments Manual.* In the United States, the Balance of Payments Division in the Office of Business Economics of the Department of Commerce is responsible for securing the data that enter into United States balance of payments accounting. Where "hard" data are unavailable, various statistical estimating techniques are used, including questionnaire surveys. Amounts determined in this fashion include foreign travel and transportation, foreign expenditures of military personnel, private remittances, and income on foreign investments.

Here is some indication of how the underlying accounting system works:

1. An increase in United States investment abroad is a debit item, inasmuch as it involves the acquisition of a claim on a foreign person, company, bank, or government.
2. A service performed by a United States resident for foreigners (e.g., the sale of services to foreign travelers in the United States) is a credit item, and a service performed by foreigners for United States residents is a debit item.
3. United States merchandise exports are credit items. The matching debit may be recorded as an increase in liabilities of foreigners to United States residents or as a decrease in foreign holdings of assets in the United States (e.g., payment made from a foreign deposit in a United States bank).
4. Foreign assets in the United States are listed as credits. Capital raised abroad by a United States corporation in the Eurodollar market for expansion overseas is a credit, listed under "transactions in foreign assets in the United States." If the money is not used immediately but deposited in a foreign bank, a debit is made under "foreign transactions in United States private assets."

Classification Problems. As one would expect from the foregoing examples numerous classification difficulties plague balance of payments accounting:

1. When one flies overseas on an American airline, one's fare is ignored for purposes of balance of payments accounting. When one flies on a foreign airline, one's fare is estimated as a transportation payment.
2. The balance of payments category "exports of goods and services" includes, in the United States, income from Panama Canal tolls, fees earned by American embassies from processing visas, receipts from the rental of United States films in foreign countries, receipts from operations of United States engineering firms contracting abroad, and receipts from United Nations operations.
3. Again, from the United States point of view, "imports of goods and services" include wage remittances to their home countries by foreign migrant workers employed in the United States, rental payments for United States embassy buildings overseas, and salaries to State Department employees assigned to United States embassies abroad.

Still other classification problems relate to identifying capital transactions as long-term or short-term flows, as direct or indirect investments or as securities transactions or loans. For example, securities with an original maturity of over one year are considered long-term assets, even if they mature in less than a year from the date of the accountable transaction. Similarly, loans of over 1 year remain long-term assets until they are paid, even if they have less than 1 year to run as of a given accounting date.

Another perennial classification concern arises over whether data ought to be categorized according to the *type* of transaction (such as travel) or according to the entity giving rise to it (such as the United States government, when official travel is involved). Obviously, the classification matter becomes all-important when "balances" are calculated between various items in a balance of payments statement.

Exhibit 10 – 3 portrays a recent international balance of payments statement of the United States.

What does it all mean? If the aggregate balance of payments always "balances," why are policy-makers so critically concerned over so-called surpluses or deficits? The answer is straightforward. The concern is not over *whether* the statement balances but *how* it is brought to balance. As an example, if an international payments deficit arises, there is a critical policy difference between measures taken to *reduce* such a deficit and measures taken that *finance* the deficit. Therefore economists distinguish between

1. *Regular* items: international payments and receipts arising from normal foreign currency deficits or surpluses arising from imbalances between tional economic relationships.
2. *Settlement* items: international payments or receipts needed to balance foreign currency deficits or surplus arising from imbalances between regular items of a nation's financial transactions with other countries.

Many different balance of payments concepts have been suggested due to controversy over what should not be regarded as a "regular" item in balance of payments accounting. Exhibit 10 – 4 sets forth three concepts widely used at the present time. Note that the official balance definition is relatively the most inclusive on the inflow side—meaning that it tends to produce equilibrium (where the other two concepts would show deficits) when a currency comes under outflow pressures.

The balance on basic transactions shows all current transactions and long-term capital movements as regular items and considers financing transactions, short-term capital movements, errors and omissions, and gold movements as settlement items. This balance concept was used in the United States through the 1940's, but was officially abandoned when short-term capital movements came to have a strong impact on the international financial positions of major countries. For the sake of illustration, it is calculated and included in Exhibit 10 – 3.

The balance on liquidity basis places short-term capital movements, as well as errors and omissions, into the regular classification. This leaves as settlement items changes in official United States reserves (including the United States position with the International Monetary Fund) and changes in United States liquid liabilities to all foreigners.

EXHIBIT 10 – 3. United States Balance of Payments Summary By Area^a, 1975 (In billions of United States dollars)

	GLOBAL	EUROPEAN COMMUNITY	JAPAN	CANADA	OTHER DEVELOPED COUNTRIES^b	LESS DEVELOPED COUNTRIES^c	EASTERN EUROPE	INTERNATIONAL ORGANIZATIONS AND UNALLOCATED^d
Exports^e	107.3	17.0	7.2	17.4	7.8	27.8	1.6	....
Imports^e	-98.1	-12.3	-8.4	-15.9	-4.7	-30.4	-0.5	....
Net trade^e	9.1	4.8	-1.2	1.5	3.1	-2.6	1.1	....
Military sales	4.0	0.4	Negl.	0.1	0.2	2.2	....	....
Military expenditures	-4.8	-1.7	-0.6	-0.1	-0.2	-1.0	Negl.	....
Net military	-0.8	-1.3	-0.6	-0.1	Negl.	1.2	Negl.	....
Investment income receipts	16.9	2.3	0.9	1.9	1.3	6.0	0.1	0.2
Investment income payments	-11.7	-3.4	-0.8	-0.5	-1.5	-2.3	Negl.	-0.3
Net investment income	5.2	-1.1	0.1	1.4	-0.2	3.7	0.1	-0.1
Travel income	6.1	0.6	0.6	1.3	0.3	1.7	....	....
Travel expenditures	-8.8	-1.8	-0.2	-1.1	-0.9	-2.5	-0.1	Negl.
Net travel	-2.7	-1.2	0.4	-0.1	-0.6	-0.6	-0.1	Negl.
Other services, net	4.8	1.2	0.4	0.4	0.5	1.2	0.1	-0.2
Balance on Goods and Services	15.6	2.4	-0.8	3.4	2.6	2.9	1.2	-0.3
Remittances (excluding military)	-1.7	Negl.	Negl.	-0.1	-0.2	-1.0	Negl.	....
U.S. Government grants	-2.8	....	Negl.	....	Negl.	-1.8	....	....
Balance on Current Account	11.1	2.4	-0.8	3.3	2.4	0.1	1.2	-0.5
U.S. Government capital flows	-2.0	-0.1	0.1	-0.1	-0.2	-1.1	0.1	-0.2
U.S. direct investments abroad	-5.9	-1.0	-0.1	-0.2	-0.3	-3.0	....	-0.2
Foreign Direct Investments in the United States	1.2	0.1	0.1	0.1	Negl.	0.6	....	....
Net Portfolio Investments	-2.3	1.0	-0.2	-1.6	0.6	0.4	....	-1.9
Other long-term private capital	-1.7	0.1	0.1	Negl.	-0.2	-0.7	-0.1	-0.3
Net long-term private capital flows	-8.7	0.3	-0.1	-1.7	0.1	-2.7	-0.1	-1.8
Balance on Basic Transactions	0.4	2.5	-0.8	1.5	2.3	-3.7	1.2	-3.1

^a Area data are for the first 9 months of 1975.
^b Australia, New Zealand, South Africa, and other Western Europe.
^c Latin America, other Western Hemisphere, and other Africa and Asia.
^d Includes transactions with shipping companies operating under the flags of Honduras, Liberia, and Panama.
^e Excluding military.

Sources: Department of Commerce. Adapted from: U.S. Government Printing Office, *International Economic Report of the President—1976.*

EXHIBIT 10 – 4.   Grouping of U.S. International Transactions Under Three Balance-of-Payments Concepts

I. BASIC BALANCE	II. LIQUIDITY BALANCE	III. OFFICIAL BALANCE

Goods and services
Remittances and pensions
U.S. Government grants and
  capital movements
Private long-term capital,
  U.S. and foreign (except
  foreign holdings of U.S.
  Government bonds
  and notes)
 	
*Balance on Basic
Transactions*
	Goods and services
	Remittances and pensions
	U.S. Government grants and
	  capital movements
	Private long-term capital,
	  U.S. and foreign (except
	  foreign holdings of U.S.
	  Government bonds
	  and notes)
		Goods and services
		Remittances and pensions
		U.S. Government grants and
		  capital movements
		Private long-term capital,
		  U.S. and foreign (except
		  U.S. government bonds
		  and notes held by foreign
		  official monetary
		  institutions)

Private short-term capital,
  U.S. and foreign
Errors and omissions
Foreign holdings of U.S.
  Government bonds
  and notes
Foreign official short-term
  capital
U.S. gold and convertible
  currency reserves and
  IMF position
	U.S. private short-term
	  capital
	Foreign commercial credits
	Errors and omissions
	
	Balance on Liquidity Basis
	
	Foreign private short-term
	  capital (except
	  commercial credits)
	Foreign holdings of U.S.
	  Government bonds
	  and notes
	Foreign official short-term
	  capital
	U.S. gold and convertible
	  currency reserves and
	  IMF position
		Private short-term capital,
		  U.S. and foreign
		Errors and omissions
		Foreign official short-term
		  capital (except that of of-
		  ficial monetary institutions)
		
		*Balance on Official Reserve
		Transactions*
		
		Foreign official monetary
		  institutions' holdings of
		  U.S. Government bonds
		  and notes
		Foreign official monetary
		  institutions' short-term
		  capital
		U.S. gold and convertible
		  currency reserves and
		  IMF position

Note: In each case, the sum of the items above the line equals the sum of the items below the line, with the opposite sign.

Source: Review Committee for Balance of Payments Statistics, *The Balance of Payments Statistics of the United States*

Finally, the balance on official reserve transactions includes private foreigners' liquid dollar assets (i.e., domestic United States dollar liabilities) as part of the regular position and thereby reduces the list of items in the settlement category even further.

Both the balance on liquidity basis and the balance on official reserve transactions are indicators of the international balance of payments position that are currently compiled and periodically published by the U.S. Department of Commerce.

To summarize, your authors contend that there is no single statistic that can completely summarize any given country's international balance of payments position at a particular date. There is simply no "right" or "wrong" single indicator. Edward M. Bernstein states

> It is quite true that the balance of payments deficit (i.e., the balance of payments problem) can't be measured. It can only be analyzed. That is to say that there will be big differences of opinion as to the size of the deficit.

But the periodic international balance of payments statements tell citizens, business decision makers and governmental policy makers (at least within the realm of statistical feasibility) what the size and nature of international financial transactions are. As we have already indicated, this creates an important information base. However, dogmatic use of particular combinations among statement categories seems ill-advised. Specific uses contemplated should dictate the type of information or the combinations of pieces of information which should be extracted for that particular use from the applicable balance of payments statement. Different decisions require different information—a slogan well worth remembering when it comes to using information contained in international balance of payments statements.

ACCOUNTING AND ECONOMIC DEVELOPMENT

Owing to ever-growing rates of literacy among the world's population, a more and more comprehensive network of worldwide communication and apparent manifestations of Dusenberry's "demonstration effect," developing countries are actively seeking to narrow existing disparities in relative consumption patterns (i.e., standards of living). While it took many of the economically advanced countries centuries to acquire their present levels of economic development, acute acceleration of timetables for economic growth has become a panacea for the nations of the Third World. Fortunately, for all concerned, it is today feasible to circumvent somewhat the traditional time constraints holding development progress in check. This feasibility comes about, at least in part, from the possibility that developing countries can benefit from the large accumulation of technology and knowledge built up in their industrially advanced neighbor countries.

Of course, many voices have been raised against subordinating all else to output of economic goods and services. One such voice is Willem P.J. Boichel's, editor of *Survey of International Development* (March, 1970, p. 5):

> Mankind is marching towards materialistic and utilitarian societies where abdication to the growth index mania has become the guiding principle. Deep incompatibilities with the human psyche are being generated in the process, for man does not find his salvation in technology and concrete alone.

There is increasing awareness in the world's development community that man's sense of well-being is derived to an important degree from natural factors which escape easy quantification, that quantity alone does not mean quality, and that technology and economic growth for . their own sakes are alienating man from his fundamental self.

Whatever one's philosophy about economic development, accounting plays a certain and positive role in it. This was first postulated by the German economist, Werner Sombart, who contended that the system of double entry bookkeeping was an active catalyst in the industrial development of Europe near the end of the Middle Ages. Some have belittled the Sombart thesis by asserting that single entry methods would have been just as effective in economic development as double entry methods, but this really misses the point. The fundamental issue bears on the relationship between accounting development and economic development (or vice versa.).

Fairly recently, Professor James O. Winjum used historiography to test Sombart's thesis by analyzing a large number of accounting treatises and records from the 16th through the 18th century in England. Here is his basic conclusion:

> Sombart was correct in directing attention to the relationship between accounting and the rise of capitalism. The system of double entry bookkeeping does have the capability of making a positive contribution towards economic growth. Although the ability of double entry to reveal the success or failure of a business enterprise for a specific period of time was not valued by the early English merchants, double entry's capacity to accumulate data on individual operating activities, combined with its ability to bring order to the affairs of these merchants, stimulated and rationalized the economic activities of the early English merchant.

This does not yet answer the query, though, whether accounting development is a precondition to economic development or whether it follows as an aftermath. This question is of critical importance to the Third World and has not yet received an answer.

Why is a reasonable amount of accounting capacity essential to a developing economy? While there are many answers, we single out five reasons to make the point.

Macro Accounts. Most industrialized Western countries determine priorities for the use of national resources through competitive economic processes. On the other hand, developing countries must rely more heavily on centralized planning, because their market processes are generally too narrow to become efficient and/or their resource bases are so singular (e.g., a single mineral or agricultural product export economy) that they depend heavily on world market conditions or consumption patterns in other countries over which they have little or no control. As one development official put it, tongue in cheek, "A few consumers in the industrialized countries sneeze, and half of the Third World catches pneumonia."

With effective national planning often critical to developing countries, they must rely heavily on complete and accurate financial data to facilitate the preparation of national income accounts and the enforcement of individual and corporate taxation policies. The financial information compiled for these purposes, in turn, facilitates decisions with regard to a government's monetary and fiscal policies, management of international balances of payments, establishment and control of international trade policies, and, of course, general economic planning. Most observers are convinced that the absence of reliable macro accounting data hampers severely any orderly economic development progress.

Management Accounting. Little needs to be said to support the contention that managerial accounting systems are likely to contribute to a country's economic development. All the arguments that are made for the benefits of good managerial accounting standards and techniques in the industrialized environments probably hold even more so in development situations. To be sure, subsystems, such as individual cost behavior analyses, may not need to be refined in the extreme for the typically very labor-intensive enterprise in a developing country. But cost accumulations and planning and control processes effected in a reliable manner are surely critical to reasonable resource allocation, both within an enterprise and in the economy at large. On balance, complete and reliable cost accumulations are probably more important for a company in a developing country than for one in an industrialized country. The reason is simple. Price-setting mechanisms in the Third World must rely heavily on cost data because markets for products and services are not efficient enough on their own to act as dependable price setters.

Financial Accounting. In the absence of large and very competitive public markets for corporate and governmental securities, financial accounting certainly plays less of a role in the developing countries than in Canada, Japan, the United Kingdom, and the United States, where the large securities markets are located. Nevertheless, relevant and timely financial reporting certainly has a contribution to make as a generator of investor and creditor confidence as well as a stimulant to the eventual development of broader money capital markets in developmental settings. All too often, households' and businesses' savings generated in the Third World are invested in marginally productive forms or nonproductive money equivalents or exported altogether. Any of these alternatives impedes a developing country's capital formation process. This, then, is the element in which financial accounting can be most helpful. Of course, it should also be able to contribute to the equitable enforcement of various governmental regulations, collective bargaining by labor unions, and a host of other processes essential to development activities.

Compliance Accounting. Many economic assistance programs depend on compliance with a potential creditor's financial monitoring system. In this respect, the requirements of the International Finance Corporation were mentioned earlier. Other economic development banks and agencies, both public and private, have similar needs for (a) reliable projections and forecasts to evaluate the financial feasibility of the project to be undertaken, (b) control systems that reliably guide investment projects during construction and start-up periods, (c) periodic financial reports to show the performance of a project after it has begun to operate, and (d) comparative financial statistics of various types for the purpose of using past actions in investments as guides to future commitments.

If a developing country, at least in cursory fashion, fails to comply with the financial control and reporting requirements of international banks and agencies, it will surely limit the amounts of economic assistance capital becoming available to it. Moreover, it will not be able to make its case, in special situations as with the United States Export/Import Bank in connection with the purchase of railroad equipment or commercial airliners from a United States-based producer.

Indigenous Expertise. To date, Anglo-Saxon countries are the major suppliers of accounting talent the world over. Widespread and easily accessible accounting education networks exist in these countries that feed the relatively attractive employment prospects for accountants in the far corners of the globe. So far, this holds true for accountants in both the private and public sectors as well as for internal and independent auditors. Yet, it is clearly not in the best interest of the Third World to have accounting talent either imported from other countries or accounting training provided for their own nationals in those other countries.

Massive efforts are under way, in the developing nations, to produce and hold indigenous accounting talent. These efforts reach from Korea to Tanzania and from Pacific Rim Islands to Persian and Arab countries. There is a firm belief in the Third World (in which your authors concur) that high quality locally provided and trained accounting talent is a significant building block in economic development endeavors.

Accounting Development Strategy

Despite the extremely urgent need for accounting development in the Third World, progress in this respect in the last few decades has been quite modest. One problem surely is that Third World leadership probably is unaware or unwilling to recognize the contributions that accounting can make to the development process. If the tradeoff is between a new flag-carrying airliner and a reasonably well-financed school of accountancy, the choice is very likely to go to the airliner. This is understandable but not necessarily optimal. As long as near-term visibility and payback are paramount, accounting development will not receive any high priority and therefore suffers relative to other development projects.

There is a second point, though, and it relates to strategy for accounting development. Despite some academic research and a fair amount of institutional attention to this issue, we still do not have a good understanding of the efficiency and the effectiveness among possible alternatives. Four basic approaches can be distinguished.

The ICAC Approach. The International Committee on Accounting Cooperation and its objectives and activities were briefly described at the end of Chapter 5. The approach taken is primarily to stimulate local accounting development through outside sources and agencies—both by training of nationals abroad and by using outside support to develop accounting education and professional accounting organizations on the local scene. If the ICAC experience is any indicator, then this approach must be described as unsuccessful.

Worldwide Standardization. Again this topic is explored at some length in Chapter 5—even though predominantly from the financial accounting perspective. But there is evidence that many associated with the international accounting standards movement feel that the Third World will be a particular beneficiary from their efforts. This came to the fore especially in the address Sir Henry Benson delivered to the 1976 Dutch Institute Accountants' Daag (also referenced in Chapter 5).

The most deliberate and most consistent advocate of accounting standardization as an aid to developing countries is Professor Enthoven. Here is a theme-setting quote from his March 1973 article in *Finance and Development* [reprinted in the Feburary, 1976 issue of *Management Accounting* (U.S.)]:

> A greater degree of standardization in accounting would be of particular benefit to developing countries. They are often faced with deficient and disorganized economic and financial data and may lack, at all levels of the economy, both effective accounting systems and related administrative skills. Because of limited natural financial and human resources, their governments may need to undertake increasingly centralized cost-benefit analyses and to involve themselves, through planning and control systems, in all socioeconomic activity.

Effective uniform standards of accounting are therefore required throughout the economy of developing countries—in enterprise accounting, government administration, social accounting, in national and international evaluations of industrial structures, in project and factorial appraisals, and in the assessment of capital markets and development finance.

Your authors find no intellectual fault with the standardization approach, but its implementation is all but a short-term proposition! We do not think that the Third World can wait this long.

Local Government Effort. If one recognizes that centralized economic planning and control are essential for the takeoff stages of economic development, one can readily make the parallel argument that accounting development should be a part of any initial central planning and control activities. Professor Scott is the key proponent of this approach.

It stands to reason, we feel, that central economic planners and controllers need accounting expertise and that, from their ranks, an initial cadre of professional management and financial accountants can be developed. From central planning agencies, these accounting experts would then filter into various national enterprises that would slowly evolve into private enterprises as the economy grows and its market mechanisms become effective. Israel, Mexico, North Korea, and Taiwan are possible cases in point. Once a reasonably strong private sector in an economy begins to emerge, financial accounting, together with an independent CPA profession, appears quite likely to follow in its wake. This accounting development strategy has both short-term and long-term advantages and would appear to be one of the viable alternatives.

Direct Indigenous Development. Probably the strongest case can be made for the strategy that seeks to develop accounting through the local priority system on the basis of local resources and firmly under local controls. The hallmarks of this particular strategy are resources allocated to higher educational facilities devoted to accounting, national accountancy legislation, regulation of professional quality, and establishment of sanctions against infringements. Also required, in our opinion, are regulatory or administrative requirements (possibly via companies legislation) to establish at least average levels of public periodic financial reporting, as well as independent auditing and appropriate review procedures for the public sale of corporate and/or public securities. The approach taken by the government of Tanzania is a good illustration of this strategy. It has much to recommend it.

BEHAVIORAL DIMENSIONS

During the past 2 decades, accountants have been able to establish that different types of accounting information affect certain aspects of human behavior and that human behavior in turn has a certain impact on the compilation and use of accounting data. Researchers have studied how managers and employees perform when budgets are either set too tight or so that they can be met with relative ease. Likewise, new insights into human information processing have given us clues on how people treat overloads of information, including accounting information. We know that some managers build personal aspirations into financial budgets and standards applied to others. Moreover, it is quite clear that managers in different cultures not only use different decision information but use the same information differentially. Of considerable interest in this respect is Professor Jaggi's flat statement, "It can be said that the experience of economically developed countries in the development of accounting principles cannot be transferred to the developing countries."

To date, virtually no work has been done on the behavioral dimensions of multinational accounting. Professor Burke, in a singularly pioneering study, has measured the reactions of different culture groups to dissonance created between directors' reports in annual accounts and the financial statements contained in the same accounts. Dissonance comes about when directors' reports are optimistic in tone and outlook while financial statements convey a declining (negative) profitability and financial position picture. Professor Burke found that dissonance occurs only when the financial statements convey a negative picture, in which case readers turn to the directors' report more than in the case with "positive" financial statements. Furthermore, cross-cultural differences were discovered in the reactions to various financial situations portrayed in annual accounts.

In time, multinational accounting should provide a rich lode for behavioral study. All the cultural, economic, legal, political, and social differences that are so widely cited in analyses of multinational business operations come to bear in equal force on multinational accounting. To what extent do financial accounting standards influence business decision-making in the multinational firm? How do managers suggest multinational financial reporting—let us say, in home countries and local currencies? Do behavioral differences warrant different budgeting procedures and financial control systems from country to country? Are local managers really more sympathetic to local internal auditors, or would they just as soon have the status and visibility that might come from a headquarters auditor? Can one measure behavioral costs and benefits from imposing a single uniform accounting system on all nine member countries in the EEC? How different are the personalities and socioeconomic characteristics of persons attracted to the accounting profession from country to country? Is professional accounting perceived as a social status ladder in most societies? Is it true that financial statements expressed in one language convey a different meaning from the same statement expressed in a different language?

We are firmly convinced that the behavioral dimensions of multinational accounting will flourish probably more than they have in uninational accounting affairs. Of course, the critical prerequisite to such flourishing is the combination of expertise not only in international matters but in accounting and behavioral matters as well. Where such a combination can be secured, attractive payoffs seem to be waiting.

A MULTINATIONAL PERSPECTIVE
ON PUBLIC SECTOR ACCOUNTING

In 1975, the financial straightjacket that the City of New York found itself in triggered an interest in public sector accounting never experienced before. Upon some checking, many local tax districts, municipalities, counties, and even state governments found, for example, that funding of their known pension obligations was grossly inadequate. Even the long-term viability of the Federal Social Security System came into doubt. Many business accounting principles, such as accrual accounting, were urged upon public sector accountants. One source even prepared illustrative financial position revenues and expenses and changes in cash and cash equivalent statements for the United States Government as a whole. With public sector expenditures in most industrialized countries ranging generally between 30 and 50 percent of the respective gross national product, it would seem safe to predict that the interest in public sector accounting is unlikely to disappear soon.

What does this have to do with multinational accounting? For one thing, macro accounts the world over need to be brought to the same common denominator. At present, neither national income accounts nor international balance of payments accounts are prepared on comparable bases the world over. In terms of national and international economic policies, this causes the same disparities that different national accounting standards and principles cause at their micro level for money capital markets, credit institutions, business management, and all others interested in enterprise financial accounting.

There are other concerns as well. As public sector activities grow, so grow national and international debts of various governments and governmental agencies. As these debts are incurred and refunded from time to time, they compete for money capital with private enterprises. It is entirely possible that public debt financing may eventually limit further growth of private enterprise. Thus, the financial reports used to tap public money markets are certainly of interest, as are the yields that must be provided to those furnishing new money capital. This is certainly an area of strong interest to multinational accounting.

A third dimension relates to doing business with the public sector. As public sector economic activities increase, multinationals are more and more likely to be selling goods and services to public sector units. In turn, they must then be willing to meet the often multitudinous conditions and regulations that go with sales of goods or services to the public sector. If these conditions and regulations vary significantly from country to country, multinational accounting will again be directly involved. Financial statements may have to be translated so that foreign public officials can readily scrutinize them. Cost-plus contracts will depend on cost information produced by a given accounting system, and new risks will have to be evaluated—for example, when payment will have to be accepted in a currency or currencies not of the vendor's choice.

Finally, the public sector is likely to produce some of its own accounting, financial reporting, and auditing rules, which simply will have to be observed if one wishes to do business with public sector units. The Cost Accounting Standards Board (CASB) in the United States and the Public Housing Authority in West Germany are examples of standard setting by the public sector for purposes of contracting with private enterprise. For one thing, such standards may well find adoption throughout an enterprise that does a lot of public sector business, e.g., an aerospace firm in the United States. For another, if such standards differ significantly from country to country and simultaneous compliance with all of them is impossible, then local companies might well become the only enterprises capable of complying with the established standards and thus garnering all the business offered by the public sector in question. This could affect multinational enterprises adversely. This possibility, among others, is foreshadowed by the insistence of the industrialized countries to have governmental economic units brought within the jurisdiction of the U.N. Commission on Transnational Corporations just as private enterprises are.

The public sector, we judge is fast becoming a frontier for financial and managerial accounting as well as opinion-type auditing. We assert that multinational accounting should be a part of this new interface.

SELECTED REFERENCES

10.1 AMERICAN ACCOUNTING ASSOCIATION, "Report of the Committee on Non-Financial Measures of Effectiveness," *Accounting Review,* Supplement, 1971, pp. 165–211.

10.2 AMERICAN ACCOUNTING ASSOCIATION, "Report of the Committee on Behavioral Science Content of the Accounting Curriculum," *Accounting Review,* Supplement, 1971, pp. 247 – 85.

10.3 AMERICAN ACCOUNTING ASSOCIATION, "Report of the Committee on Accounting in Developing Countries, 1973 – 1975," *Accounting Review,* Supplement, 1976, pp. 199–212.

10.4 ARTHUR ANDERSEN & CO., *Sound Financial Reporting in the Public Sector,* Chicago, Author, 1975, 35 pp.

10.5 BELFI, JOHN R., "Transferring Technology in a Multinational Service Industry," *Arthur Andersen Chronicle,* January 1975, pp. 16 – 21.

10.6 BELKAOUI, AHMED, Review of "Accounting and Developing Nations," by George M. Scott, *CA Magazine,* November 1974, pp. 16 – 18.

10.7 BERESFORD, DENNIS R., and STEWART A. FELDMAN, "Companies Increase Social Responsibility Disclosure," *Management Accounting* (U.S.), March 1976, pp. 51 – 55.

10.8 BURKE, RICHARD C., "Some Parameters of Financial Analysis Behavior: An Intercultural Evaluation under Experimental Conditions," Unpublished Ph.D. dissertation, University of Washington, 1976, 134 pp.

10.9 CONFERENCE BOARD, *Understanding the Balance of Payments,* New York: Author, 1970, 31 pp.

10.10 DE LA MAHOTIERE, STEWART, "The Multinational's Role in a Changing World," *Accountancy,* March 1976, pp. 28 – 30.

10.11 ENTHOVEN, A. J. H., "Standardized Accountancy and Economic Development," *Management Accounting* (U.S.), February 1976, pp. 19–23. (Reprinted from *Finance and Development,* March 1973.)

10.12 ENTHOVEN, ADOLF J. H., "Social and Political Impact of Multinationals on Third World Countries (and Its Accounting Implications)," Plenary Session Paper, 60th Annual Meeting, American Accounting Association, Richardson, Texas: University of Texas at Dallas, 1976, 36 pp. (monograph).

10.13 LINOWES, DAVID F., "The Accounting Profession and Social Progress," *Journal of Accountancy,* July 1973, pp. 32–40.

10.14 MILLER, J. IRVIN, "Multinational Corporations: The U.N. Report," *Arthur Andersen Chronicle,* October 1975, pp. 4– 12.

10.15 NATIONAL FOREIGN TRADE COUNCIL, INC., "The Balance of Payments," *Memorandum No. 9845,* April 22, 1971, 8 pp. (mimeographed).

10.16 SAUVANT, KARL P., and FARID G. LAVIPOUR, *Controlling Multinational Enterprises,* Boulder, Colo.: Westview Press, 1976, 342 pp.

10.17 SCOTT, WILLIAM R., Review of "Accountancy and Economic Development Policy," by A. J. H. Enthoven, *CA Magazine,* July 1974, pp. 8–9.

10.18 SEIDLER, LEE J., and LYNN L. SEIDLER, *Social Accounting: Theory, Issues, and Cases,* New York: Melville Publishing Co., 1975, 547 pp.

10.19 SICHEL, WERNER (ED.), *The Economic Effects of Multinational Corporations,* Michigan Business Papers No. 61, Ann Arbor, Mich.: The University of Michigan, 1975, 91 pp.

10.20 WINJUM, JAMES O., "Accounting and the Rise of Capitalism: An Accountant's View," *Journal of Accounting Research,* Autumn 1971, pp. 333–50.

DISCUSSION QUESTIONS

10.1 Today, the general public interest seems well on its way to becoming an "invisible hand" affecting business enterprise. How should multinational companies deal with the surging public interest in corporate activities and corporate governance?

10.2 A recent book referred to in the text identifies multinational enterprises as the "frightening angels." Write a concise essay on both the positive and the negative implications of this title.

10.3 Identify and elaborate briefly upon the three specific accounting responses that have been put forward to meet the challenge of greater socioeconomic control over the worldwide network of multinational enterprise operations.

10.4 Exhibit 10–1 provides excerpts from the 1976 OECD "Code of Conduct" for multinational enterprises. The excerpt deals specifically with suggested guidelines for the disclosure of information. Do presently published annual reports of large United States-based companies meet the suggested OECD disclosure guidelines? Who would benefit most if the suggested guidelines were fully observed?

10.5 The text refers to an example of binational cooperation in the area of enforcement of antitrust legislation. Similar cooperation between nations exists in the area of taxation. Identify and briefly describe one other accounting-related endeavor in which transnational cooperation seems desirable and practicable.

10.6 Identify the common interests between the United Nations Center on Transnational Corporations and the International Accounting Standards Committee (see Chapter 5). Compare and contrast the two with regard to (a) data collection and (b) accounting policy-making.

10.7 What is meant by social responsibility reporting for multinational enterprises? First, write a one-paragraph definition of "social responsibility reporting." Then list 10 reporting areas for which this type of reporting would be particularly germane for multinational companies.

10.8 Differentiate by means of illustrative examples, a table, or concise definitions: (a) corporate financial accounting, (b) accounting for a state government, (c) national income accounting, and (d) international balance of payments accounting. What is the point of closest similarity between these four? Also identify at least three points of significant differences between the four accounting applications cited.

10.9 Explain the item called "errors and omissions" that typically appears in any formal statements of a country's balance of international payments at a specified date.

10.10 How can a country have a "negative" balance of trade and at the same time a "positive" international balance of payments position? Can you list at least three different ways in which a country might settle an international payments imbalance, i.e., differences between foreign receipts and payments? (This question is not specifically covered in the text and thus the student needs to draw upon general knowledge or outside references.)

10.11 Some well-placed observers of the international scene feel that the availability of good accounting services is a prerequisite for (or even stimulates) economic development. Other equally qualified persons feel that accounting grows as an aftermath of economic development (e.g., in response to direct foreign investment). Write a short essay relating your views of this issue.

10.12 What is the so-called Sombart thesis? Can such a thesis be tested somehow? What would you advise a newly independent African nation to do regarding the implications of Sombart's thesis?

10.13 Summarize the five reasons given in the text as to why a certain amount of accounting capacity is essential to a developing economy. Are there other similar reasons that you could add to this list on your own?

10.14 Develop a list of six research projects (suitable for a term paper in a multinational accounting class) dealing with behavioral dimensions for multinational accounting. What we have in mind here is the application of any concepts or methodologies from the behavioral sciences to multinational accounting issues and/or problems.

10.15 Within the totality of the accounting discipline, multinational accounting and public sector accounting are two subfields or specialty areas. Is the multinational dimension of public sector accounting likely to be the same as the public sector dimension of multinational accounting? Notwithstanding the discussion in the text, what is your own view of bringing any public sector considerations into a multinational accounting text?

ANNOTATED TEACHING MATERIALS

10.1 *Russel Karagosian* (Robock and Simmonds, *International Business and Multinational Enterprises,* pp. 552–62). Russel Karagosian is introduced as a principal of a leading Boston firm of business consultants. He is engaged by the Minister for Industry of a small Latin American country to outline the basic features of a measurement system designed to "factualize" the contributions and/or detriments of multinational operations from the viewpoint of the recipient country. Measurement systems currently employed by the Central Bank of the Philippines, Manila, and the Government of Mexico are presented for analysis and comment.

10.2 *The Rio Tinto Zinc Corporation* (ICCH Case 9–175–259). Rio Tinto Zinc Corporation (RTZ) is a United Kingdom-based conglomerate mining company with worldwide activities. Its extractive operations have recently been assailed by various national and international groups on environmental, social, and political grounds. In response to mounting criticism, RTZ's Chairman and Chief Executive Officer makes explicit his company's position on a number of environmental and social responsibility issues. The case serves as an excellent vehicle for extended study of social responsibility accounting by multinational enterprises.

10.3 *Acme Manufacturing* (Robock and Simmonds, *International Business and Multinational Enterprises,* pp. 550–51). The Vice-President of International Operations of the Acme Manufacturing Company is evaluating a capital budgeting proposal from his Indonesian field manager. A choice must be made between investing in automatic extractive equipment versus hiring local labor for Acme's Indonesian mining operation. The company is cognizant of Indonesia's chronic unemployment situation. On the other hand, the equipment alternative appears financially attractive in light of the potential social overhead investment that must be made if Acme chooses the labor option. At issue here is whether a multinational company is responsible only to itself for profits or whether it indeed has broader social responsibilities to which it must respond.

10.4 *Balance of Payments Exercises* (Case 2, Vernon, *Manager in the International Economy,* 2nd ed., pp. 265–71). This exercise presents the system of accounts used in United States balance of payments accounting together with detailed explanations. A series of financial transactions is then presented calling for appropriate entries into the United States accounts. The exercise provides a convenient yet effective avenue for familiarizing students with balance of payments accounting.

10.5 *Lamont Industries, Inc.* (Case 4, Zenoff and Zwick, *International Financial Management,* pp. 97–98). To facilitate management of its foreign exchange risks, Lamont Industries decides to experiment with balance of payments projections. Country managers (student actors) are asked to provide headquarters management with a local balance of payments analysis. Information on past and future payments trends, as well as the interrelationships between a country's payments position and the world economy are required.

10.6 *Anco Inc.* (Case B, Robock and Simmonds, *International Business and Multinational Enterprises,* pp. 565–67). Anco Inc. (United States) is considering the feasibility of expanding its manufacturing capacity in a small Mediterranean country where anti-American sentiment prevails. Nationalistic fervor is continually fanned by four local family-owned competitors whose owners are both wealthy and politically influential. Management of these local operations, however, is characterized as "a joke." Cost controls and planning systems are lacking. The families maintain five sets of books with the result that no one knows anything about costs. Paralleling Anco's investment decision is the broader policy issue of the kinds of legislation, accounting or otherwise, that the Mediterranean government should promulgate to attain maximum economic efficiency and income for the country.

INDEX